POWER AND STABILITY IN BRITISH FOREIGN POLICY,
1865–1965

RENEWALS 458

DATE DUE

BOOKS OF RELATED INTEREST

POWER, CONFLICT AND TRADE
Military Power, International Commerce and Great Power Rivalry
By M.P. Gerace

THE MUNICH CRISIS, 1938
Prelude to World War II
Edited by Igor Lukes and Erik Goldstein

THE WASHINGTON CONFERENCE, 1921–22
Naval Rivalry, East Asian Stability and the Road to Pearl Harbor
Edited by Erik Goldstein and John Maurer

PERSONALITIES, WAR AND DIPLOMACY
Essays in International History
Edited by T.G. Otte and C. Pagedas

PESSIMISM AND BRITISH WAR POLICY, 1916–1918
By Brock Millman

WINSTON CHURCHILL AND THE ROAD TO ARMAGEDDON
Edited by John H. Maurer

THE BRITISH EMPIRE AS A WORLD POWER
By Edward Ingram

Power and Stability
British Foreign Policy, 1865–1965

Edited by
ERIK GOLDSTEIN
AND
B.J.C. McKERCHER

FRANK CASS
LONDON • PORTLAND, OR

First published in 2003 in Great Britain by
FRANK CASS AND COMPANY LIMITED
Crown House, 47 Chase Side, Southgate, London N14 5BP, England

and in the United States of America by
FRANK CASS
c/o ISBS, Suite 300, 920 NE 58th Avenue, Portland, OR 97213, USA

Copyright c 2003 Frank Cass & Co. Ltd

British Library Cataloguing in Publication Data

Power and stability : British foreign policy, 1865–1965
1. Great Britain – Foreign relations – 20th century 2. Great
Britain – Foreign relations – 1837–1901 3. Great Britain
Military policy
I. Goldstein, Erik II. McKercher, B. J. C. III. Dockrill,
Michael L. (Michael Lawerence), 1936–
327.4′1′009034

ISBN 0 7146 5560 0 (cloth)
ISBN 0 7146 8442 2 (paper)

Library of Congress Cataloging-in-Publication Data

Power and stability : British foreign policy, 1865/1965 / editors Erik
Goldstein, B.J.C. McKercher.
   p.cm
Includes bibliographical references and index.
   ISBN 0-7146-5560-0 (Cloth) – ISBN 0-7146-8442-2 (Paper)
   1.Great Britain–Foreign relations–20th century. 2. Great Britain–Foreign
relations–1837–1901
I. Goldstein, Erik. II.
McKercher, B.J.C., 1950– III. Title.
DA566.7.P69 2003
327.41′009′034–dc21
                                            2003010626

This group of studies first appeared in a Special Issue of *Diplomacy & Statecraft*
(ISSN 0959-2296), Vol.14, No.2 (June 2003), [Power and Stability: British Foreign
Policy, 1865–1965].

All rights reserved. No part of this publication may be reproduced, stored in a
retrieval system, or transmitted in any form, or by any means, electronic,
mechanical, photocopying, recording or otherwise without the prior written
permission of Frank Cass and Company Limited.

Printed and bound by Antony Rowe Ltd., Chippenham, Wiltshire

FOR MIKE DOCKRILL

Contents

Abbreviations		ix
Introduction	Erik Goldstein and B.J.C. McKercher	1
British Power and Stability: The Historical Record	Zara Steiner	23
Power, Sovereignty, and the Great Republic: Anglo-American Diplomatic Relations in the Era of the Civil War	Brian Holden Reid	45
'Almost a Law of Nature'? Sir Edward Grey, the Foreign Office, and the Balance of Power in Europe, 1905–12	T.G. Otte	77
'Après la Guerre finit, Soldat anglais partit…': Anglo-French Relations, 1918–25	Alan Sharp and Keith Jeffery	119
'Far Too Dangerous a Gamble'? British Intelligence and Policy during the Chanak Crisis, September–October 1922	John R. Ferris	139
The British Official Mind and the Lausanne Conference, 1922–23	Erik Goldstein	185
Austen Chamberlain and the Continental Balance of Power: Strategy, Stability, and the League of Nations, 1924–29	B.J.C. McKercher	207
The British Government and the Sale of Arms to the Lesser European Powers, 1936–39	Glyn Stone	237

Invading Europe: The British Army and its Preparations for the Normandy Campaign, 1942–44	David French	271
Killing the MLF? The Wilson Government and Nuclear Sharing in Europe, 1964–66	John Young	295
Abstracts		325
Notes on Contributors		330
Select Bibliography		333
Index		347

Abbreviations

AA	Auswärtiges Amt (German Foreign Ministry)
AAP	*Akten zur Auswartigen Politik der Bundesrepublik Deutschland*
AD	Allied Demands Committee
ADM	Admiralty
AFHQ	Allied Forces Head Quarters
AG	Adjutant General
AIR	Air Ministry
ANF	Atlantic Nuclear Force
BEF	British Expeditionary Force
BelD	*Die Belgischen Dokumente zur Vorgeschichte des Weltkrieges, 1885–1914*
Benckendorffs Schriftwechsel	*Graf Benckendorffs Diplomatischer Schriftwechsel, 1907–1912*
BD	*British Documents on the Origins of the War, 1898–1914.*
CAB	Cabinet
CC	Cabinet Conclusion
CID	Committee of Imperial Defence
CIGS	Chief of the Imperial General Staff
C-in-C	Commander-in-Chief
COS	Chiefs of Staff
CP	Cabinet Paper
DBFP	*Documents on British Foreign Policy, 1919–1939*
DAFV	Director of Armoured Fighting Vehicles
DC	*Diplomatic Correspondence*
DCAS	Deputy Chief of the Air Staff
DCIGS	Deputy Chief of the Imperial General Staff
DCOS	Deputy Chiefs of Staff
DDF	*Documents diplomatiques français*
DDSD(O)	Deputy Director of Staff Duties, Operations
DEFE	Ministry of Defence
DMI	Director of Military Intelligence

DMO&P	Director of Military Operations and Plans
DMOI	Director of Military Operations Intelligence
DMT	Director of Military Training
DPR	Defence Policy and Requirements Committee
DSD	Director of Staff Duties
Entente Diplomacy	*Entente Diplomacy and the World: Matrix of the History of Europe*
FAO	Foreign Armaments Orders Committee
FO	Foreign Office
FRUS	*Papers Relating to the Foreign Relations of the United States*
GC&CS	Government Code and Cypher School
GHQ	General Headquarters
GOC-in-C	General Officer Commanding-in-Chief
G(Ops)	General (Operations)
GP	*Die Grosse Politik der Europäischen Kabinette, 1871–1914*
GS(I)	General Staff Intelligence
GSO	General Staff Officer
HC Debs, 5th Series	*House of Commons Debates*, Fifth Series
HW	Records of the Government Code and Cypher School
IIC	Industrial Intelligence Centre
Kiderlen NL	*Kiderlen-Wächter, der Staatsmann und Mensch: Briefwechsel und Nachlass*
L/MIL	India Office Library and Records
LHCMA	Liddell Hart Centre for Military Archives
MID	Military Intelligence Division
MISC	Miscellaneous Committee
MGGS	Major General General Staff
MLF	Multilateral Force
MOD	Ministry of Defence
nd	no date
NID	Naval Intelligence Division
NL Aehrenthal	*Aus dem Nachlass Aehrenthal: Briefe und Dokumente*

NPT	Non-Proliferation Treaty
ÖUA	*Österreich-Ungarns Aussenpolitik, 1908–1914: Diplomatische Aktenstücke*
PREM	Prime Minister's Files
PUS	permanent under-secretary
RAF	Royal Air Force
RASC	Royal Army Service Corps
REME	Royal Electrical and Mechanical Engineers
SIS	Secret Intelligence Service
T	Treasury
VCIGS	Vice Chief of the Imperial General Staff
WO	War Office
WOG	Wireless Observation Group

Power and Stability in British Foreign Policy, 1865–1965

ERIK GOLDSTEIN AND B.J.C. McKERCHER

> The British argued [at the Paris Peace Conference] that foreign policy must evolve in the light of changing circumstances, especially in the context of her economic and financial difficulties, and the need to over-see a world-wide empire with inadequate military and naval forces.
>
> Michael Dockrill, 1984[1]

Even before 1865, it was an axiom that British foreign policy was designed and pursued to ensure international stability. Stability not only gave security to the British Isles and to its global empire; it minimized disruptions to trade and commerce – the life-blood of 'Great' Britain.[2] In the century after 1865, the pursuit of international stability remained at the heart of diplomatic initiatives supported by capable armed forces and a strong economy. The grand strategy by which successive British governments endeavoured to achieve these national and imperial ends involved the maintenance of a balance of power – both in Europe and in the wider world, where the protection of British interests in the form of prestige, markets, strategic outposts, and lines of communication preoccupied cabinets, the Foreign Office, the service ministries, other departments of state, and, sometimes, public opinion. In one sense, there were a number of individual balances of power – in Western Europe, in the western and eastern Mediterranean, in the Western Hemisphere, in South Asia, and in the Far East and Pacific Ocean. In the British diplomatic parlance of the late nineteenth and early twentieth centuries, these balances were represented as 'questions', like the 'Eastern Question';[3] and the answers to these questions combined in the minds of those responsible for British foreign policy as representing a global balance of power.⁴ In this context, the European balance of power had decided importance because any continental disequilibrium could imperil the security of the home islands, the centre of the Empire, and the well-being of Britain's people and economy. Of course, on occasion, war could occur either because British policy failed or ambitious Powers decided that they could imperil Britain's vital interests. Indeed, as Disraeli did in January 1877 when Russian armies neared the Straits in the Russo-Turkish war, the British might themselves threaten war if doing so was the only way to protect their interests. However, once war began, the British fought to win – a not unnatural course of events; but their war aims always looked to establish a post-conflict stability that augmented their narrow national and imperial interests.

Michael Dockrill's succinct observation about the nature of British foreign policy as the First World War ended is germane not only to the difficult period of 1918–20. It brings to the fore a series of truisms that underscored British foreign policy between 1865 and 1965 and which the contributors to this volume explore: that international politics, and Britain's diplomatic and military response to them, was an evolutionary process conditioned by changing circumstances; that British policy was flexible; and that from the British perspective and in line with British interests, stability was the *sine qua non* of diplomacy. Thus, as late as 1896, Lord Salisbury, the Conservative prime minister and foreign secretary, could eschew alliances because 'in 1892, as now, we kept free from any engagement to go to war in any contingency whatever. That is the attitude prescribed to us on the one hand by our popular constitution which will not acknowledge the obligations of an engagement made in former years – on the other by our insular position'.⁵ In Salisbury's estimation, stretching back to the 1870s – and even in that of his contemporary political adversaries like the Liberal, William Ewart Gladstone, who wanted morality to underpin the country's external policies⁶ – Britain lay safe behind the Channel and the strength of the Royal Navy; and no Great Power or coalition of Powers threatened the Empire. Thus, concluding alliances meant making promises it might be impossible to keep in an unknown future. It profited Britain, instead, to concentrate on trade and commercial expansion.⁷ Yet between 1902 and 1904 a different generation of British leaders with Salisbury's successor, Lord Lansdowne, as foreign secretary concluded the Anglo-Japanese alliance and an entente with France.[8] They did so because the Boer War showed Britain to be dangerously isolated at a moment when other Great Powers had coalesced into opposing alliances and looked to exploit British concentration on the crisis in southern Africa; this was a situation that could rebound unfavourably on its global interests.

Significantly, Lansdowne steered clear of joining either of the two alliance coalitions in Europe – the Dual Alliance of France and tsarist Russia, on one side, and the Triple Alliance of Germany, Austria-Hungary, and Italy, on the other. The Anglo-Japanese alliance concerned regional security in East and South Asia; the arrangement with France looked to eliminate Anglo-French colonial differences in the Western Hemisphere, North Africa, and Southeast Asia.[9] The situation between 1900 and 1904 saw British policy 'evolve in the light of changing circumstances'. But 1904 was not an end point. Desirous of an overseas empire and wanting Germany to be a 'world' power, Kaiser Wilhelm II's government had initiated a massive programme of naval construction beginning in 1899 that aimed to undermine the hegemony of the Royal Navy. London responded with its own naval construction programme in an atmosphere of embittered Anglo-German relations.[10] In 1905, worried about encirclement by the Dual Alliance now augmented by the Anglo-French entente – and just as desirous of dominating the continent – Wilhelmine Germany moved to break the entente and, thereby, weaken France. It failed because of British resolve, with the result that the entente hardened through the initiation of Anglo-French staff talks which, by 1914, had committed British military support for France in the event of a German attack westwards.[11] Similarly, in 1905, Britain's great imperial rival, tsarist Russia, was weakened because of military and naval defeat in the Far East at the hands of the Japanese force of arms. Within two years, and despite the Anglo-Japanese alliance, an Anglo-Russian convention was concluded looking to maintain the balance of power in Persia, Afghanistan, Tibet, and Nepal – the nexus of the British and Russian empires in South Asia. In this matter, the Liberal foreign secretary, Sir Edward Grey, had a particular view about the international stability suffusing British policy in the wider world. Stable Anglo-Russian relations remained essential for the security of the British Empire. Yet, like its Anglo-French equivalent, the Anglo-Russian colonial entente had European implications; hence, while the never easy Anglo-Russian relationship became strained after 1907, as St Petersburg regained its political strength via modernizing its armed forces and expanding Russian industrial capacity,[12] the 1914 'July crisis' saw the British support Russia and its French ally against Germany. Supported by the conservative Unionist opposition, Grey and the Liberal government in 1914 did so for reasons of pure *realpolitik*: it could not allow the continent to be dominated by Powers antagonistic to Britain.[13]

After Central Power defeat in the Great War – a struggle in which Italy switched sides, tsarist Russia collapsed in revolution, and the United States joined the Allied coalition – France re-emerged as the chief threat to British interests.[14] The reason was simple. France was now the leading Power on the continent; its political and military leadership sought increased security from a revanchist Germany; and possessing the second largest Empire in the world, it wanted to extend its overseas holdings.[15] It is also easy to understand why France, Britain's entente partner for a decade after 1904 and its ally from 1914 to 1918, should become a major strategic concern for London as the 1920s began. Where the variegated course of British foreign policy has at times brought the obloquy of 'perfidious Albion' upon its record – especially from the French[16] – British leaders have with some exceptions always been consistent in their defence of narrow British interests. They have subscribed to Lord Palmerston's famous dictum that the British had 'no eternal allies and no perpetual enemies, our interests are eternal, and those interests it is our duty to follow'[17] – and they did so before Palmerston began learning the art of diplomacy during the Napoleonic wars. In the years immediately after the end of the Great War, from London's perspective, French policy seemed only to create instability on the continent and, in vital places like Turkey and the Near East, destabilize regional balances of power – or, at least, regional balances that touched British interests.

Led by David Lloyd George, the post-war British government found itself at odds with France over the shape of defeated Germany; the British wanted a de-militarized but economically strong Germany – German recovery was essential for reviving trade dislocated by the war – while the French wanted a disarmed and economically weak

Germany – the better for French security.¹⁸ And as the Treaty of Sèvres – the treaty forced on Germany's wartime Ottoman ally – unravelled, Anglo-French animosities in south-eastern Europe and the Near East grew.¹⁹ Admittedly, a conference at Washington in 1921–22 brought stability to the Far East through the negotiation of three agreements recognizing the post-1918 status quo in the Pacific Ocean, limiting the battle fleets of the major naval Powers, and guaranteeing China's sovereignty.²⁰ But tied to war debts and reparations, French desires for security, and the Turkish imbroglio, European stability proved elusive. Only France's disastrous occupation of the Ruhr Valley in January 1923 – designed to seize German industrial production in lieu of reparations payments and, of course, keep Germany weakened – scuppered Paris' forward policies.²¹ Coupled with the fall of Lloyd George and the advent of a different approach to policy, British leaders looked to find diplomatic means to bring stability to both the continent and those places in the world where Great Power interests intersected. It was not easy but, by July 1923, the Conservative foreign secretary, Lord Curzon, proved instrumental in replacing Sèvres with the Treaty of Lausanne.²² Two years later, continental stability was achieved when Curzon's Conservative successor, Austen Chamberlain, reconciled Franco-German security differences through the Locarno treaty.²³ The British did all of this without concluding alliances, their primary international responsibilities deriving from their membership in the new League of Nations and its concept of collective security.²⁴

From the mid-nineteenth century onwards, those responsible for British foreign policy worked to ensure that London had a 'free hand' in maintaining balances of power, especially on the European continent. In the period from at least the end of the Crimean war to the Boer war, Benjamin Disraeli, Salisbury, and Gladstone, and those that advised them, looked to provide British diplomacy with a 'free hand'.²⁵ This translated into flexible foreign policy initiatives that allowed manoeuvre without the conclusion of formal alliances. Less prosaically, it meant pragmatism in pursuit of the balance of power, now supporting one group of Powers, now the other, in ensuring international stability.²⁶ The lack of first-class threats to the balances in Europe and elsewhere allowed this flexibility. But when the international situation merited, for instance, in 1886–87, when the

'Eastern question' flared up over Russian ambitions concerning the Straits, limited agreements with other Powers sharing the British desire for stability were not impossible. Hence, Salisbury concluded the so-called 'Mediterranean agreements' with Italy and Austria-Hungary, which, supported by Germany, looked to deter Russian exploitation of Ottoman weakness.[27] As always, however, Salisbury sought to avoid a commitment to go to war. As he told Queen Victoria, British support for these agreements left 'entirely unfettered the discretion of Your Majesty's Government, as to whether, in any particular case, they will carry their support of Italy as far as "material co-operation"'.[28] And when British security was threatened, as occurred over a crisis in the Ottoman province of Egypt in 1881 touching the Suez Canal, even the moralistic Gladstone did not shirk from using British power to protect narrow national interests. British forces occupied Egypt and, despite the near rupture of Anglo-French relations, incorporated this vital region into the Empire.[29] After 1902, changing international circumstances caused by Anglo-German rivalry and the need to avoid British isolation required new means to maintain stability: in the Far East, against Russian ambitions; and in Europe, from the two alliance coalitions that had formed. New means meant the alliance with Japan and, beginning in 1904, an increasing commitment to France. The 'free hand' had begun to disappear.[30]

After the First World War, with Britain's obligation to uphold the Paris Peace Settlement and its leading position in the new League of Nations,[31] Lloyd George and his successors looked to revive the 'free hand'. Their quest proved impossible, something seen in both the Washington treaties respecting the Pacific Ocean and China, on one hand, and Locarno, on the other. In 1930, Austen Chamberlain observed of Britain's position just before the Boer War: 'With Germany unfriendly, France embittered, Italy uncertain and Russia hostile, we were indeed isolated, and even though the loyalty and support of the Colonies made that isolation splendid it did not render it safe.'[32] To the same degree, the new international order that emerged from the Great War meant that while the traditional British grand strategy of pursuing balances of power in Europe and the wider world remained, the course of allowing other Powers to determine the shape of international politics could not be sustained.

International circumstances would not allow a return to the heyday of Salisbury and Gladstone. Germany had been defeated, tsarist Russia had fallen into revolution and civil war, and Austria-Hungary splintered into the 'successor states'; France seemed stronger than ever; and two regional Great Powers, Japan and the United States, had the economic and industrial capacity to imperil British imperial interests.[33] It followed that British diplomatists after 1919 had to adjust British foreign policy to meet change. Importantly, such change did not result only from the machinations of the major Powers. It also derived from lesser Powers, like Nationalist Turkey and revived Poland, manoeuvring to extend their territories and maintain what they perceived to be their sovereignty.

In the 1920s, this adjustment saw, first, competition with the French in Europe and the Near East and, then, after the conclusion of the treaties of Lausanne and Locarno, the concerted effort to work with Paris in ensuring international stability. To a degree, Austen Chamberlain could consider his diplomacy to have some freedom of manoeuvre, if not a free hand. He consciously worked to be 'the honest broker' in the Franco-German relationship,[34] which he held to be the lynch-pin of continental security and, thus, of the world. This attitude might have been illusionary, but for all of its faults, the 'Locarno era' proved to be the highpoint of international stability in the period between the two world wars of the twentieth century.[35] Moreover, stability in Europe allowed the British to meet successfully crises arising in other regions of the globe vital to their imperial interests and security. One example of this was in China, where the British and Japanese established a *modus vivendi* between their competing spheres of interest at the moment when Chinese nationalism emerged to threaten foreign concessions.[36] A second concerned London's success in meeting the desire of the Republican United States to force the British to concede complete Anglo-American naval parity.[37] However, the onset of the Great Depression in October 1929 generated a process by which the foundations of the international economy, especially trade, began to disintegrate. And as the Depression spread across the globe, but especially in Europe, and as it took hold for more than five years, it undermined what proved to be the fragile international structures emplaced after 1918: the Paris Peace Settlement, the Washington treaties, Locarno, and the

League.[38] Liberal democratic governments could not cope with the economic crisis, with the result that there occurred in the 1930s the radicalization of domestic politics in a number of states, chiefly Germany and Japan, which produced nationalist right-wing regimes.[39] With these regimes propounding aggressive foreign policies both to obviate the economic dislocation caused by the Depression and to meet the territorial and other demands of frankly expansionist leaderships,[40] a new international situation emerged after 1931.

In the 1930s, the goal of British foreign policy remained the pursuit of international stability. In reaction to changing circumstances – the re-ordering of the Far Eastern balance of power by Japan's force of arms in China in 1931 and in 1937; the destruction of the Treaty of Versailles by Nazi Germany after 1933; and, with Italian action in Abyssinia in 1935–36, the emasculation of the League – the determination of British leaders to achieve that goal had to balance strategic ends with diplomatic means. Confronting these policy-makers was the problem that, for the first time in its long history as a Great Power, Britain encountered three first-class adversaries in three vital regions of the globe: on the European continent, in the Mediterranean, and in the Far East.[41] While Britain possessed the military and financial resources to meet any one of these threats, its civilian and military leaders understood that it could not take on two or all three threats simultaneously. The initial British strategic decision to meet the threat to their manifold national and imperial interests occurred in early 1934 in response to the Japanese conquest of Manchuria and to Adolph Hilter taking Nazi Germany out of the League. This was to continue to pursue the balances of power in Europe and the Far East, but to do so by undertaking to strengthen the British armed forces – given public revulsion to the human and fiscal cost of the Great War, the desire to retrench, and the advent of international disarmament discussions in the late 1920s, the Army, Royal Navy, and Royal Air Force had had their budgets cut. With Italy's attack on Abyssinia in 1935, the pursuit of the balance was re-defined, while defence spending was further increased. Then, in May 1937, Neville Chamberlain rose to the premiership. He had long been critical of the balance – it held danger because if it broke down, war was inevitable.[42] He also deprecated other strategic alternatives: League collective security because the League had failed to stop Italy in 1935; multilateral conference diplomacy because in recent history such efforts were unsuccessful; and alliances with other Powers that, in 1937, meant working with the unreliable French to contain German and Italian ambitions. Instead, Chamberlain opted for what he called 'better relations with the dictators' until full-scale rearmament gave Britain's diplomatic voice greater strength.[43] Indeed, under Chamberlain, British rearmament continued apace, with a spending target of £1.625 billion by 1941, an increase of more than 3,000 per cent over that first made in 1934.[44] 'Better relations with the dictators' translated into the policy of appeasement.

Chamberlain looked to resolve British differences with Nazi Germany, fascist Italy, and militaristic Japan through bilateral agreements allowing for territorial adjustments to be made without resort to arms. There were limits to which Britain would appease, and they lay with the rearmament programme to deter Berlin, Rome, and Tokyo from seeking too much. Appeasement had been part of the British diplomatic arsenal since at least the middle of the nineteenth century,[45] and its 1930s variant constituted *realpolitik* of a high order: it placed British security and interests above all else, primarily over those of minor states like Czechoslovakia, for instance, whose western reaches contained ethnic Germans. It also looked to ensure stability because, in the view of Neville Chamberlain and his supporters, Britain could not afford to fight a second 'Great War'. Despite British victory, the economy would be irretrievably weakened, the Empire would be undermined and probably fall away, and, within Britain, the Labour Party with its dangerous socialist policies would be the political beneficiary.[46] But appeasement was a colossal failure. In March 1938, Hitler forced Austria to unite with Germany. Chamberlain's government acquiesced with some misgivings, accepting Hitler's argument that the Treaty of Versailles contradicted the important doctrine of national self-determination. Then, in September 1938 at Munich, the height of Chamberlain's appeasement policies, Britain joined with France in permitting the annexation of the German-speaking regions of western Czechoslovakia into the Reich.[47] Hitler said he had no more ambitions. But his territorial appetite went beyond righting the wrongs of Versailles, something starkly seen on 15 March 1939 when his army absorbed all of Czechoslovakia in violation of Munich. The diplomatic die had been cast. Chamberlain's government joined with the French at the end of March to guarantee Polish sovereignty – Poland then seemed to be the focus of Nazi irridentism.[48] When Italy suddenly annexed Albania in early April, additional Anglo-French guarantees were given to Greece and Romania. The British re-committed themselves to France to maintain the European and Mediterranean balances of power. When Hitler's armies attacked Poland on 1 September 1939 following a cynical non-aggression pact with Bolshevik Russia, Britain found itself fighting another 'Great War' 25 years after the 'July crisis'.[49]

Although his strategic prescription to protect British interests had been wrong, or, at least, followed too long, Chamberlain proved correct in assessing what would befall Britain and its empire should it fight a Second World War. Britain did count itself amongst the victors when that war ended in September 1945 with the defeat of Italy, Germany, and Japan. Its empire also remained intact. But the financial cost of fighting the war – especially between June 1940 and June 1941 when the British fought Germany and Italy alone and worked to meet Japanese pressures in the Far East – irretrievably enfeebled the economy.[50] Tied to massive and costly domestic reforms initiated by a majority Labour government in office from July 1945 to October 1951, the British lacked the fiscal resources to sustain a global presence. Concurrently, the onset of the Cold War produced a new world order in which London – already junior to Washington and Moscow by the time the Second World War ended – found itself increasingly marginalized by the advent of 'superpower' politics dominated by the United States and the Soviet Union. And as the Empire began to disintegrate through the successful demands for independence by colonial nationalists in Africa, the Middle East, the Caribbean, and South and South-East Asia, Britain transformed from a world to a regional Power in less than a quarter of a century. This fact became clear in late 1956, when the Egyptian regime of Gamel Abdel Nasser seized control of the Suez Canal. Britain's collaboration with the French and Israelis to re-take the Canal foundered miserably as a result of American opposition, Soviet Russian musings about intervening on the Egyptian side, and the decision of key Powers within the British Commonwealth, chiefly India and Canada, to oppose Britain in the name of opposing old-style colonialism. Over the next decade, successive British governments, whether Conservative or Labour, understood that Britain's diplomatic focus now lay in Europe. This recognition of changed international circumstances translated into seeking British membership in the new European Economic Community and tailoring Britain's military commitments to meet regional European needs, primarily within the confines of the North Atlantic Treaty Organization.

Stability remained the fundamental objective of British foreign policy in the 1960s. And Palmerston's adage about permanent interests and impermanent allies remained equally true: Soviet Russia – with its Warsaw Pact allies in tow – was now the adversary; and after fighting two world wars between 1914 and 1945 to eliminate the German menace, West Germany was a British and French ally within NATO. If they had been living in 1965, Gladstone, Salisbury, Grey, and other British diplomatists like Austen Chamberlain would not have liked the low level to which British fortunes had plunged. However, they would have understood and sympathized with the efforts newer British leaders were making to protect more narrowly defined national interests in the form of prestige, markets, strategic outposts, and lines of communication. Admittedly, new policies were needed to meet the requirements of a new international situation – membership in the Common Market, say, or a more effective British voice within NATO. The 'free hand' had certainly gone. But the strategy to protect British interests remained the same because its essential goal was immutable.

The contributors to this volume have explored issues of 'power and stability' in British foreign policy between 1865 and 1965 to honour Michael Dockrill, who retired as Professor of Diplomatic History in the War Studies Department at King's College, the University of London, in September 2001. Over the past 30 years, Professor Dockrill emerged as one of the leading historians of twentieth century British foreign policy, his written work spanning the period from before 1900 to the end of the Cold War. After working for a bank and the Foreign Office, Professor Dockrill began his serious academic career as a graduate student in the Department of International History at the London School of Economics. He wrote his doctoral dissertation on Anglo-French relations from 1902 to 1914 under the direction of the then Stevenson Professor of International History, Norton Medlicott. Following a short period teaching in Plymouth, and then at the University of Wales, Aberystwyth, he joined the War Studies Department in King's in 1972.

Professor Dockrill's contribution to the study of modern British foreign policy has several strands. The most obvious are his scholarly contributions to the field, work in which the intimate connection between the personality of diplomatists and their policies demonstrate that human agency, more than the unseen forces of societies and economies, influence the making and execution of foreign policy. Whether examining the evolution of British strategic options in the dozen years before the 'July crisis' of 1914, the development and pursuit of political and other objectives at the Paris Peace Conference, or examining British elite attitudes towards France in the late 1930s to understand better why an Anglo-French alliance did not earlier emerge,[51] his careful research and thoughtful analyses provide answers to important historiographical questions. Thus, before 1914, Grey's conception of how he, his Foreign Office advisors, and his ambassadors could maintain the European balance – while balancing domestic political forces – were, if not necessarily unique, certainly different to the remedies that might have been pursued by Unionist statesmen, like Lord Curzon or Austen Chamberlain, if they had held office. During the Paris Peace Conference, British policy took particular paths because Lloyd George distrusted the diplomatic professionals, disparaged as 'aristocrats' by the lower class prime minister, although brains and the upper classes were not mutually exclusive. In one particularly important case, Lloyd George ignored the advice of the professionals over the creation of Poland; tied to his concept of how to achieve post-war stability, his different policy prescription helped produce a situation where 'big' Poland contributed to Eastern European stability from 1919 to 1939 remaining perpetually fragile. This is not to say that the ideas of experienced diplomats like Lord Hardinge, the Foreign Office permanent under-secretary in 1919, would have necessarily been better than those emanating from 10 Downing Street. It is to say, as Professor Dockrill has shown, that they were fundamentally different ideas and could not have been worse in the quest to ensure post-war stability on the continent.

And what is true of prime ministerial control of British foreign policy in the aftermath of the First World War is equally true for that in the lead-up to the Second. In the late 1930s, the British establishment lacked a single view of France's ability to help Britain maintain continental security; as Professor Dockrill shows, the issue was not one simply of pro- and anti-French opinion – Cabinet ministers had cautious views about French reliability; the service ministries had different ones based on France's military strength; the Foreign Office generally saw France as Britain's sole ally on the continent; and the opinion of other Britons on the opposition benches, in the press, and beyond ranged amongst these disparate points of view. However, Neville Chamberlain, the prime minister, was unwilling to align with Paris until after March 1939 because he believed that Britain should avoid continental entanglements, especially a commitment to France that would isolate Germany. Chamberlain and his supporters had another vision of how to ensure international stability. Put succinctly, it was by appeasing the dictators over their legitimate grievances while building up the British armed forces to deter the Germans, Italians, and Japanese from going too far. Nonetheless, Hitler had his own ambitions. Chamberlain's policies failed to prevent war – as probably would have those advocated by his critics like Winston Churchill. The Second World War was Hitler's war, but a different approach to France after 1936 might have meant a different kind of war and, perhaps, no Dunkerque and the precipitous slide in British international fortunes thereafter.

What Professor Dockrill has argued about the period from 1900 to 1939 has a mirror in his work touching the period after 1945, when British power constricted, when the United States and Soviet Russia emerged from the Second World War as the dominant Powers in the world, and when the advent of the Cold War and American leadership of the Western Alliance placed Britain firmly in the second rank of Powers. In the quarter-century after 1945, 'Great' Britain ceased to exist as its economy struggled, its empire disintegrated, and its ability to stay aloof from the swirl of international politics proved impossible. In this context, while the goals of British foreign policy remained unaltered, the issues that preoccupied British leaders and the British public shifted. Britain became a European Power, with regional rather than global interests. British foreign and military policy had to adjust. Working alone and with other historians, Professor Dockrill has helped chart the course of this readjustment of policy;[52] in essence, he takes the view that to understand what happened after the Second World War, one must understand what happened – and why it happened – in the half-century or more before 1939. This translates into a grasp of the traditions of British foreign policy and of the nature of the debate among powerful personalities over the content and aims of policy. For instance, pursuit of the continental balance of power was an axiom of British foreign policy. But how politicians, diplomats, the military, civil servants, journalists, and others have perceived the balance, and how and with what diplomatic resources they possessed and used to maintain it, is the essence of policy-making. It is the task of the historian to make sense of this process. Although other and younger historians will fill in the details and, perhaps, even arrive at conclusions different to his following the release of more archival sources, Professor Dockrill has played an important role in setting out the parameters of the emerging historiography of British foreign policy since 1945. In this way, his work on the pre-1939 period and its post-1945 variant are tied together. Here lies the value of his contribution to the study of British foreign policy for both specialists and non-specialists.

The other strands of Professor Dockrill's contribution to the study of British foreign policy are more prosaic than research and writing; but they are just as important. As a teacher and advisor, he has helped to shape a generation of younger scholars in the fields of international and military history. With an engaging personality, a charm lacking in many academics, and a passion for the historical issues he discusses, his lectures, advice, and supervisions have tended to bring out the best in his students. He has been the mentor of a number of leading historians of modern British foreign and defence policy; he has been available when asked by other graduate students outside of King's College; and even for those students who have not gone on in 'history', he has been an influential and beloved teacher. Finally, Professor Dockrill has made a number of contributions to sustaining the general field of international history and giving it a strong reputation. Although he sometimes has said that it took an inordinate amount of his time and he hoped he had something useful to contribute – self-deprecation is one of his virtues – he served on more than 100 Ph.D. examination committees in the University of London and throughout Britain. Arguing that 'history' is not just the preserve of a relatively small group of scholars and students in academia, he also gave an unaccountable number of lectures across Britain to the general public under the auspices of the Historical Association.

Yet academe was always important. Since the 1970s, along with his colleague, Brian Bond, he helped to sustain the high reputation of the Military History Seminar at the Institute of Historical Research: providing a forum for new work in the field; allowing students to listen to leading British and international scholars; and, at times, cajoling gifted students to present their own work. More widely, he laboured for 15 years as the general editor of 'Studies in Military and Strategic History', a series of significant monographs that have covered topics as divers as the Sino-Japanese war of 1894–95, the military thinking of J.F.C. Fuller, and Anglo-American relations and Arab nationalism in the late 1950s. Perhaps one of his greatest accomplishments involved his part in the 1980s in founding the British International History Group, the only scholarly body for the field in the United Kingdom. With annual conferences and yearly prizes for the best dissertation in international history, the BIHG has emerged as the locus of international history in the United Kingdom. For the last ten years of his career, Professor Dockrill made a major contribution to the BIHG by providing effective leadership as its president.

Thus, the contributors to this book honour Michael Dockrill. But we feel, importantly, that this volume is not simply a paean to his accomplishments or to the esteem that we all feel towards him and his work. As he would appreciate – and demand – there must always be a value to historical scholarship, whether to adumbrate new interpretations, revise old ones, or offer fresh insight into how and why events happened as they did. Building these chapters around the two issues that have animated his contribution to the study of modern British foreign policy – power and stability – we each have illuminated aspects of British foreign policy between 1865 and 1965 in ways of which he would approve. We and the profession as a whole owes him a great deal.

NOTES

1. M.L. Dockrill, 'Britain, the United States, and France and the German Settlement 1918–1920', in B.J.C. McKercher and D.J. Moss (eds.), *Shadow and Substance in British Foreign Policy 1895–1939. Memorial Essays Honouring C.J. Lowe* (Edmonton, Alberta, 1984), p.217.
2. E.g., see M.E. Chamberlain, *British Foreign Policy in the Age of Palmerston* (London, 1980); H. Kissinger, *A World Restored: Metternich, Castlereagh and the Problems of Peace, 1812–22* (Boston, 1973); M. Swartz, *The Politics of British Foreign Policy in the Era of Disraeli and Gladstone* (New York, 1985); H.W.V. Temperley, *The Foreign Policy of Canning, 1822–1827: England, the Neo-Holy Alliance, and the New World* (London, 2nd edn 1966); C.K. Webster, *The Foreign Policy of Castlereagh, 1812–1815. Britain and the Reconstruction of Europe* (London, 1931).
3. For instance, M.S. Anderson, *The Eastern Question* (London, 1966); J.A.S. Grenville, 'The Eastern Question', in idem, *Lord Salisbury and Foreign Policy: The Close of the Nineteenth Century* (London, 1964), pp.24–53; J.A.R. Marriott, *The Eastern Question* (London, 1917); R. Millman, *Britain and the Eastern Question 1875–1878* (Oxford, 1965). Then cf. G.J. Billy, 'The Italian Question', in idem, *Palmerston's Foreign Policy: 1848* (New York/San Francisco, 1993), pp.85–109.
4. Cf. B.J.C. McKercher, 'Diplomatic Equipoise: The Lansdowne Foreign Office, the Russo-Japanese War of 1904–1905, and the Global Balance of Power', *Canadian Journal of History*, 24 (1989), pp.299–340.
5. Salisbury to Lascelles (British ambassador, Berlin), 10 March 1896, quoted in Grenville, *Salisbury*, p.155. Cf. M. Bentley, *Lord Salisbury's World. Conservative Environments in Late Victorian Britain* (Cambridge, 2001), pp.94–101; L. Penson, *Foreign Affairs under the Third Marquis of Salisbury* (London, 1962).
6. Gladstone argued for 'treaties of mutual benefit with every nation of earth; treaties not written on parchment, but based on the permanent wants and interests of man, kept alive and confirmed by the constant play of the motives which govern his daily life'. Quoted in H.C.G. Matthew, *Gladstone, 1809–1874* (Oxford, 1986), p.181. See the review of E. Schulyer, *Notes of a Journey in Russian Turkistan, Khokand, Bukhara, and Kuldja*, 2 vols. (London, 1876), by W.E. Gladstone, 'Russian Policy and Deeds in Turkistan', *Contemporary Review*, 28 (Nov. 1876), pp.873–91.
7. Cf. 'The doctrine that the flag draws the trade is covered and supported by the documents which are annually laid before us ...'; Salisbury in the House of Lords, 25 Nov. 1891, quoted in Bentley, *Salisbury's World*, p.226; and Gladstone to Kimberley (on inter-colonial tariff), 29 Dec. 1871, in P. Knaplund, *Gladstone and Britain's Imperial Policy* (London, 1927), pp.247–50.
8. For instance, see M.L. Dockrill, *The Mirage of Power*, Vol.I: *British Foreign Policy 1902–1914* (London, 1972), pp.1–11.
9. M. Shigeru, 'The Opening of the Twentieth Century and the Anglo-Japanese Alliance, 1895–1923', in C. Hosoya and I.H. Nish (eds.), *The History of Anglo-Japanese Relations*, Vol.I: *Political-Diplomatic Dimension, 1600–1930* (Basingstoke, 2000); I.H. Nish, *The Anglo-Japanese Alliance: The Diplomacy of Two Island Empires, 1894–1907* (London, 1967); M.H. Wilgus, *Sir Claude MacDonald, the Open Door, and British Informal Empire in China, 1895–1900* (New York, 1987). Also see G.W. Monger, *The End of Isolation: British Foreign Policy, 1900–1907* (London, 1963).
10. P.M. Kennedy, *The Rise of the Anglo-German Antagonism, 1860–1914* (London, 1980); D.M. McKale, 'Weltpolitik versus Pax Britannica: Anglo-German Rivalry in Egypt, 1904–1914', *Canadian Journal of History*, 22 (1987), pp.195–207; H. Rosenbach, *Das deutsche Reich, Grossbritannien und der Transvaal (1896–1902): Anfänge deutsch-britischer Entfremdung* (Göttingen, 1993); J. Steinberg, 'The *Novelle*

of 1908: Necessities and Choices in the Anglo-German Naval Arms Race', *Transactions of the Royal Historical Society*, 5th Series, 21 (1971), pp.25–43.
11. Cf. M.L. Dockrill, 'British Policy during the Agadir Crisis of 1911', in F.H. Hinsley (ed.), *British Foreign Policy under Sir Edward Grey* (Cambridge, 1977), pp.271–87; K. Hamilton, 'The Entente and the Status Quo', in idem, *Bertie of Thame. Edwardian Ambassador* (London, 1990), pp.125–65; T.G. Otte, 'The Elusive Balance: British Foreign Policy and the French Entente Before the First World War', in A. Sharp and G. Stone (eds.), *Anglo-French Cooperation in the Twentieth Century: Rivalry and Cooperation* (London, 2000).
12. See, generally, D. Lieven, 'Pro-Germans and Russian Foreign Policy, 1890–1914', *International History Review*, 2 (1980), pp.34–54; D.M. McDonald, 'A Lever Without a Fulcrum: Domestic Factors and Russian Foreign Policy, 1905–1914', in H. Ragsdale (ed.), *Imperial Russian Foreign Policy* (Cambridge, 1993); K.E. Neilson, *Britain and the Last Tsar: British Policy and Russia, 1894–1917* (Oxford, 1995); B.J. Williams, 'The Strategic Background to the Anglo-Russian Convention of August 1907', *Historical Journal*, 9 (1966), pp.360–73.
13. If Britain stayed out of a continental war in 1914 and Germany proved triumphant, a German-dominated Europe would be a threat to Britain. Conversely, if the British remained neutral and the Dual Alliance won, post-war Russia and France would undoubtedly threaten British security in both Europe and, because of the Russian and French empires, in the wider world. See Dockrill, *Mirage of Power*, I; M.G. Ekstein and Z. Steiner, 'The Serajevo Crisis', in Hinsley (ed.), *British Foreign Policy under Sir Edward Grey*, pp.397–410. Cf. K. Wilson, 'Sir Eyre Crowe and the Origins of the Crowe Memorandum of 1 January 1907', *Bulletin of the Institute of Historical Research*, 56 (1983), pp.238–41.
14. An indication of these complex changes can be gleaned from L.E. Ambrosius, *Wilsonian Statecraft: Theory and Practice of Liberal Internationalism during World War I* (Wilmington, DE, 1991); H.J. Burgwyn, *The Legend of the Mutilated Victory: Italy, the Great War, and the Paris Peace Conference, 1915–1919* (Westport, CT, 1993); W.B. Lincoln, *Passage through Armageddon: The Russians in War and Revolution, 1914–1918* (New York, 1986); D.M McKale, *War by Revolution: Germany and Great Britain in the Middle East in the era of World War I* (Kent, OH, 1998); N. Kawamura, *Turbulence in the Pacific: Japanese–U.S. relations during World War I* (Westport, CT, 2000); M. Rauchensteiner, *Der Tod des Doppeladlers: Österreich-Ungarn und der Erste Weltkrieg* (Graz, 2nd edn 1994). Then see D. Stevenson, *The First World War and International Politics* (Oxford/New York, 1988). Cf. A. Mombauer, *The Origins of the First World War: Controversies and Consensus* (London/New York, 2002).
15. Cf. J.R. Ferris, 'The Theory of a "French Air Menace": Anglo-French Relations and the British Home Air Force Programmes of 1921–25', *Journal of Strategic Studies*, 10 (1987), pp.62–83; W.L. Kleine-Ahlbrandt, *The Burden of Victory: France, Britain, and the Enforcement of the Versailles Peace, 1919–1925* (Lanham, MD, 1995); H.H. Hall, 'Lloyd George, Briand, and the Failure of the Anglo-French Entente', *Journal of Modern History*, 50 (1978), supplement; L.S. Jaffe, *The Decision to Disarm Germany. British Policy towards Postwar German Disarmament, 1914–1919* (Boston, 1985); J.E.L. Loyrette, *The Foreign Policy of Poincaré: France and Great Britain in Relation to the German Problem, 1918–1923* (London, 1936); W.A. MacDougall, *France's Rhineland Diplomacy, 1914–1924: The Last Bid for a Balance of Power in Europe* (Princeton, NJ, 1978).
16. E.g., see P. Chassaigne and M.L. Dockrill, '"Perfide Albion": All the Way?", in P. Chassaigne and M.L. Dockrill (eds.), *Anglo-French Relations, 1898–1998. From Fashoda to Jospin* (London, 2002).

17. See Headlam-Morley (FO historical advisor), 'Memorandum on the History of British Policy and the Geneva Protocol', 12 Feb. 1925, FO 371/11064/1252/9. There is a dissenting view: 'One strand in the argument about the "inevitability" [of the First World War] is the belief that Britain had a role to play in maintaining the balance of power in Europe and that this "traditional" policy was being fulfilled in 1914 and 1939. ... Yet where was this "tradition" between 1815 and 1914, or between 1714 and 1793 for that matter?' From J. Charmley, *Splendid Isolation? Britain, the Balance of Power and the Origins of the First World War* (London, 1999), p.1.
18. G. Bertram-Libal, *Aspekte der britishchen Deutschlandpolitik, 1919–1922* (Göttingen, 1972); S. Marks, 'Ménage à Trois: The Negotiations for an Anglo-French-Belgian Alliance in 1922', *International History Review*, 4 (1982), pp.524–52; A. Sharp, 'Repairing the *Entente Cordiale* and the New Diplomacy', *Historical Journal*, 23 (1980), pp.133–53; C. Stamm, *Lloyd George zwischen Innen- und Aussenpolitik: Die britische Deutschlandpolitik, 1921–1922* (Köln, 1977). Cf. J.P. Selsam, *The Attempts to Form an Anglo-French Alliance, 1919–1924* (Philadelphia, 1936).
19. B.C. Busch, *Mudros to Lausanne: Britain's Frontier in West Asia, 1918–1923* (Albany, NY, 1976); J. Fisher, *Curzon and British Imperialism in the Middle East, 1916–19* (London/Portland, OR, 1999); M. Hughes, *Allenby and British Strategy in the Middle East, 1917–1919* (London/Portland, OR, 1999); A.L. Macfie, 'The British Decision Regarding the Future of Constantinople, November 1918/January 1920', *Historical Journal*, 18 (1975), pp.391–400; B. Westrate, *The Arab Bureau: British Policy in the Middle East, 1916–1920* (University Park, PA, 1992).
20. T. Buckley, *The United States and the Washington Conference, 1921–1922* (Knoxville, 1970); E. Goldstein and J. Maurer (eds.), *The Washington Conference, 1921–22: Naval Rivalry, East Asian Stability, and the Road to Pearl Harbor* (London, 1994); P.P. O'Brien, *British and American Naval Power. Politics and Policy, 1900–1939* (Westport, CT, 1998), pp.149–78; S.W. Roskill, *Naval Policy Between the Wars*, Vol. I: *The Period of Anglo-American Antagonism 1919–1929* (London, 1968), pp.300–330.
21. See S.E. Fritz, 'La Politique de la Ruhr and Lloyd Georgian Conference Diplomacy: The Tragedy of Anglo-French Relations, 1919–1923', *Proceedings of the Annual Meeting of Western Society for French History*, 3 (1975), pp.61–72; E. Goldstein, *Winning the Peace: British Diplomatic Strategy, Peace Planning, and Paris Peace Conference, 1916–1920* (Oxford/New York, 1991); S. Jeannesson, *Poincaré, la France et la Ruhr, 1922–1924: histoire d'une occupation* (Strasbourg, 1998); E.Y. O'Riordan, *Britain and the Ruhr Crisis* (Basingstoke, 2001); S.A. Schuker, *The End of French Predominance in Europe: The Financial Crisis of 1924 and the Adoption of the Dawes Plan* (Chapel Hill, NC, 1976).
22. J.G. Darwin, 'The Chanak Crisis and the British Cabinet', *History*, 65 (1980), pp.32–48; K.G. Larew, 'Great Britain and the Greco-Turkish War, 1921–1922', *Historian*, 35 (1973), pp.256–70; A.L. Macfie, 'The Straits Question: The Conference of Lausanne, November 1922–July 1923', *Middle Eastern Studies*, 15 (1979), pp.211–38; A.E. Montgomery, 'Lloyd George and the Greek Question, 1918–1922', in A.J.P. Taylor (ed.), *Lloyd George: Twelve Essays* (London, 1971). Then see P. Helmreich, *From Paris to Sèvres: The Partition of the Ottoman Empire at the Paris Peace Conference of 1919–1920* (Columbus, OH, 1974); A.L. Macfie, *The End of the Ottoman Empire, 1908–1923* (London/New York, 1998).
23. E. Goldstein, 'The Evolution of British Diplomatic Strategy for the Locarno Pact, 1924–1925', in M.L. Dockrill and B.J.C. McKercher (eds.), *Diplomacy and World Power: Studies in British Foreign Policy, 1890–1951* (Cambridge, 1996); J. Jacobson, *Locarno Diplomacy: Germany and the West, 1925–1929* (Princeton, NJ, 1972), pp.1–79; G. Johnson, *The Berlin Embassy of Lord D'Abernon, 1920–1926* (Basingstoke, NY, 2002), pp.108–35; A. Kaiser, *Lord D'Abernon und die englische*

Deutschlandpolitik 1920–1926 (Frankfurt, 1989); P. Urbanitsch, *Grossbritannien und die Verträge von Locarno* (Vienna, 1968).

24. See Gregory (FO Northern Department), 'Memorandum on the Foreign Policy of His Majesty's Government, with a List of British Commitments in their Relative Order of Importance', 10 April 1926, Foreign Office, *Documents on British Foreign Policy*, Series IA, Vol.I: *The Aftermath of Locarno* (1966), pp.846–81. Of 13 specific commitments, the first four in their order of importance were: (i) the League of Nations Covenant; (ii) the Treaty of Versailles; (iii) the Treaty of Locarno; (iv) the Washington treaties. On Britain, the League, and collective security, see M. Bourquin (ed.), *Collective Security: A Record of the Seventh and Eighth International Studies Conferences, Paris, 1934, London, 1935* (Paris, 1936); G.W. Egerton, *Great Britain and the Creation of the League of Nations: Strategy, Politics and International Organization, 1914–1919* (Chapel Hill, NC, 1978); B.J.C. McKercher, 'The League of Nations and the Problem of Collective Security, 1919–1936', in U.M. Rüser (ed.), *The League of Nations, 1920–1946. Organization and Accomplishments* (Geneva, 1996), pp.66–73.

25. For an indication, see K. Hildebrand, *No intervention: die Pax Britannica und Preussen 1865/66–1869/70: eine Untersuchung zur englischen Weltpolitik im 19. Jahrhundert* (München, 1997); C.J. Lowe, *The Reluctant Imperialists*, Vol.I: *British Foreign Policy, 1878–1902* (London, 1967); Swartz, *Disraeli and Gladstone*.

26. British policy at the Congress of Berlin is a case in point. See M. Wilkinson Jones, 'Pyrrhic Victory? The Bismarck Myth and the Congress of Berlin in the British Review Press, 1878–79', in M.H. Shirley and T.E.A. Larson (eds.), *Splendidly Victorian: Essays in Nineteenth- and Twentieth-Century British History in Honour of Walter L. Arnstein* (Aldershot, 2001); W.N. Medlicott, *The Congress of Berlin* (London, 2nd edn 1963); R. Millman, *Britain and the Eastern Question 1875–1878* (Oxford, 1979).

27. W.L. Langer, *European Alliances and Alignments 1871–1890* (New York, 2nd edn 1956), pp.395–404, 434–45; C.J. Lowe, *Salisbury and the Mediterranean* (London, 1965), pp.75–7. Cf. D.R. Gillard, 'Salisbury and the Indian Defence Problem, 1885–1902', in K. Bourne and D.C. Watt (eds.), *Studies in International History. Essays presented to W. Norton Medlicott* (London, 1967), pp.245–7.

28. Quoted in Langer, *European Alliances*, p.400.

29. R.C.K. Ensor, *England, 1870–1914* (Oxford, 1936), pp.77–86; R.T. Harrison, *Gladstone's Imperialism in Egypt. Techniques of Domination* (Westport, CT, 1995); A.G. Hopkins, 'The Victorians and Africa: A Reconsideration of the Occupation of Egypt, 1882', *Journal of African History*, 27 (1986), pp.363–91; A. Scholch, '"Men on the Spot" and the English Occupation of Egypt in 1882', *Historical Journal*, 19 (1976), pp.773–85.

30. Cf. F.R. Bridge, *Great Britain and Austria-Hungary 1906–1914: A Diplomatic History* (1972); Dockrill, *Mirage of Power*; D. French, *British Economic and Strategic Planning 1905–1915* (London, 1982); Monger, *End of Isolation*; Neilson, *Last Tsar*; Z.S. Steiner, *Britain and the Origins of the First World War* (London, 1977); J.A. White, *Transition to Global Rivalry: Alliance Diplomacy and the Quadruple Entente 1898-1907* (Cambridge, 1995); S.R. Williamson, *The Politics of Grand Strategy: Britain and France Prepare for War, 1904–1914* (London, 1990). See D.G. Herrmann, *The Arming of Europe and the Making of the First World War* (London 1996); D. Stevenson, *Armaments and the Coming of War: Europe, 1904–1914* (Oxford, 1996).

31. See M.F. Boemeke, G.D. Feldman, and E. Glaser-Schmidt (eds.), *The Treaty of Versailles: A Reassessment after 75 Years* (Cambridge, 1997); G.W. Egerton, *Great Britain and the Creation of the League of Nations: Strategy, Politics, and International Organization, 1914–1919* (Chapel Hill, NC, 1978); H. Elcock, *Portrait of a Decision: The Council of Four and the Treaty of Versailles* (London, 1972); M.L. Dockrill and

J.D. Goold, *Peace Without Promise: Britain and the Peace Conferences, 1919–23* (London, 1981); M.L. Dockrill and J. Fisher (eds.), *The Paris Peace Conference 1919: Peace Without Victory?* (Basingstoke/New York, 2001); Goldstein, *Winning the Peace*; A.J. Sharp, *The Versailles Settlement: Peacemaking in Paris, 1919* (Basingstoke, 1991).
32. A. Chamberlain, 'Great Britain as a European Power', *Journal of the Royal Institute of International Affairs*, 9 (1930), pp.180–88.
33. Cf. R.A. Dayer, 'Anglo-American Monetary Policy and Rivalry in Europe and the Far East, 1919–1931', in B.J.C. McKercher (ed.), *Anglo-American Relations in the 1920s: The Struggle for Supremacy* (London, 1991); R. Henig, *Versailles and After, 1919–1933* (London, 1995); M.J. Hogan, *Informal Entente. The Private Structure of Cooperation in Anglo-American Economy Diplomacy, 1918–1928* (Columbia, 1977); M.P. Leffler, *The Elusive Quest. America's Pursuit of European Stability and French Security, 1919–1933* (Chapel Hill, NC, 1979).
34. Chamberlain to Crewe (British ambassador, Paris), 2 April 1925, Chamberlain MSS FO (Foreign Office Archives, Public Record Office, Kew) 800/258.
35. A. Cassels, *Mussolini's Early Diplomacy* (Princeton, NJ, 1970); J. Jacobson, 'The Conduct of Locarno Diplomacy', *Review of Politics*, 34 (1972), pp.67–81; E. Keeton, *Briand's Locarno Policy. French Economics, Politics, and Diplomacy, 1925–1929* (New York, 1987); F. Magee '"Limited Liability"? Britain and the Treaty of Locarno', *Twentieth Century British History*, 6 (1995), pp.1–22; S. Marks, *The Illusion of Security: International Relations in Europe, 1918–1933* (London, 1976); B.J.C. McKercher, 'Austen Chamberlain's Control of British Foreign Policy, 1924–1929', *International History Review*, 6 (1984), pp.570–91; A. Orde, *Britain and International Security, 1920–1926* (London, 1978) R. Grathwohl, *Stresemann and the DNVP: Reconciliation or Revenge in German Foreign Policy, 1924–1928* (Lawrence, KS, 1980).
36. See E.K.S. Fung, 'The Sino-British Rapprochement, 1927–1931', *Modern Asian Studies*, 17 (1983); B.J.C. McKercher, 'A Sane and Sensible Diplomacy: Austen Chamberlain, Japan, and the Naval Balance of Power in the Pacific Ocean, 1924–29', *Canadian Journal of History*, 21 (1985), pp.187–213.
37. Cf. B.J.C. McKercher, *The Second Baldwin Government and the United States, 1924–1929: Attitudes and Diplomacy* (Cambridge, 1984); idem, 'From Enmity to Cooperation: The Second Baldwin Government and the Improvement of Anglo-American Relations, November 1928–June 1929', *Albion*, 24 (1992), pp.64–87.
38. Cf. D.H. Aldcroft, *From Versailles to Wall Street, 1919–1929* (London, 1977); S.V.O. Clarke, *Central Bank Cooperation, 1924–1931* (New York, 1967); E.W. Bennett, *Germany and the Diplomacy of the Financial Crisis, 1931* (Cambridge, MA, 1962); B. Eichengreen, *Golden Fetters: The Gold Standard and the Great Depression, 1919–1939*; (1992); C.P. Kindleberger, *The World in Depression, 1929–1939* (London, 1973); D.B. Kunz, *The Battle for Britain's Gold Standard in 1931* (London, 1987); R. Skidelsky, *Politicians and the Slump: The Labour Government of 1929–1931* (London, rev. edn 1994). Then see E.W. Bennett, *German Rearmament and the West, 1932–1933* (Princeton, 1979); B. Kent, *The Spoils of War. The Politics, Economics, and Diplomacy of Reparations, 1918–1932* (Oxford, 1989); I.H. Nish, *Japan's Struggle with Internationalism. Japan, China, and the League of Nations, 1931–3* (London, 1993); K.A. Oye, 'The Sterling-Dollar-Franc Triangle: Monetary Diplomacy, 1929–1937', *World Politics*, 38 (1985), pp.173–99; C. Thorne, *The Limits of Foreign Policy. The West, the League and the Far Eastern Crisis of 1931–1933* (New York, 1973).
39. W.M. Fletcher, *The Search for a New Order. Intellectuals and Fascism in Prewar Japan* (Chapel Hill, NC, 1982).
40. On Japan, see J.B. Crowley, *Japan's Quest for Autonomy. National Security and*

Foreign Policy, 1930–1938 (Princeton, 1966); J.R. Ferris, 'Worthy of Some Better Enemy?: The British Estimate of the Imperial Japanese Army, 1919–1941, and the Fall of Singapore', *Canadian Journal of History*, 28 (1993), pp.223–56; H. Ikuhiko, *Reality and Illusion: The Hidden Crisis between Japan and the U.S.S.R., 1932–1934* (New York, 1967). On Germany, see H. James, *The German Slump. Politics and Economics, 1924–1936* (Oxford, 1986); I. Kershaw, *Hitler*, Vol.I: *1889–1936: Hubris* (1998), pp.313–427; W.N. Medlicott, *Britain and Germany: The Search for Agreement, 1930–1937* (London, 1969); G.L. Weinberg, *The Foreign Policy of Hitler's Germany*, 2 vols. (Chicago, 1970, 1980); H.A. Winkler (ed.), *Die deutsche Staatskrise 1930–1933* (München, 1992).

41. See Defence Requirements Sub-committee, 'Report' (DRC 14), 28 Feb. 1934, CAB (Cabinet Archives, Public Record Office, Kew) 16/109; DRC 'Third Report' (DRC 37), 21 Nov. 1935, CAB 16/112. Then cf. G. Post, Jr., *Dilemmas of Appeasement. British Deterrence and Defense, 1934–1937* (Ithaca, NY, 1993).
42. This and the next sentence are based on F. McDonough, *Neville Chamberlain, Appeasement and the British Road to War* (London, 1998); S. Newton, 'Appeasement as an Industrial Strategy, 1938–1941', *Contemporary Record*, 9/3 (1995), pp.485–506; R.A.C. Parker, *Chamberlain and Appeasement. British Policy and the Coming of the Second World War* (London, 1993); G. Schmidt, *The Politics and Economics of Appeasement: British Foreign Policy in the 1930s* (London, 1986).
43. In I. Colvin, *The Chamberlain Cabinet. How Meetings in 10 Downing Street, 1937–1939, led to the Second World War – Told for the First Time from the Cabinet Papers* (New York, 1971), p.46.
44. Inskip 'Interim Report on Defence Expenditure in Future Years' (CP 316(37)), 15 Dec. 1937, CAB 24/273. Sir Thomas Inskip was the minister of defence co-ordination, who oversaw a major review of defence policy between June 1937 and February 1938. Cf. S. Greenwood '"Caligula's Horse" Revisited: Sir Thomas Inskip as Minister for the Co-ordination of Defence, 1936–1939', *Journal of Strategic Studies*, 17 (1994), pp.17–38; G.C. Peden, 'A Matter of Timing: the Economic Background to British Foreign Policy, 1937–1939', *History*, 69 (1984), pp.15–28.
45. P.M. Kennedy, 'The Tradition of Appeasement in British Foreign Policy, 1865–1939', *British Journal of International Studies*, 2 (1976).
46. See Chamberlain to Ida, his sister, 4 July, 30 Oct., 26 Nov. 1937, NC (Neville Chamberlain MSS, University Library, University of Birmingham, Birmingham) 18/1/1010, 1026, 1030; Chamberlain to Hilda, his sister, 24 Oct. 1937, 5 Dec. 1937, NC 18/1/1025, 1030a. Cf. Parker, *Chamberlain and Appeasement*.
47. For examples of the disputatious historiography on this subject, see S. Aster, '"Guilty Men": The Case of Neville Chamberlain', in R. Boyce and E.M. Robertson (eds.), *Paths to War: New Essays on the Origins of the Second World War* (London, 1989); M. Hauner, 'Czechoslovakia as a Military Factor in British Considerations of 1938', *Journal of Strategic Studies*, 1 (1978), pp.221–40; D.N. Lammers, *Explaining Munich: The Search for Motive in British Policy* (Stanford, 1966); W. Murray, *The Change in the European Balance of Power, 1938–1939: The Path to Ruin* (Princeton, NJ, 1984); T. Taylor, *Munich: The Price of Peace* (London, 1979); C. Webster, 'Munich Reconsidered: A Survey of British Policy', *International Affairs*, 37 (1961).
48. This and the next sentence are based on S. Conkov, 'The British Policy of Guarantees and Greece (March–April 1939)', *Studia Balcanica*, 4 (1971); D. Lungau, 'The European Crisis of March–April 1939: The Romanian Dimension', *International History Review*, 7 (1985), pp.390–414; S. Newman, *The British Guarantee to Poland: A Study in the Continuity of British Foreign Policy* (London, 1976);
49. S. Aster, *1939. The Making of the Second World War* (London, 1973); D. Dilks, '"We Must Hope for the Best and Prepare for the Worst": The Prime Minister, the Cabinet

and Hitler's Germany, 1937–1939', *Proceedings of the British Academy*, 73 (1987), pp.309–52; E.M. Robertson (ed.), *The Origins of the Second World War. Historical Interpretations* (London, 1971); D. Cameron Watt, *How War Came: The Immediate Origins of the Second World War* (London, 1989). Cf. the iconoclastic and thought-provoking J. Charmley, *Chamberlain and the Lost Peace* (London, 1989).

50. See L.S. Presnell, *External Economic Policy Since the War*, Vol. I: *The Post-War Financial Settlement* (London, 1986), especially Chapter I, 'The Nature of the Problem'.
51. See Dockrill, *Mirage of Power*, I; Dockrill and Goold, *Peace Without Promise*; M.L. Dockrill, *British Establishment Perspectives on France, 1936–40* (Basingstoke/New York, 1999).
52. See M.L. Dockrill, *The Cold War, 1945–1963* (Atlantic Highlands, NJ, 1988); idem, *British Defence Since 1945* (New York, 1989); M.L. Dockrill and J.W. Young (eds.), *British Foreign Policy, 1945–56* (New York, 1989); A. Adamthwaite and M.L. Dockrill (eds.), *Europe within the Global System 1938–1960: Great Britain, France, Italy and Germany: From Great Powers to Regional Powers* (Bochum, 1995).

British Power and Stability: The Historical Record

ZARA STEINER

'Fog over the Channel. Continent isolated.' Regardless of the Channel Tunnel and the detailed continental weather reports on Radio 3, British attitudes towards the Continent, like those of the continental Powers towards Britain, are bound to remain ambivalent. When looking back to the history of these complex relations, two main readings stand out. The first is that Britain's attempts to underwrite European stability from Waterloo to the present day left it exhausted and stripped of its empire. The other reading perceives in these costly efforts a successful preservation of British integrity and independence. What allowed, for many years, the country to have the luxury of choices with regard to its relations with Europe was the underlying security of the home islands and the existence of a vast empire overseas. Nor was the former condition quickly forfeited. There were moments of panic – in 1908, for example, when the so-called discovery of an acceleration in German naval building led to a massive increase in the naval estimates. Throughout the 1920s, British citizens slept safely in their beds. The change came after 1933 when the possibility of a 'knock-out blow' created an 'air panic' in official circles and the belief that the Germans could launch 'a short sharp war' became a central feature of defence policy.[1] The fear of the 'knock-out blow' was very much in Prime Minister Neville Chamberlain's mind before Munich. The improvement of Britain's defensive position in 1938–39 and new air raid precaution measures increased official confidence and boosted public morale. Even so, there was a mass exodus from London in the weeks immediately after the declaration of war. Despite these fears and doubts about how the war against Germany could be won, few actually considered the possibility of invasion or defeat before 1940.[2]

This sense of security derived from a unique set of circumstances, some of which have had their American parallels – a highly favourable geographic position, supremacy on the oceans, a world empire, and an enduring commercial and financial position which outlasted the relatively short period of industrial leadership. There was also Britain's political stability. The moral authority claimed by foreign secretaries derived from the advantages of a constitutional monarchy and an ordered and free society. It was against this background in 1852, on one of those very rare occasions when a foreign secretary formulated in a single document the aims and principles of British foreign policy, that Lord Granville wrote of Britain's special place in Europe. 'It was the duty and interest of this country', he insisted, 'to encourage moral, intellectual and physical progress among all nations.'[3] When invited, Britain was in a position to settle the disputes which might arise between other nations. The patronising tone of Granville's memorandum, as Agatha Ramm has written, is only understandable from a state which felt itself safe in Europe or ascendant over it.[4]

If the former was true, the latter was not. It was not within Britain's power to establish its ascendancy in Europe. The continental stability of the mid-century was based on the domestic preoccupations of the main European Powers and their unwillingness or inability to challenge the status quo. Yet it was behind these assumptions, buttressed by Britain's world position, that Gladstone could reject a policy based on the pursuit of power and embrace national self-determination, the freedom of small countries from the domination of the large and the pursuit of free trade – the Wilsonian terminology in embryo. The true test came in Palmerston's day with the rise of Bismarckian Germany, a dramatic shift in the balance of power that Britain had no choice but to accept. It was entirely appropriate that London should follow a policy of conciliation and non-commitment, for naval strength was no longer a substitute for military power. And it was, after 1871, Bismarck's restraint that stabilized the European continent, leaving Britain at liberty to deal with the inevitable race for empire among its rivals. Salisbury felt able to use Britain's free hand in Europe to enlist Germany and Austria-Hungary to check the Russian threat to British imperial interests.[5] If there were clashes on the periphery, Britain could defend 'against all comers that which we possess, and we know in spite of the jargon about isolation, that we are competent to do so'.[6] Britain was a 'free rider' but its freedom depended on a European situation over which it had only limited control.

This special blend of illusory ascendancy and the claim to a unique moral authority outlived the Victorian age. When writing about the need for a more positive policy in 1907, Eyre Crowe wrote that 'the national policy of the insular and naval State is so directed as to harmonize with the general desires and ideals common to all mankind, and more particularly it is closely identified with the primary and vital interests of a majority, or as many as possible, of other nations'.[7] The balance of power, itself, took on moral clothing. It became Britain's 'duty' as well as its interest to preserve the equilibrium of Europe.

It is somewhat curious that the first time since the Napoleonic wars Britain actually engaged in a European war to maintain that balance in Europe, the sources of its engagement lay in the perceived threat to its empire. There is no need to review the circumstances – mainly imperial and economic – that led to a questioning of some of the assumptions outlined here. The anxieties of Lord Salisbury's last Cabinet at the turn of the century came to a height in that prolonged and expensive war against the Boers with its wide-ranging consequences on so many aspects of British political life. For a shorthand, one might take Lord Curzon's comment in 1901: 'The pessimists are abroad in the land, we can hardly take up our morning newspaper without reading of the physical and moral decline of the race. Beaten in cricket. Beaten in polo. Every man over 50 is a Cassandra.'[8] Nonetheless, between 1902 and 1905, the attacks on the Empire were contained through diplomatic manoeuvre, measured retreat, and luck. Unexpectedly, the Russian fleet was sunk at Tsuchima and the so-called 'Two Power standard' could be restored in full, with the United States again considered a possible enemy. The Russian defeat made it possible to contemplate a diplomatic settlement with the Russians, essential if the pathways to India were to be safeguarded. Lord Lansdowne began the process of rapprochement; it was completed after long and tedious negotiations under Sir Edward Grey.[9] After the summer of 1907, John Gooch writes in *The Plans of War*: 'India ceased to bulk large, indeed to bulk at all in the cycles of strategic debate in England. The fear of a Russian advance in Persia continued but the burden of preserving stability in Central Asia fell on the diplomats rather than on the soldiers'.[10]

Lansdowne's successful diplomatic efforts were imperially directed; he intended not only to begin negotiations with the Russians but to renew Britain's links with Germany. Yet his actions had European repercussions. They contributed to the restiveness of Germany and encouraged the Russian return of attention to the Balkans. It was under Lansdowne's successor that Britain began that half-committed intervention in Europe with which this chapter is concerned. Grey's policy was one of limited liability, ententes and not alliances, to contain Germany but not to isolate it. Grey believed limited support for France and Russia would contribute to the stabilization of Europe; instead they contributed to the rising sense of European unease. The ententes were nourished to defend the Empire, above all India, but the new connections affected Anglo-German relations. The alarms set off by the supposed acceleration of the German naval building programme in 1908–9 served to confirm growing doubts about Germany's future intentions. It may well be that the Grey Foreign Office overreacted. Given actual German power, the policies of the Reich were surprisingly conservative. Nonetheless, the German alarm bells were heard in King Charles Street, a measure of the post-Salisburian loss of confidence, but also the belief, so clearly articulated by Eyre Crowe, that Britain had a special responsibility for the maintenance of the stability of Europe. That stability seemed under threat. Britain became a player despite its military weakness in the continental game. Grey had seriously compromised if not abandoned the old policy of the 'free hand' while still insisting that Britain was a free agent.

There is a genuine problem about Britain's entry into the European war following the 'July Crisis' of 1914. It worried Grey and the generation that followed and still sets off historical arguments today. It cannot be shown that there was a direct threat to British security in July 1914. Two-thirds of the Cabinet at the start of the crisis was opposed to war. Yet Britain went to war with only two resignations. One of the two, John Burns, outlined the radical position: 'Splendid isolation. No Balance of Power. No Incorporation in the Continental System.'[11] But what of the other 'doves'? Most, however reluctantly, had accepted the ententes and the military and naval conversations to which they led. Faced with the outbreak of war, they proved unwilling to stand apart as the British had in 1871. National interests were involved because of the war's possible consequences for future British power. German success could lead to its domination of the Low Countries. The victory of the Dual Alliance would leave India exposed to a Russian advance. Fear of a divided Cabinet and a coalition government concentrated ministerial minds. Belgium became the fig leaf that soothed troubled radical consciences. And it was assumed that the British contribution would be limited as in the Napoleonic wars, so that the costs of intervention would not be excessive.

Had Grey's policies of the ententes helped to undermine European stability? War would have come even if Britain had eschewed his policies. Austrian action against Serbia was not shaped by the British defection from Vienna. Anglo-German rivalry was an additional rather than the central source of continental instability. The semi-committed position did, however, contribute to the fragility of the existing balance. The French and Russians gained in confidence; Germany was not deterred. Grey's balancing act was a failure because he was already committed to one side. The successful British defence of its global interests, moreover, had closed off the safety valves of extra-European expansion. When a new threat to the European equilibrium arose in the 1930s, the British Foreign Office would use colonial carrots, admittedly some belonging to the French, to try to tempt Hitler away from Central Europe. One always learns the lessons of the last war.

Britain's experience in the 1914–18 war has been read in different ways. In light of the Ludendorff–Hindenburg ascendancy and the terms of the Treaty of Brest-Litovsk, the coalition Cabinet felt they had prevented the victory of the Prussian militarists; the fear of their revival lasted well into the Hitler period and surfaced again in 1945. Britain had engaged in a great land war and emerged triumphant. Its military contribution was far more important than had been anticipated. Without British help, France might well have lost the struggle. British output of strategic industrial goods and their quality matched that of any other belligerent, including the United States. It was more successful than any other power in mobilizing the economy and, despite the massive effort, the civilian population enjoyed a higher standard of living than in the pre-war years. The Empire had come to the support of the mother country, admittedly for a price, and committed men and material to all the battlefields, including the western front. Britain's performance in the war confirmed its position as one of the world's greatest powers.

The costs were high, far higher than anyone anticipated: 730,000 dead, quite apart from the wounded and disabled and the material costs of the war. The shock was the greater because the political elite and most of the country thought that the British contribution would be a limited one and the war would be of short duration. The sense of the war's futility, so important in the pacifist and disarmament movements of the 1930s, represented a delayed reaction to the price paid. The margin of victory was narrow. In 1918, the prime minister, David Lloyd George was acutely aware of the American contribution and was fearful that if the war continued another six months, the peace would be an American one. Though Britain emerged with much of its overseas investment portfolio intact, there was the $4.7 billion owed to the United States (a levy of no more than 0.8 per cent on existing holdings would have paid off the debt), the destruction of the gold standard and the emergence of the Americans as the world's major creditors, spelling the beginning of the end of Britain's domination of world finance.

If the war experience was an ambivalent one, the peace terms both expanded the country's imperial domains and increased its influence in Europe. Britain and its empire left the peace table gorged with almost all the colonial pickings, including rich territories in the Middle East. The prime minister proclaimed that in Europe where the country had no territorial interests, the British could be the 'impartial arbiters' forgetful of the passions of war. The Welsh Wizard achieved most, if not all, of what he wanted in Paris. He sought to reconstitute the balance of power in Europe. Apart from preventing any one country from dominating the Lowlands opposite Britain, he wanted to prevent the substitution of a new hegemonic power, France, for the one that had just been defeated. This involved a series of conflicts with Clemenceau, over Luxembourg, the Saar, the Rhineland and elsewhere. Lloyd George wanted to apply the new doctrines of self-determination within prescribed limits. Quite apart from his anti-Polish prejudices, he did not want to create new Alsace-Lorraines in Poland that would leave the Germans permanently in the revisionist camp. Against Clemenceau's over-riding concern with French security, he posed his hopes for a stable Europe. Germany was to be punished but eventually allowed to return to the councils of Europe. Only a stable Europe and German recovery would allow Britain to withdraw from active intervention in continental affairs so that it could turn its attention once again to its empire. The British prime minister was convinced that German recovery and the reintegration of Bolshevik Russia into the continental economy were the essential conditions for the revival of British trade and investment and the best hope for the taming of the Bolsheviks.

The terms of the peace treaty were such that though Britain's priorities might have been imperial rather than continental, it was drawn into Europe. By disposition, Lloyd George enjoyed his mediating role and contemplated with pleasure the possibility of returning to that golden age when Britain had been the fulcrum of the balance of power. Nevertheless, he also imagined that once stability was restored, Britain could withdraw from continental affairs, leaving a peaceful France and democratized Germany to live in harmony without Britain's active intervention. Even Winston Churchill thought it possible that Britain might:

> Withdraw altogether from participation in continental affairs and imitate in this respect the attitude of the United States. She should strengthen her Navy and her Air Force. She should cultivate friendly relations equally with Germany and with France so as far as possible making it clear she will not be involved in any quarrel that may arise between them.[12]

Lloyd George never believed in a policy of continental isolation, nor did he accept the views of those who argued that British interests would be best served in a partnership with the United States. Isolation, however attractive, was not a viable option. The Committee of Imperial Defence, intent on using Britain's stripped military forces for imperial purposes, was driven to conclude in June 1920 that the dominant impulse of British policy during the last century was the defence of India: 'we cannot be free to carry out our main objects, which are Imperial and Colonial, unless we are safe in

Europe and it will be many years yet before we free ourselves from responsibility for Europe.'[13]

The British tried to restrict these responsibilities as much as they could without ceasing to have a major voice in the disposition of European affairs. They avoided guarantees to the French involving automatic support or military backing. They blocked efforts to tighten the security clauses of the League of Nations until the Labour foreign secretary, Arthur Henderson, came to the Foreign Office in 1929; and, even then, the proposed measures did not involve taking on new obligations of enforcement. The pattern had been set by the previous foreign secretaries. His immediate predecessor, the Conservative Austen Chamberlain, spelled out the limits of Britain's continental obligations in negotiating the Locarno agreements in 1925. They did not extend to Eastern Europe, where it was felt that some form of territorial revision was inevitable if a stable equilibrium was to be established. British influence depended not on military strength – the chiefs of staff repeatedly warned that there were no forces available to back up the Locarno commitments – but on the negotiating skills of its statesmen and the continuing cooperation between British and American financiers. In 1925, some form of stabilization had been achieved. At the Imperial Conference of 1926, Austen Chamberlain, engaging in an unusual speech of self-congratulation, boasted that the Locarno agreements were 'in large measure a British achievement and recognised as such by other powers ... British friendship is cultivated, British counsel asked, British aid sought and as in the days of Castlereagh, Great Britain stands forth again as the moderator and peacemaker of the new Europe created by the Great War'.[14]

How had the British achieved this position and what could they offer for the future stability of Europe given the narrow focus of the Locarno guarantees, the high point in the inter-war stabilization of Europe? In many respects, British influence was the consequence of the policies of the other players. While there was still room for manoeuvre, both Paris and Berlin looked to London. Every French premier, including Raymond Poincaré, believed that France needed British underwriting in order to deal with Germany, whose power, both existing and potential, was possibly exaggerated in Paris. French efforts at independent action, even with regard to direct

Franco-German settlements, failed to achieve their purposes. There appeared no alternative to the British card given the weaknesses of their Eastern allies and the doubts which surrounded the Soviet Union. The Germans found it highly advantageous to let the British serve as intermediaries with the French. Gustav Stresemann, the German foreign minister, looked to the United States for the restoration of German economic power, but he believed that Austen Chamberlain would bring the necessary pressure on Paris, that is, on the French foreign minister, Aristide Briand, to move faster and further along the path of treaty revision. When the limits of compromise between France and Germany were reached in 1928, the British began, partly because of their interests outside Europe, to abandon their balancing role. With the Labour victory of 1929, the pendulum swung away from France and towards Germany as the British, faced with French demands for security guarantees which London was unprepared to offer, opted to satisfy some of the German grievances as a way to promote reconciliation and disarmament.

British influence was enhanced by the semi-withdrawal of the United States from Europe and by the checking of the Soviet menace both within Europe and along the peripheries of the British Empire. American involvement in the Dawes Plan and the London agreements had important political consequences, but the Americans refused to make any commitment to the support of a European security system. The Locarno agreements were a European solution to a European problem. Austen Chamberlain had neither wanted nor solicited American cooperation. The Kellogg–Briand Pact, that international peace kiss, a promise not to go to war without any sanctions in case of violation, was as far as the Americans would go to address French security concerns. The real turn away from the Continent would come in 1933 when the new president, Franklin Roosevelt, would reject the possibilities of cooperative action to deal with the depression and use domestic remedies instead. Even the most internationally minded of his predecessors, however, recognized the limits of any American security role in Europe, not to speak of the Far East where national interests appeared more obviously engaged. The Soviet Union failed to export its revolution. British policy towards Moscow was variable and contradictory but, insofar as it had any consistency, it was to isolate Russia as far as possible. In London, two currents flowed, fear and visceral hatred of Bolshevism and an interest in Anglo-Russian trade. For Vladimir Lenin and Joseph Stalin, Britain was the most important capitalist Power and the most likely leader of an anti-Bolshevik crusade. The fear of British action, partly genuine but also critical in Stalin's intra-party fights, gave a particular importance to the decisions made in London during the 'great turn' in Soviet policy. By the second half of the 1920s, the fear of Bolshevism spreading in Europe had diminished, though the possibility of a Russo-German combination kept the Soviet Union on the diplomatic agenda. By attaching Germany to the Western world through the Locarno settlements, Austen Chamberlain believed that he had minimized this threat. Though a useful market during the depression years, the Soviet Union remained a pariah state outside the boundaries of civilized diplomatic discourse. Maxim Litvinov, the commissar for foreign affairs after July 1930, would have an uphill battle in his attempts to promote Russia's re-entry into European affairs.

There was influence but also power. Possession of empire continued to make Britain great. The peace settlements saw Britain at the highest point of its imperial expansion, though the immediate post-war years were particularly difficult for the imperial masters. Through a process of modest retreat, new techniques of association and rule, expanded trade and investment, the Commonwealth, as it came to be called, and the colonies were more secure at the end of the decade than in the immediate post-war years. Considerable police and military efforts were needed to contain the 'communal violence' in India, but British rule was not shaken, and it was hoped that the promise of Dominion status and a constitutional conference would take the edge off Gandhi's non-cooperative movement. 'As long as we rule in India', the Viceroy, Lord Curzon, declared in 1901, 'we are the greatest power in the world. If we lose it we shall drop straight away to a third rate power.'[15] The warning had lost none of its force in the 1920s. Air power helped to maintain the peace on India's north-west frontier and in the Middle East, assisted by locally recruited troops. The prestige, if not the presence of the Royal Navy, remained the foundation of British power in the Far East. It was only in China that Britain was forced to give way in the face of Chinese nationalism and Japanese expansionism, and Austen Chamberlain managed this retreat with a maximum of diplomatic dexterity. Africa, under British rule, entered a period of relative stability. Even though the United States made considerable commercial gains at British expense in the Middle East and in Southeastern Asia, the British held off their chief rivals. It was a commonplace in the political rhetoric of the day to claim that Britain only wanted to be left in the 'unmolested enjoyment' of its vast and splendid possessions whose riches unfortunately attracted the eyes of greedy foreign adventurers.

Britain still had the largest fleet in the world as the Americans failed to build up to the Washington treaty limits. While a naval race and war with the United States was ruled out of the question, even the clashes between respective admirals still left the British 'mistress of the seas' when the disputes were resolved in 1930. In European waters, the British fleet was superior to that of its only possible rivals, France and Italy, combined. In 1933, the Admiralty turned to the task of providing a fleet capable both of fighting the Japanese navy and defending the country's interests in Europe. After the Ethiopian crisis, Italy was added to the list of possible enemies. Britain's difficulties would arise from facing three geographically separated enemies at the same time.

Finally, because Britain occupied a position at the centre of world trade and finance, its actions were crucial for the stabilization of the world economy and financial structure. As the major investor abroad, funds went primarily to the Empire but sufficient amounts were directed to central and south-eastern Europe to have important, if mixed, effects on the countries in these areas. British financial power depended on cooperation with the United States; with the partial re-establishment of the gold standard, the City of London shared with New York, and after 1928 with Paris, the maintenance of its working order. The role that the ambitious head of the Bank of England, Montagu Norman, had envisioned for his country turned out to be beyond its capabilities. Yet even after the debacle of 1931, freed from gold and the ties with the United States, London became the centre of one of the most important of the world's currency blocs. Britain remained, too, the world's largest importer and this also enhanced its position as a global power.

These strengths, though they explain why British power was respected, could only be indirectly used to back Britain's continental position. This was even true of British investment, for the Americans were the major investors in Europe in the later 1920s, particularly in Germany, and far ahead of Britain in new issues. More might have been done to promote stabilization had successive British cabinets been willing to take greater risks and British traders and financiers less concentrated on the Empire. Whether Britain could have more effectively bridged the gap between German and French aspirations remains an open question, but the government's insistence on policies of limited liability weakened its continental negotiating hand. Austen Chamberlain's hope was to make the new position of Germany tolerable enough to the German people that they would prove unwilling to put their fortunes again to the desperate hazard of war. He believed that the key to the situation lay in Paris and hoped that by allaying France's fears he could encourage Briand to make the concessions to the Germans that would encourage their acceptance of the Treaty of Versailles. However sympathetic he may have been to the French, he could not go beyond the Locarno agreement, a carefully constructed guarantee with no real military back-up and restricted only to Germany's western frontiers. Given his own mounting fears about the political situation in Germany, he would not move decisively in Stresemann's direction. Neither the revision of the reparations agreement nor the evacuation of the Rhineland had the hoped for effects on German domestic opinion. The French grew increasingly restive; the Briand plan of 1929–30 for a pan-European economic union was an almost desperate French gesture to solve the Franco-German dilemma. It was one that failed to enlist the sympathies of the British government. Despite the Labour government's predilection for the League of Nations and the strengthening of its powers, Labour leaders fought off French efforts to return to the guarantees included in the rejected Geneva Protocol of 1924 as the price for French disarmament. If ultimately the Treaty of Versailles had left in place a situation where any gain in German power represented a blow to France's position, the British unwillingness to guarantee French security in any meaningful sense precluded any adjustment in the continental balance of power within the Treaty limitations.

The years between 1929 and 1933 saw the collapse of the first precarious reconstruction of Europe. During these hinge years, the

Labour and National governments not only refused to assume any new continental commitments but increasingly turned against France in the hope of buttressing the beleaguered Weimar Republic. The shock of 1931 – and the global impact of Britain's departure from the gold standard was a measure of British prestige – intensified the pull away from Europe and towards the Empire. European recovery was no longer the key to a return to British prosperity. The Manchurian crisis exposed the weaknesses in Britain's imperial defences and underlined the uncertainties of American support in maintaining the status quo in the Far East. The opening of the World Disarmament Conference on 2 February 1932 brought into prominence the public demand for disarmament. Preoccupied with the domestic crises and conscious of the weaknesses of their own defences, the British put increasing pressure on the French to meet the German demands for equal rights while refusing to offer Paris any new security guarantees or any further enhancement of the League of Nation's security functions. Reluctantly, the Cabinet came to terms with the evidence of German rearmament; but this only made it more insistent that a regime acceptable to the Germans should be put in place. When Adolf Hitler came to power and left Geneva for good, the British redoubled their efforts to secure an arms limitation agreement with Berlin. It became a settled conviction in London that it was the French who were the major stumbling block to its conclusion. Convinced that there was no way of stopping German rearmament, an arrangement with Hitler had become more rather than less imperative. As against the 1935 Stresa Front, 'a sham', the dying British prime minister Ramsay Macdonald called it, was the Anglo-German naval treaty, the first step, the British hoped, towards an air limitation pact, their first requirement against any continental danger.

It was in this critical period that Britain began to fashion the policies they would follow until 1938. Because of Hitler's preference for bilateral negotiation and his hopes, still strong, that he could strike a general bargain with the British, London welcomed direct negotiations with Berlin. French efforts in 1934 and 1935, however limited given the financial and political crises in Paris, to contain Hitler proved ineffective partly because of British obstruction. Étienne Flandin's attempt to trade off sanctions against Italy for

British underwriting of France in the Rhineland failed completely. The British were preparing to barter off the Rhineland for Germany's acceptance of an air pact when Hitler settled the matter for himself. The Rhineland crisis ended with the redefinition of Britain's Locarno obligations. In the summer of 1936, the Cabinet was prepared to frame its policy on the assumption that Britain could not help Eastern Europe but ought to resist by force any attempt against the Empire or Flanders. This was too extreme a position to become practical politics. The British adopted a policy of 'keeping Hitler guessing'; in fact, they never decided exactly where the line of resistance was to be drawn. The Foreign Office was set the task of stabilizing the situation until Britain was rearmed sufficiently to win German assent to an arms limitation programme and a revised European settlement by common consent.

Various ways were proposed to satisfy Germany's 'legitimate grievances', whether considered just or inevitable, as long as they were effected peacefully and did not endanger the security of Britain and its Empire. For at no time, even in 1939, could British leaders think only in terms of the nation's continental interests that were territorially and economically limited. Britain was a global power whose influence and strength depended on preserving its imperial position. The German problem was but a part of a global crisis in which the British Empire was threatened by both Japan and, after 1935, Italy. The burden of defending this empire fell mainly on the home country. Against these potential enemies, the British moved uneasily between hopes for a settlement and fears of future aggression. With only limited defence support from the Dominions and an uneasy and undependable relationship with the United States, the British Cabinet would try both appeasement and confrontation, mainly diplomatic, only to find that neither deterred its would-be enemies.

Haunted by the fear of fighting on three fronts, which was clearly beyond its strength, it became ever more essential to seek a peaceful settlement with Germany. As Sir Thomas Inskip, the minister for the co-ordination of defence appointed in 1937, admitted in February 1938, 'the plain fact which cannot be obscured is that it is beyond the resources of this country to make proper provision in peace for defence of the British Empire against three major Powers in three different theatres of war'.[16] The task of rearmament must also be seen within this global context. Realizing at an early stage that British financial and economic power was the 'fourth arm of defence', Neville Chamberlain, as the chancellor of the exchequer, opposed rapid or all-out rearmament. In a country haunted by the economic crisis of 1931 that saw Britain fall off the gold standard, and concerned with economic recovery and social peace, everything was to be done to maintain business as usual. Extensive rearmament, dependent on imports of raw materials (some 25 to 30 per cent of the cost of Britain's armament production) and machinery, would reduce foreign confidence in the City of London, increase the balance of payments deficit, and use up Britain's reserves of gold. It would undermine Britain's capacity to sustain a long war. The Treasury demanded a careful ordering of priorities; funds would be allotted to the air force and navy at the expense of the army for few, even the army leadership itself, were prepared to think in terms of fighting another continental war. It was safety first. Rearmament should be directed to providing safety against any bombing attack from Germany and keeping the sea lines open. Under Neville Chamberlain, who became prime minister in May 1937, the defence of Britain took pride of place in the rearmament list, protection of Britain's colonies and trade was moved up to second place and equipping the British Expeditionary Force was given the lowest priority of all. From the French point of view, at a time of financial stress and political upheaval, these decisions could only add to their fears and woes.

It was under Neville Chamberlain's leadership that Britain made its last pre-war attempt to preserve the equilibrium in Europe through the exercise of influence and global strength. It is paradoxical that his policies should have been defeated by German moves into a region that Britain had since 1919 dismissed as of little strategic interest. Germany's edge in the armaments race was recognized, its greater industrial potential appreciated and the degree of its efficiency and mobilization capacity exaggerated. There was a general consensus about the need to rearm to make the country safe and to provide a deterrent to a German resort to force. There was less agreement in Whitehall about the question of timing, that is, when Germany would be prepared to launch a war, or how far it would be necessary to conciliate Hitler without endangering British interests. At the same time, underlying the debates over tactics, there was, particularly in Chamberlain's case, a fundamental assumption about the ultimate strength of the country and its empire. If Britain had to go to war – and for the first time, after Godesberg, the British Cabinet actually contemplated war against Germany – no one actually anticipated disaster. In January 1939 when faced with the prospect, false though it proved to be, of a German invasion of Holland, the Chiefs of Staff recommended battle. 'I do not know how we can fight this war but we must', Cadogan wrote in his diary, 'else we will lose that moral position that is the source of our strength.'[17] Some, like Lord Halifax, the foreign secretary, anticipated that 'the attitude of the United States would be sufficiently favourable to us to enable us to win the war'.[18] There was the assumption, still so important during the 'phoney war' but already critical in the spring and summer of 1939, that the French army would be at Britain's disposal and provide the time needed to mobilize the global resources that would assure victory over a financially and economically weaker Germany.

There was a marked change in British thinking both at the official level and in the body politic in the months after Munich. This would result both in steps towards an alliance with France and, after German occupation of Prague in mid-March 1939, in the policy of guarantees to Romania, Greece and Poland, the latter a repudiation of the policies followed at Munich. Nonetheless, both before and after Munich, with diminishing support in the Cabinet, the prime minister believed that it was possible to convince Hitler by 'reason and diplomacy' rather than by 'menace and force' to join a new security system that would leave the continent more stable and prosperous than before. Chamberlain assumed that Britain was a great power, the most influential and important in European affairs outside of Germany. Hitler shared this view. Regarding France as Britain's satellite, an impression confirmed at Munich, underestimating the Soviet Union, and ignoring the United States as a factor in European politics, Hitler always assumed that Britain held the key to German success even after discarding his hopes for an alliance or partnership. Perceptions of power can serve as a substitute for actual strength.

The signals coming from London were mixed enough for Hitler to gamble on British non-intervention. Chamberlain never offered Hitler the free hand the dictator demanded but there was even during 1938–39 an ambiguity in his attitude towards Central Europe. Many in the Cabinet wavered in similar fashion between accepting German dominance in the region and fighting to prevent it. Once the guarantee to Poland was given, there was no question that the British would stand by their word; still, it could be hoped that some kind of settlement between Poland and Germany could be brokered. The balance in the Cabinet had shifted and the often vacillating foreign secretary, Lord Halifax, increasingly assumed the leadership of those determined that Hitler had to be stopped. What is striking about the last year of peace is Chamberlain's self-confidence that he could make a deal with Hitler. William Pitt did not make the same mistake with Napoleon. It was not only that the prime minister thought that he had secured peace and more at Munich – the difference between the attitudes of Chamberlain and Daladier in the days and weeks after the conference is highly instructive – it was also that he remained reluctant to tie Britain too closely to France and continued to oppose an alliance with the Soviet Union despite the conversion of the chiefs of staff and the overwhelming public support for its conclusion. Part of the reason Chamberlain was so unwilling to take Winston Churchill into the Cabinet, apart from the political threat the maverick Conservative might pose to his own position, was that Churchill's inclusion would send the wrong signals to Hitler. There was no loss of confidence after the announcement of the Nazi–Soviet pact as there was in Paris. On the contrary, it served to confirm the prime minister's prescience. But in a policy of 'hoping for the best and preparing for the worst', Chamberlain remained stronger on hope than on preparation. This explains the rift between the prime minister and many of his Cabinet colleagues, as well as the increasing distance, acknowledged by the prime minister when he concealed some of his actions in the direction of continued dialogue with Hitler, between Chamberlain and the electorate.

The failure of the post-Prague policy of deterrence had far more to do with Hitler than with Chamberlain, yet the latter's premises were fatally flawed. Not only had he misjudged Hitler but he had exaggerated his own influence. There was no reasoned assessment of the country's and the enemy's capabilities in August 1939. Many arguments might have been used against intervention given that it was already conceded that nothing could be done to help Poland. The intelligence services, it is true, argued in the spring and summer of 1939 that German rearmament was facing increasing economic constraints and that Germany could not sustain a successful long-term war. There was also the point made by R.A.C. Parker that 'Great Britain was approaching the point at which preparations for war might weaken the capacity for war; if war was to be risked, perhaps the risk should be taken soon'.[19] There were, however, Treasury warnings that Britain was not as well placed as Germany to conduct a long war and wished for consideration of the advantages still to be realized from the British rearmament programmes for 1939. Some historians, Williamson Murray for one, have argued that Britain's strategic situation was better at the time of Munich than in the summer of 1939.[20] Hitler himself could not understand why, having given into his demands at Munich, Britain should be prepared to fight over Danzig. It would have been impossible, however, for any government to have stayed in office had war not been declared. Political determinants and domestic pressures prevailed over any other constraints.

Once again, as in 1914, Britain went to war without an attack on its territory or empire. Once again, but without any dissimulation, there was a treaty and a moral position to uphold. But when war came, Britain's continental weakness was terribly exposed. The French army did not hold (and the late build-up of the British Expeditionary Force and the correct decision not to commit the RAF to the battle of France were contributing factors to the defeat) and so the Germans did not wear themselves out pounding upon the French defences, as both the British and French had anticipated. Strategic bombing did not break German morale or its industrial capacity until late in the war. The blockade weapon, presumed to be effective only after 18 months of war, had little bearing on the continental struggle. Little did a senior Foreign Office official, Julian Jebb, realize when he told the German diplomat, Theodor Kordt, in May 1939: 'I would infinitely prefer my country to become an American dominion than a German *Gau*' that this might be the practical alternative for an embattled country.[21] By 1940, the Treasury was warning that Britain could not fund a war without assistance for more than two years. And who in 1941, certainly not Winston Churchill, expected the Soviet Union to last more than six months against the triumphant German *Wehrmacht*.

The German sources make it abundantly clear that Hitler was anxious for a negotiated peace in 1940 and that British ministers, in the disastrous days of 26–28 May, seriously considered the possibility. Even Winston Churchill, according to the War Cabinet minutes, commented: 'if Herr Hitler was prepared to make peace on the terms of the restoration of German colonies and the overlordship of Central Europe, that was one thing' but that such an offer was 'most unlikely'.[22] Nor was it only in such moments of desperation that Churchill was willing to consider peace feelers if they were not, in Halifax's terms, 'destructive of our independence'. In public, however, Churchill took a very different line; and his extraordinary command of the English language and his matching of rhetoric to mood was a major factor in sustaining morale at a moment when its collapse could well have been fatal for the prosecution of the war. No historian disputes the importance of Churchill's intervention on 28 May, whatever their differences about its consequences. It was a decision based on miscalculations, and ultimately on faith, hope and American charity – in the first instances, leases on bases exchanged for 50 clapped-out ships. The next year represented a unique moment in British history, a singular attempt to stop a hegemonic power seizing control of much of Europe by fighting on alone. The task of actually defeating Hitler was beyond the country's capabilities, though one that refurbished its image of moral superiority so recently tarnished. It was also a necessary choice *pace* the views of those who think that a bargain with Hitler would have preserved British independence, the Empire and the balance of power in Europe.

Though the British were to recover from this low point in their fortunes and, if only temporarily from their reduction in status and influence in 1944–45, no post-war government would try again to maintain the security and stability of Europe through its own efforts. While British policy makers rejected claims that Britain was no longer a great Power, they first tried to maintain the Anglo-American–Soviet framework and when, during 1946, the Soviet Union appeared more and more as a possible enemy, again sought American underwriting only to find American support limited. There was no doubt during the terribly cold winter of 1947 that Britain was overstretched. At this low point, Britain turned to France. For a brief moment, while the Labour government decided to go ahead with the development of a British atomic bomb, the Foreign Office spoke of a role in Western Europe. The signing of the Dunkirk treaty with France in March 1947 was seen by some as the first step towards closer military and economic cooperation. Ernest Bevin, the post-war Labour foreign secretary, hoped that this agreement intended to strengthen France against a resurgent Germany and a possible Russian threat would be followed by a Western European customs union with Britain as a central member. The troubles in the Empire, some with their roots in the pre-war period but aggravated, no doubt, by the surrender at Singapore and the wartime exigencies which, for instance, changed India from a debtor into a creditor in the Anglo-Indian relationship, also played a part. With only limited American assistance, a major economic crisis, and strong domestic pressure for retrenchment, the Palestine question was referred back to the United Nations; the earlier decision to end British aid to Greece and Turkey at the end of March was confirmed; and the date for British withdrawal from India was set for June 1948. At the time, this was seen as an *ad hoc* and hasty response to a difficult situation. It was, in fact, a sign of British decline not yet recognized in Whitehall, where it was still assumed that Britain was a great power, if not one of the new 'superpowers' (the term first used in 1944). The whole situation was changed, of course, when the United States re-entered Europe in 1948 and the 'special relationship', along with the Commonwealth, became the centre of British policy overseas.

This contribution does not attempt to trace the contorted story of the British relationship with the European states when the latter took the first steps to the creation of what became the European Economic Community. It is, however, worthwhile recalling the distance between Britain and Western Europe created by the war. Britain was a victor nation; it had never been occupied; it still retained its global role. This was the reasoning behind the assumption the Britain could again resume a policy of 'limited liability' in Europe. Bevin summed up the mood in 1950 when he explained to the Americans that 'Great

Britain was not part of Europe; she was not simply a Luxembourg'.[23] It must be remembered, too, that during the war the British had worked with the Americans, and the friendships made and ties created remained important for the next decade at least. Even when the Anglo-American partnership came under strain – the 'special relationship' was clearly far more important for London than for Washington – and the contraction of Britain's global role began to gather pace, Britain's attitude towards the European Community remained an ambivalent one. There was considerable justice in the underlying assumption by the French president, General Charles de Gaulle, that the Anglo-American relationship was far more important to Britain than any association with Western Europe. When a Conservative prime minister, Harold Macmillan, finally took the decision to apply for membership in the EEC, it was, in part, to buttress the Atlantic alliance. And even when another Conservative, Edward Heath, finally led Britain into the European Community in January 1973, the British remained 'reluctant Europeans'. They are still so today. Behind that reluctance is a long history that cannot be forgotten. Cynics may claim that the present tendency to promote historical amnesia in Britain's schools has its positive side.

NOTES

This is an expanded version of a talk given for the War Studies Department at King's College, University of London, at the invitation of Michael Dockrill and the members of the department.

1. See U. Bialer, *The Shadow of the Bomber: The Fear of Air Attack in British Politics, 1932–1939* (London, 1980).
2. See C. Alexander, *Ironside's Line: The Definitive Guide to the General Headquarters Line Planned for Great Britain in Response to the Threat of German Invasion, 1940–42*, Book 2 (Storrington, 1999); M. Glover, *Invasion Scare, 1940* (London, 1990); S.P. MacKenzie, 'Citizens in Arms: The Home Guard and the Internal Security of the United Kingdom, 1940–1941', *Intelligence & National Security*, 6 (1991), pp.548–72.
3. H.W.V. Temperley, 'Lord Granville's Unpublished Memorandum on Foreign Policy, 1852', *Cambridge Historical Journal*, 2 (1928), pp.298–301. Also see J. Clarke, *British Diplomacy and Foreign Policy, 1782–1865: The National Interest* (London, 1984), pp.219–57.
4. A. Ramm, 'Granville', in K.M. Wilson (ed.), *British Foreign Secretaries and Foreign Policy: From Crimean War to First World War* (London, 1987), p.85.
5. See for instance, C.J. Lowe, *Salisbury and the Mediterranean* (London, 1964).
6. *BD*, II, No. 86.

7. *BD*, III, Appendix A.
8. Quoted in R. Scully, *The Origins of the Lloyd George Coalition* (Princeton, NJ, 1975), p.175.
9. K.E. Neilson, *Britain and the Last Tsar: British Policy and Russia, 1894–1917* (Oxford, 1995), pp.267–88. Also see B.J. Williams, 'The Strategic Background to the Anglo-Russian Convention of August 1907', *Historical Journal*, 9 (1966), pp.360–73.
10. John Gooch, *The Plans of War* (London, 1974).
11. Quoted in Z.S. Steiner, *Britain and the Origins of the First World War* (London, 1977), p.234.
12. Churchill draft Cabinet memorandum (but not circulated), 24 Aug. 1920, in M. Gilbert (ed.), *Winston S. Churchill*, Vol.IV: *Companion*, Part 2: *July 1919–March 1921* (London, 1972).
13. CID memorandum (257-B), 27 Sept. 1920, CAB 4/7.
14. *DBFP*, Series 1A, Vol.1, No.i.
15. D. Dilks, *Curzon in India*, Vol.1 (London, 1969), p.170.
16. Quoted in D. Reynolds, *Britannia Overruled: British Policy and World Power in the 20th Century* (London/New York, 1991), p.131.
17. Diary entry, Jan. 1939, in D. Dilks (ed.), *The Diaries of Sir Alexander Cadogan, 1938–1945* (London, 1971), p.xx.
18. Quoted in R. Rosecrance and Z.S. Steiner, 'British Grand Strategy and the Origins of World War II', in R. Rosecrance and A.A. Stein (eds.), *The Domestic Bases of Grand Strategy* (Ithaca, NY/London, 1993), p.142.
19. R.A.C. Parker, 'Economics, Rearmament and Foreign Policy: The United Kingdom before 1939 – A Preliminary Study', *Journal of Contemporary History*, 10 (1975), p.644.
20. This argument is the thrust of W. Murray, *The Change in the European Balance of Power, 1938–1939* (Princeton, NJ, 1984).
21. Lord Gladwyn, *The Memoirs of Lord Gladwyn* (London, 1972), p.90.
22. Quoted in David Reynolds, 'Churchill and the British "Decision" to Fight on in 1940', in R. Langhorne (ed.), *Diplomacy and Intelligence during the Second World War* (Cambridge, 1985), p.152.
23. Quoted in Reynolds, *Britannia Overruled*, p.198.

Power, Sovereignty, and the Great Republic: Anglo-American Diplomatic Relations in the Era of the Civil War

BRIAN HOLDEN REID

W.E. Gladstone once observed that foreign policy is more than just about interests. For many years diplomatic historians have eagerly embraced such issues as strategy, ideology, cultural relations, and trade in an effort to comprehend the relations between states. In the ambivalent relationship between Great Britain and the United States in the nineteenth century, the American Civil War of 1861–65 serves as a crucible into which the main issues between the two countries can be poured, brought into close relationship and put to the test. In the nineteenth century these issues revolved around independence, sovereignty and the balance of power in the Western Hemisphere. Their resolution would be determined by the relative significance attached by either side to power and the moral imperative. In this reconsideration, the main focus will be on the relative power relationship of each country rather than on the details of diplomatic exchanges. There have been many full-dress diplomatic histories of Anglo-American relations in this period and it seems unnecessary to repeat them. The approach in this chapter is thematic. It attempts to place the diplomatic history of the Civil War period into a much broader context than is frequently attempted. It therefore draws comparisons and contrasts from both before 1861 and after 1865. The American Civil War was obviously far more important to the Americans than to the British, and it is necessary to understand the effect this variance had on the development of policy by either side. Also, the moral factor was important for both sides for most of the time; but ultimately both sides lacked an interest in going to war that could outweigh their interest in preserving the peace. Despite inflammatory language, in reality, both powers reached a level of accommodation, compromise and affinity that was unusual in the nineteenth century.

Traditional diplomatic history has also been open to abuse in terms of the use of anachronism and the prevalence of a particularly American style of 'Whig' interpretation. Historians often seem to find it difficult to conceive of a world where the United States is not the most powerful state and thus does not invariably get its own way in international affairs. Furthermore, there is a distinct tendency to amplify the success and therefore the moral appeal of a liberal free, democratic United States, particularly vis-à-vis a seemingly conservative and overbearing power like imperial Britain. Moreover, a justified assumption of moral right on the part of the victors of 1865 has led (especially American) historians to criticize British policy during the Civil War as expedient and morally bankrupt because it tended to be partial towards the defeated south. The British government favoured the side that would have ruptured the splendour of the American democratic experiment. 'Lincoln appealed to *universal* principles of right and wrong', writes Howard Jones, 'and concluded that the destruction of the Southern government and way of life was necessary for the betterment of the republic.'[1] It is likely that the British prime minister, Lord Palmerston, was anxious to secure the rupture of the Union, but not at the cost of recognizing slavery. The moral question raised by these issues is not as straightforward as Jones implies.

Such an assumption of moral superiority during the Civil War itself has led to a variety of ahistorical attempts to demonstrate that the United States wrestled power and domination of the Western Hemisphere from Great Britain after 1865, and date this precisely as a self-evident result of the Union victory. Such an approach is oversimplified. It demonstrates a lack of appreciation not only of the complex nature of international relations in the nineteenth century, but also of the intricate knot of compromises that bound diplomatic activity together.

By the time Great Britain departed from many of its bases in the Western Hemisphere in the early twentieth century, it did so not out of fear, or because the United States demanded that the British leave, but because an amicable relationship had developed between the two powers over several decades of diplomacy. Terms like 'withdrawal' and 'retreat' are used by (often British) historians to gauge an American 'rise' to power and a British 'fall'. Such language conveys an incorrect impression; 'redeployment' is more accurate. Great Britain did recognize potential American strength. It was noted even during the Civil War itself, and on numerous occasions after 1865 – well before it became a hard international reality.[2]

The Civil War serves as a touchstone by which to judge these issues because it illustrates the way the United States perceived its role in international affairs. The prime issue, of course, was the maintenance of American sovereignty, both in terms of territory and commerce. Despite the successful attainment of the former aim – less so in terms of trade – there was no 'handover' of power to the United State – still less as suggested by Hugh Brogan, a Great Britain cowed into submission by a threatening American republic. On the contrary, throughout this period, Great Britain successfully pursued a policy of deterrence. At moments of crisis, for example over the *Trent* in December 1861, the United States backed down in the face of British resolve.[3] Even after the Union victory, the United States was not able to achieve the more extravagant claims demanded for compensation, which Britain successfully delayed and then reduced by prudent action.[4]

Several moves by the British government can be used to demonstrate its firm resolve: the recognition of belligerent rights for the Confederate States of America; the rapid movement of forces during the *Trent* crisis; and the refusal to guarantee the safety and primacy of American commerce. British statesmen were inclined to view the American secretary of state, William H. Seward, as a man of words rather than action, full of bluster and empty threats. Obviously, they did not neglect the possibility of war with the United States – but it was *not* an obsessive preoccupation. Avoiding entanglement with the American war in 1861–63 was not a sign of weakness but sound calculation. Entering the Civil War – and thus transforming it into a world war by inviting other powers to follow its lead – would have been bad policy. British leaders had other, more pressing matters to worry about, and American intervention would have been a costly diversion from these. Whether Great Britain would have prevailed in any war with America is a matter for conjecture. Seward believed that British intervention would have involved devastation and possibly ruin for the United States. He maintained consistently that he did not want war with Great Britain.[5]

That the global balance of power was in a state of flux during this period can largely be attributed to the secession of the southern states after December 1860. This attempt to create a second republic on American soil (with perhaps a third or fourth to follow) effectively disrupted the United States effort to create an *imbalance of power* in its favour vis-à-vis other North American polities. Its most immediate result was an increase in the likelihood of more European interventions in support of their clients.[6] Napoleon III's deployment of French troops in 1861 to buttress the regime of the Emperor Maximilian in Mexico was a case in point. Once the South had been subdued, the United States brought military pressure to bear on France to withdraw, and all French troops had been evacuated by 1866. Yet American success – and Seward's consistent pursuit of a reconstruction of this imbalance in American favour – can only be judged within the overall context of global affairs in the nineteenth century.[7]

Throughout this period there were other areas of the globe that were of greater significance to Great Britain – and France – than the Western Hemisphere. After all, the European continent was the power centre of the world. Its preoccupations affected the thinking of British leaders in both direct and indirect ways. The pursuit of British interests within the context of shifting patterns of European power had three central results. First, Her Majesty's Government was unwilling see the European equilibrium disturbed on account of affairs in the United States. Consequently, intervention in a costly American war appeared a less attractive policy if it resulted in a weakening of the British position in relation to other European powers.[8] A central pillar of British policy in the Americas was the exclusion of rival European powers from the Western Hemisphere. Great Britain colluded in the maintenance of the Monroe Doctrine by providing the naval power that alone gave it weight.[9] Richard Cobden feared the results of the breakdown of this policy due to the 'disruption of the United States'. He considered French intervention in Mexico 'a great mistake'.

> This enterprise would never have been undertaken if the United States had not been in the difficulties of this civil war. ... But it only required that the North should have been a little weaker,

and then these silly people would have been going about for an interference in America, and then they would have carried out their project, and you would have had France and other Powers going over to America to meddle in that quarrel.[10]

In Cobden's opinion, as a critic of British policy working outside the government, intervention in the Civil War would thus imperil British policy.

Second, contrary to the impression given by historians such as Howard Jones, European powers had much to gain from the Union remaining united. A fragmented and quarrelsome series of American republics would easily have become a hotbed for a power struggle between competing European interests. Indeed, a persuasive if rather exaggerated argument was advanced that the British needed to consolidate, if not extend, American influence as a counterpoise to Russian power in the region as well as globally.[11] Russian territory was restricted to a trade and fur colony in Alaska, but this detracts little from the possibility that a greatly weakened Union competing with the Confederacy could provide a great playground in North America for European powers attempting to increase their own influence in the region at the expense of Great Britain – such as Napoleon III's France. The extent to which the attention of the Great Powers was focused on strictly European rivalries can be gauged by the following. In 1812, when Great Britain was last at war with the United States, the former was preoccupied by the overthrow of Napoleon. Britain and France opposed Russia during the Crimean War of 1854–56; and in 1859 the Franco-Austrian War erupted. The 1860s, the decade of secession and civil war in the United States, saw convulsions of equal magnitude in Europe: the German Wars of Unification (Prussia's war against Denmark in 1864 and Austria in 1866); and the Polish Insurrection of 1863 against Russia, which raised the question of another Anglo-Russian War. The growing tensions between Britain and Russia were discussed in parliament on 6 and 13 July, at a time when the American Civil War reached a climactic stage. The problems of Poland, especially after the brutal crushing of the Poles in 1864, were more often discussed than American affairs.[12]

The end of the decade saw the unification of Italy and the unexpected defeat of France in the Franco-Prussian War 1870–71, culminating in the establishment of the German Empire. For the following 30 years, Britain was preoccupied by colonial rivalries and wars, and especially rivalry with France, culminating in the 'confrontation' at Fashoda in 1898; following the South African War of 1899–1902, rivalry with Germany consumed its attention. The impression sometimes given by United States historians that Europeans stood with their mouths agape, as preoccupied as Americans themselves with the greatest war of the nineteenth century, should be set aside.[13]

Third, imperial issues played a significant part in British – and French – strategic calculations. The Royal Navy had been deployed off the coasts of Greece during the Civil War years. Debates over Greece, the Eastern Question, and the expenditure required on fortifications both in the colonies and at home, took up much more time than American affairs. Kenneth Bourne has suggested that British foreign policy-makers always tended to place European above American interests; their eyes were invariably fixed on other European powers and the threat they presented to the Empire. Purely American affairs 'though by no means unimportant were always subordinate'.[14] This attitude remained a constant feature of the second half of the nineteenth century. At the end of the century, the freedom of action enjoyed by the United States during the Spanish–American War of 1898 was due as much to the preoccupation of other European powers with their own ambitions and rivalries as with increasing British friendliness towards the Americans. Certainly, during the last years of the nineteenth century, Great Britain was under increasing pressure from other European powers. A rapprochement with the United States had begun as early as 1896. It has been argued that the United States was fortunate that Britain was so hard pressed by France and Russia and needed to concentrate its military and naval resources. Consequently, the British Cabinet was ready to lend a sympathetic ear to American ambitions, especially during the Venezuelan Crisis.[15]

This latter factor explains why Lord Salisbury's attention was so far removed from the issues that provoked this crisis – a dispute between Venezuela and Great Britain over the frontier with British Guiana, the former enlisting American support. It was the Kaiser's telegram of 1896, indicating support for the Boer predicament, rather than American military and political pressure that determined the British course. Indeed, it soon became a matter of recruiting support against Germany, not the United States. Even Samuel Flagg Bemis acknowledges that it would have been the 'height of folly' for Britain to add the United States to the 'hostile camp'.[16] Indeed, British policy-makers made a conscious choice as to which powers were most dangerous to British interests and which was the power with which Great Britain could least afford to clash: Russia, Germany and France were in the former category, and the United States in the latter.[17]

In short, even when resurgent at the end of the nineteenth century, the United States was not feared as a direct threat to British interests. The interest in bimetallism, the use of gold and silver at regulated values agreed by both powers, is evidence of their convergence despite the Venezuela Crisis. Yet simultaneously the latent power of the United States was recognized. This might reflect a long-term design of securing an understanding with the United States along the lines of the *entente cordiale* eventually agreed with France, although this should be a subject of further research. Consequently, by the time that Great Britain confronted a major threat in Europe involving a redeployment of forces, the Western Hemisphere presented no problems. Canada had been made safe, Britain had concluded a number of treaties with the United States, and its western flank was protected. London could attend to other threats that presented a more grave and immediate danger. The British, in other words, were not forced out of the Western Hemisphere by a resurgent United States as a result of the Union victory in the Civil War. In fact, the costly development of the key naval base at Bermuda in this period demonstrated a commitment to upholding the status quo in the Western Hemisphere.[18]

Any effort to place and date something as ephemeral as one power replacing another as dominant in a given region leads the historian into a contentious area. The matter is curiously undefined in its terms: is the new American dominance political, military, commercial or ideological? Did these four aspects become predominant simultaneously? Partisanship tends to characterize the writings of historians. Earlier aspects of the Anglo-American relationship before 1861 are often reinterpreted in the light of later events. For example,

R.M. Hathaway believes the war of 1812 resulted in a passably successful termination for the United States. Hugh Brogan claims it taught the British that war with the United States was almost invariably not worthwhile. Such an approach has its merits: the war of 1812 reaffirmed for Britain the financial and logistic burdens of waging a war across the Atlantic while simultaneously conducting a great war in Europe. More contentious is the claim that American leaders learned that the only way to make progress in the harsh world of diplomacy was by adopting a bellicose and dogmatic manner, although the intercourse of Anglo-American relations by mid-century demonstrates that there is a lot of truth in it.[19]

There are two problems with this kind of interpretation. First, it overlooks important aspects of the Napoleonic Wars that were Britain's prime concern, the impact of the Royal Navy, and how from the British point of view, a war of winning without conquering could be fought.[20] Second, it sets the scene for an erroneous interpretation of later events. For example, asserting that Britain and France were intimidated by Seward's bellicose language during the Civil War, Hugh Brogan argues that Seward's policy underwrote the Monroe Doctrine, which served as an effective warning and deterrent to the British. Yet Britain had explicitly supported and exploited the Monroe Doctrine for its own ends and had built up its colonies in Canada. If the British were indifferent to the warnings implicit in the Monroe Doctrine, they cannot have been anxious over American threats to maintain it. In 1861, unsupported by Britain, the US Navy could not have enforced the Doctrine against France and Spain, let alone against the might of the Royal Navy. Such a low level of anxiety appears constant throughout the nineteenth century. Great Britain obliged the United States to compromise on its more extravagant claims along the 49th parallel, rather than 54o 40m, in the controversy over Oregon in 1846 and, as late as the Venezuelan Crisis of 1895, as demonstrated by treaties over bimetallism and protection.[21]

Dating the more conciliatory attitude of Great Britain towards the United States also raises problems. Brogan suggests the first half of the century. Certainly British leaders were not above interfering in American elections to serve their own ends.[22] Bemis points to the significance of the Civil War.[23] Neale suggests 1895, and Kenneth

Bourne, conscious of the complexities of attempting to put precise dates on such alterations in the power structure, suggests that the Clayton–Bulwer Treaty (1850) was a 'presentiment' of an improved atmosphere that was to develop after 1898–1902. Indeed, he argues that, as far as the British were concerned, the United States remained an 'enemy' during the Civil War era and its long aftermath until the resolution of the Venezuelan Crisis 1895–96. This is surely too harsh a verdict.[24] Of course, some significance can be attached to all the dates suggested by previous historians, but unless clarified, they hamper an understanding of the totality of the Anglo-American relationship. Treaties were signed with the United States touching upon the Canadian frontier as early as the Treaty of Ghent (1814). Neither should it be forgotten that the Monroe Doctrine was viewed by the British as a means of maintaining a closer connection with the Americans, and even an alliance.[25] It has already been suggested that the Monroe Doctrine advanced British interests (while it did not meet them exactly) by keeping others out while the British flourished where they were already present after 1783.

For most of the nineteenth century, with the exception of the Civil War years, the United States exerted power beyond its military strength. The United States Army and Navy were tiny. In 1860, the United States Army was only 16,215 strong, scattered among frontier outposts and coastal forts. In 1877, even after the Civil War and the military occupation of the southern states during Reconstruction, it still numbered only 24,140 officers and men. Throughout the century, the United States Navy was, by European standards, weak. Even as late as 1890, it had no battleships.[26] Peter Maslowski describes American military power as 'feeble'; he believes that American power expanded because it was 'raw'. It was sufficient to overcome or defeat Indians and Mexicans but, during the century, the United States had difficulty in creating and maintaining regular, trained forces of a significant size.[27] Consequently, American policy tended to mirror British policy: it depended on bluff, deterrence, and influence, the latter involving a mental or spiritual effect: the ability to modify or persuade by indirect methods.

Consequently, the vulnerability of Canada has been exaggerated. Both in 1775 and 1812–13, rash American attacks ended disastrously. Whilst great potential is an important consideration, so also is the force available to support diplomatic action. It takes time and skill to transform potential or 'raw' energy into 'kinetic' energy, and even longer for this to be hammered into a successful military instrument. Lacking stature as a great military power, the United States after 1865 prudently avoided going to war with the British Empire. Both sides therefore found it sensible, as well as expedient, to reach an accommodation over outstanding issues rather than fight over them. Palmerston wrote in 1842 that concessions made in Ashburton's Treaty were 'districts which they could never have acquired by the sword', a statement indicating his calm contemplation of American military weakness. Lord John Russell believed that an American invasion of Canada was too expensive a prospect. Affirming rightly that American military expansion would be southwards at the expense of Mexico, he further added that the honour of the British Crown was pledged to defend the Queen's Dominions in North America. In other words, there are good grounds to doubt the American ability to use Canada as a counterpoise to the strength of the Royal Navy. Holding Canada to ransom was a strategic advantage enjoyed by the United States only in theory. The idea of war with the United States *in itself* held few horrors for British statesmen, but they nursed severe doubts as to whether such a war was sound policy.[28]

A great deal is often made by historians of the inability of Britain to aim at naval supremacy everywhere. The 'legions' would have to be redistributed, and they departed first from North America waters. Nevertheless, the key to understanding British strategy after 1890 can be found in the flux developing in the world balance of power, and the options available to support the one and cope with the other. Such an approach lends strength to the fundamental pragmatism of British policy, and a straightforward rationale: a desire not to become involved in an American war because of the cost and relative loss of power vis-à-vis other European powers. The lesson of 1778 and 1812, in the eyes of British foreign policy-makers, amounted to the belief that on both occasions European rivals simultaneously had exploited British difficulties in the Americas *and* Europe. Therefore policy was directed at keeping Old World rivals separate from the ascendant rival in the New World.

Some historians consider the Civil War to be *the* event that most influenced Anglo-American relations in the nineteenth century. The war itself attracted a fair amount of British attention, although it was eclipsed by other more pressing matters closer to home. While relations in 1861 were in some ways more auspicious than at any time since 1783 (given a boost by the private visit of the Prince of Wales in the autumn of 1860), the Civil War did set them back seriously.[29] Relations did return to a relatively harmonious state after 1865, a condition that with the odd ruction, continued friendly for the remainder of the century.[30]

Peter Maslowski has noted that American expansionist urges were cloaked in the self-righteous language of Manifest Destiny. The United States was endowed, so its citizens claimed, with an exceptional status. The bedrock of American ideology was the natural rights of man; therefore civilized peoples could have no more cherished possession than liberty. American belief in the unique values of their society – because they had translated this liberty into practice – lay behind a mission to uphold, protect and spread their way of life. Americans were proud that the Union shone like a beacon upholding liberty and rights for the many.[31] The main objective of American policy before 1861 was to secure the 'new nation' as a strong and independent nation state; its special character would be invested with great moral authority and place it in a position to contribute to the settlement of global conflicts unsullied by the wicked ways and grubby methods of European power-brokers. Thus the United States could serve as an example to Europe and beyond, broadcasting the values of the Declaration of Independence.[32] The latter acquired a symbolic, ideological significance in the nineteenth century that it had not enjoyed at the time of its signing – especially when compared with the perceived values of Europe.[33]

The Civil War acquired significance as the supreme example of the time when these values were challenged, put to the test, only to triumph by heroic feats of arms. Yet this war also exposes the flaws in the conception that flatters the American self-image – agreement over the nature of liberty was by no means universal within the United States itself. An entire section of the country, the southern slave states, believed that their liberties rested on the right to hold other human beings as chattels. Such a disagreement over the character of American destiny was resolved by many ideologues of Manifest Destiny by casuistry. For example, in 1845, New Hampshire

Democrats justified the annexation of Texas on the grounds that although they considered slavery 'a great moral and social evil', they did not believe themselves 'more wise than Washington, Franklin and their associates' and they were therefore constitutionally obliged to acquiesce in its existence. (Abraham Lincoln also accepted such a stance for many years.) Thus they accepted the entry of Texas as a slave state into the Union because it 'will guaranty the blessings of a republican government to millions of patriotic and kindred beings who might otherwise be reduced to become the oppressed and unprivileged subjects of European despotism'.[34] The trouble with this form of self-flattery was that many of the old British Whigs who served in Lord Palmerston's Liberal government had far better anti-slavery records than any member of President Lincoln's Cabinet, save Secretary of the Treasury Salmon P. Chase.[35] They do not deserve the 'antirevolutionary and self-interested, reactionary', opprobrium heaped on them by Howard Jones and other historians who have inherited the 'New World–Old World' antithetical approach.[36]

American leaders believed that the United States was the representative of a new republican system (overlooking France's role that would be resumed after 1870). When in April 1861 it was stopped in its tracks, the effort required to prevent the disruption of the Union assumed, in some quarters, the nature of an almost holy cause. Lincoln himself stated that the north 'could nobly save or meanly lose the last best hope of earth' – not the United States – and that hope was liberty in republican form.[37] Such views were not absent from the opinions of some British leaders. The radical liberal politicians, John Bright and Richard Cobden, believed that the United States gave expression to all the ideals they had fought for during their political lives. Bright had been pleased by the evidence of amity in Anglo-American relations witnessed in 1850 by the signature of the Clayton–Bulwer Treaty. He thought it 'a noble prospect to see a great continent under one central republican government'. Cobden shared Bright's optimistic view of the American experiment. Mention of the two most vociferous supporters of the Union cause serves to underline that opinion in Britain over the issues raised by the American Civil War was like a kaleidoscope, with complex, shifting opinions, sometimes moving in opposite and contradictory directions. For example, even Cobden acknowledged the south's legal right to secede and the apparent pointlessness of forced reunion. Bright's views, too, oscillated as events unfolded. He had never visited the United States and relied for information on correspondence with an American cousin and friends like Senator Charles Sumner. Bright believed initially that the south was too large a tract of territory to permit much 'chance of anything like a conquest of the insurgent states'. In July 1863, he still detected 'a strange want of foresight and of force in Washington' which bred a sense of powerlessness. Only by the end of that year was he convinced of the 'resolution of the American people to preserve the integrity of their government & country & to make freedom universal over the continent committed to their rule'.[38]

Seward believed strongly in the 'mission' of the United States. As a former senator from New York, he had spoken on behalf of Irish independence and denounced British 'tyranny'. Like many other leading Republicans, he believed that an American absorption of Canada was inevitable. He believed, too, that the vast resources of the United States rendered a northern victory in the Civil War a foregone conclusion. He thus looked ahead to the time when the United States could resume its march to 'greatness'. In Seward's opinion, the war had one prime objective, the restoration of the Union. He became increasingly conservative on the question of slavery emancipation. As late as the Hampton Roads Conference in February 1865, he argued that both the Emancipation Proclamation and the Thirteenth Amendment, which had passed on 31 January 1865, were expedient wartime measures that would cease to be operative once the war ended. Seward's dedication to the Union guided his actions when dealing with foreign powers. He desired to prevent them from recognizing the Confederacy.[39] The Civil War provided European states with the first major demonstration of the potential power behind the moral imperative of the United States. Charles Francis Adams, Seward's anglophile, loyal political ally, appointed to the crucial post of American minister to the Court of St James, believed that he had a historic mission.

> It is to show by our example to the people of England in particular and to all nations in general, the value of republican institutions ... the greatest triumph of all would be to prove the

calculations (of the incompetence of republican institutions) in vain ... the progress of the Liberal cause ... all over the world is, in a measure, in our hands.[40]

The Union victory in the Civil War preserved the independence and sovereignty of the United States. It guaranteed that the latter would become a great, and then the greatest power, because of the vast, indivisible resources available to it. The Federal Government would henceforth enjoy undisputed sovereignty over both individual states and the Union as a whole. Professor Maslowski emphasizes that by using a 'mighty display of military prowess', the Union forestalled foreign intervention. However, an alternative explanation exists for the Civil War remaining a straightforward domestic quarrel. Other powers did not intervene not necessarily because of fear of American threats or armed strength, but because intervention was poor policy; this conclusion was reached by independent, pragmatic reasoning.[41]

The British viewed Seward's threats as just so much bluster. Their ambassador in Washington, DC, Lord Lyons, thought Seward was 'disposed to play the old game of seeking popularity here by displaying violence towards us'.[42] Taken in the round, British policy was based on the premise that entry into the war should be avoided. Palmerston consistently opposed involvement; the commercial imperative behind British policy was that the south should be opened to free trade, for this would offset the trading costs of the war. Palmerston hoped that southern exertions would enable this to come to pass without the complications and further expense of military intervention. Lord John Russell opposed intervention at the beginning of the war, but veered towards believing that British intervention in the form of mediation would be beneficial after the series of Confederate victories in the summer of 1862. American historians, notably Howard Jones, have seized on this as evidence of his craven desire to see the Union collapse; and Henry Adams, who worked for his father in London, certainly gives this impression in his autobiography.[43] Nonetheless, by mid-1863 Russell had abandoned the idea. Palmerston believed that Great Britain should steer clear of the conflict. He warded off all attempts by Confederate sympathizers in his government and in the House of Commons to promote full diplomatic recognition of the Confederacy.

Palmerston's reasons for reaching this conclusion will be discussed shortly. The moral ramifications of a united (or divided) Union had no appeal for him, policy calculations were what counted. At the end of the Civil War in May 1865, he told the House that Her Majesty's Government had no intention of becoming involved in American internal affairs.[44]

France was reluctant to intervene without British consent and aid, but did, of course, become involved in Mexican affairs. Seward was consistently hostile towards these efforts, warning the French ambassador, Baron Mercier, that the United States would go to war with any power that threatened its vital interests. In 1863, Lyons wrote to Russell that the American government had declared itself so violently against France that it represented a curious change of direction and mood. For the moment, the cry against France diverted more attention than any denunciation of British moves.[45] Seward's threats did not carry much weight while Confederate arms were still resurgent. But after the spring of 1864 when Union armies launched an offensive onslaught that demonstrated the immense military power of the Federal Government, requests that the French evacuate Mexico carried more conviction. The Red River Campaign of March 1864 was designed by Lincoln in part as an attempt to wave the Union flag in Texas and warn against interference in American affairs.[46] After Appomattox, General Ulysses S. Grant evinced hostility towards the French Mexican adventure. He believed it was an expression of the rebellion against the Federal Government; a necessary part of its suppression was to extinguish French military occupation. He advised arms sales to the Mexicans.[47] Grant's correspondence illustrates the different attitudes that prevailed within the American government towards Great Britain and France. French protests over the arms sales only provoked Grant's disdain. He retorted that the French had been far less neutral during the Civil War than the Americans when dealing with the Mexican opposition to Maxmilian, led by Benito Juarez.[48] Grant expressed the view that war with France should be avoided; yet if conflict broke out it would suit the United States if it occurred soon, while the US Army remained strong and a little aid to the Mexican insurgents would go a long way. He sarcastically advised 'the same sort of neutrality that has been observed towards us for the last four years'.[49]

The American attitude towards the British was far less aggressive. When the British government protested over the Fenian Raids on Canada, Grant believed that although the British had not observed a full neutrality during the Civil War, the United States should nonetheless act to prevent the raids, since British wrong-doing was no justification for following their example. Grant's attitude is indicative of the American recognition that Great Britain was more powerful than France, and war against the former would not be a pleasant prospect – even after the Union triumph in 1865.[50] In short, the United States was wary of war with Great Britain throughout the war years. Seward wrote to Adams that his prime task 'apparently so simple and easy involves the responsibility of preventing the commission of an act [by HMG] which would be fraught with disaster, perhaps ruin to our country'. Seward maintained this line constantly throughout 1861–65. His aim was not achieved without difficulty. For, as Seward complained to Adams in 1864, 'no neutral power was ever more unyielding and more exacting towards a belligerent than Great Britain has been towards the United States'.[51]

Seward's position was fraught with difficulty. Although he understood that war with Britain would be disastrous, he had to maintain the sovereignty of the United States. He was forthright in asserting 'that in this war they [the United States] are a whole sovereign nation, and entitled to the same respect as such that they accord Great Britain'.[52] Seward had to labour to prevent recognition of the Confederate States, ward off foreign intervention, and protect American commerce. At home, his path was equally treacherous. He needed to make the most of his popularity – which might explain some of his more belligerent statements; but his prestige was a wasting asset. His rivals, led by Chase, circled, intent on destroying him. He was only saved in the Cabinet Crisis of December 1862 by the president's political adroitness.[53] Seward mixed threats with friendliness. He was keen to temper the more bellicose threats or demands that might be made in speeches in Congress, on the stump, or in the newspapers. He was anxious to show himself a friend of the British (after all, in 1859 he had been given temporary membership of the Reform Club during a visit to London). 'We cannot forget that we are a younger branch of the British family; that we have not been especially reverential of the senior branch, and', he admitted, 'have ever been ambitious to surpass it in wealth, power and influence among the nations.' Seward took pains to point out that he had been, until the last moment, the only person in the American government to be in favour of the surrender of two captured Confederate emissaries, James Mason and John Slidell, during the *Trent* Crisis.[54] Lyons noticed this friendliness, which is hardly surprising because Seward deliberately sought to cultivate him and gain his friendship.[55]

Lyons reported to the British foreign secretary that Seward intended his messages and correspondence to have 'a very friendly aspect'.[56] His ploy appeared to work, as Lyons confided that Seward appeared 'anxious to remove the impression that he is not a friend of peace and a warm friend of England'.[57] Seward's approach, Lyons wrote with evident satisfaction, appears to be 'to overwhelm England and France with a demonstration of friendship and confidence'.[58] At the end of 1862 Seward decided that it was a 'propitious' moment 'for the restoration of harmonious relations between the United States and Great Britain'.[59] Adams was also instructed to postpone the question of the depredations wreaked by the CSS *Alabama* on Union shipping, until the matter could be discussed calmly and without acrimony. Seward also made offers permitting British troops to land at Portland, Maine, on their long journey to Canada.[60] Seward's personal and public amity did not prevent him from bombarding the British with demands, threats and protests, especially over the matter of attacks on Union commerce by Confederate raiders built in British ports. These demands focused around the maintenance of American paramount sovereignty and reminders of the dangers of war and the power of the Union.[61] Seward insisted on the 'freedom of the seas' and the safety of United States borders from violent incursions. Particularly urgent was the issue of recognition of the Confederate States of America as a belligerent granted by Great Britain in the spring of 1861, followed swiftly by France, as this obviously undermined the sovereignty of the Union. Seward repeatedly pressed Great Britain and France to withdraw their recognition of the Confederacy's belligerent status, but to no avail.[62] Finally, Seward reminded the British that American naval power was growing and that in the future the United States would be in a position to take all necessary measures to protect its interests.[63]

The British response to Seward's policy was not diffident and was based on the dual principles of being firm in the defence of British interests and not giving in to American demands. Lyons wrote at the beginning of the Civil War that 'one might laugh at his [Seward's] blustering words if one were not afraid that if they be in the least yielded to they will be followed by violent deeds'.[64] British policy, therefore, was based on deterrence; any military threat made by the United States should be deterred by a stance based on resolution. Russell advised Palmerston that he believed the British should not be intimidated by American military power. Hence the military and naval preparations that were set in train for the defence of Canada. Yet Canada had only three substantial fortifications, Quebec, Halifax, and Kingston; they were key naval bases, and thus signalled the idea that the British Army supported the Royal Navy rather than served as an offensive instrument.[65] Within this overall context of deterrence, the British felt reasonably secure and were not overly anxious about the outcome should a war with the Americans erupt. In 1862 Russell remarked perceptively to Lord Clarendon that 'if they want a quarrel of course they can do it [go to war]. But I think that if we are calm and firm they will not do it. The cost would be immense and they are not as fond of being taxed as our people'.[66] The following year he did not 'apprehend anything unless our naval forces on the American station and our troops in Canada are diminished. Such a reduction might, I think, produce a serious state of danger'.[67] Faith in deterrence seemed to bring its own rewards and was consistent with British imperial and European policy.

As for American belligerence, although Lyons was often unsure whether Seward meant his threats – the secretary of state was a capable actor – he usually concluded, as already mentioned, that he was 'full of braggadocio'.[68] Lyons confided to Russell that Seward had not the 'least idea of really going to war with either England or France but they would go to the verge of it for the sake of making political capital at home and they may be carried over the verge before they see where they are'.[69] Such 'brinkmanship' had its dangers, but Lyons believed that the relative position of Great Britain was a strong one and that its policy should consequently remain steadfast in defence of British interests. 'I can perceive little or no understanding in ... Seward either of the comparative power of the great countries of Europe and the remains of the United States or the importance to this government of conciliating the European powers or at all events not forcing them into hostility'.[70] Seward believed that the pro-Confederate thrust of British policy was more likely to bring war than any American act because it presented a temptation to intervene in the conflict. The first important step in this direction came in May 1861 with a British declaration of neutrality – followed by a similar French pronouncement a month later – that included the recognition of Confederate belligerent status which Seward found so annoying. The British argued that the Civil War shared features characteristic of wars between nation states. Belligerent status, of course, recognized the Confederacy's status and permitted it to raise loans, to employ manpower for military purposes that did not infringe neutrality laws, and purchase military equipment so long as it was not employed in areas enjoying allegiance to the Crown. In addition, the Confederacy could sail naval prizes into British ports, although on 1 June the privateers of both sides were prevented from selling their prizes in British ports. Howard Jones recognizes that the 'overriding factor' in British policy 'was to stay out of the American war – as long as that war posed no threat to Britain's vital interests'. Nevertheless, he goes on to denounce British leaders as 'either incredibly naïve or very disingenuous', and hints at hypocrisy because 'the push for intervention reveals that self-interest provided the most likely determinant for British policy-makers, even when they espoused humanitarian rationales'. The latter judgement serves, needless to say, as an apt summary of American policy. Yet the crucial point is that lucid British calculation of those interests led them to embrace a policy that denied the value of intervention.[71]

As it happened, the Confederacy failed to exploit fully the opportunities that belligerent rights offered them, as the Union desire to blockade Southern ports implied that the Confederacy represented a legitimate government. Seward was thus able to turn the matter to his advantage, and overlook the complication that the Constitution prohibited the closure of ports unless they were not part of the United States. For all Seward's denunciation of it, the British Declaration of Neutrality, by acquiescing in the blockade, allowed him to ignore the issue of port closure.[72] In August the Confederate Congress passed a resolution accepting the Declaration of Paris of

1856 regulating maritime relations – which the United States had refused to sign – although it reaffirmed its determination to continue to accept privateering 'as established practice and recognized by the law of nations'. Yet despite this and other initiatives, all Confederate efforts for the remainder of the war resulted in British recognition of the legal character of the Union blockade. Accordingly, the Declaration of Neutrality was more sternly enforced. British leaders were often wrong about the outcome and shape of the Civil War; so, too, it must be recalled, were many American politicians. This was the product of what one historian has called their 'massive ignorance' of the United States. Such ignorance is hardly surprising given the enormous distances involved, an inevitable time-lag which resulted in belated decisions over matters already decided, and the numerous distractions that resulted from more pressing concerns nearer to home. Yet one-sided and rather self-righteous denunciations such as those of Howard Jones, conceal an important background factor, namely, that the case for sympathizing with the drive for Confederate independence was stronger in nineteenth-century liberal thought than he allows. It was axiomatic that any political movement that demonstrated its cause was sustained by popular support should enjoy the rights of 'self-determination': Russell felt very strongly that he could not treat 'five millions of free men as pirates'; Napoleon III had posed self-consciously throughout his reign as the champion of self-determination among nationalist groups in Europe.[73]

Consequently, a list of reasons justifying support for the south would include its desire for self-rule, its stance against overweening centralization or swaggering intervention by the Federal government in local affairs, and the Southern preference for free trade. Moreover, a very British sympathy developed for the 'under-dog', who appeared, at least in Virginia, to be triumphing over great odds. These attitudes underwrote what Peter Parish has called a 'pervasive, if not necessarily profound, feeling in favour of the Southern Confederacy'. All of these broad emotional or ideological responses overlooked the evils of slavery, but the latter could be explained away by reference to initial northern declarations that the war was not for slavery. The political expediency of the Lincoln administration in denying the centrality of slavery to the conflict had severely constricted the moral appeal of the north's cause abroad. Curiously,

British sympathizers began to find parallels with the 13 colonies during the War of Independence. They did this not because they found such parallels convincing, but because the historical analogy turned the North's case against itself.[74]

Many British politicians who sympathized with the Confederacy felt that the sheer size and diversity of the United States had led to its disintegration. The same factors, especially the physical difficulty of subduing such vast stretches of territory that had overcome the British Army eventually in 1775–83, would apply to the Union Army. Sympathizers assumed, too, that once intent on separation nothing could prevent the Confederacy from achieving its aim and establishing itself as an independent state. W.E. Gladstone, the chancellor of the exchequer, felt that even if the north did defeat the south militarily, the Union would be so transformed as to have lost its liberal appeal and moral rectitude. The original experiment in republican democracy, however admirable in some ways, was doomed from the start. Consequently, Gladstone jumped to the conclusion that the effort to restore the Union was futile and its cost unbearable. In short, Confederate sympathizers assumed the mantle of moral right, not expediency or hypocrisy. In Gladstone's case, his position was supported by the illusion that should Great Britain attempt to mediate in the conflict, British influence could be brought to bear on the Confederacy to improve the lot of the slaves or to abolish slavery altogether. Here, it must be said, Gladstone indulged a vision of America too common in British leaders for the next century and a half, the creation of an image suited to their own preconceptions and vanities.[75] General views like Gladstone's form the background to his famous speech at Newcastle in July 1862 in which he declared 'there is no doubt' that southerners 'have made a nation'. Consequently, the European powers should mediate with the aim of ending the war; Gladstone assured the Duke of Argyll, a strong Union sympathizer in Palmerston's cabinet, that 'the South cannot be conquered'. He eloquently denounced 'the wholesale slaughter' and its 'thoroughly purposeless character'. Howard Jones in turn denounces Gladstone's 'shallow approach' but interprets it too narrowly.

Both Gladstone and Lord John Russell found solace in humanitarian arguments to end the Civil War. It is perhaps too easy to forget that although the nineteenth century saw many local wars, great wars on the scale of the American Civil War seemed to have vanished. It appeared therefore to be a noble end to prevent the Civil War from becoming even more violent than it already was. Gladstone arrived at this conclusion by twisted logic and false premises, but it seems unfair to criticize him for shallowness. Russell was also alarmed by the possibility that a servile war might develop – especially after the issue of the Preliminary Emancipation Proclamation in September 1862 – fuelled by frequent slave rebellions. Our own time has witnessed a tendency to cast doubt on the value of the causes fought for in civil wars; to dismiss them as futile or the product of mindless, headstrong obstinacy, and to call for their immediate cessation on the humanitarian grounds of saving human life. Recent experience of mediation and peacekeeping perhaps illuminates the motives of those that called for mediation in the Civil War; they were not hypocrites. What is beyond doubt is that any intervention (or even mediation) in the Civil War by outside powers would tend to favour the weaker side.[76] In short, the equation of morality and power in the American Civil War, especially when it involved outside powers, is by no means as straightforward as is sometimes assumed by some historians. What Gladstone and Russell advocated in the autumn of 1862 was not military intervention by Great Britain on the Confederacy's behalf, which was what many Confederates hoped and expected; they counselled mediation involving mainly France, but also Austria-Hungary, Prussia, and Russia, and doubtless would have been followed by outright diplomatic recognition of the Confederacy as an independent, sovereign state. Gladstone assumed that the latter was only a matter of time. Lacking Gladstone's consistency, Russell approached this question more timorously, but he also accepted the argument that the Confederacy was capable of achieving its independence by feat of arms.[77] The policy they advocated would have made it easier for the south to achieve this aim by its own exertions.

In the event, this policy was not accepted by Lord Palmerston's Cabinet – mainly because the prime minister, the ultimate 'realist' in the conduct of foreign and military affairs, was not persuaded by the humanitarian arguments. Gladstone's remark about foreign affairs being more than just about interests, curiously, applies to his prime minister. Palmerston was vehemently anti-slavery, an attitude that dominated his policy and diluted his support for the free trade, agrarian south. He really despised all Americans, although he found southern manners preferable; for instance, he expressed outrage at Benjamin F. Butler's New Orleans order, as he misinterpreted it to mean that arrested southern ladies would be used as prostitutes; and he refused to talk to C.F. Adams for some time. Palmerston would not allow such sympathies to sway his calculations. He would only contemplate some form of intervention in American affairs if it could guarantee a complete and cheap success along the lines of the 1856–60 Arrow War in China. This was a war about trade and reveals the mainsprings of his policy clearly. Palmerston had then very successfully manipulated British public opinion into accepting intervention on the most spurious grounds, and he had fought and won a general election on the issue. Palmerston sensed that the American Civil War would not provide such opportunities, and any initial commitments would grow in complexity and expense. As he accepted Tocqueville's view that Russia and the United States would eventually dominate the world, he worked to slow the process down. He preferred that the Civil War would continue so that the two warring American republics would exhaust themselves and the south would be opened to free trade.[78]

British leaders were reluctant to intervene militarily in the Civil War, but this should not be confused with an unwillingness to fight if they were attacked. There was a general anxiety until 1863 that Seward might misjudge the effect of his bluster and plunge the two countries into war. The presumed 'defencelessness' of Canada worried Lyons, as it would continue to alarm British leaders, like Gladstone, after 1865. Palmerston thought that three battalions should be sent to Canada in 1861 to help deter Seward. Fears of a possible retaliatory strike once the Union had won the Civil War gradually subsided. The House of Commons felt no sense of urgency by May 1865 in increasing expenditure on Canadian fortifications. Far from striking at British possessions while drunk with victorious ardour, Lyons's successor, Sir Frederick Bruce, drew the justified conclusion 'that Seward does not want war with anyone'.[79] Thus able to deter major threats against Canada, British statesmen kept up diplomatic pressure on the United States, although in a restrained and tactful manner. Recruiting for the Union Army in Canada and Ireland was stopped.[80] At the British request, aggressive American naval tactics outside ports in Crown territory were modified.[81] The order issued in 1864 by the Judge Advocate General, John A. Dix, empowering US marshals to cross the Canadian frontier, was also revoked.[82] The clearest indication of British firmness was the continuance of Confederate belligerent rights, which was sustained until July 1865. Far from being intimidated by a resurgent United States, the British prevailed on most important policy points at issue. Seward uttered the truth – and expressed a realistic appreciation of the power relationship between the two countries – when he claimed that Anglo-American relations had been 'practically restored to the condition in which they stood before the Civil War'.[83]

During the American Civil War, the British pursued pragmatic and on the whole sensible policies to protect their interests. They made errors in calculating the likelihood of Confederate independence but their motives seem to have deserved less censure than they have sometimes received. Finally, despite the military resurgence of the United States, Great Britain was not intimidated, as neither side *wanted* war; on the contrary, both sides wanted to avoid it. It was against this background that the congruence of liberal opinion in both countries promoted the idea of 'Kin Across the Sea' in the years after 1865.

The theme of American belligerence tempered by British pragmatism and restraint can be discerned after 1865. The settlement of the *Alabama* claims postponed until after the end of the war commenced with a flourish of highly inflammatory language on the American side. Voices were heard calling for compensation not just for damage inflicted on Union shipping by Confederate cruisers built in British yards, but adjudication over more general claims arising from British policy during the Civil War. Gladstone had succeeded as prime minister, leading the great Liberal reforming ministry of 1868–74. His Newcastle speech was by this date an embarrassment to him, for he had begun to develop a notion of an English Speaking Union. While in opposition in the years 1886–92, he wrote about a dozen articles for journals such as the *North American Review*, *Youth's Companion*, and the *Nineteenth Century* on this and related themes.[84] Nonetheless, Gladstone remained defensive over his views on the Civil War. He would never admit to having felt pro-Confederate sympathies. Such denials carried little weight in Washington, DC. A groundswell of opinion demanded the cession of Canada, calls that revived British fears over the security of the frontier north of the 49th Parallel. Longstanding disputes over fisheries and tariffs were exacerbated by an upsurge in Fenian Raids. Senator Charles Sumner, the chairman of the Senate Foreign Relations Committee, gave eloquent voice to the more extreme American demands. Sumner had previously enjoyed a reputation as an Anglophile and had convalesced in England after Preston Brooks's brutal assault on him in the Senate Chamber in 1857. To the consternation of his British friends, Sumner claimed that British policy had doubled the length of the Civil War and the amount of effort and expense required by the north to win it. American claims for $110 million – a calculation of the total losses to the US merchant marine – were 'only an item on our bill'. Sumner estimated total Union war costs at $4 billion, therefore the British were responsible indirectly for half this sum, and claims for compensation should equal $2 billion.[85]

Sumner basked in unaccustomed praise. His speech was congratulated for revealing the 'perfidy, offensive arrogance and grasping selfishness' of Great Britain. Sumner exploited the issue as a means of intimidating the new administration of Ulysses S. Grant. Denied a seat in Grant's Cabinet, Sumner attempted to dominate the foreign policy of the Grant administration through the Senate Foreign Relations Committee; he aimed to browbeat Secretary of State Hamilton Fish. Sumner had opposed and helped defeat the initial effort to resolve the *Alabama* question, the Johnson–Clarendon Convention of January 1869. There was an additional complication. Grant sought to aid Cuban rebels against Spain. He realized that it was not sensible to denounce Britain for pursuing a policy he wished to imitate. Sumner's effort to dominate Grant's administration failed; but in a memorandum he expressed a widely held view that the United States should demand British withdrawal 'from this hemisphere, including Provinces and islands'.[86]

Judged by extremity of the claims, American policy was ultimately unsuccessful. Sumner could offer no method whereby his huge claim could be attained. Neither side wished to push the matter to the brink of war. Slowly but surely an accommodation emerged from protracted bouts of negotiation. Hamilton Fish did not condemn Sumner's speech because he believed it would offer Sumner a pretext to oppose the Treaty of Washington of May 1871. This provided a virtual British apology for supporting the wrong side. David Donald considers that this treaty, because it provided for the withdrawal of British troops from the St Lawrence basin, 'implied a recognition of the military superiority of the United States on the continent'. Perhaps. Yet it also implied recognition of the legitimacy of Canada. Henceforth the United States Army would patrol the Canadian frontier for the British and round up Fenians. The implicit American acknowledgement that Washington had no desire to seize Canada by force, and was willing to carry out frontier policing, were important concessions. An apology was a small price to pay for them. The British had struck a bargain. Moreover, Anglo-American relations were fundamentally amicable; for example, that year Great Britain arbitrated in a wrangle between United States and Brazil.[87]

Gladstone also counselled a maintenance of our 'present composed temper' during the final arbitration of the *Alabama* claims in Geneva in September 1872. Gladstone believed that such arbitration should be the method that states resolve their disputes by peaceful means. His view that arbitration was a 'good prospective system' had been written into the Treaty of Washington. In the event, Gladstone persuaded the Americans to drop the suit for 'indirect' claims. He was helped (despite several public disagreements) by the intervention of the American minister to London, General Robert C. Schenck, and by the American arbitrator, Charles Francis Adams. The United States was awarded compensation totalling £3,200,000 ($15,500,000). This was hardly an insignificant sum, but appears tiny by comparison with the claims for 'indirect' costs, or even $110 million. Gladstone was so pleased with the outcome that he adopted an uncharacteristic flippant tone, telling the chancellor of the exchequer to look cheerful and ask for a cash discount for prompt payment.[88]

This contribution has argued against a simplistic interpretation of Great Britain being driven out of the Western Hemisphere by a resurgent United States. It has also argued against trying to date this transition precisely. For most of the nineteenth century, despite belligerent and sometimes outlandish statements by both sides, the two countries had no interest in going to war. The American Civil War does form an important staging-post in this process, but not in the way that many historians have assumed. It is frequently held that as a result of the Union victory in 1865, and British support for the defeated side, the United States was determined to supplant Britain. The experience of the Civil War, on the contrary, confirmed to leaders of both countries the desirability of maintaining and further developing close relations. In any case, because American military power was latent rather than actual – the great armies of 1865 soon melted away, and the United States lacked a great navy until after 1898 – the British could not be forced out of the Western Hemisphere. During the second half of the nineteenth century, a series of British statesmen, Gladstone, Joseph Chamberlain, and Lord Salisbury, pushed for better Anglo-American relations. They grasped the full extent of American potential which offered opportunities for increased trade, but also the great danger to the future security of the British Empire should a hostile European power seek an alliance with the United States.

Consequently, in the 1870s America was 'discovered' by British Liberal politicians. Relations between states should be judged by standards other than the exchange of diplomatic agreements like treaties. This social and intellectual affinity provided the basis for understanding overall British policy at the end of the century. In 1872 Benjamin Disraeli was aware of the impact of the New World on the distribution of power. Many upper class British visitors made their way to the United States in the early 1870s and felt at home. When in New York in December 1873, Lord Rosebery made his way to a party in honour of Nellie Grant, the president's daughter, 'There were a whole lot of old Etonians there and I am afraid we cronied together too much'.[89] Gladstone realized that 'the daughter was much more powerful than the mother'. The great majority of British leaders began to think in these terms even before the strategic redeployment at the end of the century.[90] An awareness of this potential and a desire not to allow the United States to complicate existing knotty problems with European rivals resulted in British policy seeking fundamentally good relations. For the United States' part, expansionist enthusiasms were tempered by the caution imposed by comparative military weakness and a wish not to quarrel with a power that could still command formidable military strength, not least the world's greatest navy. Salisbury's comment that 'it is sad, but I am afraid that America is bound to forge ahead and nothing can restore the equality between us', is prescient – but he was referring to the distant future. Confident in actual rather than potential strength, and by the pursuit of pragmatic and restrained policies, the British were able to secure their objectives throughout the century. The main exception, the surrender over the Venezuelan Crisis, was mainly due to the fact that it was not a key British interest. Such levels of accommodation and cooperation were to lay the foundations, despite mutual suspicion and condescension, for the Anglo-American relationship during the twentieth century.

NOTES

I would like to thank Mr Andrew Monaghan for all his help in the gestation and writing of this essay, and the late Professor Peter J. Parish for suggesting the topic and his numerous helpful comments on an earlier draft. I am also greatly obliged to Professor Andrew Lambert and Dr Susan-Mary Grant for coming to my aid after the eleventh hour, and the members of the United States History Seminar at the Institute of Historical Research, who listened to an abridged version and made a number of shrewd suggestions.

1. H. Jones, *Abraham Lincoln and a New Birth of Freedom: Union and Slavery in the Diplomacy of the Civil War* (Lincoln, NE, 1999), pp.6, 55 (my italics) [hereafter *New Birth of Freedom*].
2. For example, C.J. Bartlett, *The Long Retreat* (London, 1972).
3. On the mechanics of British deterrence and the global context of British action, see A. Lambert, 'The Admiralty, the *Trent* Crisis of 1861 and the Strategy of Imperial Defence', in *Les Marines Française et Britannique Face aux États-Unis: De la Guerre d'Independence a la Guerre de Secession* (Vincennes, 1999), pp.305–23.
4. H. Brogan, *The Longman History of the United States* (London, 1985), p.333.
5. Seward's most belligerent statement, 'Some Thoughts for the President's Consideration', 1 April 1861, Robert Todd Lincoln Papers, Library of Congress, sought 'explanations' from Great Britain, France, and Spain as to their intentions, but only advocated war against France and Spain if these were unsatisfactory. G.G. Van Deusen, *William Henry Seward* (New York, 1967), pp.282–3; B. Holden Reid, *The Origins of the American Civil War* (London, 1996), pp.346–8.
6. G. Connell Smith, *The United States and Latin America: An Historical Analysis of Inter-American Relations* (London, 1974), pp.2–4, 38, 78 9.
7. Jones, *New Birth of Freedom*, pp.xii, 2, tries to offer such an interpretation, but his assumptions, and a one dimensional approach to European statesmen, rather undercut his laudable aim.
8. M. Silberschmidt, *The United States and Europe: Rivals and Partners* (London, 1972), p.62.

9. K. Bourne, *The Balance of Power in North America, 1815–1908* (London, 1967), pp.409–10.
10. J. Bright and J.E.T. Rogers (eds.), *Speeches on Questions and Public Policy by Richard Cobden*, Vol.II (1870), Appendix 1, p.108.
11. Ibid., p.76.
12. See *HC Debs.*, Vol.171, 1 July–28 July 1863; A.J.P. Taylor, *The Struggle for Mastery in Europe, 1848–1918* (Oxford, 8th edn, 1988), pp.133–41.
13. J. Gooch, 'The Weary Titan: Strategy and Policy in Great Britain, 1890–1918', in W. Murray, M. Knox, and A. Bernstein (eds.), *The Making of Strategy: Rulers, States and Wars* (Cambridge, 1994), pp.278–306.
14. Bourne, *Balance of Power in North America*, pp.406–7.
15. R.G. Neale, *British and American Imperialism, 1898–1900* (Brisbane, 1965), pp.34, 173; J.A.S. Grenville, 'Diplomacy and War Plans in the United States, 1890–1917', *Transactions of the Royal Historical Society*, 5th Series, 2 (1961), pp.1–21.
16. S.F. Bemis, *A Diplomatic History of the United States* (New York, 5th edn, 1936), p.420.
17. Bourne, *Balance of Power in North America*, p.403; B. Perkins, *The Great Rapprochement: England and the United States, 1895–1914* (London, 1969), pp.20, 48–59.
18. M. Gerlach, *British Liberalism and the United States: Political and Social Thought in the Late Victorian Age* (London, 2001), pp.176–85.
19. R.M. Hathaway, *Great Britain and the United States: Special Relations Since World War I* (Boston, 1990), p.1; Brogan, *Longman History*, pp.261, 448
20. Bourne, *Balance of Power in North America*, p.404, suggests, on the basis of Palmerston's assessment, 'massive retaliation', the use of the Royal Navy to devastate American cities on the eastern seaboard to strike at American commerce, morale, and loyalty.
21. T.R. Hietala, *Manifest Design: Anxious Aggrandizement in Late Jacksonian America* (Ithaca, NY, 1985), pp.81–3; Gerlach, *British Liberalism and the United States*, p.258.
22. For example, when President John Tyler tried to influence the electorate of Maine to accept a negotiated compromise with Britain over the disputed Canadian frontier, the source of the funds – some $14,500 – was the British emissary, Lord Ashburton. See S.F. Knott, *Secret and Sanctioned: Covert Operations and the American Presidency* (New York, 1996), pp.123–4.
23. Bemis, *Diplomatic History of the US*, p.411.
24. Bourne, *Balance of Power in North America*, pp.408–9; on the Clayton–Bulwer Treaty, see R.A. Humphreys, 'Anglo-American Relations in Central America', *Transactions of the Royal Historical Society*, 5th Series, 18 (1968), pp.174–208.
25. H.C. Allen, *The Anglo-American Relationship Since 1783* (London, 1959), p.198.
26. R.F. Weigley, *History of the United States Army* (London, 1968), p.567; K. Hagan, *In Peace and War* (New York, 1978), Chapters 6–8.
27. P. Maslowski, 'To the Edge of Greatness: The United States, 1783–1865', in Murray et al. (eds.), *Making of Strategy*, pp.207, 225; B. Holden Reid, 'Civil Military Relations', in S.-M. Grant and P.J. Parish (eds.), *The Legacy of Disunion* (Baton Rouge, 2003), pp.151–72.
28. Bourne, *Balance of Power in North America*, p.412; Earl Russell, *Recollections and Suggestions 1813–73* (London, 1875), p.441; Allen, *Anglo-American Relationship*, p.203.
29. Allen, *Anglo-American Relationship*, p.218; P. Magnus, *King Edward the Seventh* (London, 1964), pp.32–41. The visit to Canada was official but, although the visit to the US was made at the invitation of President James Buchanan, it remained unofficial. The Prince of Wales travelled as Lord Renfrew, a pseudonym ignored by all.

30. Gerlach, *British Liberalism and the United States*, p.5.
31. Maslowski, 'To the Edge of Greatness', pp.209–10, 229.
32. Silberschmidt, *The United States and Europe*, p.72. For a brilliant critique of American exceptionalism, see M. Cunliffe, 'New World, Old World: The Historical Antithesis', in R. Rose (ed.), *Lessons from America* (London, 1974), pp.19–43. The antithesis tends to underwrite Jones, *New Birth of Freedom*, see especially pp.2–3, where Lord Palmerston and Napoleon III are presented as comic book villains. On the Declaration of Independence as a 'civic religion', see G. Wills, *Inventing America: Jefferson's Declaration of Independence* (London, 1980), pp.xvii–xxii.
33. J.J. Ellis, *American Sphinx: The Character of Thomas Jefferson* (New York, 1998), pp.28, 57, 100, 123, 358–9.
34. Quoted in R.F. Nichols, *Franklin Pierce: The Young Hickory from the Granite Hills* (Philadelphia, 2nd edn, 1958), pp.136, 139; Jones, *New Birth of Freedom*, pp.38–9. The theme of the American self-image is explored in Connell-Smith, *United States and Latin America*, pp.8–12; and the justification that Manifest Destiny lent to expansion, ibid., pp.71–2.
35. P. Scherer, *Lord John Russell* (London, 1999), pp.70, 94, 118.
36. Jones, *New Birth of Freedom*, pp.3, 55. Although not so cynical, Lincoln shared with Palmerston a cold, hard realism that is not acknowledged in Jones's interpretation of a 'caring' Lincoln.
37. Maslowski, 'To the Edge of Greatness', pp.229, 241. Cf. A. Lincoln, 'Annual Message to Congress', 1 Dec. 1862, *Collected Works*, ed. R.P. Basler, Vol.5: *1861–1862* (New Brunswick, NJ, 1953), p.537.
38. K. Robbins, *John Bright* (London, 1979), pp.78, 108, 114, 156–8, 166, 167; Jones, *New Birth of Freedom*, p.50, relies too heavily on C.F. Adams's view of British opinion.
39. Van Deusen, *Seward*, pp.292–3, 326, 329, 370. On the Hampton Roads Conference, see ibid., 384–7. Seward was a devious negotiator, it is difficult to believe that he had such a casual view of a constitutional amendment.
40. In E.D. Adams, *Great Britain and the American Civil War*, Vol.I (New York, 1925), p.296.
41. Maslowski, 'To the Edge of Greatness', pp.205, 241.
42. Lyons to Lord John Russell, 7 Jan. 1865, in Lord Newton, *Lord Lyons: A Record of British Diplomacy* (London, 1913), p.30.
43. H. Adams, *The Education of Henry Adams* (New York, 1931), pp.149, 152–3.
44. Lord Palmerston, 19 May 1865, HC Debs, Vol.179; J.M. McPherson, *The Battle Cry of Freedom: The Civil War Era* (New York, 1988), pp.384, 554.
45. Lyons to Russell, 18 Feb. 1863, FO 30/22/37; Lyons to Russell, 24 Feb. 1863, FO 30/22/29.
46. Although the Union commander, Nathaniel P. Banks, appeared unaware of this objective; see A. Jones and H. Hattaway, *How the North Won* (Urbana, IL, 1983), p.522.
47. Grant to Andrew Johnson, 15 July 1865, in J.Y. Simon (ed.), *The Papers of Ulysses S. Grant*, Vol.15 (Carbondale and Edwardsville, IL, 1969–), p.264.
48. Grant to Edwin M. Stanton, 6 Nov. 1865, ibid., p.394.
49. Grant to Philip H. Sheridan, 15 July 1865, ibid., p.286.
50. Grant to Edward O.C. Ord, 26 Nov. 1865, ibid., pp.420–21; also see C.F. Adams to Seward, 24 March 1865, in *DC, 1865*, Part 1, No.908.
51. Seward to Adams, 10 April 1861, in *DC, 1861*; Seward to Adams, 22 April 1864; *DC, 1864*, Part 1, No. 917.
52. Seward to Adams, 8 Dec. 1862, in *DC, 1863*, Part 1.
53. A. Nevins, *The War for the Union*, Vol.II (New York, 1960), pp.354–62; Van Deusen,

Seward, pp.343–48; F.J. Blue, *Salmon P. Chase: A Life in Politics* (Kent, OH, 1987), pp.189–94; D. Donald, *Lincoln* (London, 1995), pp.399–406.
54. On the reasons why this dispute was resolved peacefully, see Holden Reid, *Origins*, pp.387–90.
55. Van Deusen, *Seward*, pp.211, 293; Seward to Adams, 2 Aug. 1862, *DC, 1862*, Nos.314, 418; Newton, *Lyons*, p.81.
56. Lyons to Russell, 1 Dec. 1863, FO 30/22/37.
57. Lyons to Russell, 3 Feb. 1862, FO 30/22/29.
58. Lyons to Russell, 7 Feb. 1862, FO 30/22/36.
59. Seward to Adams, 8 Dec. 1862, *DC, 1863*, Part 1, No.418.
60. See *HC Debs.*, Vol.179, p.876.
61. See, for example, Seward to Adams, 2 Aug. 1862, *DC, 1862*, No.314.
62. Van Deusen, *Seward*, pp.303, 357, 360, 372.
63. Ibid., pp.356–8.
64. Lyons to Russell, 23 May 1861, FO 30/22/35.
65. Russell, *Recollections and Suggestions*, pp.275–6; Lambert, 'Admiralty and the *Trent* Crisis', pp.320–23.
66. Russell to Clarendon, 22 April 1862, in G.P. Gooch (ed.), *The Later Correspondence of Lord John Russell, 1840–1878*, Vol.II (London, 1885), p.324.
67. Russell to Sir George Cornewall Lewis, 24 March 1863, in ibid., p.333.
68. Lyons to Russell, 26 March 1863, FO 30/22/35.
69. Lyons to Russell, 10 March 1863, FO 30/22/37.
70. Lyons to Russell, 6 May 1863, FO 30/22/35.
71. Jones, *New Birth of Freedom*, pp.16–17, 46–9, 60; Scherer, *Russell*, p.291.
72. For an able discussion, see C.M. Hubbard, *The Burden of Confederate Diplomacy* (Knoxville, TN, 1998), pp.38–40, 44–5, 52, 80, 110, 147 for the remainder of the paragraph. British efforts in 1856 to reach a deal on outlawing piracy, an issue actually raised by the United States but neatly turned against it by Palmerston, are discussed in Nichols, *Pierce*, p.354.
73. P.J. Parish, 'Gladstone and America', in P.J. Jagger (ed.), *Gladstone* (London, 1998), p.88; Holden Reid, *Origins*, p.391; Taylor, *Struggle for Mastery*, pp.19–20; J.A.S. Grenville, *Europe Reshaped, 1848–1878* (Brighton, 1976), pp.177–9, also notes his caution; Russell is quoted in Scherer, *Russell*, pp.290–91.
74. Parish, 'Gladstone and America', pp.87, 89; Jones, *New Birth of Freedom*, pp.16, 62; for Confederate efforts to exploit the northern stance on slavery, see Hubbard, *Confederate Diplomacy*, pp.38, 41.
75. Scherer, *Russell*, p.294; Parish, 'Gladstone and America', pp.90, 92, 94; M. Beloff, 'The Special Relationship: An Anglo-American Myth', in Martin Gilbert (ed.), *A Century of Conflict: Essays for A.J.P. Taylor* (London, 1966), pp.153–8.
76. Parish, 'Gladstone and America', pp.96–8; Scherer, *Russell*, p.293; Jones, *New Birth of Freedom*, pp.83, 93–4, 97, 121, 141, 176; Hubbard, *Confederate Diplomacy*, pp.79, 123–4. Russell believed that Lincoln's action gave the south an opportunity to emancipate its slaves even more quickly than under his own plan for mediation.
77. Hubbard, *Confederate Diplomacy*, pp.115–23. Jones, *New Birth of Freedom*, pp.84, 98–109, argues, contrary to received wisdom, and persuasively, that the carnage of the Battle of Antietam, 17 September 1862, made British intervention more rather than less likely. For the opposite view, see Scherer, *Russell*, pp.294–5. He also exaggerates Russell's consistency; see ibid., p.297.
78. J.Y. Wong, *Deadly Dreams: Opium and the Arrow War (1856–60) in China* (Cambridge, 1998), pp.167, 170, 172, 226, 250–54, 463, 464; Jones, *New Birth of Freedom*, pp.129, 167; Holden Reid, *Origins*, pp.392–4.
79. *HC Debs.*, Vol.179, p.876; Bruce to Russell, 11 July 1865, FO 30/22/38.

80. Russell to Adams, 16 April 1863, *DC, 1863*.
81. Van Deusen, *Seward*, p.354.
82. Ibid., p.359.
83. *HC Debs*, Vol.179, p.876.
84. H.G.C. Matthew, *Gladstone, 1809–98* (Oxford, 1997), p.188; Parish, 'Gladstone and America', pp.101–2; Gerlach, *British Liberalism and the United States*, p.145.
85. D. Donald, *Charles Sumner and the Rights of Man* (New York, 1970), p.376; A. Cook, *The Alabama Claims: American Politics and Anglo-American Relations, 1865–1872* (Ithaca, NY, 1975), pp.74–6; the speech did not appear anti-British to Sumner, see ibid., pp.91–7.
86. Donald, *Sumner*, pp.377, 380, 390, 394–5, 406, 484; J.A. Carpenter, *Ulysses S. Grant* (New York, 1970), pp.100–101. For Cook's harsh verdict on the Johnson-Clarendon Convention, see Cook, *Alabama Claims*, p.63, also see pp.160–62.
87. Donald, *Sumner*, p.506; Cook, *Alabama Claims*, pp.101, 129, 134, 154–6.
88. Mathew, *Gladstone*, pp.189–90; P. Magnus, *Gladstone* (London, 1954), p.206.
89. A.R.C. Grant and C. Combe (eds.), *Lord Rosebery's North American Journal, 1873* (London, 1967), p.119.
90. Bourne, *Balance of Power in North America*, p.199; Gerlach, *British Liberalism and the United States*, p.xiv.

'Almost a Law of Nature'? Sir Edward Grey, the Foreign Office, and the Balance of Power in Europe, 1905–12

T.G. OTTE

In his famous 1907 memorandum, Eyre Crowe noted that it had become 'an historical truism to identify England's secular policy with the maintenance of [the] balance of power. ... [It] assumes almost the form of a law of nature, as has been theoretically demonstrated, and illustrated historically by an eminent writer on English national policy'.[1] A few years earlier, the then assistant undersecretary of state at the Foreign Office expressed his hope that Britain would 'remain the country holding the balance between Dual and Triple Alliance'.[2] What the more systematic and methodical Crowe had advanced in somewhat rigid terms, Sir Francis Bertie expressed as merely an aspiration. The thrust of their argument, however, was the same: the maintenance of the balance of power in Europe was a British strategic interest.

Few concepts have preoccupied students of international affairs more, and fewer still present more problems to them, than the notion of the balance of power. Many scholars have identified it as a *force majeure et profonde*, the fundamental mechanism of international politics.[3] Nevertheless, as two recent historians rightly stated, it is also a concept that has never been properly explored, and has tended to be used in vague and largely descriptive terms.[4] That the concept of the balance of power has a long intellectual pedigree needs hardly to be emphasized. Although diplomatic or international history as an academic discipline was still in its infancy before 1914, late Victorian and Edwardian historians of European diplomacy tended to hold as axiomatic that Britain had always pursued an equilibrist policy. Thus, E.S. Beesly argued that Queen Elizabeth I's shrewd balancing of the rivals France and Spain had guaranteed England's national security.[5] Montagu Burrows, naval officer-turned-Chichele professor of modern history, noted that '[t]he meaning of the term of Balance of Power is really Self-Defence; it is not too much to say that it has been the saving of Europe'. Burrows praised the wholesale adoption of a balance of power policy by Britain in the course of the eighteenth century as 'the result of self-sacrifice and far-seeing public spirit'.[6] Similarly, J.R. Seeley, regius professor at Cambridge, identified the idea of the 'balance of power' as an 'old English tradition', continued by William III who 'in a still more effectual manner restored the European balance'.[7] In more general terms, H.W.V. Temperley identified 'the struggle for the balance of power' as one of the hallmarks of Great Power relations since the eighteenth century.[8] 'That Great Britain should occupy a commanding place in the councils of Europe was with Canning an article of faith', the Oxford don and Conservative MP J.A.R. Marriott noted approvingly.[9] W.A. Phillips, a pioneer of international history, similarly wrote of Canning's foreign policy that '[t]he function of England, in fact ... was to hold the balance between extreme principles'; and of Castlereagh that his diplomacy 'was the traditional one of establishing and maintaining the balance of power'.[10] Of course the present-day historian must beware not to assume too great an intellectual influence of such works on foreign policy-makers.[11] Nevertheless, many of the underlying assumptions had seeped into the political consciousness of the educated classes of late Victorian and Edwardian Britain. Thus, for example, an anonymous writer in the *Quarterly Review* observed a few months before the cataclysm of July 1914: 'The preservation of the "Balance of Power on a peace footing" ... is still the main object of British diplomacy.'[12] A few months later, a group of Oxford historians invoked the principle of the continental 'balance of power' to justify Britain's involvement in the war.[13] The *topos* of the 'balance of power' featured prominently in the public discourse on past and present foreign policy in the years before 1914. This, in turn, begs a number of questions: were the policy-makers in Britain worshipping 'the false idol of the balance of power'?[14] Did the notion of a continental equilibrium serve as a convenient 'smokescreen' for Britain's real concerns, its Asiatic imperial interests?[15] Did Grey's 'fixed version of the "balance of power"' prevent him from appreciating the shifts in the relations amongst the Great Powers after 1906?[16] And, lastly, was the notion of the 'balance of power' a *wise* policy? – the question to which, as Herbert Butterfield once observed, Grey's defenders did not give the answer.[17]

British foreign policy before 1914 lay in the hands of a small, socially relatively homogenous group of men. The views and actions of this small elite were shaped by the prevailing modes of thought and behaviour of their age. The high degree of social homogeneity produced a relative uniformity of outlook, a firm, though not always fully articulated, understanding of the basic principles of British policy, what Harold Nicolson later called the 'Foreign Office mind'.[18] For the historian of this period, this implies the need to establish the 'unspoken assumptions', to recreate the 'cognitive maps', upon which the 'Edwardian generation' based its policy decisions.[19] Lastly, the historian has to bear in mind that the assumptions upon which decision-makers act are not necessarily the result of systematic or even profound thought; that they may be haphazard and lacking in consistence; and that the actual policy-making process may be more ragged around the edges than many later reconstructions tend to suggest.[20] The equilibrist notions entertained by Britain's foreign policy elite were no exception: they reflected general analogies derived from British and European history. Furthermore, of these broad assumptions and judgements the statesmen and diplomats were often only dimly aware themselves. Thus, Sir Edward Goschen, when ambassador at Berlin, could in all sincerity ridicule the speculations in the foreign press about 'our deeply laid plans and our long prepared coups'; and Grey himself would later dismiss in a similar vein 'the carefully laid plans, the deep, unrevealed motives' that were often attributed to British diplomacy.[21] However, while British diplomacy undoubtedly tended to react to the exigencies of the moment, such statements ought not to be construed into assumptions of an altogether haphazard and *ad hoc* policy-making process and its underlying concepts. In Michael Dockrill's succinct characterization, Grey was 'a cautious Foreign Secretary, disinclined, like Salisbury and Lansdowne, to take risks, and highly conscious of the element of continuity in British foreign policy'.[22] Grey, indeed, attached great importance to continuity. Already in October 1905, with the Unionist government clearly disintegrating and the Liberals' return to power imminent, Grey was anxious to dispel the impression that a Liberal government would unsettle Lansdowne's *entente* agreement with France: 'I think we are running a real risk of losing France & not winning Germany, who won't want us, if she can detach France from us.'[23] In his 'City Speech' of 20 October 1905, Grey identified the Anglo-French *entente* as a 'cardinal point in our foreign policy', and argued 'that the spirit of the agreement is more important than the letter of the agreement'.[24] Unlike Lansdowne, Grey 'had worked out a rationale for his foreign policy'; and, again unlike the more empire-centric, former colonial governor Lansdowne, 'Grey ... was more concerned with Europe'.[25] One recent historian has taken Grey to task for this preoccupation with the 'spirit' of the *entente* with France – in contrast to Lansdowne, to whom the 'exact terms' of the agreement were more important – with the implication that Grey neglected Britain's imperial interests.[26]

Such criticism is misplaced. Impermanence is the main characteristic of international affairs. They do not reach a plateau, only there to rest, but are in constant movement; and, unlike a contractual agreement between private individuals, international understandings not only reflect the particular circumstances that produced them, they also have an internal logic that develops as circumstances change. The French *entente* was no exception. Originally conceived as the settlement of a series of colonial disputes – with the Egypt–Morocco barter at its core – it was a pragmatic attempt at a negotiated and mutually beneficial removal of potential sources of conflict between the two countries, without, Lansdowne hoped, incurring major European obligations; though the French foreign minister, Théophile Delcassé, undoubtedly had more far-reaching ambitions for the *entente*.[27] Indeed, within 18 months of its conclusion, the *entente* had evolved into something more than merely a colonial agreement. This was caused not so much by actions on the part of the two signatories, but rather reflected changes in the constellation between the Great Powers. Two factors combined to bring about this evolution: first, the impact of the *entente* on Great Power relations in general; and, second, the temporary disruption of the international system by the Russo-Japanese War.

The *entente* changed the dynamics of European diplomacy. The power most affected by its conclusion was Germany. French acquiescence in Britain's predominance on the Nile removed the

'Egyptian lever' from Germany's diplomatic toolbag. For as long as successive French governments had refused to accept Britain's *de facto* control of Egypt after 1882, British policy-makers tacitly acknowledged, 'the necessity of working with Germany. Berlin, and not Cairo, is the real centre of gravity of Egyptian affairs'.[28] Germany's loss of leverage over Britain was keenly felt at the Wilhelmstrasse; and attempts were made to extract compensation from Britain so as to regain some of the lost leverage. German diplomacy had reverted to type, as King Edward VII minuted: 'This political "blackmailing" ... occurs to me to be as unfair as it is as unnecessary.'[29] Ultimately, the exchanges between London and Berlin resulted in little more than an arbitration agreement which, despite the soothing noises made by Lansdowne, fell well short of German expectations.[30] Nevertheless, the episode reinforced the now growing suspicions of German ambitions.[31] It also highlighted once again Britain's earlier vulnerability to political blackmail, and, secondly, that the *entente*, though on paper a strictly colonial agreement, had repercussions for Britain's relations with the other powers. Edward Grey understood this. As Michael Dockrill has argued convincingly, his outlook on foreign affairs was shaped 'by his experiences ... in the 1890s, when it seemed to him that Germany had used England's difficulties with France and Russia to extract concessions as a price for her support'.[32] Such was the impact of these earlier experiences on the Edwardian generation of British diplomats that there were only few 'in London or in Europe who were not imbued with deep suspicions of German policy'.[33] Indeed, the problems of the last two decades of the nineteenth century were never far from the minds of Grey and his officials throughout his tenure of the Foreign Office. In the spring of 1909 Grey reflected on the 1880s and 1890s when successive British governments 'used "to lean on Germany". ... [W]e were kept on bad terms with France & Russia. We were sometimes on the brink of war with one or the other; & Germany took toll of us when it suited her'.[34] Thus, when in September 1912 Crowe warned that proposals for an Anglo-German understanding, if accepted, would ultimately allow Berlin to indulge again in the 'policy of political blackmail', Grey minuted: 'I have always felt that this was the real reason of the change of our policy.'[35] The perceived dangers inherent in any return to Britain's exposed pre-*entente* international position were a recurrent theme in internal Foreign Office thinking.

The second factor which profoundly influenced Grey's diplomatic calculations was the international fall-out of the Russo-Japanese War. Russia's defeat at the hands of Japan had a significant impact on European diplomacy. For a decade, until 1904–5, the Franco-Russian alliance, alongside the German-led Triple Alliance, had been the key variable in the calculations of the chancelleries of Europe. The alliance acted as a kind of vice on Germany, restricting the latter's diplomatic freedom of manoeuvre in Europe. The outward signs of this were the absence of those war-scares which Bismarck engineered repeatedly between 1875 and 1887, and Germany's, albeit clumsy, attempts at overseas expansion under the auspices of *Weltpolitik*. In 1905 the Franco-Russian Dual Alliance was effectively disabled: the vice had cracked open. It was a considerable reversal of Germany's international fortunes so shortly after the earlier perceived setback in the shape of the Anglo-French understanding. For the foreseeable future, as Britain's chargé d'affaires at St. Petersburg pointed out, Russia was unlikely to pursue a policy antagonistic to Germany, and would, in fact, 'temporize between Germany & England'.[36] Grey shared this view, but he also saw Russia's weakness in wider balance-of-power terms. Despite his later claim that he had 'never consciously set [the balance of power] before me as something to be pursued, attained, and preserved', he was, in fact, keenly aware that in 1905–6 the European equilibrium was disturbed to Germany's advantage.[37] Thus, shortly after assuming the seals of the Foreign Office, he wrote to Spring-Rice at St Petersburg: 'I want to see Russia restored in the councils of Europe, & I hope on better terms with us than she has yet been.' Two months later he reiterated his impatience 'to see Russia reestablished as a factor in European politics. Whether we shall get an arrangement with her about Asiatic questions remains to be seen'.[38] Two important inferences can be drawn from this as to Grey's foreign policy: he clearly saw Russia in a European as well as an Asiatic context, but not necessarily a linkage between them; and he perceived there to be an imbalance in European politics that had to be redressed.

German diplomacy amply demonstrated the disruption of the balance of power in Europe. The Kaiser's Baltic summer surprise at

Bjørkø could be dismissed as farcical bungling;[39] not so, however, Germany's earlier decision to challenge French aspirations in Morocco. By the time Grey entered office in December 1905, the crisis had already passed the moment of greatest danger. However, given Grey's insistence on continuity in foreign policy, it is appropriate briefly to examine Lansdowne's handling of the Moroccan dispute. It seems unlikely that the German leaders had any territorial ambitions there, or that they actively prepared a preventive war against France, though Field Marshal Alfred von Schlieffen and the general staff were clearly alive to the opportunities of the moment.[40] The German chancellor, Prince Bernhard von Bülow, and his chief adviser, Friedrich von Holstein, provoked the Moroccan crisis as part of a diplomatic offensive, camouflaged as the defence of international treaty rights under the 1880 Madrid Convention. Their actions were actuated by concerns about what they perceived to be the beginnings of Germany's 'encirclement'. Their objective was to exploit the perhaps unique moment of military advantage caused by Russia's weakness, and to force France to make terms on Morocco with Germany rather than Britain. In the longer term, they hoped, France would adhere to a Russo-German continental bloc against Britain.[41]

Ironically, Germany's Moroccan offensive was also a confirmation of Britain's new position in Great Power politics. The fact that a potential international question, the future of Morocco, had been settled without German consultation underlined that Britain was now the linchpin of European diplomacy. Louis Mallet, Lansdowne's and then Grey's private secretary, pointed out that the Anglo-French understanding 'has put us in a position which Germany has held for many years, and we must do everything in our power to keep it'.[42] Lansdowne saw matters in a similar light: 'It is a bad thing that the Germans should have been able to discredit the entente.' German diplomacy would 'put a spoke in our wheels' whenever possible.[43] It is true, initially Lansdowne and the Admiralty were primarily worried about the possibility of Germany acquiring a naval base somewhere along the Moroccan coast as compensation for recognition of French predominance there. Nevertheless, from a British as well as a German perspective the dispute was not confined merely to the future of the Moorish lands. Allowing German interference in Morocco, and treating exclusively with France, implied an acceptance that Germany was after all the predominant power in European diplomacy. Thus, the *entente* had become bound up with Britain's international position. Germany's diplomatic offensive, then, was superficially a challenge to France, in reality a test of the *entente*, and thus a challenge to Britain's position. To preserve it, the *entente* had to be maintained, and so British diplomacy had to support France. In the absence of such support France might turn to Germany for a bilateral settlement, which would very likely be unfavourable to British interests.[44] Far from removing Morocco from Britain's diplomatic agenda, the combination of French *entente* and heavy-handed German diplomacy ensured that it would remain there until the Quai d'Orsay and the Wilhelmstrasse settled their differences. However, any Franco-German settlement that came about without Britain's consultation would have ended Britain's position as the new linchpin of European politics. Lansdowne, therefore, indicated his willingness to join with France 'in offering strong opposition' to possible German demands for Moroccan territory, subject to prior consultation.[45] In an effort to allay existing French anxieties about Britain's support, Lansdowne suggested to the French ambassador, Paul Cambon, that the two governments 'should, as far as possible, discuss in advance any contingencies by which they might in the course of events find themselves confronted'.[46] Following a further enquiry by Cambon, however, Lansdowne hurried to remove any hopes the French might have had of Britain's full and unconditional support against Germany as a result of what Cambon had called Lansdowne's 'déclaration la plus nette et la plus spontanée': there was to be consultation 'only in anticipation of any complications to be apprehended during the somewhat anxious period through which we are at present passing'.[47] Lansdowne's offer of support was confined to the present crisis only. At the same time, he warned the German ambassador, Count Metternich, that in the event of a German attack on France public opinion would not allow the government to remain neutral.[48] Crucially, Lansdowne never informed the French of his warning to Metternich. Paris had to be given assurances of British support only to the extent that it did not yield to German pressure, and conclude a bilateral deal with Berlin to Britain's disadvantage. But it was imperative not to encourage France too much, lest it provoke Germany into an act of aggression, and so embroil Britain in a continental war. It was therefore vital to exercise a calming influence at Paris, while restraining Berlin.

Lansdowne's diplomatic strategy was only partially successful. Delcassé's enforced resignation dented the prestige of the *entente*; and had Bülow reciprocated in kind to French Prime Minister Pierre Maurice Rouvier's offer in November of territorial compensation – an offer of which Lansdowne and his diplomats were quite ignorant – then his strategy might have unravelled altogether. However, while Lansdowne had failed sufficiently to steady French nerves against German pressure, he succeeded in restraining Germany. Uncertain as to the full extent of the *entente* agreement, and unpersuaded by Lansdowne's emphatic denial of an Anglo-French alliance, Bülow agreed to an international conference to settle the Moroccan dispute.[49] German diplomats might complain that, in the event of a complication involving Germany and another power, they 'would inevitably find England on the other side'.[50] But for as long as Berlin and Paris could not settle their differences directly, no movement was possible in the matter without British participation.

On coming to office Grey reiterated the essential continuity in British foreign policy. He reminded the ambassador at Berlin, Sir Frank Lascelles, to impress upon Bülow 'our intention to keep in letter & spirit our engagements to other countries'. He rejected Bülow's tentative suggestion of British mediation between Berlin and Paris prior to the convening of the conference at Algeciras. The German chancellor's 'fine words', he observed, 'butter no parsnips, and if the parsnips are to be buttered, it must be done at the Conference. If that ends in conclusions not adverse to the Anglo-French Entente there will be a real clearing of the sky and assurance of peace'.[51] Like Lansdowne, Grey was convinced that in a Franco-German war 'we certainly should not be able to remain neutral. The public feeling would be too strong'.[52] To Metternich he repeated Lansdowne's warning that, 'if the circumstances arose, public feeling in England would be so strong that it would be impossible to remain neutral'. He assured the German ambassador that 'we did not intend to make trouble. ... We wanted to avoid trouble between Germany and France' – another recurring theme in Grey's conversations with foreign diplomats throughout his period of office.[53] Grey also followed the line laid down by Lansdowne in his policy towards France, though he ventured a step further when Cambon saw him on 10 January 1906 to 'put *the* question ... directly & formally': could France count on British military support in the event of 'une aggression brutale'? Grey promised nothing more than 'benevolent neutrality if such a thing existed', but volunteered the observation that 'public opinion would be strongly moved in favour of France'.[54]

Cambon's enquiry came as no surprise. At the end of December Grey had been informed by Lieutenant-Colonel Charles à Court Repington, the raffish but brilliant military correspondent of *The Times*, of informal enquiries by the French military attaché, Major Victor Huguet, about the new government's attitude in the event of a continental war.[55] The possibility of war was on the minds of many diplomats in Europe. Although Russia had by now made peace with Japan, it was clearly in no position to undertake any offensive military operations.[56] From the hustings of the general election campaign Grey wrote to the new secretary of state for war, R.B. Haldane: 'Persistent reports and little indications keep reaching me that Germany intends to attack France in the spring.'[57] Under these circumstances, Cambon's enquiry was not only to be expected; in making it the French ambassador also merely took up Lansdowne's offer in May to discuss 'any complications to be apprehended'. In fact, in the course of the first week of January 1906, before his conversation with Cambon, Grey discussed the possibility of war with Haldane, and afterwards authorized informal talks between the director of military operations and the French military attaché.[58] These staff talks have earned Grey the opprobrium of those contemporary Liberal politicians critical of the French *entente* as well as of some later historians. However, the military talks are easily exaggerated.

The key members of the Cabinet were clearly informed, though the talks were not formally reported to the full Cabinet. Indeed, there seems to have been more support for Grey's policy and wider knowledge of the talks among his colleagues than some historians are prepared to concede.[59] Moreover, as the service departments had already begun seriously to consider the possibility of a continental war involving Britain, staff talks with the French made sense. Any plans to render armed assistance to France depended for their feasibility on detailed information about French military plans; and such information was only to be had through military talks. The conversations ultimately resulted in contingency plans for the despatch of a 100,000 strong British force to France. However, there was no binding commitment on the part of Britain to intervene; and the French general staff never made a British intervention part of its war plans.[60] From a purely military point of view, staff talks with the British were of only limited value to France. The conversations, then, ought to be seen not so much in a technical but rather in a political context. They were an integral part of Grey's diplomatic strategy. They were intended to reassure the French government of Britain's support without incurring any firm commitments. At stake was Britain's position in Egypt as well as its role in international diplomacy. Even after the conclusion of the French understanding, Grey and the Foreign Office did not regard Britain's position on the Nile as wholly secure. Thus, were the Egyptian question ever to be raised while the *entente* with France was intact, French support could confidently be expected to be forthcoming.

If, however, the *entente* were allowed to collapse, Britain would be internationally isolated, and thus vulnerable to pressure by other powers. Sir Charles Hardinge, the permanent undersecretary, endorsed Grey's argument: 'If France is left in the lurch an agreement or an alliance between France, Germany and Russia in the near future is certain. This ... is the Kaiser's ideal, France and Russia becoming satellites within the German system.'[61] If, however, the *entente* remained intact, then Britain's position as the linchpin of European politics would also be secure. To attain his objectives, Grey had to preserve peace, and prevent independent action on the part of France. If war broke out, Britain would be forced to declare its hand, thus inevitably losing influence over one of the two parties involved; and if France entered into a bargain with Germany by making concessions at Britain's expense, or provoked it into an act of aggression, and Britain remained aloof from the conflict, then it would again be confined to the sidelines of European diplomacy. Grey had to perform a delicate balancing act. France had to be buttressed against German pressure. But assurances had to be vague enough to dissuade France from being too unaccommodating to Germany.[62] On no account, Grey explained to Bertie, now ambassador at Paris, was France to be encouraged to take 'independent action ... which might lead to a war with Germany without keeping us informed and hearing what we have to say'. For that reason, he refused to give a firm undertaking of British armed support: '[A] promise in advance committing this country to take part in a Continental war is ... a very serious [matter] ... it changes the Entente into an Alliance – and Alliances, especially continental Alliances are not in accordance with our traditions.'[63] Grey's studied vagueness paid off. French anxiety that Britain might not support France, and German fears that it would, meant that, as Bülow resignedly observed, 'the key to this Moroccan situation is in England's hands'.[64] Britain was 'holding the balance', as Bertie and other British diplomats had hoped it would. This was not traditional 'balance-of-power' politics. It was a form of British neo-Bismarckianism to which the Edwardian generation inclined, a conscious effort to hold the balance, rather than a merely passive support for the *status quo* powers in European politics.

The first Moroccan crisis set the pattern for British diplomacy during future Franco-German crises until the outbreak of the Great War. Moreover, the Bülow–Holstein policy of pressurizing the French had transformed what was a purely colonial settlement into a virtual diplomatic alliance between Britain and France, though it would be fallacious to argue that the *entente* paved the way for war with Germany in 1914. Britain's position after 1906 was much more complex. Grey never wanted a military confrontation with Germany. In the aftermath of the Bosnian annexation crisis of 1908–9 he noted: 'Real isolation of Germany would mean war: so would the domination of Germany in Europe. There is a fairly wide course between the two extremes in which European politics should steer.'[65] Yet, in practice, steering this wide course proved to be fraught with difficulties. Above all, it was acknowledged by British diplomats that the French *entente* and the later convention with Russia could not be seen in isolation, but within the context of the equilibrium between the Great Powers. In Gerald Spicer's analysis: 'The "Ententes" will have ... a tendency towards becoming alliances in proportion as the Powers concerned have grounds to fear that Germany desires to play the predominant part in Europe.'[66]

The object of Grey's policy was to preserve peace in Europe by recreating a European equilibrium. The period after Algeciras was, however, considerably more fluid than later historians have tended to acknowledge. Grey and his senior officials recognized that France was a weak reed to lean upon; and so continually reassured their counterparts at the Quai d'Orsay of Britain's continued support in order to buttress them against future German pressure.[67] Nevertheless, concerns about French reliability were never far from the surface. Commenting on the reported desire in ministerial circles in Paris for some form of 'working arrangement' with Germany, Eyre Crowe drew a parallel with the Ferry–Bismarck colonial *entente* of the early 1880s, and warned 'that the political friendships concluded by [Germany] have always had a "point" directed against some other power or combination of powers'.[68] André Tardieu's advocacy of closer Franco-German cooperation caused similar flutters of anxiety; and Clemençeau's financial and commercial Moroccan agreement with Germany was regarded in Whitehall as a potential precursor to a political understanding.[69] The Foreign Office was certainly aware that the very vagueness of Britain's pledges of support was at the root of France's perceived vacillation. Nevertheless, this was part of Britain's diplomatic strategy, as Hardinge noted: 'The present elastic situation is more satisfactory for us.' Grey himself was wary of a firmer commitment to France that some diplomats suggested. A military alliance with France was fraught with risks; chief amongst them was the possibility 'that Germany might attack France at once, while Russia is helpless. ... She might make an alliance between us & France a pretext for doing this as her only chance of saving her future'.[70]

The 'encirclement' of which German leaders now increasingly spoke was neither so threatening nor so firm as they supposed. Still, Germany's first diplomatic offensive had alerted the Foreign Office to the danger of future attempts to break up the *entente*. Indeed, German diplomats made no secret of it. The future state secretary at the Auswärtiges Amt, Heinrich von Tschirschky, expounded to the British consul-general at Hamburg 'that it was a cardinal principle of German policy to break up all coalitions between other powers which might tend to affect German prestige' – a statement that rapidly earned him the distinction of being the Foreign Office's chief *bête noire*.[71] That Germany would try, whenever possible, 'to make mischief between England & France' was held as almost axiomatic by the Foreign Office. The possibility of such 'mischief', the Austrian ambassador Count Albert Mensdorff warned, 'makes them suspicious here more than anything else. ... About that one should have no illusions at Berlin'.[72] Indeed, evidence was mounting that Germany was increasingly relying on its alliance with Austria. The posthumous publication of the memoirs of Bülow's predecessor, Prince Chlodwig von Hohlenlohe-Schillingsfürst, caused a stir. They revealed that Wilhelm II had given Austro-Hungarian Emperor Franz Joseph a firm undertaking that in the event of an Austro-Russian conflict Germany would 'go with Austria even at the risk of war with France and Russia'.[73] While Austro-German relations seemed to be getting closer, Italy's position within the Triple Alliance became increasingly doubtful. Already during the Algeciras conference the Italians had given a clear signal that they were unlikely to support Germany in the event of a Franco-German war over Morocco.[74] Such information shaped British diplomatic calculations, which remained focused on the maintenance of the *status quo* and the equilibrium of Europe. These calculations were subtle and nuanced, and by no means aimed at the crude containment of Germany. Thus, for instance, when the French ambassador at Rome, Camille Barrère, suggested to his British colleague, Sir Edwin Egerton, an agreement between the Mediterranean powers – France, Spain, Italy, Britain, and Austria-Hungary – in order to 'paralyze [German] influence in Mediterranean affairs', Hardinge and Grey poured cold water on the idea. Such a combination, the permanent undersecretary warned, might lead to the break-up of the Triple Alliance. This was unwelcome 'since it would open up possibilities of other combinations which might prove more dangerous than those actually existent. By the two alliances and our "entente" with France the balance of power is fairly maintained'. The proposed agreement, however, had wider implications. As any agreement to maintain the *status quo* in the Mediterranean would pertain to the Turkish Straits, Hardinge warned, a future Anglo-Russian rapprochement would be a much more difficult proposition.[75]

Though weakened, the Triple Alliance was unlikely to collapse. Indeed, British diplomats wished to preserve it, as Hardinge elaborated in early 1909:

It is very much to the interest of France & England that Italy should continue as a source of weakness to the Triple Alliance. It would be a misfortune if the Alliance were denounced. Should the "Drei Kaiserbund" ever be reestablished Italy must inevitably lean on France & England as she does now in fact to a considerable extent.[76]

The last point is significant. The senior officials at the Foreign Office were convinced that, with Italy's alliance-worthiness declining, 'the reestablishment of the "Drei Kaiserbund" is the main object of German foreign policy'.[77] The recrudescence of the combination of the three Eastern monarchies, however, would have tilted the balance of power in Germany's favour and might have pushed Russian ambitions towards Central Asia once more.

Many international developments were judged against this possible scenario, as is illustrated by the abortive Balkans initiative by the new Austro-Hungarian foreign minister, Count Alois Lexa von Aehrenthal, in May 1907. Aehrenthal, 'prototype du diplomate suffisant, irréaliste',[78] had approached the Russian foreign minister, Alexander P. Izvolsky, with a view to cooperating along with Germany and France in the Macedonian question. Whether Aehrenthal intended to extend this regional combination so as to regroup the European powers is a matter of some debate amongst historians, though his private correspondence would tend to support a more far-reaching interpretation.[79] When news of the Austrian initiative reached London through French and Russian sources, Grey and the Foreign Office were alarmed at the prospect of Aehrenthal's 'noyau des puissances conservatrices'. Goschen, who had received part of the information, warned that 'there is good ground ... for the surmise that the plan was made in Berlin, and that its ultimate object is the formation of a quadruple alliance which, beginning in a small way in the Near East, might eventually lead to a rearrangement of European alliances'.[80] At the beginning of May information had been received by the Foreign Office that Aehrenthal, on a visit to Berlin, had advised his German colleague to be conciliatory to France 'so as to detach her from England'.[81] Combined, the two pieces of information seemed to suggest that moves were under way to exclude Britain from important international issues. Grey and Hardinge lost no time to nip the initiative in the bud. The unfortunate Austrian ambassador – who had no knowledge of Aehrenthal's moves – was informed in rather forceful terms of Britain's displeasure at being excluded from the discussions. Mensdorff was warned that the initiative 'gained the appearance as though [Aehrenthal] were aiming at a new grouping of the Powers'.[82] Grey's intervention crossed Aehrenthal's plans, and the matter ultimately came to nothing. The British reaction may seem exaggerated. Certainly, Goschen and the Foreign Office misjudged Aehrenthal, who, far from being Berlin's poodle, was his own rottweiler. The fear that the envisaged Balkans combination of four powers to the exclusion of Britain and Italy might lead to a regrouping of the alliances, however, was not so unrealistic. After all, Germany's approaches to Britain around 1900 had always openly envisaged regional cooperation as a first step towards a later alliance.[83] The *entente* itself was proof that regional agreements could grow beyond their original confines.

Despite this contretemps, Austria continued to play an important role in Britain's equilibrist diplomacy. Grey and his senior advisers were loath to disrupt the Austro-German alliance. This passive policy did not always go unchallenged. In August 1908, Sir Fairfax Cartwright, ambassador-designate at Vienna, writing from his old post at Munich, submitted a lengthy survey of Austro-Hungarian foreign policy. Cartwright, who had Austrian and Italian family connections, and who was highly suspicious of German policy and motives,[84] suggested that the Hapsburg monarchy was not doomed to decline; and that Britain's unquestioning acceptance of 'the effaced position of Austria-Hungary in European politics' was unwarranted. The Ballhausplatz, he argued, had 'taken the road to Berlin' since the 1870s 'from force of habit'. However, given Russia's current weakness, existing Austro-Russian differences in the Balkans could be settled. Britain, on the strength of the Anglo-Russian agreement of August 1907, should act as a latter-day 'honest broker' to facilitate this *rapprochement*. Vienna, he concluded, should be encouraged to pursue a policy more independent of Berlin. If the German leaders were convinced that 'Austria's fidelity could no more be depended upon in the event of a crisis ... than that of Italy', Germany would be forced 'to join a genuine league of peace' which operated through diplomacy rather than the threat of force.

Cartwright's wide-ranging proposals met with a sceptical reception by the Western Department. Ronald Campbell identified Cartwright's assumption of German quiescence as the main flaw in the ambassador's argument. 'The balance of power in Europe', he warned, 'would be completely upset and Germany left without even her nominal allies. Is it not more likely that she would consider this humiliating position intolerable and risk everything in defence of her honour, dragging Europe into what would be the most terrible war in all history?' Walter Langley, the assistant undersecretary, agreed: 'we should be in some danger for if Germany resents and is frightened at our friendly relations with Russia, any overtures to Austria ... would be calculated to produce a much greater effect.' The foreign secretary was equally dubious, and reiterated his equilibrist principles: 'an attempt to isolate Germany by setting Austria against her might precipitate a conflict. ... At present there is a fair equilibrium & we should not try to make a break between Germany & Austria.'[85] The notion that Germany might precipitate a general war in Europe if ever Austria were to drift away had become firmly lodged in the official mind in London. When in early 1909 Cartwright reported that Aehrenthal was apparently dissatisfied with the current arrangements under the Triple Alliance, the Foreign Office urged caution. The assistant chief clerk of the Western Department, Gerald Spicer, warned that any rapprochement between Vienna and 'the so called "Triple Entente" Powers ... might easily bring about a very dangerous situation, for if Germany is deserted by the only ally on whom she feels able to depend, she will ... regard this as the final link in the "Einkreisung" policy of Great Britain, & may be seriously tempted to resort to the fortunes of war to burst through the iron ring encircling her'. In this Spicer merely mirrored Grey's views. The foreign secretary had told Cartwright 'originally to be careful to do nothing which would make mischief between Germany & Austria'.[86]

To a large extent Grey's attitude towards the Triple Alliance powers reflected the growing importance of Russia for British diplomacy. Russia's double crisis of 1905 was both a challenge and an opportunity for Britain. Japan's victory, coupled with the renewed and now much tighter Anglo-Japanese alliance of 1905, blunted the Russian advance in Asia and thus increased the security of the Britain's imperial possessions there. Russia's evident desire for a *recueillement* afforded an opportunity to begin the search for a settlement of Anglo-Russian differences; joint concerns about Germany's involvement in Persian affairs provided an opening. The Anglo-Russian convention of August 1907 brought to a conclusion the efforts of successive British foreign secretaries to reach some form of *modus vivendi* with Russia. It either settled or eased outstanding disputes between the two governments ranging from Persia to Tibet. At least officially it ended the nearly century-long rivalry between these two Asiatic empires, though it could not extinguish local rivalries.[87] Still, the convention reduced Russia's perennial threat to Britain's Indian possession and its other Central Asian interests, and so reduced the dangers of imperial overstretch. Nevertheless, the conclusion of the convention did not mean that Anglo-Russian relations were secure. Izvolsky's talks with Germany on the Baltic and North Seas questions and with Austria-Hungary on the Balkans suggested to some British diplomats the decline of the Franco-Russian alliance.[88] If relations between the three Eastern powers improved at the expense of the French alliance, they reasoned, then the Anglo-Russian convention, too, might be jettisoned. British diplomacy, therefore, had to ensure that any Russo-German rapprochement did not come about at the expense of British interests.[89] This was given even greater urgency in light of the marked decline in Anglo-German relations, caused by the accelerated naval race. However, Grey's policy towards Russia was of necessity reactive, since Grey 'could neither compel Anglo-Russian relations to be cordial nor force Russo-German relations to be distant'.[90]

This essentially reactive stance, coupled with the desire not to disrupt Germany's alliances, was also much in evidence during the six months of European tensions produced by the Austrian annexation of Bosnia-Herzegovina. The crisis was the result of the efforts of two unscrupulous men, Aehrenthal and Izvolsky, to take advantage of the Young Turk revolution, and to out-Bismarck each other in the mistaken belief that double-dealing was the surest way to diplomatic success.[91] Both men miscalculated. Izvolsky, whose vanity and affectation frequently got the better of his intelligence, failed to anticipate the speed with which Aehrenthal, the cooler of the two, would move in an effort to keep foreign interference at a minimum.[92] The Austrian foreign minister, in turn, seriously misjudged the strength of southern Slav nationalism and the vehemence of its response. Since Austria's annexation of Bosnia was in breach of the 1878 Treaty of Berlin, to which Britain was a signatory, the British government could not well turn a blind eye to the Near Eastern developments. Considerations of international law apart, there were other factors to be taken into account. Within a week the Bosnian annexation was followed by Bulgaria's declaration of independence. Both events were a serious blow to the stability of the new Turkish regime. By extension this also seemed to have the potential of affecting Britain's own regional position. Decades of declining British influence at Constantinople had been reversed, albeit only temporarily, by the Young Turk revolution in July 1908 which installed in power there a liberal, reformist and largely pro-British group of army officers and intellectuals.

To maintain Britain's newly gained influence and privileged position in the Turkish capital was a key object of Grey's policy throughout the crisis and after.[93] The gravest danger, however, lay in a local military conflict, for it had the potential of embroiling the continental alliance systems. Grey himself thought that it would be difficult for Britain to stay neutral in such an event.[94] The task of maintaining peace and safeguarding British interests at Constantinople was not facilitated by Izvolsky's frantic personal efforts to gather support in Paris and in London for a change in the Straits regime so as to salvage as much of his own personal reputation as possible. Indeed, in his desperation, the Russian foreign minister attempted to blackmail Grey into supporting Russia's ambitions at the Straits: if the British were to fail him, a more reactionary government would be formed at St Petersburg and the course of Russian foreign policy would change to Britain's disadvantage.[95] Izvolsky's bluster had only limited effect on Grey. It is true, the government, as Prime Minister H.H. Asquith noted, 'attach very little strategic value ... to the maintenance of the existing restrictions [the Black Sea clauses]: and this is the opinion of our naval and military advisers'.[96] However, open support for Russian demands for some rectification of the Straits regime would inevitably have reduced British influence at Constantinople and might have pushed the Young Turks towards Germany. Grey once more had to perform a balancing act to ensure that his Russian and Turkish policies did not collide; and in this he was successful. Izvolsky was persuaded to defer his Straits initiative until the Bosnian crisis was settled; and in return received little more than rather vague promises of support for a compromise solution to be discussed at some future international conference.[97] Izvolsky, of course, was in a weak position. He had been given no mandate for his jolly Balkans adventure. However, this did not mean that Russian interests could be ignored. Grey's freedom of manoeuvre was further circumscribed by a Franco-German row over deserters from the French Foreign Legion, who had sought refuge in the German consulate-general at Casablanca. Combined with the outburst of public indignation in Germany which greeted the Kaiser's injudicious *Daily Telegraph* 'interview', it made for a volatile situation. The German leaders, as Grey warned Goschen, might be tempted to use the Casablanca incident 'as a means of diverting attention from the results of the interview: but it is playing a dangerous game, and this is not a time when any nation can safely strike sparks'.[98]

In an effort to pour oil on troubled water, Grey tried to facilitate a solution of the protracted Austro-Turkish and Bulgaro-Turkish disputes. In the latter crisis, Grey's earlier efforts to maintain friendly relations with Russia bore positive results. British support for Constantinople, though short of the full alliance that Turkey had hoped for, combined with Russian financial assistance for Bulgaria brought the Turko-Bulgarian aspect of the Near Eastern crisis to a close by the early months of 1909. Throughout the crisis, as Hardinge elaborated to the new ambassador at Constantinople, Sir Gerard Lowther, Grey's diplomacy had been inspired by a desire to prevent an Austro-Bulgarian combination. If an arrangement could be come to between the two countries through the mediation of Britain and Russia:

> Bulgaria would then be encouraged to be on friendly terms with Turkey, and if Bulgaria at the same time made friendly ententes with Servia and Montenegro, the position of the Balkan States, supported by a friendly Turkey, would be a very strong one, and would practically spell checkmate to Aehrenthal's policy of obtaining Austria's supremacy in the Balkans.[99]

Indeed, though Anglo-Russian relations remained fairly steady until early 1909, relations between London and Vienna deteriorated rapidly. While British diplomats kept a close watch on the Austro-

Russian 'sort of political duel ... for predominant influence' in the Balkans, Aehrenthal had convinced himself that Grey was at the bottom of all his troubles.[100]

Nevertheless, Anglo-Russian ties were tested when Izvolsky decided to support Serbian claims for compensation. Early in January 1909 Aehrenthal had conceded Turkish demands for financial compensation, thereby eliminating the Austro-Turkish dispute. The demands by Serbia, however, were a more serious matter for the Ballhausplatz; and Aehrenthal was not prepared to encourage Serbia's southern Slav ambitions by agreeing to compensation. The deadlock caused by the Austro-Serbian dispute was the most intractable aspect of the whole crisis. By mid-February 1909, Aehrenthal began to increase pressure on Belgrade. Indeed, rumours abounded that 'Austria intends to present shortly an ultimatum to Serbia, which, if not obeyed, will probably be followed by a punitive expedition'.[101] Earlier mediation efforts by France and Italy had led nowhere.[102] Aehrenthal was in a strong position. On 21 January 1909 the German Kaiser had expressed his full approval of Austria's foreign policy to the Austrian ambassador at Berlin, Ladislas von Szögyény-Marich. More significantly, the Austro-Hungarian chief of staff, Franz Conrad von Hötzendorff, had been given assurances by his German colleague of full German support against any Russian intervention.[103] Although, of course, none of this was known in London, it was never seriously doubted that Austria had Germany's support. Any attempt to restrain Vienna, then, depended on cooperation with Germany. The king's visit to Berlin on 9 February provided an opening for Hardinge to discuss the crisis with Bülow. The latter protested his willingness jointly with Britain and France to mediate between Vienna and Belgrade. The rationale behind Grey's initiative was for Berlin to exercise a moderating influence on its ally. In return, Grey would press Izvolsky to force Serbia to yield, especially with regard to its demands for territorial compensation. Moreover, it was a chance to test the value of Bülow's protestations of friendly sentiments.[104] There was no fundamental disagreement between Downing Street and the Wilhelmstrasse as to the desired outcome of the crisis. There was, however, a difference as to the preferred *modus procedendi*. To an extent, London and Berlin were locked into a diplomatic 'duel': for as long as Bülow was reluctant to use his influence at Vienna to induce Aehrenthal to buy off the Serbs with economic concessions, Grey refused to make representations at St. Petersburg to induce Izvolsky to make Serbia renounce its demands for territorial compensation.[105]

Already in November 1908, Grey had pointedly refused to commit himself when the Russian ambassador, Count Alexander von Benckendorff, raised the question of Britain's attitude in the event of an Austro-Russian war. Now, Izvolsky once more tried to put pressure on Grey by hinting that the *entente* with Britain was bound to collapse if Britain failed to support Russia in the present crisis. Certainly, Sir Arthur Nicolson, the ambassador at St Petersburg, was convinced that Russia would intervene militarily despite the lack of French support.[106] Still, Izvolsky's crude attempt at political blackmail does not seem to have influenced Grey's attitude. On the contrary, the foreign secretary continued his efforts to persuade Russia to bring pressure to bear on Serbia, though he was cautious not to associate himself with the latest German proposal for a joint *démarche* by all the powers to force Belgrade to acquiesce in the changed status quo in the Balkans.[107] Of the two original plotters, Izvolsky not only did not have Aehrenthal's cool head, he also did not have his steady nerves. While the Austrians were sabre-rattling, Izvolsky decided to advise Belgrade to disengage.[108] It is unlikely that Aehrenthal seriously entertained the idea of a war against Serbia, although he gave Cartwright to understand that he would send an ultimatum to Belgrade unless Serbia reversed its own military preparations.[109] In fact, Aehrenthal was anxious to explore Grey's suggestion for a solution to the crisis. In light of Izvolsky's collapse into apathy, Grey now became more directly involved in the last phase of the crisis. Still, the various drafts and counterdrafts that were exchanged between London and Vienna ultimately failed to move the matter forward. In a further twist, Izvolsky's apparent loss of nerve now also drew Bülow and Tschirschky's deputy, Alfred von Kiderlen-Wächter, into the dispute – the latter being anxious to reassert Germany's leadership of the Dual Alliance. In a curious parallel to events in the 1905 Moroccan crisis after Delcassé's fall, Izvolsky's palpably more conciliatory utterances to the Austrian and German ambassadors prompted the German *démarche* of 22 March. The note amounted to a de facto ultimatum dressed in friendly verbiage.[110] Izvolsky's hurried surrender broke the deadlock, but also reduced Grey's diplomatic efforts to nought. Dismay at Izvolsky's somewhat undignified climb-down was widespread amongst British diplomats, though they acknowledged that Britain itself had been freed from an increasingly difficult and embarrassing situation. Still, Germany's forceful and unilateral solution of the Bosnian crisis was deeply resented by British diplomats. Grey's sharp exchange with Metternich on 25 March was little more than a rearguard action. The final outcome was a foregone conclusion.[111]

By general consent, the Bosnian annexation crisis had ended in a diplomatic victory for Germany and Austria and humiliation for Russia. It was also a set-back for Grey's continental diplomacy. Whereas in the Moroccan crisis the key to its solution had lain in Grey's hands, German willingness to exploit Russia's weakness and push matters to extremes in February 1909 meant that the Wilhelmstrasse had now regained the diplomatic initiative. Thus, the outcome of the crisis was generally seen to have had an effect on the balance of power in Europe. In the Near East, it also led to the supplanting of British by German influence at Constantinople. The aftermath of the crisis brought relations with Germany into sharper focus again. The events of the winter of 1908/9 had demonstrated the essential military and financial weakness of the Franco-Russian alliance vis-à-vis the Central Powers, Hardinge argued in a lengthy memorandum in April 1909. His analysis was predicated on the assumption that Germany aimed at 'a position of predominance in Europe', and that it would use its navy to attain that object. He anticipated that in any future Austro-Russian confrontation Russia would have to disengage and seek an accommodation with the Austro-German combination. The Franco-Russian alliance would thus be devalued, and France would follow Russia's lead and seek terms with Germany. In light of the Franco-German Morocco agreement of February 1909 the idea of a general Franco-German compromise was not so far-fetched. In essence, the memorandum restated Hardinge's belief that under present circumstances Britain held the balance between the two alliance groups. He regarded an agreement with Germany as a 'more serious and insidious danger' than isolation. An understanding with Berlin, he argued, might entail a British neutrality pledge in the event of a continental conflict, and so enable Germany to consolidate it continental position, perhaps later to turn on Britain itself. At the same time, Hardinge admitted that a full alliance with Russia was rendered impossible by public hostility to Tsarist autocracy.[112] Both Grey and Hardinge feared that a formal commitment to Russia would be taken by Germany's leaders as a confirmation of a conscious policy of encirclement, and that Germany might then seek its future security in a continental war while Russia was weak. The clear implication, then, in terms of practical politics, was that British diplomacy would have to continue its current equilibrist policy by informal means: 'If we stick close to France ... we can hold Russia', Mallet observed.[113]

Grey's own concerns about German aspirations and the implications of Germany's naval build-up are well-documented.[114] Yet he was well aware of the possible benefits, both domestic and diplomatic, which might accrue from an Anglo-German understanding. British foreign policy, he explained confidentially to US President Theodore Roosevelt in late 1906, 'is not anti-German. But it must be independent of Germany. We wish to keep and strengthen the Entente with France'.[115] Grey's willingness to explore cautiously the possibility of an agreement with Germany was one thing; his key objective, the maintenance of a balance of power in Europe, quite another. This was demonstrated by the often tortuous talks on a naval agreement in 1909. Mutual suspicions, aroused by a series of genuine misunderstandings as well as Berlin's ham-fisted intrigues, had for years burdened Anglo-German relations. From the point of practical diplomacy, moreover, the often chaotic situation inside the Wilhelmstrasse, with its petty rivalries and culture of calculated leaks, engendered little confidence in the reliability of German diplomacy. Still, at the root of the Anglo-German 'cold war' was the question of naval armaments.[116] While the diplomats were preoccupied with the gathering war-clouds in the Balkans, the Admiralty had picked up evidence that Germany's naval building programme was to be accelerated.[117]

At the Foreign Office it was noted that the German naval estimates made no allocations for coastal defences, despite the official German line that the naval programme was essentially a defensive measure. Indeed, official and semi-official statements in Germany made uncomfortable reading for the British. Thus, articles on modern warfare on land and at sea by Schlieffen, the former chief of the German general staff, and by Vice-Admiral von Ahlefeldt alluded to British hostility to Germany as the guiding principle of German strategy.[118] Yet, the controversy over Germany's suspected acceleration also produced the first serious suggestions by German diplomats for a naval agreement. Grey's interviews with Metternich between January and March 1909 were in the nature of *pourparlers*. The foreign secretary gave clear hints that Britain would match the acceleration in Germany's ship-building, but also suggested that 'we should, if we found that Germany was not building as fast as we had anticipated, be quite prepared to go more slowly with our shipbuilding'. A little later he also suggested the exchange of technical information.[119] Grey's evident desire for some kind of naval agreement led Bülow to conclude in June that an understanding on the reciprocal reduction of the speed of construction was within grasp. From the beginning, however, he linked this to an 'an agreement of a general political nature, such as a neutrality agreement'.[120] It was left to Bülow's successor, Theobald von Bethmann Hollweg, to make a definite 'scheme for a general good understanding' of which a naval agreement would be a key component.[121] Grey ultimately accepted Bethmann's diplomatic initiative as the basis for further negotiations. His earnest desire to come to an understanding notwithstanding, Grey was cautious lest Germany used the naval talks in an effort to break up the existing *ententes*. The nature of the German proposal certainly did not come as a surprise. Already in mid-April 1909 Goschen had alerted him to the hints dropped by Bülow's mouthpiece, Kiderlen-Wächter, that Germany desired a neutrality and non-aggression agreement as part of an understanding.

Grey was suspicious since an 'entente such as M. Kiderlen-Wächter sketches would serve to establish German hegemony in Europe & would not last long after it had served that purpose. It is in fact an invitation to help Germany to make a European combination which could be directed against us when it suited her to use it'. That was the advice he received from the Western department throughout the spring and summer of 1909.[122] Bethmann's eventual proposal confirmed British suspicions of German intentions. More importantly, in addition to the unpalatable demand for British neutrality in the event of a continental war, the Germans now offered only a 'relaxation of the tempo' of their construction programme rather than its restriction. The chasm between what Bethmann demanded and what he was prepared (or able) to offer was too wide for Grey. Hardinge noted that especially the suggested political agreement was 'so far-reaching as to be likely to disturb the political equilibrium of Europe'.[123] The talks were suspended in November 1909, and although they recommenced in the spring of 1910, the impasse caused by Germany's demand for a political agreement could not be broken. They petered out after Haldane's abortive mission to Berlin in February 1912. The fact that Grey continued negotiating with Metternich demonstrates his willingness to come to an understanding with Germany and accommodate its legitimate demands. However, he was not prepared to treat with Germany at the price of vital British strategic interests: 'We cannot enter into a political understanding with Germany which would separate us from Russia and France, and leave us isolated while the rest of Europe would be obliged to look to Germany.'[124]

How fragile the relations with St Petersburg still were was demonstrated by the Potsdam *entrevue* between Kaiser and Tsar and the new Russian foreign minister, Sergei D. Sazonov, in November 1910. The meeting resolved Russo-German disputes, especially regarding the Baghdad railway, though the final agreement was not signed until August 1911. The rapprochement between the two Eastern empires indicated how uncertain the future of Anglo-Russian relations was. It also rekindled the fears of senior diplomats, such as new Permanent Undersecretary Sir Arthur Nicolson, that Berlin intended to instrumentalize the Potsdam agreement to 'rearrange the European grouping'.[125] Nicolson in particular was haunted by the spectre of renewed isolation: 'were the Triple Entente to be broken up, we should be isolated and compelled to do the bidding of the Power which assumed the hegemony in Europe.' Indeed, the outcome of the 1908/9 Near Eastern crisis, the tortuous course of the Anglo-German naval talks, and the Potsdam meeting demonstrated the extent to which Germany was able to dominate the diplomatic agenda. As the ever-pessimistic Nicolson noted: 'our position is not very strong abroad. Owing to our internal troubles and also to our military weakness. ... I sometimes get uneasy at the outlook, & I fear that someday we shall find ourselves isolated, and compelled to attach ourselves as a satellite to some powerful European combination.'[126]

Britain's weakened international position was highlighted by the early phase of the Agadir crisis, the second Franco-German clash over Morocco. In the spring of 1911 Grey had tried in vain to restrain the actions the French government proposed to take in response to a revolt of Moroccan tribesmen.[127] France's hasty despatch of troops to Fez provided Kiderlen-Wächter, since 1910 Germany's foreign secretary, with a welcome pretext to re-open the Moroccan question and improve the terms granted under the 1909 Morocco agreement. Throughout May and June Kiderlen increased the diplomatic pressure on Paris. Although the Franco-German dispute was superficially a colonial and commercial one (centred on German interest in Moroccan mineral resources), it was part of Kiderlen's longer term diplomatic strategy to compel France to accept German predominance in Europe while Russia was still too weak to take an active part in European politics. Moreover, a weakening of the *entente*, Kiderlen reasoned, would also aid his energetic efforts to force a reorientation of British foreign policy.[128]

Grey once again followed the established pattern of urging moderation on the French while supporting legitimate German demands for compensation. In so doing he ignored his senior officials, men like Crowe and Nicolson, who counselled in favour of firmer ties with France. France, after all, was about to alter the *status quo* in north-west Africa, and Berlin could legitimately claim compensation. Moreover, Grey was only too aware that a majority of the Cabinet would not wear a full alliance with France. He refused to pledge Britain's full support for the French action in Morocco, but hinted to Metternich that 'through the [1904] agreement with France [Britain] was bound in the Moroccan question and obliged to support France'.[129] Provided that Germany did not acquire a foothold in the Mediterranean, Grey and Asquith initially took a detached view of the dispute.[130] However, the German leaders raised the political temperature with the despatch on 1 July of the gunboat *Panther* to the Moroccan port of Agadir. When by mid-July the Franco-German talks were on the brink of collapse, Grey, in spite of the Cabinet's reluctance to intervene in the crisis, could no longer afford to remain aloof.¹³¹ The acrimonious dispute on 15 July between Kiderlen and the French ambassador at Berlin, Jules Cambon, in which the German minister demanded the whole of the French Congo as compensation, was widely reported in the continental press. Crowe warned that Kiderlen was 'playing for the highest stakes'. The acceptance of Germany's demands would mean 'the subjection of France. ... Concessions mean not loss of interests or loss of prestige. It means defeat, with all its inevitable consequences'. Nicolson was equally alarmed: 'If Germany saw the slightest weakening on our part her pressure on France would become intolerable so that eventually she would have to fight or surrender. In the latter case German hegemony would be solidly established.'¹³² War seemed a distinct possibility. Kiderlen's ambition to imitate Bismarck, the leader of Germany's socialists warned the Foreign Office privately through a contact in Switzerland, might manoeuvre Germany and France down the slippery slope towards war.¹³³

Even if war could be avoided, Britain was in danger of being sidelined. Failure to support France, Nicolson argued, would finish the *entente* and 'we should have a triumphant Germany, and an unfriendly France and Russia and our policy since 1904 of preserving the equilibrium and consequently the peace of Europe would be wrecked'.¹³⁴ It would have ended Britain's role as a key decisive factor in the European equilibrium. No settlement could therefore be tolerated without British participation, as Grey informed Metternich on 21 July, with the approval of the still nervous Cabinet.¹³⁵ Lloyd George's dramatic intervention in the crisis with his speech at the Mansion House later that same evening emphasized Grey's private statements in the most public manner. The speech was not at all spontaneous, but was made after discussions with Grey and Asquith.¹³⁶ *Pace* A.J.P. Taylor, it was not so much a warning to France not to negotiate a separate deal with Germany;¹³⁷ nor was it exclusively aimed at Berlin. Rather it was a reassertion of British claims to be the key to the balance of power in Europe. The chancellor's public intervention had an electrifying effect. Indeed, as Michael Dockrill wrote, the supposedly pro-German Lloyd George's 'speech had more influence on the Germans than any comparable effort by Grey would have done'.¹³⁸ It transformed what had been a Franco-German dispute into an Anglo-German crisis. Tensions remained high, but gradually the Wilhelmstrasse sought to disengage. Grey and Asquith were now anxious further to reduce tensions and to facilitate Franco-German negotiations.[139] Grey and Lloyd George agreed that, in so far as Germany was concerned, 'after the crisis is over the whole question of [the] future development of foreign policy will have to be considered very carefully & coolly in the light of recent events'.[140]

It may, then, be assumed that Grey's subsequent efforts to improve relations with Germany were not simply an effort at appeasing his critics in Cabinet and parliament, but were part of his diplomatic strategy. Indeed, the attempts by Bethmann-Hollweg and Tirpitz during the Haldane mission in the spring of 1912 to extract some kind of assurance of British neutrality in the event of a continental war in return for a naval agreement confirmed that Britain was the linchpin of the European system; upon Britain rested the question of war and peace. A neutrality pledge was too high a price for any naval arms limitation agreement since it would have reduced Britain's role; and in this respect the naval question, while not the central issue in Anglo-German relations, was of symptomatic significance. It demonstrated the incompatibility of German and British aims. Grey wanted to maintain the *status quo* in Europe. Germany's attitude during the negotiations, however, indicated that it wished to be given a free hand in continental affairs. Grey's refusal to promise more than a non-aggression commitment ultimately rendered the mission fruitless, though it did not stop Anglo-German colonial talks over the next two years.[141]

Still, the Agadir crisis played a catalytic role in Anglo-French relations. Paradoxically, with the Franco-German agreement of November 1911, which brought the crisis to a formal conclusion by allowing a French protectorate over Morocco, Britain's obligations towards France under the 1904 agreement had ceased. But the *entente* was no longer a purely colonial understanding. The first Moroccan crisis had transformed it into a virtual diplomatic alliance; the Agadir crisis had hardened it further. It revitalized the staff talks which had languished since 1906 and provided a stimulus for naval cooperation in the Mediterranean.[142] By spring 1913 the staff talks had produced a series of comprehensive agreements on military and naval cooperation between the two countries. However, Grey once again refused to give a binding and unconditional commitment to the French. The ambassador at Paris echoed Grey's concerns. The *entente*, he later explained to Grey, acted as 'a restraint on the French government', whereas an alliance 'might encourage [it] ... to be too defiant to Germany'.[143] The naval convention of November 1912 was somewhat vague, merely confirming that naval consultations had taken place, but that these were not to be regarded as 'an engagement that commits either government to action in a contingency that has not arisen and may never arise'. Arguably, however, the resulting respective redeployment of the two navies entailed a moral obligation by Britain to defend the French Channel coast in the event of a continental conflict.[144]

The outcome of the Agadir crisis helped to transform the international landscape further. The final settlement of the Moroccan question encouraged Italy to fill the Tripolitanian power vacuum, as Rodd accurately predicted in September 1911. In terms of Great Power relations, Italy's North African adventure reduced it alliance value for Germany and Austria-Hungary: 'With Egypt on one side and Tunis on the other the good will of Great Britain and France will be of paramount importance to her.'[145] The strains especially in Austro-Italian relations had been carefully noted by the Foreign Office over the years. By 1911, moreover, the full text of the secret Barrère–Prinetti 'agreement' of 1902 was known, under which agreement Italy effectively 'opted out' of its Triple Alliance obligations in the event of a continental war.[146] Indeed, by 1912, the reinvigorated Franco-Russian alliance put further pressure on Germany, and underlined Britain's position as the link to the weakening Triple Alliance.[147] These developments throw into sharper relief the Anglo-German talks of 1912. Germany's reduced position seemed to imply increased British leverage, and so made talks a more attractive proposition for Grey. Moreover, the offer of talks should have alleviated German fears of 'encirclement'. In both these respects, however, Grey miscalculated.

Under Grey's stewardship British diplomacy pursued equilibrist aims. It did not do so out of utilitarian motivations. But then, states are not philanthropic institutions. It did so because Britain's national and imperial interests required it. However, the notion that British foreign policy was dictated by overseas imperial interests, with the implication of some kind of appeasement especially of Russia, is an oversimplification of the case. It is true, the French *entente* was an attempt to solve existing colonial disputes with France, and then to utilize improved relations with France to reach that elusive goal: an understanding with Russia. All of this was undertaken with a view to reducing tensions with the other Great Powers. The European powers, by contrast, judged the value of any agreement with Britain by its utility in forcing Britain to take part in continental affairs. They were right to do so. Extra-European affairs and continental diplomacy were fused into one system. Since around 1900 it had become common currency amongst the British political elite that Britain could no longer solely rely on the navy to safeguard its manifold interests. Diplomacy had to fulfil that role. Still, the formative experience of the 1880s and 1890s had convinced the Edwardian political generation that 'isolation' implied vulnerability to political blackmail. There was no credible alternative to playing an active role in European politics, especially in light of Russia's temporary weakness after 1905. For all the noise created by the naval race, Britain and Germany were locked into a diplomatic 'duel' for diplomatic influence. Both pursued in all-but-name a neo-Bismarckian strategy; both aimed to be the 'honest broker' without whom no international question could finally be settled, though both had perhaps rather different notions as to what constituted honesty in international dealings. For Britain, the maintenance of a continental equilibrium meant a positive power balance, as opposed to an overdrawn one. If the continental groups of powers remained finely balanced, then Britain was the potential linchpin of European politics, and, in turn, better placed to protect its interests. This, however, necessitated a willingness to walk onto the crease and bat. Standing on the sidelines only meant accepting that wickets would fall, and, in the worst case, that the pitch might be rolled up altogether.

The continental equilibrium was not merely a reflection of the military balance between the powers, though that certainly was a key ingredient. Maintaining the equilibrium entailed nuanced and subtle efforts to influence the diplomatic dynamics of Europe. Grey was keenly aware of the shifts in the relations between the two Great Power groups and within them. His policy calculations were not based on a fixed version of the 'balance of power'. Grey had skilfully manipulated Great Power relations, albeit with varying degrees of success. By 1911, after the Agadir crisis, Britain's international position was much enhanced. In fact, over the next two years Grey's diplomacy reached the zenith of its influence; and Grey's handling of international problems before 1911/12 throws into sharper relief his actions in the last two years before 1914. His balanced policy eschewed firm commitments to either of the two power groups, for this would have made the disruption of Europe's peace more likely, and would have reduced Britain's international influence. To that extent, Grey's caution was also wise. Nevertheless, as the scholar-diplomat Sir Ernest Satow remarked six years before the Great War: '[T]he utmost attainable by prudence and love of peace is the *postponement of the evil day*. That delay may be longer or shorter ... owing to the incalculable effect of individual speech or action.'[148] Ultimately, the evil day could only be postponed if all the chancelleries of Europe wished it. Grey's policy since 1906 did not bring that day forward.

NOTES

1. Crowe, 'Memorandum on the Present State of British relations with France and Germany', 1 Jan. 1907, in *BD*, Vol.III, App.III, p.403.
2. Bertie to Spring-Rice, 26 Dec. 1902, Spring-Rice CASR I/1/2; Cranborne to Bertie, 12 April 1903, Bertie Add MSS.63015.
3. L. Dehio, *The Precarious Balance: The Politics of Power in Europe, 1494–1945* (London, 1963); F.H. Hinsley, *Power and the Pursuit of Peace: Theory and Practice in the History of Relations between States* (Cambridge, 1982); D.E. Kaiser, *Politics and War: European Conflict from Philip II to Hitler* (Cambridge, 1990).
4. M.L. Roi and B.J.C. McKercher, '"Ideal" and "Punch-Bag": Conflicting Views of the Balance of Power and Their Influence on Interwar British Foreign Policy', *Diplomacy & Statecraft*, 12 (2001), pp.48–9, 51.
5. E.S. Beesly, *Queen Elizabeth* (London, 1892), p.35.
6. M. Burrows, *The History of the Foreign Policy of Great Britain* (Edinburgh, rev. edn, 1897), pp.7, 41.
7. J.R. Seeley, *The Growth of British Policy: An Historical Essay*, Vol.II (Cambridge, 1895), pp.307–8.
8. H.W.V. Temperley, *Frederic the Great And Kaiser Joseph: An Episode of War and Diplomacy in the Eighteenth Century* (London, 1915), p.9. Although not published until 1915, the book was written in 1911; cf. G.P. Gooch, 'H.W.V. Temperley, 1879–1939', *Proceedings of the British Academy*, 25 (1940), pp.10–11.
9. J.A.R. Marriott, *George Canning and His Times* (London, 1903), p.144.

10. W.A. Phillips, *George Canning* (London, 1903), p.119; and idem, *The Confederation of Europe* (London, 1914), p.88.
11. It can, however, be established that Crowe was familiar with the works of Beesly, Seeley and Marriott. Cf. 'Lesebuch', Crowe MSS Eng.d.2909, entries for 1892, 1895 and 1903.
12. Anonymous, 'British Foreign Policy in the Last Century', *Quarterly Review*, 220/439 (April 1914), p.312.
13. E. Barker *et al.*, *Why We Are At War: Great Britain's Case* (Oxford, 3rd rev. edn., 1914), pp.83–5 and 121–2.
14. G. Barraclough, *From Agadir to Armageddon: Anatomy of a Crisis* (London, 1982), p.181.
15. K.M. Wilson, 'British Power in the European Balance, 1906–1914', in D. Dilks (ed.), *Retreat from Power*, Vol.I (London, 1981), pp.21–41; idem, 'Grey', in idem (ed.), *British Foreign Secretaries and Foreign Policy* (London, 1987), pp.172–97.
16. J. Charmley, *Splendid Isolation?: Britain and the Balance of Power, 1874–1914* (London, 1999), p.379; K.M. Wilson, *The Policy of the Entente: Essays on the Determinants of British Foreign Policy, 1904–1914* (Cambridge, 1985), esp. pp.85–99.
17. H. Butterfield, *History and Human Relations* (London, 1951), p.217.
18. Nicolson House of Commons speech, 5 Nov. 1938, from a copy in the Attlee MSS Dep.1. His colleague Owen O'Malley, *The Phantom Caravan* (London, 1954), p.157, spoke of the 'brotherhood'; cf. Z.S. Steiner, 'Elitism and Foreign Policy: The Foreign Office before the Great War', in B.J.C. McKercher and D.J. Moss (eds.), *Shadow and Substance in British Foreign Policy, 1895–1939* (Edmonton, 1984), pp.19–55.
19. Steiner, 'Elitism', pp.44–51. On 'cognitive maps', cf. J. Joll, '1914: The Unspoken Assumptions', in H.W. Koch (ed.), *The Origins of the First World War: Great Power Rivalry and German War Aims* (London, 1972), pp.307–28; K. Neilson, *Britain and the Last Tsar: British Policy and Russia, 1894–1917* (Oxford, 1995), pp.48–51; T.G. Otte, 'Eyre Crowe and British Foreign Policy: A Cognitive Map', in T.G. Otte and C.A. Pagedas (eds.), *Personalities, War and Diplomacy: Essays in International History* (London, 1997), pp.14–16.
20. For a general discussion of the problem, cf. R.E. Neustadt and E.R. May, *Thinking in Time: The Uses of History for Decision-Makers* (New York, 1986), pp.xx–xx, 1–2; also H.A. Kissinger, *The White House Years* (Boston, 1979), pp.54–5.
21. Goschen to Hardinge, 25 July [*sic*, June] 1910, Hardinge FO [Foreign Office Archives, Public Record Office, Kew] 800/192; Viscount Grey of Fallodon, *Twenty-Five Years, 1892–1916*, Vol.I (New York, 1925), p.6.
22. C.J. Lowe and M.L. Dockrill, *The Mirage of Power*, Vol.I (London, 1972), p.17.
23. Grey to Spender, 19 Oct. 1905, Spender Add MSS. 46389.
24. The foreign policy part of the speech is reproduced in G.M. Trevelyan, *Grey of Fallodon* (London, 1943), pp.90–92.
25. Lowe and Dockrill, *Mirage of Power*, I, p.18.
26. Charmley, *Splendid Isolation?* p.332; Wilson, *Policy of the Entente*, pp.86–99.
27. Lansdowne to Lascelles (No.76), 11 April 1904, FO 244/636; Cambon to son, 16 April 1904, in H. Cambon (ed.), *Paul Cambon: Correspondance, 1870–1924*, Vol.II (Paris, 1940), pp.134–5; T.G. Otte, 'The Elusive Balance: British Foreign Policy and the French Entente Before the First World War', in A. Sharp and G. Stone (eds.), *Anglo-French Cooperation in the Twentieth Century: Rivalry and Cooperation* (London, 2000), pp.16–17; C.M. Andrew, 'The Entente Cordiale from Its Origins to 1914', in N. Waites (ed.), *Troubled Neighbours: Franco-British Relations in the*

Twentieth Century (London, 1971), pp.16–18.
28. Baring to Rosebery, 9 Feb. 1886, Cromer FO 633/6; also Salisbury to Queen Victoria, 10 June 1890, in G.E. Buckle (ed.), *The Letters of Queen Victoria*, 3rd Series, Vol.I (London, 1928), p.613.
29. Edward VII minute, nd, on Lascelles to Lansdowne, 22 April 1904, FO 64/1593.
30. Lansdowne telegram (No.46) to Lascelles, 3 June 1904, FO 64/1595; Whitehead to Lansdowne (nos.170, 178), 1, 16 July 1904, FO 64/1594. Cf. D.M. McKale, '*Weltpolitik* versus *Pax Britannica*: Anglo-German Rivalry in Egypt, 1904–1914', *Canadian Journal of History*, 22 (London, 1987), pp.195–6.
31. Lansdowne to Lascelles, 7 Sept. 1904, Lascelles FO 800/12.
32. Lowe and Dockrill, *Mirage of Power*, I, p.18; cf. Grey, *Twenty-Five Years*, I, pp.10–11.
33. M.L. Dockrill, 'The Formation of a Continental Foreign Policy by Great Britain, 1908–1912' (unpublished Ph.D. thesis, University of London, 1969), p.15.
34. Grey minute, nd, on Goschen to Grey (No.141), 16 April 1909, FO 371/673/14511; cf. Crowe and Barrington minutes, both 9 April 1906, on Lascelles to Grey, 5 April 1906, FO 371/77/12103.
35. Grey and Crowe minutes, both 17 Sept. 1912, on Granville to Grey (No.407), 12 Sept. 1912, FO 371/1371/38804.
36. Spring-Rice to Lascelles, 2 Oct. 1905, Lascelles FO 800/12; for the background cf. Neilson, *Last Tsar*, pp.268–9; B.J. Williams, 'The Revolution of 1905 and Russian Foreign Policy', in C. Abramsky (ed.), *Essays in Honour of E.H. Carr* (London, 1974), pp.105–7; D. Lieven, 'Pro-Germans and Russian Foreign Policy, 1890–1914', *International History Review*, 2 (1980), pp.34–54. The German General Staff had come to similar conclusions, cf. D. Stevenson, *Armaments and the Coming of War: Europe, 1904–1914* (Oxford, 1996), p.68; H. Raulff, *Zwischen Machtpolitik und Imperialismus: Die deutsche Frankreich-Politik 1904–1906* (Düsseldorf, 1976), pp.128–9.
37. Grey, *Twenty-Five Years*, I, p.5.
38. Grey to Spring-Rice, 22 Dec. 1905, 19 Feb. 1906, Spring-Rice FO 800/241; K. Neilson, '"Control the Whirlwind": Sir Edward Grey as Foreign Secretary, 1906–1916', in T.G. Otte (ed.), *The Makers of Foreign Policy: From Pitt to Thatcher* (London, 2001), pp.129–30.
39. Lansdowne to Tower, 20 Aug. 1905, Lansdowne FO 800/130; Bompard to Rouvier (No.78, secret), 9 Aug. 1905, *Documents diplomatiques français*, Serie 2, Vol.VII, No.323 [hereafter in the style *DDF*, S2, VII/323].
40. G. Ritter, *The Schlieffen Plan: Critique of a Myth* (London, 1958), pp.104–12; E. Kessel (ed.), *Generalfeldmarschall Graf Alfred von Schlieffen: Briefe* (Göttingen, 1958), pp.54–5; S. Förster, *Der doppelte Militarismus: Die deutsche Heeresrüstungspolitik zwischen Status-Quo-Sicherung und Aggression, 1890–1913* (Stuttgart, 1985), pp.144–7. The Kaiser drew an ominous historical parallel with the build-up to the Seven Years' War: Wilhelm II to Bülow, 23 Nov. 1904, in *GP*, XIX/1, No.6126.
41. Stevenson, *Armaments*, pp.66–9; Raulff, *Frankreich*, pp.123–4; N. Rich, *Friedrich von Holstein: Politics and Diplomacy in the Era of Bismarck and Wilhelm II* (Cambridge, 1965), pp.696–702, 718–19; Belgian circular despatch, 13 Jan. 1906, *BelD*, III/31.
42. Mallet to Bertie, 13 April 1905, Bertie FO 800/162.
43. Lansdowne to Balfour, 23 April 1905, Balfour Add MSS 49729; Lansdowne to Lascelles, 9 April 1905, Lascelles FO 800/12. Cf. G.W. Monger, *The End of Isolation: British Foreign Policy, 1900–1907* (London, 1963), pp.187–92.
44. Lansdowne minute, nd, on Nicolson telegram (No.19) to Lansdowne, 11 April 1905, FO 99/434; Grey to Bertie (No.22, very confidential), 10 Jan. 1906, *BD*, III/210.

45. Lansdowne telegram to Bertie (No.61), 22 April 1905, *BD*, III/90; Lansdowne to Balfour, 23 April 1905, Balfour Add MSS 49726; Bertie *aide memoire*, 24 April 1905, *DDF*, S2, VI/347.
46. Lansdowne to Bertie (No.307), *BD*, III/94.
47. Cambon to Delcassé, 18 May 1905, in *Cambon Correspondance* II, pp.195–6; and Cambon to Delcassé, (No.182), *trés confidentiel*), 18 May 1905, *DDF*, S2, VI/443; Cambon to Lansdowne, 24 May 1905, ibid., VI/455; and reply, 25 May 1905, *BD*, III/95.
48. Metternich to Bülow, 28 June 1905, *GP* XX/2, No.6860; Lansdowne to Lascelles, 5 Aug. 1905, Lascelles FO 800/12; cf. Monger, *End of Isolation*, pp.203–4.
49. Lascelles to Lansdowne (No.160), 12 June 1905, and reply (No.136), 16 June 1905, *BD*, III/97 and 99; on the continued uncertainty at Berlin about the exact nature of the *entente*, cf. Raulff, *Frankreich*, pp.106–9.
50. Lascelles to Lansdowne (No.204), 2 Aug. 1905, FO 64/6417.
51. Grey to Lascelles, 1 Jan. 1906, Lascelles FO 800/8.
52. Sanderson to Lascelles, 2 Jan. 1906, Lascelles FO 800/13.
53. Grey to Lascelles (No.11), 9 Jan. 1906, *BD*, III/229.
54. Grey memorandum, 10 Jan. 1906, Campbell-Bannerman Add MSS. 41218; Cambon to Rouvier (No.4), 11 Jan. 1906, *DDF*, S2, VIII/385.
55. Repington to Grey, 29 Dec. 1905, in A.J.A. Morris (ed.), *The Letters of Lt.Col. Charles à Court Repington, 1903–1918* (Stroud, 1999), No.19. Cf. Huguet to Étienne (No.81), 20 Dec. 1905, *DDF*, S2, VIII/256.
56. Spring-Rice to Grey (No.112), 7 Feb. 1906, *BD*, III/272; report Moulin, 6 March 1906, *DDF*, S2, IX/371.
57. As quoted in R.F.V. Heuston, *Lives of the Lord Chancellors* (Oxford, 1964), p.205; *procés-verbal* of meeting between French and Russian chiefs of staff, 8/21 April 1906, *DDF*, S2, X/119. The Belgian minister at London judged the British attitude to be calmer, cf. Belgian circular despatch, 29 Jan. 1906, *BelD*, III/32.
58. S.R. Williamson, *The Politics of Grand Strategy: Britain and France Prepare for War, 1904–1914* (London, 1990), pp.59–88; J. McDermott, 'The Revolution in British Military Thinking from the Boer War to the Moroccan Crisis', in P.M. Kennedy (ed.), *The War Plans of the Great Powers, 1880–1914* (Boston, 1979), pp.99–117.
59. Ripon to Fitzmaurice, 11 Jan. 1906, Ripon MSS [British Library, London] Add MSS 43543. Cf. the important re-examination of the issue in J.W. and P.F. Coogan, 'The British Cabinet and the Anglo-French Staff Talks: Who Knew What and When Did He Know It?', *Journal of British Studies*, 24 (1985), pp.110–31.
60. Stevenson, *Armaments*, p.72; Williamson, *Grand Strategy*, pp.116–27; J. Snyder, *The Ideology of the Offensive: Military Decision-Making and the Disaster of 1914* (Ithaca, NY, 1984), pp.41–6.
61. Grey memorandum, 20 Feb. 1906 and Hardinge minute 23 Feb. 1906, *BD*, III/299. Cf. Grey to Campbell-Bannerman, 29 March 1906, Grey FO 800/100; Grey's statement in the House of Commons on 26 April 1906, *HC Debs.*, 5th Series, Vol.CLVI, Col.24.
62. Grey to Bertie (No.76), 31 Jan. 1906, *BD*, III/219; Cambon to Rouvier (No.11), 15 Jan. 1906, *DDF*, S2, VIII/417.
63. Grey to Bertie, 15 Jan. 1906, Bertie Add MSS 63018.
64. Bülow to Speck von Sternburg, 16 Jan. 1906, quoted in S.L. Mayers, 'Anglo-German Rivalry at the Algeciras Conference', in P. Gifford and W.R. Louis (eds.), *Britain and Germany in Africa: Imperial Rivalry and Colonial Rule* (New Haven, CT, 1967), p.226.

65. Grey minute, nd, on Rodd to Grey (No.47), 10 Feb. 1909, FO 371/599/6296; Grey to Lascelles (No.196), 31 July 1906, FO 244/663/26335.
66. Spicer minute, 21 Jan. 1909, on Rumbold to Grey (No.9), 18 Jan. 1909, FO 371/670/2719; Crowe minutes, 18 Aug. 1908, 2 Feb. 1911, FO 371/461/28785 and 1117/3884.
67. Hardinge and Grey minutes, nd, on Bertie to Grey (No.407), 27 Oct. 1906, FO 371/74/36423; Grey to Bertie (No.620), 8 Nov. 1906, FO 371/74/37870; Grey to Lascelles (No.178), 11 July 1906, FO 244/663/23570.
68. Crowe minute, 20 Nov. 1906, on Bertie to Grey (No.453), 19 Nov. 1906, FO 371/74/38956.
69. Bertie to Grey (Nos.109, 146), 28 Feb. and 23 March 1907, FO 371/253/6682 and /9555; Oppenheimer memorandum, 24 Feb. 1909, FO 371/672; E.W. Edwards, 'The Franco-German Agreement on Morocco, 1909', *English Historical Review*, 79 (1963), pp.483–513.
70. Hardinge and Grey minutes, nd, on Pearson memorandum, 18 Sept. 1906, FO 371/74/31864. Cf. Mallet memorandum, 20 June 1906, Grey FO 800/92; Bertie to Grey (No.30), 13 Jan. 1906, *BD*, III/213.
71. Crowe minute, 29 Jan. 1906, on Lascelles to Grey (No.37), 26 Jan. 1906, FO 371/76/3439; Cartwright to Hardinge, 16 March 1910, Cartwright MSS [Northamptonshire Country Record Office] C(A)45. Hardinge later called him 'the evil genius of German diplomacy': Lord Hardinge of Penshurst, *Old Diplomacy* (London, 1947), p.118.
72. Mensdorff to Aehrenthal, 17 June 1907, in *NL Aehrenthal*, II/364; Grey minute, nd, on Cartwright to Grey (No.79), 21 Aug. 1907, FO 371/253/28172.
73. Boothby to Grey (No.158), 19 Oct. 1906, FO 371/8/35517. Cf. F. Curtius (ed.), *Memoirs of Prince Chlodwig of Hohenlohe-Schillingsfürst*, Vol.II (London, 1906), p.413. On the importance of 'minor' incidents cf. K. Neilson, 'Incidents and Foreign Policy: A Case Study', *Diplomacy & Statecraft*, 9 (1998), pp.53–4.
74. Egerton to Grey (No.29), 19 Feb. 1906, Grey minute, 24 March 1909, both FO 371/82/6674. Cf. E. Decleva, *Da Adua a Sarajevo: La politica estera italiana e la Francia, 1896–1914* (Bari, 1971), pp.297–306.
75. Hardinge and Grey minutes, nd, on Egerton to Grey, 9 June 1906; Grey to Egerton (No.100), 21 June 1906, all FO 371/82/20308. Ultimately the matter came to nothing after the Quai brought Barrère to heel; cf. Egerton to Grey (No.114), 27 June 1906, FO 371/83/22216. Barrère repeated the idea a year later; cf. Bertie to Grey, 1 Nov. 1907, *BD*, VIII/20.
76. Hardinge minute, nd, on Rodd to Grey (No.74), 22 March 1909, FO 371/683/11613; Hardinge minute, nd, on Rodd to Grey (No.47), 10 Feb. 1909, FO 371/599/6296; Hardinge minute, nd, on Cartwright to Grey (No.133), 13 Oct. 1906, FO 371/79/34841; Crowe minute, 10 Oct. 1906, on Bertie to Grey (No.381), 9 Oct. 1906, FO 371/74/34195.
77. Hardinge and Campbell minutes, both 20 April 1909, on Goschen to Grey (No.141), 16 April 1909, FO 371/673/14511. Reconstitution of the Three Emperors' League was a recurring theme with Hardinge; cf. Cambon to Bourgeois (No.317), 24 Oct. 1906, *DDF*, S2, X/241, Hardinge to Nicolson, 11 Nov. 1908, Nicolson FO 800/341.
78. F. Fejtö, *Requiem pour un empire défunt: Histoire de la destruction de l'Austriche-Hongrie* (Paris, 1993), p.40.
79. Aehrenthal to Khevenhüller, 25 May 1907, in E. Walters (ed.), 'Unpublished Documents: Aehrenthal's Attempt to Re-Group the European Powers', *Slavonic and East European History*, 30/73 (1951), No.5; Berchtold to Aehrenthal, 20 May 1907,

NL Aehrenthal, II/364. Wank is sceptical on this point; see ibid., p.504, n.2; as is F.R. Bridge, *The Hapsburg Monarchy among the Great Powers, 1815–1918* (Oxford, 1990), p.273. For a mediating position, cf. I.F. Pantenberg, *Im Schatten des Zweibundes: Probleme österreichisch-ungarischer Bündnispolitik, 1897–1908* (Vienna, 1996), pp.381–96. For the Macedonian background, see D. Dakin, *The Greek Struggle in Macedonia, 1897–1913* (Thessalonika, 1993), pp.340–46.
80. Goschen to Grey (No.671), 31 May 1907, FO 371/377/18027. The information came from Prince Demidov, secretary of the Russian embassy, Vienna, and reached Goschen through the journalist W.T. Stead: Goschen diary, 18 May, 8 June 1907, in C.H.D. Howard (ed.), *The Diary of Sir Edward Goschen* (London, 1980), pp.146, 149. Cf. Redlich diary, 26 June 1912, in F. Fellner (ed.), *Schicksalsjahre Österreichs, 1908–1919: Das politische Tagebuch Josef Redlichs*, Vol.I (Graz, 1954), pp.138–9; Ourusov to Izvolsky, 31 May/13 June 1907, in H. Izvolsky (ed.), *Au Service de la Russie: Alexandre Iswolsky, Correspondance Diplomatique, 1906–1911*, Vol.I (Paris, 1937), pp.158–9.
81. Bertie to Grey (No.243), 10 May 1907, Hardinge minute, nd, both FO 371/254/15629; Crozier telegram to Pichon (No.33), 5 May 1907, DDF, S2, X/491.
82. Mensdorff to Aehrenthal (No.34B), 31 May 1907, in Walters, 'Unpublished Documents', p.231; Grey to Goschen (No.49), 4 June 1907, FO 371/377/19412; Benckendorff to Izvolsky, 26 May/8 June 1907, *Izvolsky Correspondance*, II, pp.49–50.
83. It is rather a sign of the myopia of some historians who merely see British diplomacy under Grey in the context of the years 1904–14. The perception of Aehrenthal soon changed; see. Nicolson to Grey (No.315), 18 May 1909, FO 371/683/19349.
84. Cartwright to de Bunsen, 1 Oct. [1908], De Bunsen Box 14. Cartwright had made his name by 'delug[ing] the F.O. with much doubtful & even incorrect information, and with preposterous proposals as to policy', Findlay to Rumbold, 11 Feb. 1909, Rumbold Dep.14.
85. Cartwright to Grey (No.86), 1 Aug. 1908, and Campbell, Langley and Grey minutes, all 5 Aug. 1908, FO 371/399/27154. Cartwright had been encouraged by Grey's new Private Secretary, William Tyrrell, to submit this despatch; see Tyrrell to Cartwright, 21 July 1908, Cartwright MSS C(A)42. Cf. K.M. Wilson, *Empire and Continent: Studies in British Foreign Policy* (London, 1987), pp.76–8. Dr Wilson's criticism of British 'unwillingness to credit Vienna with a will independent of Berlin', ibid., p.91, mistakes Aehrenthal's desire to demonstrate Austria's ability to act unilaterally with a willingness to loosen ties with Berlin. For a useful corrective, cf. Aehrenthal to Berchtold, 26 June 1908, *NL Aehrenthal*, II/439.
86. Spicer minute, 8 Feb. 1909, and Grey minute, nd, on Cartwright to Grey (No.18), 5 Feb. 1909, FO 371/599/5138. Grey's abhorrence of 'mischief' is well documented; see Mensdorff to Aehrenthal (No.34B), 31 May 1907, in Walter, 'Unpublished Documents', No.10, p.232.
87. The best assessment of the forging of the Anglo-Russian convention is Neilson, *Last Tsar*, pp.267–88; cf. B.J. Williams, 'The Strategic Background to the Anglo-Russian Convention of August 1907', *Historical Journal*, 9 (1966), pp.360–73.
88. Hardinge to Lascelles, 6 Aug. 1907, Lascelles FO 800/13; Hardinge and Grey, nd, minutes on Dumas to Lascelles (No.6), 7 March 1907, FO 371/259/7836. Cf. D.W. Spring, 'Russia and the Franco-Russian Alliance, 1905–1914', *Slavonic and East European Review*, 66 (1988), pp.588–9; D.W. Sweet, 'The Baltic Question in British Diplomacy before the First World War', *Historical Journal*, 13 (1970), pp.454–74; S. Jungar, *Ryssland och den Svensk-Norsk Unionens Opplösning* (Åbo, 1969), pp.25–8, 88–91.

89. Nicolson to Grey (No.532), 23 Oct. 1907, *BD*, IV/544.
90. Neilson, *Last Tsar*, pp.289–90.
91. Aehrenthal memorandum, nd, in ÖUA. Cf. F.R. Bridge, 'Izvolsky, Aehrenthal, and the End of the Austro-Russian Entente, 1906–8', *Mitteilungen des österreichischen Staatsarchivs*, 29 (1976), pp.331–8; B.E. Schmitt, *The Annexation of Bosnia, 1908-1909* (Cambridge, 1937), pp.20–33; J. Angelow, *Kalkül und Prestige: Der Zweibund am Vorabend des Ersten Weltkriegs* (Cologne/Vienna, 2000), pp.175–95.
92. For useful pen-portraits of Izvolsky, see H. Nicolson, *Sir Arthur Nicolson, Bart, First Lord Carnock: A Study in the Old Diplomacy* (London, 1930), p.216; G.P. Gooch, *Before the War: Studies in Diplomacy*, Vol.I (London, 1936), pp.291–2.
93. Lowther to Grey, 4, 11 Aug. 1908, Lowther FO 800/193B; Mallet minute, nd, on Lowther to Hardinge, 6 April 1909, Hardinge FO 800/192; Benckendorff to Izvolsky, 12/25 Oct. 1908, *DDF*, S2, XI/569; Mensdorff telegram to Aehrenthal (No. 58), 3 Oct. 1908, ÖUA, I/115; M.B. Cooper, 'British Policy in the Balkans, 1908–9', *Historical Journal*, 7 (1964), pp.267–8; D.W. Sweet, 'The Bosnian Crisis', in F.H. Hinsley (ed.), *British Foreign Policy under Sir Edward Grey* (Cambridge, 1977), pp.181–2.
94. Grey to Nicolson, 10 Nov. 1908, *BD*, V/441. Cf. Hardinge (?) memorandum, 'Commitments by Treaty', 11 Nov. 1909, Grey FO 800/92; Izvolsky to Nelidov, 23 Oct./5 Nov. 1908, in *Benckendorffs Schriftwechsel*, No.6.
95. Hardinge to Nicolson, 13 Nov. 1908, *BD* V/372; Balfour to Asquith, 14 Oct. 1908, Asquith 11; Belgian circular despatch, 10 Nov. 1908, *BD*, IV/25. To Bülow he complained that he had been tricked by *'l'affreux juif* Aehrenthal': B. von Bülow, *Denkwürdigkeiten*, Vol.I (Berlin, 1930), p.395.
96. Asquith to Balfour, 15 Oct. 1908, Asquith MSS 11; cf. Neilson, *Last Tsar*, p.300.
97. Grey to Lowther (No.434), 15 Oct. 1908; Grey to Nicolson (No.319), 19 Oct. 1908, 26 Oct. 1908, all *BD*, V/383, 394, 409(b); Huguet to Picquard, 9 Nov. 1908, *DDF*, S2, XI/550.
98. Grey to Goschen, 5 Nov. 1908, Grey FO 800/61; Aehrenthal telegram to Mensdorff (No.81), 6 Nov. 1908, ÖUA, I/514. Cf. G.E. Silberstein, 'Germany, France and the Casablanca Incident, 1908–9: An Investigation of a Forgotten Crisis', *Canadian Journal of History*, 11 (1976), pp.331–4; T.G. Otte, '"An Altogether Unfortunate Affair": Britain and the *Daily Telegraph* Affair', *Diplomacy & Statecraft*, 5 (1995), pp.296–333.
99. Hardinge to Lowther, 1 Dec. 1908, Lowther FO 800/193A; reply, 3 Feb. 1909, FO 800/193B; Poklevsky-Koziell to Izvolsky, 4/17 Feb. 1909, *Izvolsky Correspondence*, II, pp.201–2; Mensdorff to Aehrenthal (No.2A), 8 Jan. 1909, ÖUA, I/863. Cf. Schmitt, *Annexation*, pp.125–43; Sweet, 'Bosnian Crisis', pp.183–4.
100. Buchanan to Hardinge, 6 Jan. 1909, Hardinge FO 800/192; Cartwright to Grey, 19 Dec. 1908, Grey FO 800/39; Archduke Franz Ferdinand to Aehrenthal, end of February 1909, NL Aehrenthal, II/499.
101. Nicolson telegram to Grey (No.69), 13 Feb. 1909, *BD*, V/567; Khevenhüller telegram to Aehrenthal (No.8), 19 Feb. 1909, ÖUA, I/1017; Crozier telegram to Pichon (No.56), 19 Feb. 1909, *DDF*, S2, XII/24; Schmitt, *Annexation*, pp.149–52.
102. Schoen memorandum, 20 Jan. 1909, *GP*, XXVI/1, No.9365. Cf. Goschen to Grey (No.8), 7 Jan. 1909, *BD*, V/507; Decleva, *Politica estera*, pp.343–9, 354–5; Schmitt, *Annexation*, pp.147–8.
103. Szögyény to Aehrenthal, 21 Jan. 1909, ÖUA, I/ 912; Kiderlen memorandum, 23 Jan. 1909, *GP*, XXVI/2, No.9367; Field Marshal Conrad von Hötzendorff, *Aus meiner Dienstzeit, 1906–1918* (Vienna, 1923), Vol.I, pp.68–70; N. Stone, 'Moltke-Conrad:

Relations between the Austro-Hungarian and German General Staffs, 1909–1914', *Historical Journal*, 9 (1966), p.207.
104. Hardinge to Nicolson, 15 Feb. 1909, Nicolson FO 800/342; Hardinge memorandum, 11 Feb. 1909, *BD*, V, ed. note, 608–9 and No.574; Bülow memorandum, 10 Feb. 1909, *GP*, XXVI/2, No.9330; Hardinge, *Old Diplomacy*, pp.173–5.
105. Grey telegram to Nicolson (No.181), 16 Feb. 1909, Goschen to Grey (No.42), 18 Feb. 1909, Cartwright telegram to Grey (No.51), 24 Feb. 1909, *BD*, V/573, 583, 603; Sweet, 'Bosnian Crisis', pp.188–9.
106. Nicolson to Grey, 24 Feb. 1909, Grey FO 800/73; Nicolson telegram to Grey (No.76), 15 Feb. 1909, *BD*, V/572; Touchard note to Izvolsky, 13/26 Feb. 1909, in *Entente Diplomacy*, No.257; Neilson, *Last Tsar*, p.304.
107. Memo. Kiderlen-Wächter, 26 Feb. 1909, *GP*, XXVI/2, No.9398; Touchard telegram to Pichon (No.35), 18 Feb. 1909, *DDF*, S2, XII/231. There is no sufficient documentary evidence to support the contention by Schmitt and Sweet that Grey's hand was forced by Izvolsky's thinly veiled threat. Cf. Schmitt, *Annexation*, p.150; Sweet, 'Bosnian Crisis', p.188.
108. Izvolsky telegram to Hartwig (No.251), 14/27 Feb. 1909, *Entente Diplomacy*, No.261; Nicolson telegram to Grey (No.106), 27 Feb. 1909, and reply (No.257), 1 March 1909, *BD*, V/619, 626; Aehrenthal to Berchtold, 19 Feb. 1909, *ÖUA*, I/1018. On Austro-Hungarian military preparations in the border provinces, cf. Stevenson, *Armaments*, pp.120–21.
109. Cartwright to Grey (No.43), 18 March 1909, *BD*, V/715; *Diary of Edward Goschen*, entry 15 March 1909, p.189; Stevenson, *Armaments*, p.121. Hötzendorff certainly pressed Aehrenthal for a preventive strike against Serbia; cf. K. Peball (ed.), *Conrad von Hötzendorff: Private Aufzeichnungen* (Vienna, 1977), p.63.
110. Pourtalès to Bülow, 17 March 1909, *GP*, XXVI/2, No.9451; Kiderlen journal, 20 March 1909, in *Kiderlen NL*, II, pp.26–7; Szögyény to Aehrenthal (No.104), 24 March 1909, *ÖUA*, II/1336; Touchard telegram to Pichon (No.98), 23 March 1909, *DDF*, S2, XII/127; O.H. Wedel, *Austro-German Diplomatic Relations, 1908–1914* (Stanford, CA, 1932), pp.91–3.
111. Nicolson to Grey, 24 March 1909, Nicolson to Grey telegram (No.169), 25 March 1909, *BD*, V/764, 768; Cambon telegram to Pichon (No.86), 24 March 1909, *DDF*, S2, XII/130. Nevertheless, British diplomacy lobbied for Izvolsky to be retained in office by the Tsar so as to avoid another Declassé-style incident; cf. Nicolson telegram to Grey, 7 April 1909, Grey FO 800/73.
112. Hardinge memorandum, 'On the Possibility of War', ? April 1909, *BD*, V, App.III; for the background, see Neilson, *Last Tsar*, p.307.
113. Mallet minute, nd, on Buchanan to Grey (No.29), 26 April 1909, FO 371/605/16587; Hardinge to Nicolson, 25 May 1909, Nicolson FO 800/342; D.W. Sweet, 'Great Britain and Germany, 1905–1911', in Hinsley (ed.), *Foreign Policy*, pp.225–7.
114. Geoffray to Bourgeois (No.260), 22 Aug. 1906, *DDF*, S2, X/187; Grey minute, nd, on Cartwright to Grey (No.3), 8 Jan. 1908, FO 371/457/1308; Hardinge minute, nd, on Lascelles to Grey (No.243), 28 May 1907, FO 371/259/17976; P. Hayes, 'Britain, Germany and the Admiralty's Plans for Attacking German Territory, 1906–1915', in L. Freedman *et al.* (eds.), *War, State and International Politics: Essays in Honour of Sir Michael Howard* (Oxford, 1992), pp.96–116.
115. Grey to Roosevelt, ? Dec. 1906, quoted in Trevelyan, *Grey*, p.114. On domestic opposition cf. H.S. Weinroth, 'British Radicals and the Balance of Power,

1902–1914', *Historical Journal*, 13 (1970), pp.653–82; G.H.S. Jordan, 'Pensions Not Dreadnoughts: The Radicals and Naval Retrenchment', in A.J.A. Morris (ed.), *Edwardian Radicalism, 1900–1914* (London, 1974), pp.163–79.
116. Hardinge minute, nd, on Goschen to Grey (No.26), 16 Jan. 1909, FO 371/670/2231. Cf. Mensdorff to Aehrenthal, 13 Dec. 1907, *NL Aehrenthal*, II/409.
117. P.M. Kennedy, *The Rise of the Anglo-German Antagonism, 1860–1914* (London, 1980), pp.444–7; J. Steinberg, 'The *Novelle* of 1908: Necessities and Choices in the Anglo-German Naval Arms Race', in *Transactions of the Royal Historical Society*, 5th Ser., 21 (1971), pp.25–43.
118. Spicer minutes, 11 Jan. 1909, on Goschen to Grey (No.10), 8 Jan. 1909, FO 371/671/1212; Villiers and Spicer minutes, both 11 Jan. 1909, on Trench to Goschen (No.2), 8 Jan. 1909, FO 371/671/1215; Goschen to Grey (No.17), 12 Jan. 1909, FO 371/671/1799. CF. A. von Schlieffen, 'War at the Present Day', *National Review*, LII/312 (1909), pp.928–41.
119. Grey to Goschen (Nos.9 and 73), 4 Jan., 18 March 1909, *BD*, VI/151, 156; *GP*, XXVIII/10249, 10266, 10269, 10273.
120. Minutes of interdepartmental conference, Reich chancery, 3 June 1909, in Bülow, *Denkwürdigkeiten*, II, p.430. Kiderlen-Wächter developed more fully the rationale of such a deal for Bülow's successor; cf. Kiderlen-Wächter memorandum, late September 1909, *Kiderlen NL* II, pp.48–59.
121. Goschen to Grey (No.93), 21 Aug. 1909, *BD*, VI/186.
122. Grey minute, nd, on Goschen to Grey (No.141), 16 April 1909, FO 371/673/14511; cf. Spicer and Crowe minutes, both 13 April 1909, on Goschen to Grey (No.131), 8 April 1909, FO 371/6731/13621; Cambon to Pichon (No.159), 6 May 1909, *DDF*, S2, XII/181.
123. Hardinge minute, 10 Sept. 1909, on Goschen to Grey (No. 371), 4 Sept. 1909, *BD*, VI/204.
124. Grey minute, nd, on Goschen to Grey (No.102), 11 April 1910, *BD*, VI/344; Goschen to Nicolson, 28 Oct. 1910, FO 371/901/41807; Goschen to Grey, 24 March 1911, FO 371/1123/12050; Goschen to Grey, (No.70), 10 Feb. 1912, FO 371/1372/4980. Cf. Grey to Bertie, 12 July 1911, Bertie Add MSS 63026; Nicolson to Rodd, 27 Feb. 1911, Rennell of Rodd MSS [Bodleian Library, Oxford] box 14; Sweet, 'Britain and Germany', p.230.
125. Nicolson memorandum, 2 Jan. 1911, Grey FO 800/93; Nicolson to Bertie, 14 Nov. 1910, Bertie Add MSS 63025; Sazonov to Nicholas II, 4 Nov. 1910, in *Un Livre Noir: Diplomatie d'avant-guerre d'aprés les documents des Archives Russes, Novembre 1910– Juillet 1914*, Vol.II (Paris, s.a.), pp.331–4; Benckendorff to Sazonov, 24 Nov./7 Dec. 1910, *Benckendorff Schriftwechsel*, II/308. Ironically Bethmann Hollweg had calculated that a rapprochement with Russia would improve Anglo-German relations, Bethmann Hollweg to Eisendecher, 27 Dec. 1910, in E. von Vietsch, *Bethmann Hollweg: Staatsmann zwischen Macht und Ethos* (Boppard, 1969), p.125.
126. Nicolson to Goschen, 28 Feb, 1911, Nicolson FO 800/342; to Rodd, 27 Feb, 1911, Rodd MSS box 14.
127. Grey telegram to Bertie (No. 95), 5 May 1911, *BD*, VII/252; Cambon to Jules Cambon, 27 April 1911, *Cambon Correspondance*, II, pp.315–18, Izvolsky to Sazonov, 15/28 March 1911, *Entente Diplomacy*, No.669.
128. Kiderlen-Wächter to Bethmann Hollweg, 28 Nov. 1910, *GP*, XXVIII/10424; Kiderlen-Wächter memorandum, 9 July 1911, *Kiderlen NL*, II, pp.123–6; Shebeko to Neratov, 15/28 April 1911, *Benckendorff Schriftwechsel*, II/394. Cf. E. Oncken, *Panthersprung nach Agadir: Die deutsche Politik während der zweiten Marokkokrise*

1911 (Düsseldorf, 1981), pp.46–63, 219–78; H. Pogge-von Strandmann, 'Rathenau, die Gebrüder Mannesmann und die zweite Marokkokrise', in I. Geiss and B.J. Wendt (eds.), *Deutschland in der Weltpolitik des 19. und 20. Jahrhunderts: Festschrift für Fritz Fischer* (Düsseldorf, 1973), pp.251–7; J.-C. Allain, *Joseph Caillaux*, Vol.I (Paris, 1978), pp.377–9.
129. Bertie to Nicolson, 14 March 1911, and reply, 17 May 1911, *BD*, VII/269, p.275; Metternich to Bethmann Hollweg (No.430), 22 May 1911, *GP*, XXIX/10561; Benckendorff to Neratov, 10/23 May 1911, *Benckendorff Schriftwechsel* II/403. The best account of British diplomacy during this period is M.L. Dockrill, 'British Policy during the Agadir Crisis of 1911', in Hinsley (ed.), *Foreign Policy*, pp.271–87.
130. Grey to Bertie, 12 July 1911, Bertie Add MSS 63026; Cambon telegram to De Selves (No.187), 10 July 1911, *DDF*, S2, XIV, No.48; Dockrill, 'Agadir', p.274; A.J. Marder, *From Dreadnought to Scapa Flow: The Royal Navy in the Fisher Era, 1904–1919*, Vol.I (London, 1966), pp.240–41.
131. Crowe to Bertie, 20 July 1911, Bertie Add MSS.63026; Asquith to George V, 22 July 1911, CAB 41/38/3; Neratov telegram to Benckendorff (No.811), 19 June/2 July 1911, *Entente Diplomacy*, No.680; cf. H.Marchat, 'L'Affaire Marocaine en 1911', *Revue d'histoire diplomatique*, 77 (1963), pp.193–235.
132. Crowe and Nicolson minutes, both 18 July 1911, on Bertie telegram to Grey (No.103), 18 July 1911, *BD*, VII/392; Schoen telegram to *Auswärtiges Amt* (No.207), 19 July 1911, *GP*, XXIX/10612; Marchat, 'L'affaire Marocaine', pp.218–19.
133. Angst to Tyrrell, 15 July 1911, Grey FO 800/104. Cf. H. Bley, *Bebel und die Strategie der Kriegsverhütung, 1904–1913: Eine Studie über Bebels Geheimkontakte mit der britischen Rgeierung* (Göttingen, 1975), pp.160–62; R.J. Crampton, 'August Bebel and the British Foreign Office', *History*, 58 (1973), pp.222–3.
134. Nicolson minute, 21 July 1911, *BD*, VII/409; Metternich telegram to *Auswärtiges Amt* (No.79), 19 July 1911, *GP*, XXIX/10615; I.C. Barlow, *The Agadir Crisis* (Durham, NC, 1940), p.292.
135. Grey to Goschen, 21 July 1911, *BD*, VII/411; Metternich to Bethmann Hollweg (No.528), 21 July 1911, *GP*, XXIX/10617; Benckendorff to Neratov, 6/19 Aug. 1911, *Entente Diplomacy*, No.688.
136. M.L. Dockrill, 'David Lloyd George and Foreign Policy before 1914', in A.J.P. Taylor (ed.), *Lloyd George: Twelve Essays* (London, 1971), pp.14–17; Lord Riddell, *More Pages from My Diary, 1908–1914* (London, 1934), pp.20–21; A.C. Murray, *Master and Brother: The Murrays of Elibank* (London, 1945), p.84. For general context, cf. M.G. Fry, *Lloyd George and Foreign Policy: Education of a Statesman, 1890–1916* (Montreal, 1977), Ch.7; T. Boyle, 'New Light on Lloyd George's Mansion House Speech', *Historical Journal*, 22 (1980), pp.431–3; R.A. Cosgrove, 'A Note on Lloyd George's Speech at the Mansion House, 21 July 1911', *Historical Journal*, 12 (1969), pp.698–701.
137. A.J.P. Taylor, *The Struggle for Mastery in Europe, 1848–1918* (Oxford, 8th edn, 1988), p.471.
138. Dockrill, 'Agadir', p.278; Nicolson to Goschen, 24 July 1911, *BD*, VII/418; Tyrrell to Spring-Rice, 1 Aug. 1911, Spring-Rice FO 800/241; Metternich to Bethmann Hollweg (No.530), *GP*, XXIX/10621; Barlow, *Agadir*, pp.300–313. Cf. K.O. Morgan, 'Lloyd George and Germany', *Historical Journal*, 39 (1996), pp.755–66.
139. Grey to Goschen (No.168), 25 July 1911, Asquith statement in the House of Commons, 27 July 1911, *BD*, VII/419, 426; Cambon to de Selves (No.252), 22 July 1911, *DDF*, S2, XIV/94; Kiderlen-Wächter telegram to Metternich (No.99), and

reply (No.87), 24 July 1911, *GP*, XXIX/10623–24; Osten-Sacken to Neratov, 3/16 Aug. 1911, *Benckendorffs Schriftwechsel*, II/435.
140. Grey to Lloyd George, 5 Sept. 1911, Lloyd George C/4/14/5.
141. Grey to Churchill, 29 Jan. 1912, Lloyd George MSS C/4/15/14; Grey to Bertie, 2 Jan. 1912, Bertie Add MSS 63026.
142. Bertie to Nicolson, 9 May 1912, Crowe memorandum, 8 May 1912, *BD*, X/2, Nos.388, 386; cf. Mallet to Bertie, nd [but 8–9 May 1912], Bertie Add MSS 63029; Admiralty memorandum, March 1912, Asquith MSS 24.
143. Bertie memoranda, 26 March 1913, 8 March 1914, Bertie Add MSS 63032 and 63030.
144. Grey to Cambon, 22 Nov. 1912, *BD*, X/2, No.416; P.G. Halperin, *The Mediterranean Naval Situation, 1908–1914* (Cambridge, MA, 1971), pp.99–109; Otte, 'Elusive Balance', pp.26–7. Cf. T. Wilson, 'Britain's "Moral Commitment" to France in August 1914', *History*, 54 (1979), pp.380–90.
145. Rodd to Grey, 4 Sept. 1911, Rodd MSS box 14; and Rodd to Grey (No.149), 19 Sept. 1911, *BD*, IX/1, No.230.
146. Rodd to Grey, 16 Oct. 1911, Rodd MSS box 14. London had been aware of the agreement in its outlines since 1907; cf. Orde minute, nd, on Rodd telegram to Grey (No.150), 3 Nov. 1912, FO 371/1384/46542. For the text, see *DDF*, S2, II/329.
147. G. Krumeich, *Armaments and Politics in France on the Eve of the First World War* (Oxford, 1984), pp.26–30; S.R. Williamson, 'The Origins of World War I', *Journal of Interdisciplinary History*, 18 (1988), p.798.
148. E.M. Satow, *An Austrian Diplomat of the 'Fifties: The Rede Lecture for 1908* (Cambridge, 1908), p.57.

'Après la Guerre finit, Soldat anglais partit …':[1] Anglo-French Relations 1918–25

ALAN SHARP and KEITH JEFFERY

This article investigates a number of issues and problems about which Michael Dockrill has written extensively in his career – the end of wars and the problems of victorious alliances, the control of foreign policy, the conundrums raised by defence policy, and, in particular, Anglo-French relations in the inter-war period.[2] It illuminates some of the difficulties of diplomatic, strategic, and military policy towards a great power that was simultaneously an ally and a rival in the wake of a great war in which there had been a close alliance. In their fine study of Britain and the peace conferences, Dockrill and Goold argued that the Anglo-French relationship was of central importance to international relations after 1918. Observing that while both Britain and France 'were more or less able to thwart the other's German policies', neither country on its own was able 'to impose a coherent long term unilateral solution'. It was not the Treaty of Versailles, they asserted, 'that was at the root of the problems of the inter-war period. It was the inability of France and Britain, the two great powers with most at stake in the settlement, either to agree to uphold the Treaty or to find some means of alleviating it'.[3] There are obvious parallels between the Anglo-French and Anglo-American experiences during and after both the twentieth-century world wars, but this investigation is focused on the post-1918 Anglo-French relationship. It is also a case study for the important problem faced by all major governments – the extent to which it is possible to plan a realistic and effective defence strategy linked to the priorities of foreign and domestic policy aims.

Britain's relationship with France after the First World War was complex and multi-layered. It was based on a series of concentric circles that began with Germany and Western Europe and gradually widened via Eastern Europe, the Near and Middle East and from the Atlantic to the Pacific, eventually encompassing almost all major aspects of international relations in the post-war era. The interplay between the differing aims and ambitions of Britain and France in these geographical spheres was made more complex by a series of policy disputes that ranged from the settlement of their inter-indebtedness to the interpretation and the enforcement of the peace treaties. During the war itself, their rivalries had been somewhat tempered by a mutual interest in the defeat of Germany (although each accused the other of being prepared to fight to the last drop of the other's last soldier's blood). Once the war was over, some of this restraint vanished. The 1921 response of David Lloyd George, the British prime minister, to the complaint of Georges Clemenceau, his wartime and post-war French counterpart, has become almost a cliché. Clemenceau declared that, at the end of the war, Britain had immediately reverted to a stance of enmity to France: 'Well', replied the Welshman, 'was it not always our traditional policy?'[4] Yet the need to cooperate remained extremely desirable even though the end of military operations made this less obvious.

The paradox that France was now, simultaneously, Britain's most considerable ally and yet, potentially, its most formidable Great Power enemy was not lost on British decision-makers or on historians. The future foreign secretary, George Curzon, stated on 2 December 1918: 'I am seriously afraid that the great power from whom we have most to fear in the future is France.'[5] Yet three years later, as foreign secretary, he painted the other side of the picture:

> As a result of the war there remain only two really great powers in Europe – France and ourselves. ... For a considerable period, therefore, a combination of Great Britain and France would be so strong that no other likely combination could successfully resist it. It follows that a definite and publicly announced agreement between the two countries to stand by one another in case either were attacked would offer a guarantee of peace of the strongest kind.[6]

John Ferris confirms this, reminding us that 'until 1936 an Anglo-French alliance would have been the strongest military force on earth, dominant in Europe and easing indirectly Britain's problem of the Pacific. Even after 1936 such an alliance would have remained a formidable combination'.[7]

Yet this did not materialize, even though on several occasions British decision-makers offered pacts of guarantee or alliance. Indeed, the early post-war years saw Britain constructing part of its armed forces against a perceived threat from France.[8] This created many dilemmas. How could military planning against France be justified, both in terms of the continuing Anglo-French partnership and domestically? Suspicion of France was tempered by the knowledge that some measure of post-war cooperation in almost every aspect of diplomacy was probably essential if Britain wanted to make its policies successful. There was the further consideration – as Winston Churchill, aware of the growth of battlefield pilgrimages, reminded Lloyd George: 'It would be an enormous shock to the British public, who have 600,000 graves in France, if the statesmen were to tell them that we backed the wrong horse.'[9]

It was indisputable that each perceived the other as a rival as well as a friend. Like Britain and the United States in the Second World War, they were 'allies of a kind'.[10] Even though British leaders often qualified their warnings by admitting that Britain was much more secure than before the war[11] – and added disclaimers that war between France and Britain would be a calamity or unthinkable – a number of statesmen and defence analysts raised this spectre, in some cases for cynical ends. The veteran lord president of the council, Arthur Balfour, was typical of these warning voices. On 24 May 1922, he told the Committee of Imperial Defence (CID) that a French air attack was 'hardly conceivable, except on the extreme assumption of the adoption by France of a policy which French public opinion was never likely to approve'. Already in 1921 he had stated: 'the only country which can seriously menace us is France. A war with France would be a world calamity which seems almost unthinkable: but where national security is concerned even the unthinkable must be faced, and we must sometimes assume that to be possible which, in existing circumstances, seems only an evil dream.'[12] Lloyd George agreed that 'it was necessary to make preparations against such a contingency because, even if it did not occur, the fear of it would weaken British diplomacy, and the knowledge of that power would be a weapon in the hands of French statesmen which they would not refrain from using'.¹³ Discussing the possible types of investigation that an imperial staff or war college might undertake, Admiral Richmond suggested in September 1922 that these could include a number of issues that might arise in case of a war with France: the defence of Malta; countermeasures against French air bases in North Africa; the defence of trade in the Mediterranean; the defence of the Suez canal; attacks on French bases in Africa and Asia; the consequences of a dispute with France in the Middle East.¹⁴

Commenting in November 1923 on a CID paper on 'The Menace', Curzon insisted – 'in order to obviate any suggestion that France was considered to be a likely enemy at the present time' – that a sentence be added stating: 'In this paper attention is drawn to France only because at the present moment she is the strongest Air Power.' Balfour's conclusion was nonetheless stark. He had originally reported in 1922 that France could drop at least 75 tons of bombs daily on London for an indefinite period, now the Air Ministry raised its estimate to 168 tons on the first day, 126 tons the next day and 84 tons daily thereafter. 'Day after day, and night after night, the capital of the Empire would be subject to an unremitting bombardment of a kind which no city effectively acting as the Military, Naval and Administrative centre of a country engaged in a life-and-death struggle has ever had to endure.' Curzon added that if 'France [had] a preponderance of air power and an increased strength in submarines ... it would be possible for her to dictate her policy to the whole world'. Despite believing that war with France was remote, Balfour still wished to maintain Britain's defences because 'he was doubtful if we possessed sufficient confidence in the French nation who were at present in a somewhat hysterical condition'.¹⁵ Yet the Treasury was aware of the French financial and economic situation which seemed to preclude great expenditures on armaments.¹⁶ This discussion thus raises interesting questions about the effectiveness of the CID in fulfilling its role of bringing together the best estimates and intelligence of the various British government agencies to facilitate coordinated defence and foreign policy planning.

Many in Britain did not like France. As Robert Vansittart, a bastion of the inter-war Foreign Office, pointed out:

> the Victorian England in which I was brought up was almost entirely anti-French ... Victorian England was vaguely convinced that nineteenth century France had too good a time; that France laughed too much and cooked too well for this vale of tears. ... More serious still, Victorian England suspected that the French somehow put more into, and got more out of, sex than the English. Victorian England had not the vaguest idea how this was done, but was fairly sure that the advantage was not fair, and quite sure that it was not nice.[17]

Despite the *entente cordiale* and the First World War itself, there were memories that went back for centuries and, like Lord Raglan during the Crimean campaign, still some for whom 'the French' was synonymous with 'the enemy'.[18] Robert Graves, up at Oxford after the war, recorded that

> Anti-French feeling amongst most ex-soldiers amounted almost to an obsession. Edmund [Blunden], shaking with nerves, used to say at this time: "No more wars for me at any price! Except against the French. If there's ever a war with them, I'll go like a shot". ... Some undergraduates even insisted that we had been fighting on the wrong side: our natural enemies were the French.[19]

Such sentiments could be matched in France, though there is also ample evidence on both sides of the channel that there was much mutual sympathy and admiration. It would be unwise to attach too much importance to the sentiments of Graves and his friends when matters of state were at stake.

Balfour, when British foreign secretary in March 1919, summed up many of the paradoxes at the heart of British decision-making, displaying the common British exasperation with a France that refused to see matters from a British perspective and that persisted in adopting unwise policies towards Germany. He would later express this frustration with the French in a colourful manner, declaring they 'were so dreadfully afraid of being swallowed up by the tiger, but would spend their time poking it'.[20] In 1919, he declared that the French were defeatist, assuming demographic inferiority to a *revanchiste* Germany and the impotence of the League. His assessment was: 'They may be right; but if they are, it is quite certain that no manipulation of the Rhine frontier is going to make France anything more than a second-rate Power, trembling at the nod of its great neighbours on the East, and depending from day to day on the changes and chances of a shifting diplomacy and uncertain alliances.'[21]

There were obvious, yet confusing, contradictions. Balfour judged that France was now inescapably a second-rate power and yet he still warned of the frightening prospect of French saturation bombing. Balfour's analysis acknowledged Germany as a potential disturber of the peace, but most of his contemporaries believed that Germany no longer represented the most pressing threat to the European balance of power; rather it was France's ambition to be, in Curzon's words, 'the mistress of Europe in respect of coal, iron and steel ... and also ... the military monarch'.[22] British suspicions were sustained by the maintenance of a large French standing army, the encouragement of Rhineland separatism, and the consistent demands of successive French governments to punish real or perceived German infractions of the Treaty of Versailles by an occupation of the Ruhr. Lord D'Abernon, the first British post-war ambassador to Germany, wrote in 1923:

> many of the arguments which were valid in 1914 against Germany are valid today against France. ... Anyone who supposes that a French Government dominating the Continent as Napoleon dominated it after Tilsit will remain friendly to England must be a poor judge of national psychology. ... Desiring the maintenance of the Anglo-French Entente, I am compelled to desire the existence of a strong Germany.[23]

This was a tragic misreading of reality from the perspective of Paul Cambon, the veteran French ambassador in London, who believed that 'The misfortune is that the English are not yet aware that Napoleon is dead'.[24]

Economic and territorial considerations in Europe and imperial rivalries elsewhere – particularly in the Middle East[25] – also fuelled Britain's suspicions of France. According to Curzon, 'the lure of the Ruhr' was irresistible to France.[26] It was thus Britain's usual policy to resist French attempts to extend the occupation of Germany, although Lloyd George had acquiesced in such an extension in March

1921 and agreed to the threat of a further extension in April 1921.²⁷ As Curzon declared: 'We are at the present moment ... the only moderating influence in respect of France. We go about arm in arm with her, but with one of our hands on her collar, and if we relax that control I myself should be very much alarmed at the consequences that would ensue.'²⁸

In a typically lengthy and authoritative review of the international situation prepared for the 1923 Imperial Conference, Curzon discussed relations with France. He dwelt on 'the difficulty of working in absolute sincerity and friendship with our great neighbour across the Channel, the frequent desertions and the almost chronic lack of loyalty in great emergencies of the Government of France'. He went on to illustrate French failings, including the trials he had endured with regard to Near Eastern affairs and at the Lausanne conference, where he 'found her a faithless ally, deserting me at the pinch everywhere'.²⁹ Curzon complained at France's current policy of grinding Germany down, observing that it was 'far from being favourable to the recovery of the world'. Yet he also assured the Dominion premiers that he had not 'the smallest animus against our great neighbour and ally'.

> No one is a more profound believer than myself in the policy of the *Entente*; and I do not rest that belief merely on the memories of the war, or on principles of self-interest; my conviction is based on the widest considerations of world peace and world progress. If France and ourselves permanently fall out, I see no prospect of the recovery of Europe or the pacification of the world.

He went on to stress how very much Britain had attempted to secure the entente. Over the past two years it had 'made innumerable sacrifices'. He himself had endeavoured 'at every stage with laborious hands' to build up unity between Britain and France. But he had received scant return for what he described as his 'loyalty' to France. 'I cannot say truthfully that this loyalty has received any encouragement, still less any imitation. These are things', he added, 'which I cannot possibly say in public.'³⁰

Yet the question remained of how best to achieve a satisfactory Anglo-French relationship. British leaders were not persuaded by the moral obligation to renegotiate the abortive Anglo-French guarantee of 1919.[31] They were uncertain whether such a pact would encourage French intransigence or magnanimity towards Germany. In 1921 Sir Maurice Hankey, the secretary to the cabinet, took a simple line. Even if the French were 'bought' by an alliance, they would not 'stay bought'. 'We should constantly be in the dilemma of having to choose between breaking off an Alliance and associating ourselves in a policy utterly distasteful to us and liable to lead to a breach of the peace.'[32] Arthur Henderson expressed the opposition of the Labour party on 7 January 1920:

> we hold most decidedly that a commitment of this kind is unnecessary, since the Covenant of the League of Nations imposes already the obligation to defend the territorial integrity and independence of all its members. Further, although this alliance may be in form defensive, it must have the effect of diminishing the motives which would otherwise incline French policy to courses of prudence and conciliation.[33]

The influential South African leader, J.C. Smuts, wanted Britain to withdraw from Europe and to concentrate on its imperial role. 'I would rather assume a position of independence, putting the British Empire entirely aside from all of them', he told the 1921 Imperial Conference.[34] This echoed earlier advice to Lloyd George from his private secretary, Philip Kerr, who advocated leaving 'Europe to itself with such assistance as the League of Nations can give to it'.[35]

Harold Nicolson of the Foreign Office, reminded the CID in 1920 that 'the events of the last twenty years have shown that we cannot be free to carry out our main objects which are Indian and Colonial, unless we are safe in Europe, and it will be many years yet before we can free ourselves of responsibility for Europe'.[36] Isolation was not an option for most decision-makers. Some were committed to a treaty with France. Of these Lord Derby, British ambassador in Paris 1918–20 and war minister in the Conservative government of 1922–24, was the most vociferous and devoted.[37] Sir Henry Wilson, the chief of the imperial general staff from 1918 to 1922, was another enthusiast, declaring: 'I conclude that a close offensive and defensive Alliance should be entered into between the British, French and Belgian Governments.'[38] Austen Chamberlain, the chancellor of the exchequer in 1920, asked 'if it be once admitted that we cannot afford to see Germany dominating Belgium and Holland or overwhelming France, is it not far better that this vital object of British policy should be consecrated and defended by a public treaty?'[39] In 1920 Winston Churchill, the colonial secretary, believed that an alliance was the necessary price of French flexibility towards Germany. He was supported by Charles Hardinge, a former PUS at the Foreign Office and Derby's successor in Paris, who wrote 'I feel that until France obtains some guarantee of assistance by us against possible aggression by Germany, she will continue to be unreasonable and tiresome over all questions affecting her relations with Germany'.[40]

Opinions thus differed within the British establishment as to the correct stance to take towards France. Most were non-committal, recognizing the force of both sides of the argument, anxious, if possible, to retain the traditional 'free hand' in foreign policy but prepared to be persuaded that it might be necessary to make a gesture towards France. In return, however, they would expect French concessions in key political and diplomatic disputes. It suited some to argue for a firm British military and diplomatic commitment even if few shared what they saw as a French obsession with the menace of a revived Germany. For others France was a useful yardstick against which British military planning and preparedness should be measured, usually as part of a campaign to increase government spending in these areas.

There was, however, a wider dimension to this debate – the place of defence in the priorities of post-war government. On his return from Paris Lloyd George was anxious to move scarce resources away from the armed forces and towards social and industrial reconstruction. Given his peculiar political situation as the head of a coalition government in which his own party was the junior partner and unsure of its future support, he was especially aware of the role of public opinion. On 5 August 1919, he asked his cabinet colleagues to consider what the popular response would be to a continued high level of military expenditure. Britain 'had destroyed the only enemy we had in Europe'. If the country now 'maintained a larger Army and Navy and Air Force than we had before we entered on the War, people would say, either that the War had been a failure, or that we were making provision to fight an imaginary foe'. The external threat may have been eliminated, but there were now domestic dangers. Lloyd George was not prepared to 'take risks with labour. If we did, we should at once create an enemy within our own borders, and one which would be better provided with dangerous weapons than Germany'. The first priority, therefore, was to provide for 'the health and labour of the people and to lay at once the sure foundations of national health and industrial prosperity'.[41]

Confronted by this uncompromising statement the service ministers assured the cabinet that economies could be made. Churchill, secretary of state for both war and air, thought, optimistically, that by 1920 'events would no longer govern expenditure which would then be controlled by the policy decided upon by the Cabinet'. He ventured to make a forecast, 'which was necessarily very vague', that expenditure on both the army and the air force in the coming year would not exceed £100 million. He thought that the size of the army, which had stood at two million at the beginning of the year could be the following spring be reduced to about 320,000. This compared with a pre-war figure of about 255,000. When the prime minister asked why so much larger a force was required than in 1914, Churchill remarked that 'our responsibilities during the War had considerably increased, especially in regard to Ireland and the East'.[42]

Arising from this discussion came the definition of the famous 'ten year rule', which was agreed at a cabinet meeting ten days later. The rule instructed the service ministries when framing their estimates to assume 'the British Empire will not be engaged in any great war during the next ten years, and that no Expeditionary Force is required for this purpose'. It was confirmed that the 'principal function' of the army and air force was 'to provide garrisons for India, Egypt, the new mandated territory (other than self-governing) under British control, as well as to provide the necessary support to the civil power at home'. It was finally agreed that the navy should aim at a maximum estimate of £60 million, and the army and air force at a joint estimate not exceeding £75 million.[43]

The cuts which the service ministries introduced in 1919–21 were both painful and impressive; between 1919/20 and 1921/22, total defence expenditure fell from £766 million to £189 million. But they were not enough. In 1920/21, inflation, continuing high levels of government expenditure, and the collapse of the brief post-war economic boom, together with the solemnly held principles of economic orthodoxy shared by the cabinet and its financial advisers, led to further demands for reductions in expenditure. 'Finance dominates everything', wrote Hankey at the beginning of 1921. 'At the very moment when we are threatened with so many perils in these regions [the Middle East] we find it impossible to continue the overwhelming burden of cost which our military forces entails.'[44] Casting around for some 'sop to Anti-Waste',[45] Lloyd George hit upon the stratagem of a committee of businessmen, chaired by Sir Eric Geddes, to review all government expenditure.

The Geddes committee worked quickly. By the end of the year it had produced interim reports on service spending. Generally critical of the services' lavish provision of manpower, the committee recommended that the army should be reduced by 50,000 men and the estimates brought down from £75 million to £55 million (in 1922/23). Taking the ten year rule at its face value, they argued that a clear area for economy was in the War Office's provision for an expeditionary force to meet possible overseas emergencies. Although the expeditionary force could theoretically go anywhere abroad, in practice it was the only basis for any continental commitment Britain might assume, and for the French a symbol of Britain's bona fides should they be threatened by a revived Germany.[46] The committee concluded that 'considerable room' for economy existed in the air force, and suggested that the estimates be reduced from £15 million to £10 million. The navy fared no better: Geddes recommended a reduction in personnel from 121,000 to 88,000 with a spending cut from £81 million to £60 million, and still lower in the subsequent year.[47]

Naturally the armed services responded fiercely to the Geddes Report – Sir Henry Wilson described it as containing 'fantastic proposals for reducing the Army to futility'[48] – and Lloyd George appointed a committee under Churchill to adjudicate between the services and Geddes. Although Churchill accepted that 'the forces at the disposal of the Empire are now reduced to a weakness unprecedented since the South African War', his committee largely confirmed the Geddes cuts, reducing the navy vote to £62 million, and the army to £58.6 million.⁴⁹ The air force fared better, impressing both Geddes and Churchill with its modern potential and thrifty attitude to affairs. In fact, during the 1920s, the air force increased its share of total defence spending, from eight per cent in 1922 to 14 per cent in 1928, when its expenditure was just over £16 million. Part of this success of Hugh Trenchard, the chief of the air staff, can be explained by his use of the supposed French threat (which he later admitted he did not credit) to maintain the independence of the RAF and to secure its expansion.⁵⁰

The cuts left the army the main victim. Its role was conceived as imperial policing and it had only a small expeditionary force of two infantry and one cavalry divisions at full strength. The War Office conceded that the army was the least necessary service for 'any war with a Continental Power'.⁵¹ Thus, even had an alliance between Britain and France been negotiated, it is difficult to see what immediate military value this would have been to Britain's ally. Things would have reverted to the pre-war position when Foch had told Wilson: 'After all it doesn't matter what you send us, we only ask for one corporal and four men, but they must be there right at the start. You will give them to me and I promise to do my utmost to get them killed. From that moment I will be at ease since I know that England will follow them as one man.'⁵² Yet Wilson believed that there might, in any future war, no longer be time for such a symbolic act, particularly if it were decided to build a Channel tunnel connecting Britain and France.

Discussing the strategic implications of such a construction in 1919, he argued that it would concentrate German attacks on the tunnel exits rather than Paris. 'To put this point in another and more correct way, an offensive directed against the Tunnel exits would bring on a decisive battle with more certainty that a similar offensive in the direction of Paris; and we should be forced to stand and fight, however inferior our strength.' Wilson added:

> From past experience it would appear unwise to rely on the French entirely, and we must therefore be ready to despatch a force capable of securing an area of deployment well in advance of the exits from the Tunnel and this emphasises the point already stated that the Tunnel is not only useless, but a

positive danger unless there is a military force of sufficient size ready to use it.⁵³

His personal preference was for a 'close offensive and defensive alliance with France' and he favoured a 'consistent and well-defined foreign policy of friendship for France, of determination to defend France and Belgium from German aggression and of a plan for fighting on the Continent on a continental scale'.⁵⁴ In July 1919, the War Office suggested two schemes allowing it to field 50 or 41 divisions, while Wilson argued for the establishment of the post-war army 'on a broader basis and one which will admit of considerable expansion in the future'.⁵⁵ Yet it is clear that he did not succeed in convincing the British government on this score and, argues Ferris, left the army in a poor state when he retired in 1922.⁵⁶

As early as August 1914 the French were joking: 'If the English get into Calais they will never leave it at the end of the war. They were much too upset when they lost it before.'⁵⁷ The reality was different. At the moment of the armistice there were over 1.5 million British troops in Italy, France and Flanders; within a year the number was 46,000; by the spring of 1920 there were 21,000 and a further year later fewer than 1,000 men remained. By January 1922 no British troops remained in these areas, where they had mainly been employed in clearing the battlefields and reburying the dead.⁵⁸ The Army of the Rhine had also declined from over 236,000 in early 1919 to 9,000 by the autumn of 1922.⁵⁹ Very rapidly after the war finished, the British soldiers had gone.

What had not gone were a series of personal connections at the top and subordinate levels of command which had begun before the war and been fostered by it. General Huguet commented:

> At the same time [that is, after 1906] the link between the military authorities of the two countries became closer and closer and not a year passed without the exchange of missions which grew in frequency and greatly contributed to the birth and growth of a spirit of good comradeship, marked more and more by a spirit of confidence and kindly feeling.⁶⁰

That there was a 'special relationship' at this level is well attested. Henry Wilson's correspondence is littered with affectionate references to 'the Old Marshal' – Foch – and each did his best to accommodate the other in practical matters wherever possible and to keep the other informed when circumstances did not permit this. Faced with a potential domestic crisis in April 1921, Wilson believed that he might have to withdraw British troops from Europe just as the Allies were seeking to pressurize the Germans into accepting the reparations settlement and into fulfilling their disarmament obligations. He asked Charles Sackville-West, the British military attache in Paris, to show Foch a letter which spelled out his logistical dilemma and wrote in his diary that the General Staff would only send troops to the Rhine 'to show loyalty to the Old Marshal'.

Foch himself had proved very cooperative over problems in Constantinople in November 1920. Fred Kisch, Sackville-West's deputy, wrote to Wilson: 'I think he would stand on his head if you were to ask him to do so!' In May 1921 Sackville-West wrote to Wilson: 'The FO are jealous of the rapidity with which you and Foch fix things up. Curiously enough Weygand told me the French Frocks are just as jealous of this.' Wilson responded: 'It really is the greatest pleasure to deal with men like the Old Marshal himself and his subordinates and I only wish, and I sincerely hope, that one of these days we may be able to do something to please him.' As Wilson approached retirement, Sackville-West wrote on 2 January 1922:

> Foch I know has written to you. He is anxious about the future – if only England and France hold together all will be well, if not the deluge. Meanwhile I suspect the Frocks and without you at the military helm I fear the soldiers of the two nations will gradually drift apart. No one seems to look very far into the future and of course the little Frenchmen are intensely irritating at times and then we get sulky.[61]

There is clearly scope here for greater investigation of the role played by the personal contacts and friendships of men like Edward Spears who undertook important Anglo-French liaison duties in both world wars.[62]

Failing to look far into the future was indeed part of the Anglo-French problem. The British tended to offer, initially at least, pacts and guarantees for the next ten years, yet their own military planning assumed no major confrontations in that period. The French were quick to point out that it was precisely at the point at which the British guarantees would expire that Germany might realistically once more pose a threat to their security. It was a normal part of most such negotiations between them that the British would raise the term to 20 years. Yet, although as David French has argued, the British military did try to retain a continental mentality in their doctrine and organization,[63] the reality was that the British army was designed to be small and professional, for imperial rather than continental service. It seems to have been part of Wilson's make-up that he never believed he knew what was in the government's mind. There is little evidence, however, in the files of the Foreign Office at least, that the practical implications of the offers of guarantees, pacts and alliances made had been translated into logistical requirements or incorporated into military planning. Given the economic and political circumstances that the services found themselves it is difficult to see how any realistic plans involving British troops on a scale useful to France could have been made.

In December 1924 the War Office had argued:

> The true strategic frontier of Great Britain is the Rhine; her security depends entirely upon the present frontiers of France, Belgium and Holland being maintained and remaining in friendly hands. The great guiding principle of the German General Staff in making plans for a future war will be, as in the last war, to try to defeat her enemies in detail. Any line of policy which permitted Germany (with or without allies) first to swallow up France and then to deal with Great Britain would be fatal strategically.[64]

It was, however, hard to translate such clear views into policies that had the necessary logistical backing. There were, for example, no Anglo-French staff talks. As it was, most historians agree that the obligations that Britain entered into under the Locarno agreements represented the maximum that could be expected, given the attitudes and political circumstances of the time, though they disagree as to whether Locarno increased or limited British continental commitment.[65] In military terms, planning to implement the guarantee offered to all the potential adversaries was impossible. As Leo Amery, the Dominions secretary, told the Dominion premiers in

August 1925, Britain could not send 'its officers simultaneously to Paris and Berlin to work up arrangements for fighting with the French and against the French!' Indeed Austen Chamberlain, the foreign secretary, rejected any strategic investigation of his policy by the CID because he 'did not wish to wreck his policy on the technicalities of military consideration'.[66] The reality of the requirements of Locarno (and of obligations under the League) was, according to the chiefs of staff, that 'so far as commitments on the Continent are concerned, the Services can only take note of them'.[67] Anglo-French relations in the post-war period were thus complicated and ambiguous. Ferris's historical verdict is that

> French and British security were indivisible: the fall of the British Empire was a necessary if delayed concomitant of the fall of France. Only by an understanding with France could Britain have achieved its central aim in Europe: to revise the Treaty of Versailles in such a way as to reconcile Germany while maintaining an acceptable balance of power in Europe.[68]

In October 1942, J.C. Smuts argued that 'the almost total loss of the entire Allied possessions in the Far East and in South-East Asia was due to the fall of France'.[69] The Vichy government established in French Indo-China 'opened the door' for the Japanese to Singapore, Siam, Malaya, and Burma. There is much evidence to suggest that contemporary British decision-makers and policy advisers were aware of the problem but there were so many variables and issues involved that they could create no satisfactory arrangements to cement what all agreed would be a formidable alliance. President Lyndon Johnson encapsulated the post-1945 Anglo-American relationship in characteristically earthy terms: 'Britain may dicker around in the nightclubs and dance with a few of the girls but in the end you'll always come home to bed with the same old girl.'[70] The problem after the First World War was that Britain and France did not grasp their need for each other. The 'standard bearers of democracy' got themselves in a fearful tangle and contributed to the realization of their ultimate nightmare, a new continental war against Germany.

Reflecting on the fall of France in 1940 Marshal Petain stated: 'Too few children, too few arms, too few allies – those were the reasons for our defeat.'[71] Earlier Clemenceau told the Senate in 1919:

The Treaty does not say that France must undertake to have children, but it is the first clause which should be included in it. For if France turns her back on large families, one can put all the clauses one wants in a treaty, one can take all the guns of Germany, one can do whatever one likes, France will be lost because there will be no more Frenchmen.[72]

Meanwhile, British policy was based too much on aspirations, wishful thinking and the hope that Baldwin was mistaken when he feared that 'some day the cheque would be presented and we should have to honour it'.[73] There were not enough mademoiselles in the family way 'après la guerre finit', the English soldiers did indeed depart, and France was left in the lurch.

NOTES

We are grateful to Elizabeth Greenhalgh of the Australian Defence Force Academy, first for suggesting that we contribute an earlier version of this paper to a panel at the Society of Military History's annual conference (in Calgary in May 2001) and, second, for offering material and references from her paper, 'Diplomacy in the Field: The French and British Liaison Services, 1914–1918', which is part of her wider doctoral study.

1. 'Après la guerre finit, Soldat anglais partit, Mademoiselle in the family way, Après la guerre finit.' Soldiers' song from the First World War.
2. See, for example, Z. Steiner and M.L. Dockrill, 'The Foreign Office Reforms, 1919–21', *Historical Journal*, 17 (1974); M.L. Dockrill and Z. Steiner, 'The Foreign Office at the Paris Peace Conference in 1919', *International History Review*, 2 (1980); M.L. Dockrill and J.D. Gould, *Peace Without Promise: Britain and the Peace Conferences 1919–1923* (London, 1981); M.L. Dockrill *British Defence since 1945* (Oxford, 1988); M.L. Dockrill, *British Establishment Perspectives on France, 1936–1940* (Basingstoke, 1999).
3. Dockrill and Goold, *Peace Without Promise*, p.86.
4. G. Clemenceau, *Grandeur and Misery of Victory* (London, 1930), p.113; J.-B. Duroselle, *Clemenceau* (Paris, 1988), p.879.
5. Eastern Committee minutes, CAB 27/24.
6. Curzon memorandum, 28 Dec. 1921, in *DBFP*, 1st Series, XVI, p.862.
7. J.R. Ferris, *The Evolution of British Strategic Policy, 1919–1926* (Basingstoke, 1989), p.186.
8. 'Report of the Sub-Committee of Imperial Defence on National and Imperial Defence' (Salisbury Committee), 9 March 1923, CAB 16/46. Published, in a slightly edited form, as *1924 Cmd. 2029*.
9. Churchill to Lloyd George, 28 Nov. 1921, Lloyd George F/10/1/48. House of Lords Record Office. For battlefield pilgrimages, see D.W. Lloyd, *Battlefield Tourism: Pilgrimage and the Commemoration of the Great War in Britain, Australia and Canada,*

1919–1939 (Oxford, 1998).
10. The term adopted by Christopher Thorne to characterize Anglo-American relations in his *Allies of a Kind: the United States, Britain and the War against Japan, 1941–1945* (London, 1978).
11. Report of the Sub-Committee of the Committee of Imperial Defence on National and Imperial Defence (Salisbury Committee), 15 Nov. 1923, CAB 16/46.
12. CID 157th meeting, 24 May 1922, CAB2/3; CID 108A, 29 May 1922, CAB16/47.
13. CID 158th meeting, 5 July 1922, CAB2/3.
14. Richmond memorandum, September 1922, CAB16/45. Richmond also suggested that the College be tasked with studying the main strategy of a war with Japan.
15. Meetings of a CID Sub-Committee, 16 May, 15 Nov. 1923, CAB/46.
16. See M. Horn, *Britain, France and the Financing of the First World War* (Montreal/Kingston, 2002) for the wartime background. On the post-war situation, see A. Turner, 'Anglo-French Financial Relations in the 1920s', *European History Quarterly*, 26 (1996), pp.31–55; idem, *The Cost of War: British Policy on French War Debts, 1918–1932* (Brighton, 1998).
17. R. Vansittart, *Lessons of My Life* (1943), pp.21–2. Vansittart was permanent under-secretary at the Foreign Office from January 1930 to December 1937.
18. A. Wood, *Nineteenth Century Britain 1815–1914* (London, 1960), p.194.
19. R. Graves, *Goodbye to All That* (London, 1963), p.240.
20. CID 195th meeting, 13 Feb. 1925, CAB 2/4.
21. Balfour memorandum, 18 March 1919, Balfour Add MSS 49751, British Library.
22. 1921 Meeting of the Imperial Conference E4, 22 June 1921, CAB 32/2/E4.
23. Lord D'Abernon, *An Ambassador of Peace*, Vol.II (London, 1929), pp.238–9.
24. Comte de Saint-Aulaire, *Confession d'un Vieux Diplomate* (Paris, 1953), p.536.
25. See C.M. Andrew and A.S. Kanya-Forster, *France Overseas: The Great War and the Climax of French Imperial Expansion* (London, 1981), pp.180–251.
26. 1921 Meeting of the Imperial Conference E4, 22 June 1921, CAB 32/2/E4.
27. See the helpful summary in S.E. Crowe and E. Corp, *Our Ablest Public Servant: Sir Eyre Crowe 1864–1925* (Braunton, 1993), pp.430–33.
28. 1923 Meeting of the Imperial Conference E3, 5 Oct. 1923, CAB 32/9/E3.
29. Curzon's troubles with the French were accentuated by the revealing information he received from secret intelligence sources. See K. Jeffery and A. Sharp, 'Lord Curzon and Secret Intelligence', in C. Andrew and J. Noakes (eds.), *Intelligence and International Relations, 1900–1945* (Exeter, 1987), pp.103–26.
30. Stenographic Notes of Meetings, Imperial Conference, 5 Oct. 1923, CAB 32/9/E3.
31. See Anthony Lentin, 'Lloyd George, Clemenceau and the Elusive Anglo-French Guarantee Treaty: "A Disastrous Episode"?' in A. Sharp and G. Stone (eds.), *Anglo-French Relations in the Twentieth Century: Rivalry and Cooperation* (London, 2000), pp.104–19; and his other writings on this question, notably 'The Treaty That Never Was: Lloyd George and the Abortive Anglo-French Alliance of 1919', in J. Loades (ed.), *The Life and Times of David Lloyd George* (Bangor, 1991), pp.115–28; and '"Une aberation inexplicable"? Clemenceau and the Abortive Anglo-French Guarantee Treaty of 1919', *Diplomacy & Statecraft*, 8 (1997), pp.31–49.
32. Hankey to Lloyd George, 25 June 1921, Lloyd George MSS F/25/1/48.
33. Henderson to Lloyd George, 7 Jan. 1920, Lloyd George MSS F/27/3/39.
34. 1921 Meeting of the Imperial Conference E6, 24 June 1921, CAB32/2/E7.
35. Kerr memorandum, 2 Sept. 1920, Lloyd George MSS F/90/1/18.
36. CID Paper [251-B], 10 July 1920, CAB 4/7.

37. R.S. Churchill, *Lord Derby: 'King of Lancashire'* (London, 1959), *passim*. His letter to Lloyd George of 10 June 1921, quoted in ibid., pp.397–8, is typical.
38. Wilson memorandum [CP 919], 20 March 1920, CAB24/101.
39. Note, 28 June 1920, by Austen Chamberlain [Chancellor of the Exchequer] 'Our Future Relations with Belgium', CID Paper 246-B, CAB4/7.
40. Churchill's remarks are in CC 40(21)4, 24 May 1921, CAB23/25; Hardinge to Lloyd George, 22 June 1921, Lloyd George MSS F/53/1/63.
41. War Cabinet meeting 606A, 5 Aug. 1919, CAB23/15.
42. Ibid.
43. War Cabinet meeting 616A, 15 Aug. 1919, CAB 23/15. See also Ferris, *Evolution of British Strategic Policy* for a useful and provocative account.
44. Hankey diary, 3 Jan. 1921, Hankey MSS, HNKY 1/5, Churchill College, Cambridge.
45. This is H.A.L. Fisher's phrase. See Fisher diary, 2 Aug. 1921, Fisher MSS, Bodleian Library.
46. See M. Howard, *The Continental Commitment: The Dilemma of British Defence Policy in the Era of Two World Wars* (Harmondsworth, 1972).
47. 'Interim Report of the Committee on National Expenditure' [CP 3570], 14 Dec. 1921, CAB 24/131.
48. Henry Wilson diary, 24 Oct. 1921, Imperial War Museum microfilm DS/MISC/80 reel IX, Wilson MSS Imperial War Museum.
49. 'Report of the Committee appointed to examine Part I of the Report of the Geddes Committee on National Expenditure' [CP 3692], 4 Feb. 1922, CAB 24/132.
50. See Boyle, *Trenchard*, especially Chapter 16.
51. Ferris, *Evolution of British Strategic Policy*, pp.112–33.
52. General Huguet, *Britain and the War: A French Indictment* (London, 1928), p.26.
53. Memoranda on the War Office's views on the desirability of building a Channel Tunnel by Sir Henry Wilson [Chief of the Imperial General Staff] 23, 16 Dec. 1919, with a covering note from Winston Churchill, 9 Feb. 1920, printed as CID Paper 98-A in FO 371/3765.
54. Note, 6 Feb. 1920, WO 32/5302.
55. See D. French, *Raising Churchill's Army: The British Army and the War against Germany 1919–1945* (Oxford, 2000), p.15.
56. Ferris, *Evolution of British Strategic Policy*, p.116.
57. E.L. Spears, *Liaison 1914: A Narrative of the Great Retreat* (London, 1930), p.84.
58. Figures for 11 Nov. 1918 in 'Statistical abstract of information regarding the army at home and abroad', WO 161/82; 'Strength of the British Army' [CP 55], 15 Nov. 1919, Appendix B, CAB 24/92; 'Statistical Abstract', 3 April 1920, WO 161/82; 'Distribution of the total of all ranks at home and abroad', April 1921, WO 73/114; 'Distribution of the total of all ranks at home and abroad', Jan. 1922, WO 73/116.
59. 'Statistical Abstract', 3 May 1919, WO 161/82; 'Distribution of the total of all ranks at home and abroad', Oct. 1922, WO 73/117.
60. Huguet, *Britain and the War*, p.26.
61. K. Jeffery (ed.), *The Military Correspondence of Field Marshal Sir Henry Wilson 1918–1922* (The Bodley Head for the Army Records Society, London, 1985), pp.258–9, 269, 330. The other letters from Kisch (British Deputy Military Attache, Paris) and Sackville-West (British Military Attache, Paris) are in the Wilson MSS 2/12G/8 and 2/12G/37.
62. See, for example, Spears, *Liaison 1914*; M. Egremont, *Under Two Flags: The Life of Major General Sir Edward Spears* (London, 1997).

63. French, *Raising Churchill's Army*, pp.12–47.
64. Ferris, *Evolution of British Strategic Policy*, p.150.
65. See A. Sharp, 'Anglo-French Relations from Versailles to Locarno', in Sharp and Stone, *Anglo-French Relations*, pp.132–3.
66. Ferris, *Evolution of British Strategic Policy*, p.154.
67. COS 41, 22 June 1926, CAB 53/12.
68. Ferris, *Evolution of British Strategic Policy*, p.186.
69. Quoted in Nicholas Mansergh, *Survey of British Commonwealth Affairs: Problems of Wartime Co-Operation and Post-War Change, 1939–1952* (Oxford, 1958), p.191.
70. Quoted by P. Arthur, *Special Relationships: Britain, Ireland and the Northern Ireland Problem* (Belfast, 2001), p.120.
71. Broadcast of 20 June 1940, quoted by R. Tomlinson, 'The "Disappearance" of France, 1896–1940: French Politics and the Birth Rate', *Historical Journal*, 28 (1985), pp.405–15.
72. Ibid., p.409.
73. Ferris, *Evolution of British Strategic Policy*, p.154.

'Far Too Dangerous a Gamble'?[1] British Intelligence and Policy during the Chanak Crisis, September–October 1922

JOHN R. FERRIS

Between 26 August and 11 September 1922, the Turkish Nationalist Army threw the Greek Army out of Anatolia. This surprised Whitehall – on 29 July the War Office told the Cabinet neither Turk nor Greek could defeat the other[2] – and wrecked its attempts to end the war in Turkey through moderate revision to the Treaty of Sèvres. Whitehall assumed that stalemate in Anatolia would continue indefinitely. It hoped – prayed – this might let Britain manoeuvre Allies and belligerents toward a diplomatic solution that would preserve British interests in the area, as embodied in the Allied proposals of March 1922. According to these proposals, Turkey would receive Istanbul and Anatolia (subject to protection for Christian minorities) but lose half of its European territories, including Adrianople, to Greece; most of Thrace and the Asiatic shores of the Dardanelles would be demilitarized; the Turkish Army would be kept tiny; while a small Allied garrison would remain forever in the Gallipoli peninsula to maintain the 'freedom of the Straits'. The Greeks were willing to place themselves in the Powers' hands; so must the Turks. Yet these hopes were never high and, over months of stalemate, British policy drifted toward pessimism tinged with bitterness. Decisive Turkish victory in Anatolia wrecked this policy. It also produced Britain's gravest strategic crisis between the 1918 Armistice and Munich, plus a seismic shift in British politics; and it almost caused World War Two to start on the banks of the Bosphorus in September 1922. These events merit more attention than they have received.[3] They cannot be understood without realizing that Chanak was a military crisis, where political and strategic problems marched hand in hand, and to which intelligence was fundamental. The study of intelligence is essential to explain what happened during the crisis and why – as a lever of events and as a mirror for decisions. Diplomatic intelligence is rarely part of the study of diplomacy or intelligence. This account will show something of its peculiarities, and its significance.

British decisions during this crisis turned on assessments of Turkish strength in Anatolia, especially that which could be deployed near the Dardanelles and the Bosphorus. Estimates of these forces fluctuated wildly; on 17 September, the General Staff put them at 100,000 rifles, but soon it defined them as 300,000; the prime minister, David Lloyd George, at 70,000; and the British commander in Turkey, Charles Harington, at 45–50,000.[4] This uncertainty occurred for several reasons. In 1922, Turkish divisions varied dramatically in rifle strength, which British intelligence found hard to determine even when it knew the number of formations.[5] In November 1922, the War Office estimated that 20 Turkish divisions with 100,000 rifles stood near the Bosphorus and Dardanelles. Harington thought these divisions had 63,000 rifles, though the Turks had 201,000 men in total, which could easily be expanded to 300,000.[6] Britain also had an imperfect grasp of Turkish armament. Codebreaking showed that in 25 days of May 1922, Italy and France had shipped the Turks 21,000 rifles, 26 guns, 304 machine guns, 102,000 shells, and 15,600,000 rifle cartridges; these states and the USSR had no doubt sent other weapons, while gifts had been captured from Greeks. On 17 September the General Staff assumed the Turks could deploy 300 field guns, perhaps augmented by 30 howitzers from the USSR; by 23 September, it thought the Turks had 400 artillery pieces.[7] Estimates of Turkish strength overall were inaccurate, but not grossly so, and the issue generally irrelevant, since Britain rightly assumed that Turkey had great numerical superiority in infantry and cavalry. Britain suffered no harm from the one area where such problems might have mattered. The Royal Air Force (RAF) and the Army assumed the Turks had 60 aircraft, which could attack British forces or produce a 'very great' moral effect by flying over Istanbul; army and air authorities in Egypt had the 'general impression ... formed from unconfirmed reports' that 'the Kemalists appear to be making a good deal of progress in air matters'. In fact, though the Turks had some 60 aircraft, few were serviceable and none likely to have bothered Britain – they had not even fought the Greeks; in any case the RAF, confident it could handle Turks, ignored the issue, which negated the error.[8]

One problem of operational intelligence, however, did shape British decisions: Turkish strength not as a whole but at the front. From 13 to 30 September, 30,000 Turkish regulars and 100 guns moved north from Smyrna, leaving 18,000 men behind. These forces and more could be thrown against the small Allied forces in the theatre, especially at the flash-points of Chanak or Istanbul, and British intelligence could not find them until they reached the front. British signals intelligence had great success against Turkish military traffic in 1921 and, during September 1922, traced the location of Turkish Army headquarters; but it provided nothing about the movement or strength of Turkish formations, most likely because Turks did not discuss such matters over communication systems the British could intercept.[9] Meanwhile, no British aircraft in the theatre could conduct deep reconnaissance. Lack of intelligence was especially acute at Chanak, on the Asiatic side of the Dardanelles. Two mounted companies were the main source of tactical intelligence outside that town, augmented by a few British officers who knew the district.[10] Though seaplanes flew daily over the Dardanelles and Bosphorus, one commander at Chanak doubted their value and, with reason, believed the Turks were avoiding detection by moving at night: between 1 and 9 October, seaplane reconnaissance 'carried out with great boldness – the machines flying frequently within fifty feet of the ground' located just eight Turkish guns in the Neutral Zone at Chanak, when in fact 100 were deployed there. Again, this intelligence failure was irrelevant; Turkey had far fewer guns than Britain in the vicinity, too few to close the Dardanelles or crush Chanak's defences, which were established to handle the worst case, in which the Turks threw everything they could at the place the British thought most valuable and vulnerable.[11] Between 20 and 30 September, however, large Turkish forces were only days from Chanak, within striking range but undetected, and by 26 September able to operate on the Ismid Peninsula, on the Asiatic coast of the Bosphorus. Three days later, at the height of the crisis, Harington reported ten Turkish divisions with 28,000 rifles and perhaps 120 guns were in the theatre but unlocated.[12] In case of war, this power could easily be augmented by conscription in Anatolia, while thousands of armed if untrained Turkish Nationalists stood in Istanbul and Thrace – in early October 1922, Harington thought that 120,000 Turkish soldiers could strike Chanak and Istanbul, while 40,000 rose in Turkish Europe.[13] The picture was not pleasant viewing through the glasses of worst-case analysis. Harington commanded 4,700 British infantry, rising towards 10,000 at the height of the crisis between 29 September and 9 October 1922. The British believed that if hostilities occurred, their position would be perilous; they would have to evacuate Istanbul under fire, block attacks on Chanak and the Gallipoli peninsula, and fight across the Sea of Marmora. British intelligence's greatest failure during this crisis lay in the operational sphere, yet its effects were odd. It did not hamper military decisions that rested on worst-case analysis, rightly so in this case, given the Turk's overwhelming strength in infantry; but British strategy and diplomacy were shaped by uncertainty about Turkish military intentions and capabilities, which multiplied a sense of danger combined with opportunity.

Questions of capabilities were significant to Britain, but less so than intentions, strategic and diplomatic, of the other major states involved in the crisis: Italy, France, the USSR, and, above all, Nationalist Turkey. Britain needed to understand these intentions for their own sake and to change them because, seeking to enforce its will on other statesmen, it needed to know their aims. Some intentions were easy to gauge. Britain had normal relations with its erstwhile allies, France and Italy, and with two lesser players, Greece and the rump Ottoman government; conventional contacts revealed much of their policy. But no Western state had official entrée to Soviet decision-making, while Britain had poor relations with the Turkish Nationalists. Encounters with Turkish officers at the front and diplomats in Istanbul and London provided confusing reports of uncertain value; accounts by French and Italian statesmen of their discussions with Turks were open to suspicion, though in fact they proved to be generally accurate. This situation forced the British towards speculation and secret intelligence. Three secret services, all good, working independently though usually corroborating each other, influenced British decisions. In London, the Government Code and Cypher School (GC&CS), the world's best codebreaking agency of that era, easily read the diplomatic messages of France, Italy, Greece, and the Turkish Nationalists and, less handily so, those of the Union of Soviet Socialist Republics (USSR); the Secret Intelligence Service (SIS) had rather good sources across Europe; while, in Istanbul, the Army's No. 3 'Wireless Observation Group' (WOG) cracked Greek, Soviet, and Turkish diplomatic traffic. British decision-makers not only had good intelligence; they were veterans in its use. In Istanbul, Admiral Brock, commander of the Mediterranean Fleet, had been Chief of Staff to the wartime Grand Fleet, one of few officers with complete access to the intelligence from 'Room 40' and its application in war; as Chief of Staff to the Second Army in France, Harington had used all forms of military intelligence in battle and designed a sophisticated method to process it for operations; while the high commissioner to Turkey, Horace Rumbold, had managed the working of agents and Allied attempts to negotiate separate peace with Turkey, as minister to Switzerland, a centre of European espionage, in 1916–18 – he also had experienced the confusion of a crisis with the British embassy in Berlin during 1914. In London, many ministers, especially Winston Churchill, Lord Curzon, and Lloyd George, had been using intelligence in policy for years, and well – few statesmen have been more interested or expert in the matter. Unfortunately, a combination of system and circumstance saw these intelligence services present different pictures to decision-makers in Istanbul and London; hence, good evidence, well analyzed, caused the machinery of state to stutter between high performance and break-down.

The accidental factors were political – the way both power in decision-making devolved between authorities in Istanbul and London, and intelligence reached them. Levels of policy were confused – Whitehall tried to make tactical decisions, Harington made strategic ones. Without anyone intending the effect, authorities in Istanbul seized control over policy. They were united and coordinated local British power and policy, while their superiors in London were divided and too far from the scene to command it. When Whitehall pulled levers, nothing moved; Rumbold, Brock, and Harington pulled levers without trying. The structural problem was the organization within and between intelligence services. During the Great War, these services grew haphazardly and, afterward, were not well coordinated; though one key step had occurred by 1922 – the Foreign Office took responsibility for the SIS and GC&CS – many more remained to be taken. Indeed, the Chanak crisis helped to spark a reorganization of British intelligence.[14] Coordination among the SIS, the GC&CS, and No. 3 WOG was poor; the latter received none of the formers' material, and its reports reached London 12 to 24 hours after they had been generated, in part because they first went through Harington and his intelligence staff so they could inform Whitehall of how they interpreted them. The GC&CS focused exclusively on collection, paying no attention to assessment, although the SIS often commented on the meaning of its product and the reliability of reports and their unnamed sources. No. 3 WOG was, probably, heavily involved with assessment at General Staff (Intelligence) (GSI) Istanbul. Assessment was of even more mixed quality among intelligence consumers. GSI, the Military Intelligence Division (MID), and the Naval Intelligence Division (NID) had specialist officers for assessment, while Curzon had a junior member of the Foreign Office collate all news from all sources, gauge each piece in the light of the whole, and send daily 'problem files' to his superiors for immediate minutes to the minister (who demanded speed, thoroughness and accuracy in the process). His officials found the process burdensome and, myopically, abolished it when he fell from office – it gave the foreign secretary a better grasp of information than any other minister; its abandonment proved their loss a decade later.

In these four cases, assessors served one bureaucracy alone. No layer of interdepartmental assessment serviced Whitehall as a whole, or many ministers at all. During this crisis, cascades of intelligence and decisions crashed together. Some decision-makers steered this white-water with the guidance of thorough and specialist intelligence analysis. Others did so by taking a cursory glance at each report through the prism of memories of earlier messages, clouded by spray from the rapids. This matter by itself did not make disaster – decision-makers assessed most pieces of information in the same way; expert assessment on an interdepartmental basis might well have supported (as the NID and the MID in fact did) the most spectacularly bad decision of the crisis: the government's instructions that Harington deliver an ultimatum and then open fire at Chanak on 29 September 1922 – but it did create a serious problem. Significantly, the two men with the best sense of the crisis and the best intelligence on it, Curzon and Harington, were serviced by specialist assessment. Meanwhile, decision-makers were divided over access to and the interpretation of intelligence; notoriously, this matter provoked bad blood between politicians, especially Curzon and Churchill, but the greater effect was subterranean. Without anyone, including himself, appreciating the fact, Harington acquired an intelligence agency of his own and used it well, took control of the key levers of power and diplomacy, and made Britain's decisions for war and peace. This outcome, and the unexpected way in which it occurred, defined the Chanak crisis.

Further problems emerged from the relationship between two good codebreaking agencies. Army signals intelligence in the Middle East came from the remnants of two wartime WOGs (radio interception units with cryptanalytical and intelligence teams). No. 4 WOG in Iraq focused on Soviet wireless traffic but occasionally provided useful material on Turkey. For instance, in 1921, by intercepting and solving messages between Ankara and Moscow, it uncovered the Franklin–Bouillon agreement, the Franco-Turkish treaty that signalled France's break with Britain in Turkey. GSI at Istanbul relied most heavily on No. 3 WOG, formed from the radio interception units at Salonika in 1917–18, and the codebreaking team at Cairo which cracked Turkish military traffic in Palestine. In 1919, No. 3 WOG focused on radio messages between Budapest and Moscow, uncovering communications between Vladimir Illych Lenin and Bela Kun, but then it turned primarily to Turkish traffic in Anatolia.[15] Some of that material moved by telephone and radio but, the commander of No. 3 WOG noted decades later:

> We relied however for our best meat on landline interception, tapping the "secret" Nationalist line between C'ple & Ankara & by agents who took copies of messages in various telegraph offices & from the E[astern]. T[elegraph]. C[ompany]. All we could do here was the simple ciphers, ie the Turk Greek & some Russian. Most of our raw material went home & we saw or heard no more of it.

No. 3 WOG included three British intelligence officers, and 'from Egypt their Turkish team of cryptographers Hazan (Smyrna Jew), Papazozlou (Cairene Greek) Daniellian (Cairene Armenian) who went on to Sarafend & is still on the strength Utidjian (Cretan Armenian) and Chavookian (a chemist from Brighton, believe it or not)'.[16] As the crisis broke, six of Harington's intelligence personnel (possibly including the non-British members of No. 3 WOG) had just been retired as an economy measure, though he immediately rehired them.[17]

No. 3 WOG, the intelligence service most valuable during the crisis, differed from the GC&CS and the SIS in key ways. It was an integrated collection and intelligence service, whose members had specialized in Turkish diplomacy and operations for six years, developing a strong sense not only of what messages said but of what they meant. They were limited in technical terms, working from already reconstructed Turkish and Soviet codebooks ('simple ciphers') rather than cracking new systems. Still, they knew the systems at hand, usually translating Soviet messages in one to two days, and Turkish traffic in four to five, faster than the GC&CS did its work. The national status of its personnel, however, produced a problem of liaison, with unfortunate and unexpected effects – for this reason, in 1923 the GC&CS declined to give classified material to No. 3 WOG. No. 3 WOG's material went to decision-makers in Istanbul and London, but little GC&CS material was reported back; codebreaking, the best source of intelligence, gave decision-makers in the two cities radically different pictures. In principle, this need not have mattered. Whitehall, after all, had the full range of diplomatic intelligence required for high level policy, while No. 3 WOG's solutions of Turkish Nationalist traffic met Harington's need in that area. In practice, however, this situation produced chaos, as a tacticization of strategy crushed the borders between high and low policy, and decision-makers acted on the basis of different knowledge.

Yet another problem arose from the nature of the SIS. This was an able agency. Its strong suit, officers in Paris and Switzerland, monitored Turkish Nationalist diplomats in Paris and Rome, Ferid Bey and Fathi Bey; corroborated by diplomatic telegrams to and from Ankara, these reports usually circulated within two to four days of the date they occurred. SIS weakness lay in Turkey. In 1920–21, the Istanbul station was among the SIS's largest, with eight officers, six clerical staff, army and navy representatives, and unusually well-financed, receiving £2,200 per month for all operating expenses. Run by the SIS and the Government of India, the agency's main personnel, including the head, Major Vivian, were drawn from an excellent intelligence and counter-intelligence bureau, the Criminal Intelligence Department of India. The SIS chief, Mansfield Cumming, wrote: 'My agency in Constantinople is one of the most important, if not the most important, of all my agencies'; the head of his Military Intelligence section, MI1c, thought 'a better service of information has never been organised regarding events in the Near East'. In early 1922, however, the organization collapsed; the Government of India demanded the return of its personnel, including Vivian, who in turn quickly resigned to join the SIS. This event crippled the SIS in Istanbul – Cumming, 'staggered', contemplated abandoning the station and Rumbold denounced the damage, which officials in the India Office agreed was great.[18] It also shaped SIS's ability to acquire information during the Chanak crisis in a complex fashion.

During 1920–21 the Istanbul agency had assessed the Turkish Nationalists in the context of Bolshevik and Pan-Islamic schemes and the subversion of India (which Vivian described as 'the hardest worked section as it is largely the raison d'etre of the organisation'), focusing on Russians as intelligence sources; it may have run the SIS's successful penetration of Soviet bureaus between 1920 and 1924. Only one of its officers had specialized in 'local Turkish' intelligence, with limited success. The SIS intermittently tapped the rumour mill in Ankara, but mostly from sources outside Turkish Nationalist territory, with mixed results. In January 1921, for example, Vivian acquired high-level documents from the Ottoman government, through:

> an influential local Armenian from a Turk, who is believed to have access to Turkish Government papers, but who refuses to divulge his means of access. He is a disappointed politician who is believed to have given up all hope of the future of his country, and frankly obtains the information for mercenary reasons. He obtains his information so quickly after the event reported that

his reports have frequently been challenged, and this report cannot be categorically accepted without knowing the exact circumstances under which his information came into his hands, but his information has invariably proved in the end to be correct, though it has always been challenged. ... Major Vivian thinks that the original informant possibly sees papers for a short period and commits them to memory, afterwards reproducing them as accurately as he is able, and that, though they may not be minutely accurate, they probably represent the gist of the documents which he sees.[19]

Since the intermediary belonged to the Armenian Dashnak Party and had reason to distort his reports, the Foreign Office disregarded much of his material. However accurate Vivian's assessment, such material provided mere shadows of Mustafa Kemal; the failure of the Istanbul SIS station lay at Ankara. During the Chanak crisis, SIS agencies in Athens and Istanbul addressed Nationalist preparations in European Turkey, but not in Anatolia, while its reports from elsewhere (even those which illuminated Soviet policy toward Turkey, and the attitudes of Turkish diplomats abroad) do not seem to have reached Harington. Agents were useless to him except in one area – they were his main means to assess secret Nationalist preparations in Istanbul and Thrace. Reading the Turkish Nationalists from Turko-Bolshevik and pan-Islamic perspectives, SIS reports very much influenced Whitehall.[20] Characteristically, as the crisis broke, the SIS warned that Islamic and Bolshevik delegates were meeting in Berlin to coordinate an Islamic uprising in the British Empire, which was supported by Turkish Nationalist leaders.[21]

The SIS and No. 3 WOG threw no light on France or Italy, except as reflected by their Turkish sources; here, the main source of secret intelligence was GC&CS. Some of its information was trivial, providing a few hours forewarning of minor matters Britain quickly would have learned in any case: on 1 September, for instance, the instructions of the French premier, Raymond Poincaré, that his ambassador in London disclaim any French responsibility for Turkey's attack, blame Britain for the debacle, and demand the immediate calling of a peace conference to settle the issue. Some material arrived frustratingly just too late to use, such as about the decisions by France and Italy to withdraw their token forces from Chanak, and clear indications of their policy at inter-Allied meetings of 20–22 September 1922, though such information often had indirect value by illuminating past attitudes with future resonance.[22] In any case, codebreaking, combined with official sources, clearly outlined the positions of France and Italy in time for Britain to act.

Conversely, secret intelligence on Turkey and the USSR was excellent, but crippled by the lack of official access to decision-making in Moscow and Ankara – covert sources could not overcome the weakness in conventional ones. They provided a host of reliable, useful and timely material on every important issue about these states except their intentions at the highest of levels. This was an old problem. In 1920–21, for example, British diplomats in Istanbul developed a form of 'Ankara watching', routinely describing their evidence as 'facts and rumours', some of it probably deceptive, 'specially prepared for British consumption', with the situation even on basic matters, like whether Kemal was 'dictator or figurehead', as 'obscure'.[23] Britain had to guess at that issue from its reflections in three mirrors: solutions of correspondence between Ankara and its diplomats in Europe, material derived from Soviet sources by codebreaking and the SIS, and the GC&CS's work against French and Italian telegrams. Britain's best source on Turkish attitudes was French and Soviet diplomats in Ankara. Problems in assessing Turkish intentions were multiplied because Nationalist leaders were factionalized in ways the British knew they did not understand (as was also true of the Soviet elite), and physically divided between Ankara and Smyrna during September 1922. And what most concerned Britain was something beyond the realm of intelligence – to know the mind of one man, Kemal. The British received little material directly on or from him, but rather from people trying to influence him. The British were more confident in their intelligence on the USSR, even though it rested on less thorough access than with Turkey, France, or Italy. The SIS was Britain's fundamental source of information on Soviet policy; even codebreaking could cross-check from just one important tangent. No. 3 WOG mastered material to and from the Soviet legation in Ankara, but the GC&CS provided little on other aspects of Soviet policy. In the early 1920s, the SIS had good sources in the Soviet government. It believed that it had a reliable informer, with access to official documents and to the thinking of high level officials, in both the Soviet Commissariat of Foreign Affairs and the Kavbureau, the coordinating body for Communist Party agencies in the Caucasus, which influenced Soviet policy toward Turkey, along with less reliable agents in Soviet bureaus at Berlin, Helsinki and Riga. The SIS also received some information from French and possibly Polish agents in Russia and, after the crisis, from a sergeant at the Turkish Mission in Moscow.[24] Most SIS reports on Turks and Soviets were labelled 'A.1', meaning the source had proven reliable and had access to high level documents, some of which his SIS controller had seen in their original form. These agents appear to have provided genuine and important information, while No. 3 WOG demonstrated that Soviet behaviour toward Britain really was alarming; none the less, the SIS appears inadvertently to have distorted Soviet malevolence to Britain during the crisis by picking up a disproportionate number of indications of active emnity as against cautious hostility. Even more, No. 3 WOG often confirmed SIS reports, but never proved them wrong and demonstrated that SIS material on the Turkish Nationalists was excellent; hence, codebreaking increased the plausibility of the details reported by any one agent not supported by other sources and, more generally, SIS material on the USSR. The effect was unfortunate, because the SIS provided the most worrisome reports during the crisis, while its linking of Turks and Bolsheviks multiplied the effect of the most sinister material provided by codebreaking, the telegrams of the Soviet ambassador at Ankara, Aralov. This accidental outcome gave Whitehall a frightening picture of events and fuelled the most belligerent of British actions during the crisis.

These problems were multiplied by another and ironic one – British decision-makers trusted intelligence and used well what they had. Since 1920, Harington had been reading Kemal's telegrams, comparing words to deeds, learning how the Nationalist leader and his colleagues thought and argued and acted. Harington had just used intelligence and his local forces to break Greece's attempt to seize Istanbul during the Chatalja crisis. After Chanak, he noted that he had 'been very fortunate in possessing a highly efficient Intelligence Service throughout which has enabled me to keep touch not only with the military situation, but with the various organizations which have existed in the Near East. I venture to think that the information which has been obtained and forwarded has been of use to His Majesty's Government'.[25] His key steps, once realizing the Chanak crisis had broken – to act boldly so as to deter the Turks, to keep the allies united, and to commit men and prestige to Chanak – rested on intelligence. He told the War Office:

> Sources of our information are good enough to ensure our receiving early warning. Do not let us run away before danger is imminent. Let us rather stand united as we did at Chatalja. ... Secret information shows Bolshevik influence at Angora is being lost and Nureddin has declared Nationalists are not at war with England. I think Turks are waiting for a sign from England. If this is given they will be reasonable. Otherwise their attitude will change. It is therefore essential to maintain Allied unity.

He used 'secret information' of Nationalist intentions to convince his French and Italian counterparts to send forces to Chanak on 10 September, and he warned Whitehall intelligence also showed this effort might fail, because local French and Italian authorities 'favour eastern Thrace being given to Turks at once and are not disposed to scruple over neutrality to get it', 'when it comes to business they may not return compliment of allied unity which I showed over Chatalja'.[26] Harington's key decisions throughout the crisis, such as between 14–20 September to make Chanak strong enough to survive the worst case, on 24–26 September to warn the Turks that Britain would fight if attacked there, and, on 1 October to make the Turks commit themselves to talk or war, when their reserves were thought to be nine days from Istanbul but unlocated, reflected intelligence and his experience with its role in operations and politics. Like British generals in the Middle East during the Great War, Harington worked closely and informally with his codebreakers and intelligence staff; much of their advice and influence was expressed in person rather than on paper. He was fortunate to have No. 3 WOG and his chief intelligence officer, Colonel Gribbon, previously the MID's specialist in Turkish politics. Gribbon's role in Istanbul is shadowy but was substantial. Like most soldiers, he thought the diplomats' policy towards Turkey idiotic, as sometimes were his own views – he was exceptionally anti-semitic and once, in 1921, held that Kemal was secretly working for the Greeks, because his policy must destroy his country! Gribbon, apparently, was one of Harington's links to Turkish politicians. After the crisis, Curzon cursed the colonel as a 'political soldier' and forced his removal. Still, under Gribbon's direction in 1921–22, GSI Istanbul analyzed the Turkish Nationalists rather better than the embassy or the SIS; this expertise was an asset during the crisis.[27]

Harington controlled a source which collected a remarkable but manageable amount of accurate evidence, precisely on the topics which concerned him, with little irrelevant material, and a staff with experience appropriate to his problem – to manage the Turks and his local allies, to stabilize the situation around the Straits, and to bring Kemal to a negotiating table at which Britain would have cards to play. He shared the British consensus about the nature of those cards – control over Istanbul, the Gallipoli peninsula, and the Asiatic shores of the Bosphorus and the Dardanelles – but he and the General Staff were isolated over aims; he accepted without rancour that Turkey would regain its 1914 European borders, while Britain could not hope to achieve its desires on the 'freedom of the Straits'. Unlike diplomats and ministers, he had no responsibility for the failure of British policy, no need to defend his reputation, no rage at Turks for their victory, or at Italy, France and the USSR for assisting it and, apparently, less fear that Soviets or Kemal wanted war or would cause it. Conversely, if his colleagues felt strain – Rumbold held 'we must keep a stiff upper lip', but alarm sometimes broke his bluff façade; Brock's chief of staff thought his master near nervous breakdown ('I have to stop him every moment from doing silly panicky things')[28] – responsibility weighed on Harington with unique force. Sometimes ill, often tired, many of his telegrams drafted in the early hours, he was the architect of the high-risk strategy of bluff and deterrence Britain followed during the crisis, aiming for success 'with British flag flying high bars' while not himself causing 'another dreadful war', ready to open fire in defence of peace, fearing this might bring hundreds of thousands of Christians in Istanbul to what he termed 'holocaust'.[29] Underlying his assessments and actions were some understanding of and respect for his adversary. Kemal's aims and success enraged most British decision-makers, who viewed Turks as a trivial and evil race and the Turkish Nationalist programme, the

'National Pact', as a humiliation to the British nation. During 1921–22 Curzon frequently described Kemal as 'hostile and almost insolent', the word 'insolent' echoed by Churchill, a leading advocate of better relations with Turkey.[30] As the crisis broke, Lloyd George described Kemal as an alcoholic pederast, whose emissary to London had to be dragged from buggery in a brothel. In January 1921, conversely, Harington noted that venereal disease 'apparently has imbued [Kemal] with contempt and disgust for life, prohibited marriage and driven him to homosexual vice, and he has become somewhat immoderately addicted to liquor of late', but still he was charismatic and able, the only incorruptible leader in Turkey, jealous of others, hungry for fame, a patriot, a soldier, a man 'well qualified to lead the forlorn hope which on the one hand is playing with probable annexation by Reds and on the other is defying Europe'. This sketch was written when Harington thought Kemal's approach doomed but brave – now he viewed the gambler triumphant, after reading the mail which showed the working of that victory. He thought he knew Kemal and could manage him; Harington pinned British policy to that faith. It proved a damned near-run thing.[31]

Harington's actions during the crisis are universally praised, and rightly so; yet he, too, failed in important areas. He made good decisions which led others to make bad ones. He was the root cause for Britain's actions during the crisis. On 10–11 September, Lloyd George, the General Staff, and the Foreign Office all authorized the abandonment of Chanak; Harington convinced them to stay, to adopt a policy of bluffing Kemal, and then to fight at Chanak to signal determination; between 24 September and 9 October, he frequently was ready to open fire to further his policy. The latter worked, but it was risky and catching. His policy created a nervousness magnified by his messages to London. They did not report everything that mattered, while not everything they implied was entirely true. His frequent changes of opinion bewildered ministers. He phrased in an oblique fashion the notifications that he was considering the use of force under hypothetical circumstances, which led ministers and generals to believe he was seeking their permission to open fire immediately. Despite being a trained staff officer, Harington did not fully inform his superiors of the situation and his policy, which led to chaos on 28–29 September; in particular, his reports on the flash-point at Chanak were misleading. When combined with calculations of state and intelligence, they led ministers into a mess.

Whitehall faced greater problems than Harington, many of its own making. Counsels were divided – Brock and the Admiralty about what the Navy could achieve, the War Office against other departments over aims and means, ministers regarding the division of Turkish territories in Thrace, decision-makers sometimes pursuing private actions that contradicted accepted policy, the fighting services offering much bad advice, the politicians deaf to arguments which would subvert their hopes. These problems, complex enough, were multiplied by Whitehall's attempts to control more than it could do and the failure of that effort. It sought to manage everything Harington, Rumbold, and Brock did at Istanbul (not surprisingly, since these matters involved risks of war and to careers) and also the broad repercussions of the crisis on British policy across Europe and the Middle East. Harington could disregard past French and Italian actions; not Whitehall, because the past was closely linked to the present and future. The game was not yet done – must Britain let Turkey, France, Italy, and the USSR win through one inning's victory when another remained to play? The Foreign Office and ministers, responsible for the debacle, were angry at Turkey and their allies, at criticism and threats, unwilling to be pushed around and attracted to tough policy; personality became fundamental to policy. Churchill, no Turcophobe, resented Turkish challenges to British prestige and believed that, to restore its credibility, Britain must act boldly in the Straits and be seen to do so. Lloyd George, hostile to Turkey, believing Kemal had won simply because Greeks had panicked, had little appetite for more crow. Even the most realistic and pacific of major ministers, Austen Chamberlain, held Britain could neither tremble before threats nor let allies profit from treachery. Curzon's foreign policy was cool but the minister steamed, enraged by the allies and his colleagues. When the latter assailed him for cutting short his duties to return home for the weekend on 15 September, Curzon feared they would leave 'me to fight the battle and to bear the brunt of defeat'.[32] When Poincaré blamed him for the debacle on 22 September and refused to follow Curzon's line, the foreign secretary stormed from the meeting, guzzled brandy, and wept.

Whitehall was handling more issues, and harder ones, than Harington, and receiving more intelligence on a broader range of issues. Generally, the effect was positive – intelligence illuminated the crisis and its context, while statesmen assessed and used this material well. These sources were as close to perfection as is possible in any crisis; Britain read the telegrams of every participant, while officials or agents reported on most of their major decisions. Any bilateral diplomatic contact between France, Italy, and Turkey could be cross-checked through reports from two to four sources (solutions of the diplomatic traffic from, and reports through agents or officials on, both sides), though just one account existed of any Turco-Soviet talks, at best loosely confirmable with one other. Britain could see other states' attitudes, policies, and divisions, their views of the factions in third parties, and cases when junior figures contradicted the words or intentions of their seniors – or did they? It could view concealed levers and hidden hands, and decide how to manipulate or counter them before they moved. Thus, Aralov's telegrams outlined his attempts to manipulate the Turks into hostilities with Britain, and the means by which he hoped to do so. Ferid's messages outlined his intrigues with powerful elements in the French Army. All these reports concerned the Foreign Office. Thus, on 11 September, one senior official, Ronald Lindsay, interpreted Ferid to indicate 'a struggle in Paris between pro Turk marshals and other interests, who are concerned at the magnitude of the Turkish victory and the resultant arrogance of the Turk. This, says Ferid, is the moment to make a drive at the hesitating Poincaré, throw him on the side of the Marshals, and get Turkish control of the Straits'. Lindsay asked whether the British ambassador in Paris might now 'have a talk heart to heart with Poincare and find out if now there is not some common ground on which the French & British Govts [sic] could stand, both willingly, for dictating terms of peace?' This information reinforced Curzon's decision to move on Poincaré – that is, Turkey's assessment of its means for leverage helped to shape Britain's counter (and both failed).[33] Later, intelligence guided Harington and Curzon when determining how, when, and through whom to give Ankara messages of immediate peril if the Turks did not halt. Intelligence gave good news and showed the limits to bad, increasing one's certainty that unknown and unpleasant developments were not happening;

through crosschecking and corroboration one source could support (or weaken) the plausibility of important comments in another.

Nonetheless, when policy was so personalized, good intelligence also had unfortunate effects. One may see unflattering comments when reading other gentleman's mail; messages which describe their intention to defeat one's aims will seem sinister, especially when phrased in rude or threatening terms. It was mortifying simply to read telegrams which described Turkish consideration of their victory over Britain. An Ottoman diplomat at Rome, Osman Nizami Pasha, told his British counterpart that Britain must concede the 'National Pact' under threat of a Kemal 'determined to retake Constantinople and Adrianople by force of arms if necessary; he was in the midst of victorious army of 300,000 men splendidly equipped and regarded any Allied threat to stop him as mere bluff'. GC&CS and No. 3 WOG constantly solved Turkish, French, and Italian telegrams that made such comments, rubbing salt in British wounds. Curzon was bitter to read that Osman blamed him for Turkey's decision to attack, telling his ambassador 'this absurd and belated attempt to throw responsibility for recent Turkish actions upon attitude of His Majesty's Government towards Fathy Bey has received wide circulation in press and merits emphatic repudiation'. If he was so prickly when reading such comments in British traffic, he was doubly irritated to see it expressed so frequently in solutions of Turkish telegrams, his anger perhaps reinforced by Ferid's claim that he had primed the British press and 'Capitalists' to make this point.[34] Similarly, when Curzon began to break with Lloyd George, he sent five GC&CS flimsies to the prime minister, claiming they documented a history of personal diplomacy that had wrecked British foreign policy and caused the debacle.[35] Intelligence reinforced emotion; meanwhile, the crisis magnified the significance of technical difficulties. Between late 1921 and late 1922, for example, British intelligence was moving slowly from indicating Turkey a Bolshevik pawn to demonstrating the two were drifting apart. Precisely during the Chanak crisis, the SIS crossed this great divide. Secret information on Russo-Turkish relations was problematical precisely because the subject was undergoing radical change. In a year of peace, this would not have mattered; during this crisis, that issue almost led Britain to start a world war by attacking

Turkey and the USSR. Again, the normal corruptions in solutions had unusual effect. On 26 September, No. 3 WOG circulated a message, sent by Aralov to Moscow the day before: 'informed by Riza Nuri Bey of secret decision to occupy neutral zone. In opposition to this are Ali Fuad, Raouf Bey and Yussef Kemal who is hesitating. These three have left for Mustapha Kemal's Headquarters. Our friends have wired Mustapha Kemal not to be influenced by them. During Yussef's absence Riza is acting for him'.[36] This was powerful evidence of Turkish determination to escalate matters by moving on Chanak, of Nationalist intentions, Soviet manipulation, and Aralov's view of the factions in Ankara, including the belief that three key figures in the Ministry of Foreign Affairs opposed risky action – and yet the first half of the message was missing!

British decision-making was also dogged by unexpected problems of command, control, communications, and intelligence. Decisions were made by a tight triumvirate in Istanbul and a large and disparate group in London, several hundred miles apart, the latter's efforts at micromanagement frustrated by communication problems. Usually, it took seven to 12 hours from time of dispatch to time of receipt for a telegram from one body to reach the other, though a few 'very urgent' messages, often transmitted by wireless, arrived within two to three hours. Most cycles of communication between authorities in Istanbul and London took more than a day to complete. No telegram sent by Harington after 20:00, Istanbul time, for example, could reach Whitehall before 20:00 GMT (the great majority several hours later), nor be read and circulated by the recipient departments before 10:00 of the next day, nor reach ministers before the early afternoon; they would need time to assess and discuss such information, amidst the press of other material, and their comments or orders probably could not reach Istanbul until 23:00, local time – where they were unlikely to be read until the next morning, eight hours later, or 35 hours after the initial transmission! Any uncertainty over orders, or garbling in messages, would automatically worsen the situation. On 5 October, during the most chaotic moments of the Mudania conference, the Cabinet could not meet Harington's request that he receive instructions by 10:00 the next day because his key telegrams were 'very corrupt and incomplete'; in effect, he had to make British decisions for war or peace on his own.[37] All this produced a systematic problem. Whitehall was telling Harington how to act 12 hours ahead, through its reaction to a local situation 18 hours past, which led him to debate his orders, thus reopening the can of worms (or never letting it close). These problems were central to Harington's calculations and to Whitehall's confusion about them. Authorities in London and Istanbul reacted to the same wide range of political and military factors but 12 to 36 hours apart, a long time in politics, without being able completely to inform each other of details important to decisions. Ministers made tactical decisions: Harington, Brock, and Rumbold political ones. Authorities in Istanbul dominated British decision-making, which became a reaction to circumstances around the Straits. Fundamental strategy turned on one commander's reaction to tactical minutiae. In particular, Harington made the decisive political decisions: London followed him to Chanak, to the brink of war, and back again. In the process, war was averted and Lloyd George destroyed.

Intelligence was fundamental to this problem. During the crisis, as hard and fast decisions had to be made, waves of intelligence, orders, queries and assessments from London and Istanbul crashed into each other. Decision-making was swamped by the combination of Whitehall's efforts at micromanagement, its reading of intelligence, its weaknesses in assessment, and its reaction to Harington's reports; his different conclusions and his command over No. 3 WOG and local British power and policy; and from the 12 to 36 hour difference in their intelligence pictures and operational circumstances. The issue was who knew what and when, how they reacted to news, and how they could act on their views. Twelve hours' difference in time and one message might be enough to reverse this balance. On 29 September, for example, No. 3 WOG solved a message from Ferid to Ankara, in answer to queries from the Ministry for Foreign Affairs on 23 September. He declared that Italy and France wanted good terms with Turkey. Britain's

> object in being in Straits is to separate Asia from Europe and prevent Franco-Turkish co-operation and to confine France to Europe. Both press and Government realize this ... France are genuinely assisting us and Poincare wishes us to be placed on X [sic] with Europe and is right when he says Turks are not

negroes. We will be on equal terms probably at conference before which we ought to ask for evacuation of Constantinople and Thrace. The best course for us to adopt is to tell France before conference what we cannot give up politically or militarily in the same way as I asked their opinion about Straits. Majority of France is in our favour. Leave economic questions for Allied discussion and you can defend these modern principles at conference ultimately.[38]

Ministers did not have this telegram when they ordered Harington to deliver his ultimatum; but he did when he read their order. He no doubt noted that a Turk notorious for belligerence had finally come to favour conference before conflict. Indeed, a striking number of indicators of improvement arrived in Istanbul and London just after ministers issued their ultimatum.

For convenience sake, British decisions during the Chanak crisis can be divided into four phases. First, between 29 August to 20 September, authorities slowly realized they faced a problem, but believed they could overcome it by demonstrating resolve, sending reinforcements, moving diplomatic levers, and making concessions. Second, between 20 and 27 September, decision-makers gradually concluded they faced a crisis and, perhaps worse, Kemal was trembling on the decision for war and Allied unity had failed – the Admiralty saw 'no doubt that the French Government are hand in glove with the Nationalists'; Rumbold complained that Britain '*cannot* count on our gallant allies'.[39] Britain did not want to fight Turkey, or to surrender to it, France, and the USSR. Britain and the Turkish Nationalists pursued similar policies. Each deployed large forces and exhibited a determination to use them, so to bolster their prestige and ability to define the terms for the most minute aspects of negotiations. Neither preferred war as a first option but each was willing to fight if necessary, and each intended to hold the same territory of strategic value. This made conflict a real possibility. These developments magnified the sense that British prestige – the international credibility on which its power rested – was at stake and must be restored. Though it continued to follow its earlier policy, military matters became central, with the aims of deterring attack, strengthening Britain's diplomatic position, and showing resolution at Chanak for its own sake. That location was assigned increasing weight, because at Chanak, the only place where Britain stood alone and could be challenged by Turkey, it might win a prestige victory over its allies and its enemies. Attitudes on this issue were ambivalent, however, because a military position suitable for bluff confronted the risk of attack, with reinforcements days away and disaster possible; authorities knew their weakness tempted the fates and the Turks. Third, between 28 and 30 September, decision-makers became convinced they faced peril, and Whitehall ordered Harington to deliver an ultimatum followed by a preemptive strike, which he declined to do because he believed peril a few days further off. Finally, between 1 and 10 October, British and Turkish forces poured into the theatre and Britain pursued an armistice while recognizing war was likely. It generally forced its terms for the process of a peace settlement, and the crisis abated. In both its success and failure, intelligence shaped all these events.

Before 20 September, intelligence was irritating but not alarming. Sources in Turkish embassies abroad, their accounts confirmed by solutions of Turkish telegrams, reported that Paris and Rome had promised not to oppose Turkey's Anatolian offensive. French authorities had promised aid for the attack, stated that Britain intended to destroy Turkey while the Greek army was too weak to stand a heavy onslaught, and noted France would not let Britain take Istanbul as it had Egypt in 1882.[40] French and Italian telegrams loosely confirmed these accounts and showed contempt for British policy; the Italian ambassador to London wrote later: 'It is in accordance with the habit of this people to consider and settle the difficulties of the day, leaving the more remote difficulties to the future.'[41] The GC&CS showed where the allies aimed to push British policy and how, their fears at what might happen should their efforts fail, the internal debate and the discussions with each other and the Turks that they were trying to hide from Britain. On 20 September, for example, Italian material showed that French officials had just informed Italian ones:

> POINCARE has not yet decided to make, known, even in a semi-official form, the French point of view. If he declared at this moment the French opinion regarding ADRIANOPLE and

the Thracian boundaries he would on the one hand (? alienate, irritate) ENGLAND too much, while she may perhaps be induced to accept the French standpoint by degrees, and on the other hand he might perhaps evoke new and greater pretensions on the part of ANGORA.⁴²

Similarly, after the Paris meetings, the GC&CS revealed that just before them, the Italian foreign minister, Signor Schanzer, had asked his ambassador in Paris, Count Sforza, to tell Poincare but not Curzon that the most controversial issue at hand might best be solved through the temporary expedient of extending Ottoman administration over all of Turkey in Europe, because of a hidden advantage. This would essentially be a Kemalist administration, so meeting Nationalist demands that it receive all of these territories while denying Britain any chance to block that ambition or to gain a bargaining chip from the effort.⁴³

Its allies had broken the agreement of March 1922 and sold British interests to further their own, and everyone was trying to beat England again. This enraged Whitehall. It explains Chamberlain and Lloyd George's hostility to France on 18–19 September, and Curzon's accusations of treachery in his meetings with Poincare and Sforza in Paris during the following four days. The GC&CS's material reinforced the contempt British officials felt for one ally. Italy dared not act apart from France, its officials trembled at tiny problems and grasped for crumbs of prestige, ministers pointing proudly to their worth, ministers obsessed with attempts to hold the peace conference in Venice; however annoying the French, at least their telegrams were manly. The Italians were also believed to be selling machine guns to the Turks at Istanbul, which the Foreign Office regarded as 'traitorous proceedings'.⁴⁴ This illuminates Curzon's belief that the French have 'a serious political interest in a just settlement. The [Italians] are mere bagmen, who will sell either party, notably ourselves'.⁴⁵ Yet these reports were past history. Britain had expected betrayal from its allies, and indications of their present behaviour were encouraging. No intercept or agent indicated that either ally was encouraging Turks to attack British forces, or doing anything other than try to solve the crisis, in their own interests. Even when condemning British policy as 'unreasonable and stupid', and asking that Italy receive economic concessions from Ankara, a senior figure in the Italian Ministry for Foreign Affairs, Count Lago, still told Fethi Bey that Italy supported Britain's position over the freedom of the Straits; Whitehall did not want war, its policy was confused 'probably due to bewilderment caused by defeat of Greeks' , and 'in the meantime, to avoid affording any pretext to Britain, Nationalists should abstain from any hasty action against British troops until situation clears'; they must not attack Istanbul. Schanzer, too, urged the Turks to wait for negotiations: 'to try to capture Constantinople by force of arms would only have serious consequences'.[46] This intercept confirmed the Italian account given to Britain's ambassador in Rome. Indeed, codebreaking generally showed that Italian or French statements to British representatives were true, if rarely the whole truth, which reinforced the significance of their comments when there was no confirmation. There was one great exception to this rule. Fethi's messages indicated either that Poincaré was disingenuous to claim, on 1 and 22 September, that he had told the Turkish Nationalists 'how deplorable it would be if Angora were to take the offensive when an Allied Conference had been practically decided upon at Venice', or else that he did not know his subordinates had been less restrained (a worthwhile point to ponder).[47]

At least this intelligence showed the limits to bad news and revealed the aims, fears, and vulnerabilities of Britain's allies. France and Italy wished to use the political credit just gained to further their economic interests in Turkey, but feared that escalation in the crisis might wreck their hopes. Italy worried that defeat in Anatolia might spur Greeks to seize Istanbul and was angered by British efforts to mobilize the 'Little Entente' against Turkey, in both cases from concern the conflict could spread easily to the Balkans and so cripple Italian interests. Solutions consistently showed that senior French and Italian authorities feared the combination of Turkish success and British intransigence might cause Kemal to strike Istanbul, or perhaps even betray his friends. French authorities worried Kemal might attack Syria and protested Turkish atrocities against Christians. No. 3 WOG showed the Turks unsure of diplomatic support from France over Thrace, and so nervous, while Poincaré advised against any attack on Britain.[48]

Two more frightening pictures were forming by 20 September. Secret information on Russo-Turkish relations was as contradictory as the matter itself. The two states had a military agreement, and Whitehall believed the Soviets had pledged naval assistance to Turkey against Greece, especially submarines, which in turn might be used against Britain. Fragmentary information from No. 3 WOG led Harington's staff to conclude the USSR had sold submarines to Turkey, though Brock's staff doubted this had occurred.[49] The Admiralty closely monitored that issue throughout this crisis, and it fundamentally shaped decisions.[50] Believing the USSR ready to attack Britain and with submarines, on 18 September ministers in effect declared war. Any Soviet warships or submarines which approached British vessels during the crisis must be destroyed. 'It was not deemed expedient to warn the Soviet Government at present of these intentions.'[51] Five days later, the Atlantic Fleet was told to ready a commerce protection force for the Baltic Sea in case of war with the USSR while, to keep the Turks out of Europe, Brock was to prepare to seize potential Soviet transports in the Black Sea, an act of war against the USSR. Had war broken out with Turkey, Britain would almost immediately have extended it to the USSR. On 8 October Brock intended, should the Mudania Conference collapse, to send submarines to sink a Soviet submarine reported to be at the Turkish port of Ineboli.[52] The explosives were piling up; if Britain and Turkey went to war, the British would attack the USSR, and presumably Greece would join in, while Turkey would exploit its secret alliances with the USSR and Bulgaria.

These decisions stemmed from knowledge of past Soviet hostility to Britain and suspicion of more, and from some evidence of present malevolence. During 1921–22, British diplomats had varied from believing Turkey almost a Soviet puppet, to viewing this alliance as unnatural, one which ultimately Kemal must break.[53] By mid-1922, diplomats at Istanbul held that Russo-Turkish relations were strengthening. Curzon thought the SIS and codebreaking showed 'that combination has been growing much firmer – that Mustapha Kemal is tight in the grip of the Bolsheviks – that his truculence as regards the Paris terms arises from his reliance on their support'.[54] As the Chanak crisis began, however, in a halting but ambiguous manner, secret intelligence began to indicate rupture in these relations, words barely papering over conflicts. The USSR expelled Turkey's diplomatic agent in Moscow, Kemal's friend, Ali Fuad. It was thought to believe Ankara behind anti-Soviet unrest in the Caucasus and a rebellion in Central Asia, involving the wartime Turkish leader, Enver Pasha, who soon died in action against Soviet forces. These points were resonant, because the British had viewed Enver as the leader of the pro-Soviet and anti-British factions in Ankara, and as the unholy link between Bolshevism, German militarism, and pan-Islamism (which, in fact, he had been); if an Enver had broken with Moscow, what might a Kemal do? Meanwhile, reported the SIS, the Kavbureau opposed further aid to Ankara because it thought a secret clause of the Franklin Bouillon Treaty pledged Turkey to attack the Caucausus if the USSR fought France's allies in Eastern Europe. An equally secret clause of a Russo-Turkish Treaty, the SIS believed, committed Turkey to assist the USSR should it be attacked by a Balkan or Caucasian state.[55] Meanwhile, the Turkish press attacked the USSR and the Turkish Communist Party was banned.[56] The SIS indicated that the beliefs Britain was anti-Turkish, and the Soviets would betray their pledge to invade Romania at Kemal's request, had spurred Turkey's Anatolian offensive.[57] Against this, Aralov publicly committed the USSR to support Turkey against Britain at Istanbul and the Straits; the SIS took this as further proof of the 'close co-operation' between Soviets and Turks.[58] Russo-Turkish relations were confusing and alarming, and the British could not simply assume the best.

More significant was the image built up of the Nationalists. Agents and intercepts indicated Turkish policy was not absolutely fixed, but it wanted its European borders of 1914, including the Straits, perhaps with limits on its sovereignty there.[59] Solutions of Turkish, French, and Italian traffic all showed Ankara's demands that a quick peace conference end the crisis (and the First World War in the Near East!) on the terms of the National Pact. The British knew the Nationalist leadership was factionalized, though not how, save that Kemal was the key; intelligence filled in this picture. From codebreaking, the Foreign Office made shrewd guesses at the character and position of some decision-makers; the Turkish foreign secretary, Raouf Bey, for example, was 'the leader of the Moderate party', which wished to achieve Turkish aims without war, views shared by Hamid Bey and

Mustafa Reschid, the Nationalist agents in Istanbul and London with whom British figures most tended to work. All sources concurred that Ferid, a 'hothead', encouraged Kemal to treat Britain as an irreconcilable enemy. On 5 September, for example, Ferid informed Ankara (correctly) that Britain was delaying the attempts of France and Italy to call an international conference; Turkey must respond by seizing all the territories it wished to control – 'Our foot is black upon Smyrna' – and by manoeuvring to throw responsibility for any failure in negotiations on Britain; meanwhile, he would 'reinforce our war preparations by diplomacy'. After solving a message from Raouf asking Ferid for detailed information on French and Italian policy, to guide Ankara's preparations for a peace conference, GSI commented Raouf 'is being kept in the dark. Ferid always sends him provocative information'.[60] British officials, however, were blind regarding attitudes in Ankara. They thought most Turkish Nationalist leaders hostile, and the SIS defined Kemal as the leader of the 'military party', which wished to humiliate Britain and to fight it.[61] Only one report indicated Kemal had any other view.[62] This assessment was alarmist, but only slightly so – perhaps too slightly to have been avoided. In fact, Turkish Nationalist leaders were hostile to Britain, because it was the only Great Power left in their way and willing to fight if it did not concede their aims. Kemal did not plan to start another war, but this intention was hard to discern, because threat and resolve were part of his policy. In a public speech, as his men moved north from Smyrna, he told them France and Italy were friends, but Britain a foe. They were not to start a war, but they must occupy 'every inch of ground' Britain did not hold; Turkey would pursue its aims through threat and diplomacy but, if this failed, within a few months it would drive on Istanbul and close the Dardanelles with howitzers and mines.[63] British intelligence easily found proof Turks wished to wreck British interests, humiliate it, and close in on British forces and if necessary attack. All of these things were true; unfortunately, but unsurprisingly, intelligence could not get the precise time and conditions for an attack. Good intelligence was bound to be alarming because such was the situation. In this context, one SIS report of 18 September echoed over the coming 12 days: on 30 September Kemal would deliver an ultimatum that the Allies evacuate Istanbul within 24 hours or be attacked.[64] This report, magnified in the retelling and loosely corroborated from other sources, was repeated and believed by ministers, generals, and diplomats.

This intelligence shaped Britain's understanding of the situation and of the best means to defend its interests and of how diplomatic leverage and military coercion could achieve those ends. Until 10 September, secret and official reports alike were not alarming, which reinforced a tendency to wait on events; but a sense of urgency and difficulty emerged over the following week. Though official sources provided much of this picture, secret intelligence was of equal importance. Intelligence indicated a dynamic and uncertain situation, but not an entirely unpredictable one. The best outcome was that Britain would recoup its prestige by standing firm against allies and dangers and by enforcing its terms about how to settle the conflict (even though, given the Turkish victory and the Greek defeat, the National Pact must define the nature of the settlement). The surrender on content doubled Whitehall's focus on form, on the need to ensure that Turkey (and the allies) were seen to follow lines of process defined by Britain. The worst outcomes were that Kemal (and therefore, most probably, the USSR) would attack, or the allies would entirely betray Britain. Either case seemed possible but unlikely; conceivable only if the Turks believed they could safely attack Britain and that it rejected their basic aims. This should not occur if Britain signalled resolution, power, and concessions, or if the allies warned Kemal off, which they would do if they feared disproportionate British retaliation. Intelligence showed many ways to block these worst case outcomes by pursuing the best one. It was fundamental to the policy British decision-makers defined between 10 and 15 September, and pursued, with wrinkles, to the end of the crisis – to put pressure on everyone at once by playing the diplomatic equivalent of the strategy of 'chicken', when two cars drive headlong at each other, and one driver suddenly throws his steering wheel out the window. The means were to take a tough and highly publicized stand: by refusing to let Turkey take Istanbul, Thrace or the Straits without first fighting Britain, or else until a conference with legitimacy inherited from Sevres settled the issue; by sending powerful reinforcements and leaving trip wire forces between Kemal and his hearts' desires; and by accepting (*sotto voce*) the National

Pact in European Turkey. The aims were to pull its allies onto Britain's side, ideally to state that they would assist it or at least press the Turks to halt, for fear Britain unchecked would start a war, which would wreck their local aims and cause circumstances in which the Turks would betray them while England broke the entente. Such moves, in turn, would erode the allies' relations with Ankara and weaken the 'military party' there, which would meanwhile be deterred by British warnings and force, while concessions would strengthen the 'moderate party' and rebuild British relations with a resurgent Turkey. In pursuit of this policy, Harington led Britain to Chanak, and a policy of bluff and deterrence. The Cabinet extended this lead on 15 September, through decisions summarized by Curzon: '*Broadly* speaking the plan is to strengthen our position at the impending conference by mobilising as many forces as we can command, to show Kemal that we are in earnest, and to prevent a sudden and successful attack by him upon the Allied positions and a possible eruption into Europe'. Curzon and his colleagues doubted Kemal would enter the Neutral Zones (the territories around Chanak and on the Ismid peninsula which the allies had, in theory, declared out of bounds to Greeks and Turks during their recent struggle) and start a war. They thought the key to success lay in forging a joint policy with France, through meetings with Poincaré and Sforza on 20–22 September, and the strengthening of Britain's hand by despatching reinforcements to the Dardanelles.[65]

Intelligence was fundamental to the formulation of this policy, but in alloy with calculations of military power and prestige. Its influence was more particular regarding tactics. Intelligence showed Britain how to use leverage and against what targets, where to deliver messages and through whom, and helped it to measure the effect of these actions. Italy was mistress to fear – push her to his arms. Rome could not be seduced except through a *menage à trois*? Why pay there for favours which could be sampled only through Paris, but then for free? Of course, diplomatic leverage could achieve only so much. Britain had none to use against the USSR – it could respond to Soviet hostility only by preparing for war; it had to send substantial forces to the Straits as a precondition for diplomatic leverage, to build the military credibility needed to sustain bluff and deterrence, and convince allies and orientals Britain would fight. Again, intelligence could support the grasping of many levers at once, some of them seemingly contradictory. It showed Turks apparently believed Britain wished to seize the Straits forever, and were using that argument to gain support with Italy and France, with effect. One Foreign Office official asked: 'Can we not in some way explode the theory that our object is permanent British occupation of Constantinople? But it is so universal that a denial would probably be discounted.'[66] Still, the Foreign Office did try to pass such a message through the allies to Ankara. Curzon informed Paris of British concessions about Thrace, precisely so the news would reach Ferid and thus his masters, to show Britain was not anti-Turkish and so strengthen the 'moderate' party.[67] Ministers, meanwhile, hoped to manipulate these same concerns by making France and Italy fear that if they did not help Britain defend the Dardanelles, Britain would take it. In Lloyd George's phrase, seconded by Chamberlain, 'the mounting of heavy howitzers on the Gallipoli Peninsula would be very important from a diplomatic point of view. The French were afraid of our establishing a second Gibraltar on the Gallipoli Peninsula'.[68] These different modes of leverage worked to achieve one end. Again, knowledge could be used like a rapier to shape one individual's views on a specific issue – on 22 September, Curzon refuted one of Poincaré's claims by stating that 'the British Foreign Office knew in fact from their own sources of information that Ferid had actually advised Mustapha Kemal to cross the Straits and attack the Allies' (a slightly distorted statement).[69]

This lever pulling had some effect, but not immediately. England delivered the messages defining its policy, and others understood them, but did not bow to Britain. France and Italy denied its policy could work. They refused to support the impossible effort of blocking the Straits, and sought to change and defeat British aims. Still, they also met minimum British desiderata, by asking Turks not to provoke Britain and by stating Ankara could receive its demands through negotiations. Indeed, though the British did not yet fully realize it, their pressure had moved the French a fair distance; if they encouraged the British to leave Chanak, they firmly warned the Turks from that town and any provocation to Britain. How the allies would jump if the crisis escalated was uncertain, and their attitudes remained of concern, but Britain's greater problem was Turkey. Though the allies invited it to enter armistice talks and prepare for peace settlement, and their representatives in Istanbul pressed the point, the Turks did not respond formally while their forces advanced into the theatre. The only official Turkish overture to Britain during this period came on 27 September when, in response to a message from Harington, Kemal denounced British behaviour, but also expressed a 'genuine and sincere' willingness to 'avoid the occurrence of incidents'.[70]

Whitehall had started a war of nerves; now it had to suffer one. As it waited between 20 and 27 September, the intelligence picture darkened. Agents and slowly solved Turkish messages provided signs of further Allied misbehaviour, even hints that shoals of treachery lay ahead. French and Italian authorities told Nationalist representatives they would not fight Turkish forces. Poincaré gained kudos by pledging Turkey a status equal to all parties at the peace conference, and for saying 'Turks are not negroes'. Important hints emerged of earlier efforts to bribe the Allies away. Fethi pressed Ankara to meet Italian demands for economic concessions, specifically to buy Italy from Britain; not merely Curzon believed Italians bagmen, or worse![71] Again, before the Paris conference Schanzer told Sforza he hoped the French fleet would not help Britain 'to prevent any passage of the Straits'. Sforza should raise the matter with Poincaré, and state that though Italy would follow France's lead, 'we cannot ignore the danger that naval action may involve us in warlike operations and cause us to lose the favourable position which our initiative for a peace conference has won for us in relation to the Turks'.[72] Even worse, No. 3 WOG and the GC&CS solved an older message from Ferid, claiming the eminent French soldier, Marshall Lyautey, 'the most important personality in official and private politics of to-day', had given an extremely anti-British memorandum to Poincaré – 'We are under the necessity of either submitting to British aspirations or opposing them. Our freedom bids us oppose them. We were not victorious in order that FRANCE might become a slave' – recommending France systematically weaken Britain, among other means by supporting Turkey. Ferid indicated he would exploit this opportunity.[73] Yet codebreaking again showed the limits to bad signs and that some parts of British policy were working as intended. Between 15 and 20 September, Italian and French authorities advised Ferid and Fethi that Turkey should not attack

Britain, and held that Britain would cede Turkey's basic demands at a conference. A senior figure at the Quai, Jules Laroche, told Ferid 'he had studied the British temperament for twenty five years. They had no capacity for grasping a fact quickly, but when once they grasped a fact, then they took their new course instantly'. Ferid presented one his favourite arguments:

> I pointed out that the strength of FRANCE lay in her land forces, and that it was in the interests of FRANCE to use the Straits as a bridge rather than [?open sea], and so preserve a road, in her rivalry with GREAT BRITAIN, which would join FRANCE to ASIA. For these reasons, I submitted, it was FRANCE's definite interest to strengthen in the greatest degree possible our sovereignty over the Straits.
> "We cannot", replied LAROCHE, "to-day forget the relations now existing between FRANCE and BRITAIN. We are not free to follow an entirely separate policy."

Even Ferid had to inform Ankara that 'Ministry of Foreign Affairs advises [sic] us not to spoil our favourable chance by attacking the British', and warned that Britain would concede Istanbul and the Maritza line at a peace conference, but it would fight if attacked. When Ferid stated, 'This would not apply to Chanak naturally', the MFA replied that it hoped Britain would not stay there, but even with Chanak 'an occupation without firing was important'.[74]

News on the allies was annoying; that on other powers alarming. During and after the Paris conference, the only direct information available on Turkish thinking indicated the strength of the 'war party' abroad, and implied the same balance in Ankara. Codebreaking showed that Turkish diplomats, especially Ferid but also Hamid, initially described British policy as a bluff and recommended lines of policy certain to provoke explosion: Turkey should enter a conference only after Istanbul and Thrace were returned, or 'our army can walk into Chanak and probably not even meet British force. We must settle down at Chanak. I think it is best to delay our advance on Constantinople and that our going to Chanak is sufficient to force Europe to give us Thrace to Maritza. We can always drive Greeks from Thrace. It would be a good idea to ask Greeks now to evacuate Thrace'. However, by 26–27

September, these messages changed somewhat. Ferid became less forcefully hostile, though still favouring some form of confrontation, Hamid clearly recommended that Ankara accept an armistice, while, from London, Reschid warned consistently Britain was serious and would fight if provoked, which Turkey therefore must not do.[75] The significance of this key indicator was easy to miss, however, in the context of the whole. Allied assessments of Turkish intentions, for example, became more fearful, though largely by accident. Much of it rested on older intelligence, generally from just before and during the Paris conference, sent in French and Italian systems the GC&CS found harder to break, its effect felt out of its time; meanwhile, some of the most encouraging Allied telegrams from 20–27 September were not solved until after 30 September. Again, much of the news of Turkish belligerence, each piece corroborating and corroborated by all the rest, was merely an echo of earlier tough and publicized British actions. They had been intended to influence other parties, and did so, but not entirely as expected, due to the reciprocal and competitive nature of this crisis. This approach angered Turkish decision-makers, who felt the need to respond in kind, by aggressively displaying their force so to bolster the military backing for their diplomacy and by seeking to push a pin through any balloon of bluff. Their belligerent statements and actions, in turn, fed Aralov's manipulation of Ankara, alarmed France and Italy, and provided reports from multiple sources which multiplied British fears the Turks might attack, when in fact it was hearing only the sound of wheels it had set in motion.

On 21 September, the GC&CS showed Schanzer's fear that British policy, which 'throws down a challenge to KEMAL and does it at the moment when he is most ready to take it up', might provoke a disastrous war in the Balkans and a 'complete loss of [allied] prestige vis-à-vis the whole Mohammaden world'. The Italian minister in Istanbul, Signor Garroni, feared Kemal would strike unless he quickly received his demands:

> His intimates declare that he is not at all concerned about the possible action of the British fleet, recalling that, even though reinforced by ... it was not able to force the defences of the DARDANELLES. He considers that he has to-day ... sufficient

to ... on the Asiatic coast and through aeroplanes to paralyze British naval action. He also considers that he has the means to transport his troops into THRACE where the disorganisation of the Greek troops is such as to render success easy [sic].

While noting 'exaggerations' in these claims, Garroni thought any attempt to defend the Neutral Zones 'would do nothing but incur a useless sacrifice of human lives, with a grave responsibility upon whosoever destined them to certain destruction'. On 22 September, Garroni reported that the French legation in Istanbul expected the Nationalists to take Chanak, 'without however immediately attacking the neutral zone in the vicinity of CONSTANTINOPLE', where 'the Turkish army would remain for perhaps fifteen days on the watch along the frontier of ANATOLIA [sic] and the Asiatic coast, ready to advance on Constantinople if in the meantime the Allies do not make a declaration in favour of peace on the basis of the National Pact'. Thus, the French and Italian legations in Istanbul appeared to confirm SIS warnings of an imminent Turkish attack on Chanak and ultimatum at Istanbul.[76]

Even more frightening were revelations about Russo-Turkish relations. While not absolutely clear-cut – intercepts showed that on 8 September Aralov told Moscow 'Military success has turned Turkish Government's head' and diplomatic pressure alone could save the Turkish Communist Party from mass arrest[77] – these reports were very consistent. The SIS warned, 'under reserve', that a source in the Soviet Mission in Riga thought the Soviet–Turkish agreement bound Russia to support a Turkish seizure of Istanbul and the Straits, and their closure to the allies.[78] Reliable SIS reports indicated that Kemal, under Soviet influence, favoured immediate attack on Chanak and Istanbul.[79] Intercepts showed that on 14 September the Soviet leader Karakhan had told the Turkish agent in Moscow that Britain would not simply abandon the Straits, and ' we must ?evict [sic] them by force. Brigand bands in the neutral zone or a threat on Irak might, however, attain this end'.[80] On 25 September, an alarmed Rumbold cabled that 'absolute proof from usual secret sources' (probably a message from Aralov claiming that he and his Turkish friends, was endeavouring to defeat the moderate party) showed Bolsheviks were pushing Turkey to war; the MID had already reached this conclusion.[81] Rumbold hoped Britain would refrain from provoking the Turks, but that advice was not easy to swallow.[82] Information indicated the Soviets were seriously considering military intervention. Many unreliable reports from Eastern Europe and Persia indicated Soviet preparations for war, which only the British military attache in Warsaw doubted.[83] On 25 September, a major SIS report, labelled 'A.1', tied all the strings together, though much of the detail had been provided on Saturday, 23 September.[84] Kemal had asked the Soviets to attack Romania. He would drive on the Dardanelles if the reply was favourable. The Soviet leadership was split, Trotsky and Bukharin favouring intervention, Chicherin opposing it, but the USSR was making preparations for intervention, strengthening the Caucasian army and the Black Sea fleet. These reports came at the crucial moment, when Lloyd George's government made the decisions which led to its downfall. Rumours of Soviet intrigue no doubt strengthened the resolve of ministers predisposed to expecting Soviet malevolence, especially of anti-Bolsheviks like Churchill and Lord Birkenhead who were central in these decisions. Other reports indicated the Turks were preparing underground agencies for uprisings in Istanbul and Thrace, attempting to foment a war in the Balkans and a pan-Islamic conflict within the British Empire.[85]

As the crisis reached its height on 29 September, the intelligence picture was at its worst, because of uncertainty about Turkish military dispositions, some clear proof of danger from codebreaking, and SIS reports of Turkish and Soviet hostility. The changes in the picture were not fundamental, but the bad news gave an edge to a weightier matter – changes in attitudes; heightened fears for the security of British forces, emotional responses to the positions of other states, the tension produced by the war of nerves, the fact that authorities in Istanbul and London focused increasingly on capabilities and plans for war, and therefore on indications Turkey was threatening to start one. They believed a Turkish ultimatum or attack was imminent, and read ambiguous information in that light. It was easy to find what they expected to see. British decision-makers were primed for the worst case.

Two groups dissented from this view: decision-makers in Istanbul, and the Foreign Office. Curzon and his officials profited here from their weaknesses as well as strengths. Their professional deformation – their focus on intentions instead of capabilities, on diplomacy against reality – and their contempt for Turks and Bolsheviks, cost Britain in many cases, but not this one. They thought Turks would not attack Britain without French consent, which was inconceivable. Even after the clashes of 20–22 September, Curzon believed Britain's point made. Poincaré 'will now stop Kemal from any precipitate or foolhardy advance and that our strong policy will thus have been justified ... I would urge that while maintaining our position we desist from any action likely to provoke immediate hostilities'. He told colleagues of signs of 'consciousness of France of moral weakness of her own position and deserting the allies from admitted motives of fear' and 'her genuine apprehension . that we not only mean but are able to act alone'. These negotiations, and those needed to call an armistice, had 'gained' several days to strengthen Britain in Turkey: 'Before the end of this time our preparations should be complete and in any case the prospect of an attack upon Chanak and Ismid seems now to be receding.'[86] Curzon believed France would prevent Turkish attack, thus the crisis would not produce war and military problems were irrelevant. His colleagues probably read these comments as cover for another defeat of British policy by French diplomats and Turkish soldiers – with some truth. Curzon did not fully understand Kemal's resolve, Poincaré's power, and the situation in the Straits; but in essence his views were right. He and his officials were predisposed to ignore military danger and to interpret intelligence calmly; they also had an assessment system able to track key indicators, such as the more pacific tone of Turkish diplomats from 20 September, and the hints the allies were holding steady. Its intelligence assessment remained confident. 'Lyautey's alleged report and Ferid's estimate of his influence are of great interest but "Laroche's attitude is even more so"', it noted; Karakhan's advice 'typical of Russian opportunism & cynicism', but no more.[87] On 28 September, it remained calm – and confident – opposing even a minor modification in the British bargaining position, despite accepting reports '15,000 men are ready in Constantinople. ... The Nationalists are being urged both by Ferid in Paris & by Aralov in Angora to go to Chanak'.[88] The Foreign Office did not fear threats, because it thought these would not be delivered. Meanwhile, it simply held the ring, waiting on events.

Curzon granted Mustafa Reschid's request for a meeting but not in a rush, despite knowing him as the Turk abroad most constantly warning those at home not to push Britain; Curzon felt no imperative need to move, and waited for the right moment to send him a message (perhaps fearing rush would send the wrong one).[89]

Between 20 and 28 September, decision-makers in Istanbul were equally concerned with intelligence but far more with danger and the need for messages. 'We are literally living on a volcano here', Rumbold thought; a spark might set Istanbul ablaze.[90] He worried more than Harington about the potential for military disaster, and interpreted intelligence to mean Britain must hold fundamentals but pass no gas to hotheads in Ankara. Yet Rumbold, too, had to wait on events, because Harington was the main channel for negotiations over an armistice with the allies and the Nationalists. Uniting force and policy, the general's calculations became even more political. On 22 September, possibly in reaction to Ferid's first comments on the Paris conference, Harington thought the Quai d'Orsay was 'egging' the Turks on, by claiming Britain would not resist Turkey at Chanak. Almost immediately, codebreaking showed Hamid had told Ankara the garrison at Chanak 'is believed of no value' and Ferid urged its immediate occupation, the Italian admiral in Istanbul warned of imminent attack – and then Turkish forces entered the Neutral Zone at Chanak.[91] Harington assumed these events were one. At the Neutral Zone, Turks were testing Britain.[92] Aiming to use force to achieve specific political objectives, he sent his commander, Colonel Shuttleworth, a telegram *en clair* – an extremely rare procedure. Perhaps he was gambling that Turks or Allies would intercept the message and, thus, lead Ankara to understand Britain's resolution. In polite and pompous language, Harington stated Turks might think Britain would not fight for Chanak. This was wrong; but before opening fire, Shuttleworth must give his counterpart every honourable opportunity to withdraw.[93] The colonel never could deliver this message, but it may well have been intercepted by some party and made available to the Turks. In any case, Harington delivered such messages through other Allied commanders and Hamid and, by radio, direct to Mustafa Kemal.

Harington's assessment in these days was complicated. He thanked Brock for naval assistance at Chanak: 'The moral effect of the immediate and powerful co-operation of the Royal Navy in dealing with the situation cannot but give pause to MUSTAPHA KEMAL and compel him to that serious consideration of the forces he will be opposing, on which rests our greatest hope of avoiding actual conflict.'[94] Harington believed the Turks could be deterred from war and, even if one came, he could hold Chanak and withdraw his other forces to safety. He was willing though not eager to open fire himself, holding that a controlled demonstration of force would show Britain was not bluffing, while hints at diplomatic concessions would signal that the Turks could gain their ends without war. On 24, 27, and 28 September, he ordered his forces to be ready to open fire. Several days later, when the Mudania Conference seemed near breakdown, he was prepared to do so again and to attack the Turks with all his forces at Chanak and the Ismid peninsula, and twice expected to do so.[95] However, Harington did not make his calculations clear to his superiors. He led Whitehall to believe Kemal's intentions and actions at Chanak were tightly linked – in fact, they were rather disassociated at the start, though they became closer as time went by, in part because of the forceful way the British joined them; not until 6 October were they as cohesive as Harington led Whitehall to believe was so from 24 September. Even worse, he led Whitehall to think Chanak in imminent peril, which he did not think was so. He hoped that limited force combined with diplomatic concessions would prevent war, and wanted permission to shoot in order to maintain peace, but only if absolutely necessary. London thought it had to decide whether it would risk that war.

The third phase of the crisis emerged straight from these circumstances. London did not understand Harington's calculations. It thought he saw imminent danger at Chanak and the need to fight there, but feared making that decision. Hence, on 29 September, a conference of ministers told him: 'Kemalists are obviously continuing to move up troops and are making efforts to net you in. General Staff advises that the defensive position will be seriously endangered if this is allowed to continue and that the time has come to avert this disaster.' He was ordered to present an ultimatum to the Turks. If the latter did not withdraw from Chanak immediately, Harington was to fire on them with all his forces. Several hours later, in response to press reports of an improved situation at Chanak, and Curzon's view that it and his subsequent discussions with Mustafa Reschid gave grounds to postpone the bombardment by 24 hours, ministers reconsidered their decision, but retained it.[96] In all of these actions, they acted on the basis of professional advice, from military chiefs reacting to the telegrams received from Harington during the last 48 hours. Some of these evinced great pessimism and strain. He used the adjective 'impossible' to describe the situation emerging around Chanak; they thought this meant the garrison was threatened with destruction unless the Turkish position was cleared immediately. The service chiefs recommended this action be taken,[97] which they thought was merely telling Harington to do what he wanted to do. Nor were they misinterpreting the reports they had received. Harington described Kemal as unyielding over Chanak. Rumbold noted: 'Situation evidently contemplated by Mustapha Kemal is that British and Turks should watch each other whilst Turkish forces are piling up until Mustapha Kemal thinks he is strong enough to attack.'[98] On 28 September, Harington informed the War Office that he had ordered his forces to fire on the Turks should this be necessary. 'I regret very much having to take this action but I have no alternative as Kemalists have challenged me.'[99]

Harington's messages triggered the government's decisions, but in the context of a sense of crisis, and of ministers' reading of messages on operations and intelligence. On 29 September, ministers interpreted Harington and Rumbold's comments in the light of the bad reports from intelligence, especially NID assessments of Soviet naval activity and the SIS's warning that Kemal would deliver an ultimatum on 30 September – the next day. They thought a Turkish attack imminent, which might take Chanak and certainly would let Turkey into Thrace, and perhaps spark a general war in the Balkans and Eastern Europe. They believed only decisive British action could break Turkish resolve; these were not the actions of a war party, but of men convinced of peril, believing themselves to be launching a preemptive strike for security – for peace. Ministers wanted to send a diplomatic message through a blast of guns. For that matter, right after ministers reached their initial decision, in a meeting scheduled by coincidence, Curzon met Reschid. The foreign secretary criticized Kemal for his failure to act on Allied overtures for an armistice, and of the threats posed at Chanak: 'immediate action alone could prevent the outbreak of hostilities and probably the renewal of war between Great Britain and Turkey'. When informed of the ultimatum, Reschid replied: 'But this means war.' Curzon agreed, and refuted Reschid's claims that Britain was anti-Turkish; in particular, Britain intended Turkey to recover control over Thrace. Reschid agreed to inform Kemal by wireless that Britain did not desire war, and hoped this message could reach his master by the following morning. Curzon noted that it might fail to reach Kemal in time to avert an 'unfortunate incident', none the less 'it might be too late to prevent hostilities, but it might still be possible to avert a war'. Reschid did pass on this message in clear but diplomatic terms, stating that a Turkish withdrawal from the Neutral Zone was 'an absolute condition' for negotiations, and that 'even if a regrettable collision did take place then, in order not to give occasion for a declaration of war, if explanations were given that the collision was not the result of an order given by the Commander-in-Chief, they would regard the incident as if it had not happened, and the discussions could contrary to [? custom] be continued'.[100]

This message proved unnecessary, because Harington questioned his orders and refused to open fire. He had never feared immediate danger as Whitehall believed, while from the evening of 28 September he became increasingly optimistic, reinforced by waves of new information. On 29 September, Aralov told Moscow that he was attempting to bribe senior Nationalists, including Kemal, with valuable swords, jewels and gold cigarette cases. GSI read this in a counterintuitive but accurate fashion which demonstrates its expertise – as an indication Bolshevik influence was declining, which other information also indicated.[101] So much for the Soviet threat. Meanwhile, indications of Turkish intentions became more promising. In a radio message, Kemal made serious demands, including a request that the British evacuate Chanak in return for a pledge that Turkey would not threaten the Dardanelles during negotiations; but he noted signs of British goodwill, emphasizing: 'With a view to avoiding fresh misunderstandings I have issued orders to the Commander at the front for our Troops at Chanak again to enter the localities they are occupying at the present, but that they are to avoid provoking any incident.' He concluded with a reference to 'the assembly of the coming conference which we sincerely hope will lead to permanent results'. Harington characterized this message as meaning Kemal had 'given orders to avoid incidents and looks forward to an early meeting but otherwise his reply does not appear very helpful' – an understatement, since Kemal was announcing his intention to intensify the crisis at Chanak – but still it indicated no need for alarm.[102] Harington saw the prospect of a peaceful solution. The Turks might enter armistice negotiations if they were explicitly promised that they would receive the bulk of Thrace, and if Greek forces withdrew from it; he thought the position at Chanak secure. Harington's next step after refusing the government's ultimatum, however, was to deliver one of his own. Knowing Turkish forces were entering the theatre in uncertain strength, which might become overwhelming within ten days, Harington told Hamid Turkey must immediately commit itself to enter armistice talks, or else face war. The Turks formally agreed to talk.

This set in motion the last phase of the crisis, which centred on the Mudania conference. Intelligence was fundamental in bringing Britain to that point, but of minor import at Mudania (that revived during the next eight months of negotiation). Granted, old assessments continued to affect attitudes and good intelligence to come in. Some of it remained alarming – on 29 September Garroni noted his 'impression that ANGORA is not trying to facilitate a solution and that it is perhaps impelled to this course by Russian influence', and feared Kemal would drive to Thrace and attack Chanak unless Britain met its demands; French traffic demonstrated Kemal's resolution to seize control of Thrace before signing an armistice.[103] The intelligence picture available in London, however, was far more favourable than before. Between 29 September and 3 October, the GC&CS showed that in terms even more peremptory than those he used with the British, on 21 and 26 September Poincaré himself ordered his emissaries to warn the Turks from Chanak and any violation of the Neutral Zone.[104] Again, on 29 September, the SIS issued reports that Fethi Bey thought France had fulfilled its promises and would back Ankara at a conference, and believed that Kemal preferred a peaceful solution to the crisis, though in case of war Russia and Bulgaria would back Turkey, which would beat Britain. An SIS report prepared on 29 September but probably not then available – the Foreign Office's copy is marked 4 October – tamped down the fear it had done the most to stoke up, on Russo-Turkish relations. The Turks were trying to drag the Russians into war, but the latter, increasingly suspicious of Ankara, were unlikely to support them.[105] By 10 October, a Foreign Office assessment of intelligence placed far more emphasis on evidence about Turko-Soviet dissension than earlier ones, including the news that Aralov's residence in Ankara had burned down on 15 August – he suspected arson![106] This material influenced policy in London, especially the determination that it could force Poincaré in line through another set of meetings, in which it had some success; but the real decisions were made by Harington at Mudania. Though he no doubt paid careful attention to intelligence, and perhaps was influenced by material showing that Turkish concerns regarding Thrace were in part motivated by genuine fears that if not removed, Greek troops would commit massive atrocities against Turkish civilians, Harington acted above all on reports from his forces at Chanak, and his own personal assessments in negotiations with Turks and Allied generals. His intuition was his intelligence. In the end, an armistice was signed essentially on the basis of British demands, and the British ensured their prestige, but after running almost one risk too far.

NOTES

1. Harington to Maurice, 8 Jan. 1923, 23 April 1923, Maurice 3/2.
2. War Office memorandum (CP 4131), 29 July 1922, CAB 24/138.
3. The best, though flawed, account of the topic, remains D. Walder, *The Chanak Affair* (London, 1969); J.R. Ferris, '"Between Military and Political": British Power and Diplomacy From The Chanak Crisis to the Lausanne Conference, 1922', *Proceedings of the Joint Turkish-Israeli Military History Conference* (Istanbul, 2000), pp.235–84, examines government policy on the crisis.
4. General Staff Memorandum, 'Near East Situation', 17 Sept. 1922, WO 106/1503; Conference of Ministers, 18 Sept. 1922, FO 371/7892; Harington to War Office (No. 2538), 30 Sept. 1922, WO 106/1441.
5. J.R. Ferris (ed.), *The British Army and Signals Intelligence During the First World War* (London, 1992), pp.297–98.
6. WO telegram to Harington (No.91497), 20 Nov. 1922, Harington telegrams (Nos. 2999, 3051) to WO, 15 Nov., 22 Nov. 1922, WO 106/1429.
7. *DBFP*, Series I, XVII, pp.883–84; Conference of Ministers, 23 Sept. 1922, CAB 23/31; 'Near East Situation', 17 Sept. 1922, 'Notes on the Situation in the Near East' by Conwell, 18 Sept. 1922, WO 106/1503.
8. Air Intelligence Report No 28, 21 Sept. 1922, AIR 5/267/S21443; Ellington telegram (GS 105) to Trenchard, 22 Sept. 1922, AIR 8/51; Air Staff Note, 'Air Assistance in the

defence of Constantinoiple', nd [circa 12 Sept. 1922], DCAS to DMOI, 12 Sept. 1922, AIR 5/297.
9. WO 106/1495-96 have material on 1921; Burnett Stuart to Cavan, 26 Sept. 1922, WO 106/709.
10. Shuttleworth memorandum, 'Account of Operations Chanak Area', 1 Jan. 1923, WO 32/5743.
11. Ibid.; 4th Battle Squadron to C-in-C, Mediterranean Fleet, 13 Oct. 1922, ADM 137/2498.
12. Harington telegram (No.2525) to WO, 29 Sept. 1922, AIR 5/297; Harington telegram (No.2525) to WO, 30 Sept. 1922, ADM 137/2498.
13. Harington memorandum, 'British Forces In Turkey, C-in-C's Dispatch, Period 1920–1923' (CR/BFT/58410/CHH), WO 32/5743.
14. J.R. Ferris, 'Whitehall's Black Chamber: British Cryptology and the Government Code and Cypher School, 1919–1929', *Intelligence and National Security*, 2 (1987), pp.54–91.
15. This material is in 'Wireless News', contained in the ADM 223 series.
16. Notes by Brigadier F.W. Nicholls, nd [circa post-Second World War], Lycett to Tozer, 2 May 1948, both HW 3/88; for evidence on telephone tapping, cf. GHQ Constantinople to WO, I 9817, 28 Jan. 1921, FO 371/6464. Sarafend, in Palestine, was the base of No 2 Wireless Company, the army's Middle Eastern codebreaking bureau between 1923 and 1939, and a key element in its signals intelligence capacity during the Second World War.
17. Harington telegram to WO (No.2306), 18 Sept. 1922, WO 106/1503.
18. Cumming to Seton, 2 Feb. 1922, L/MIL 7/18813; SIS Section 1A to Bland, CX/7488, FO 371/7951/9945.
19. Gribbon to DMI, 7 Jan. 1921, FO 371/6464/743.
20. SIS Eastern Summary (No.638)) 21 April 1922, FO 371/8073; FO 'Memorandum respecting Co-operation of Muslim Countries and Russia', 26 Jan. 1923, FO 371/9290/481.
21. SIS report (No.854), 8 Sept. 1922, (No.866), 14 Sept. 1922, Section 1a to Oliphant, CX/1331/, 12 Sept. 1922, all FO 371/7889.
22. (No.010954), (No.011076), (No.011095), all HW 12/38.
23. *DBFP*, Series I, XVII, pp.45, 47, 224–7, 242–3, 424, 511, 529.
24. Memorandum, 5 Oct., 'Secret' (no number or source indicated), 13 Sept. 1922, FO 371/7899/10554
25. Harington memorandum, WO 32/5743.
26. Harington to WO (No.2248), 13 Sept. 1922, E 9362; Harington to WO (No.2262), 14 Sept. 1922, E 9363; Harington to WO (No.2230), 10 Sept. 1922, E 9324, all FO 3721/7888.
27. Gribbon to DMI, 7 Jan. 1921, FO 371/6464/743; Osbourne minute, 4 Feb. 1921, FO 371/6465; for one example of GSI reports, cf. General Staff 'Intelligence', 'Weekly Report No 81' (No.2797 T), 11 Aug. 1920, FO 371/5170; Curzon to Derby, 9 Nov. 1922, WO 137/5.
28. High Commission, Istanbul, telegram to FO (No.379), 4 Sept. 1922, FO 371/7885; Domville Diary, 12, 22–24 Sept. 1922, Domvile MSS.
29. Harington to WO (No.2506), 28 Sept. 1922, FO 371/7899; Harington to WO (No.2493), 29 Sept. 1922, WO 106/1441; Harington to WO (No.1222), 27 Sept. 1922; (No.1223), 28 Sept. 1922; (No.2485), 28 Sept. 1922, all FO 371/7896; CP 4234, CAB 24/139.
30. *DBFP*, Series IA, XVII, pp.301, 316, 714; Churchill minute, 9 Dec. 1920, WO 32/5743; Curzon minute, 10 Feb. 1921, FO 371/6265/1478.
31. GHQ Constantinople to WO (I.9021), 29 Jan. 1921, FO 371/6464.

32. Hankey memorandum for Baldwin, 4 Nov. 1927, Austen Chamberlain to Hankey, 2 Nov. 1933, Hankey to Chamberlain, 6 Nov. 1933, all CAB 21/334; Curzon to Hardinge, 16 Sept. 1922, FO 800/157.
33. Lindsay minute, 11 Sept. 1922, FO 371/7887/9158.
34. Rome Embassy telegram to FO (No.271), 10 Oct. 1922; FO telegram to Rome Embassy (No.271), 13 Sept. 1922, FO 371/7887; No.010930, No.011026, HW 12/38.
35. Curzon to Lloyd George, 5 Oct. 1922, Curzon F 112/224B.
36. GHQ Constantinople to WO, 26 Sept. 1922, FO 371/7896/10197.
37. Cabinet meeting, 11 pm, 5 Oct. 1922, CAB 23/31.
38. GHQ Constantinople telegram to WO (No.2509), 29 Aug. 1922, FO 371/7897.
39. Admiralty to C-in-C, Atlantic Fleet, 24 Sept. 1922, 'Appreciation of the Situation in the Near East, a.m., Sunday, 24.9'; ADM 137/1778, Rumbold to mother, 20 Sept. 1922, Rumbold Dep. 30.
40. SIS Report No.874, 16 Sept. 1922, WO 106/1503; SIS Reports No.862, 12 Sept. 1922, No.864, 13 Sept. 1922, both WO 106/1505.
41. No.011187, HW 12/38.
42. No.011101, ibid.
43. No.011125, ibid.
44. FO to WO, 16 Sept. 1922, 'Secret and Immediate'; Oliphant minute, 15 Sept. 1922, FO 371/7888/9349.
45. Curzon to Hardinge, 16 Sept. 1922, FO 800/157.
46. Harington to WO (No.2284), 15 Sept. 1922, and Harington to WO (No.2291), 17 Sept. 1922, both FO 371/7889.
47. *DBFP*, Series I, XVIII, pp.15, 43; No.010954, 011030, HW 12/38
48. No.010997, Nos.011011–12, No.011024, No.011026, No.011028, No.011030, No.011067, No.011081, No.011090, No.011094, No.011107, No.011157, all HW 12/38; Harington to WO, 19 and 20 Sept. 1922, Nos.2316, 2347 SIS Report No.866, 14 Sept. 1922, all FO 371/7891.
49. No.2 Bureau, GHQ Constantinople, 'Note on the Obtaining of Submarines by the Turkish nationalists', 15 Aug. 1922, ADM 137/2498.
50. Admiralty to Brock (No.996), 25 Sept. 1922, and 26 Sept. 1922 (No.999), ADM 137/1780.
51. Admiralty telegram to Brock (No.929), 19 Sept. 1922, WO 106/1503.
52. Brock telegram to Admiralty (No.472), 8 Oct. 1922, FO 371/7900; Admiralty to Atlantic Fleet (M.01279), 24 Sept. 1922, FHR/10; Admiralty to C-in-C Atlantic Fleet, 24 Sept. 1922, 'Appreciation of the Situation in the Near East, a.m., Sunday, 24.9', ADM 137/1778.
53. *DBFP*, Series I, XVIII, pp.6, 22, 42, 225–6, 306–7, 425, 491–2, 512–13, 574, 628, 831.
54. Curzon to Chamberlain, 26 May 1922, Chamberlain AC 23/3.
55. Edmonds, 'Summary', 10 Oct. 1922, FO 371/7902/10892; SIS report (No.895), 26 Sept. 1922, WO 106/1504.
56. SIS Section Ia to Oliphant, CX 1331, 12 Sept. 1922, FO 371/7889; Harington telegram to WO (No.2385), 23 Sept. 1922, FO 371/7894.
57. SIS report No.865, 13 Sept. 1922, FO 371/7891.
58. SIS Section Ia. to Oliphant, CX 1205, 12 Sept. 1922, FO 371/7889.
59. SIS Report No.887, 22 Sept. 1922, Military Intelligence IC HC/3918, 19 Sept. 1922, both WO 106/1504; SIS 'Eastern Summary' (No.865), 13 Sept. 1922, FO 371/7891.
60. No.010931, No.010970, No.011078, No.011105, all HW 12/38; Harington to WO, 19 Sept. 1922, 20 Sept. 1922, both FO 371/7891; Osborne minute, 22 Sept. 1922, FO 371/7891.

BRITISH INTELLIGENCE AND POLICY   183

61. See note 59, above; and Osborne minute, 22 Sept. 1922, FO 371/7891/9680.
62. SIS report No.874, 16 Sept. 1922, WO 106/1503.
63. 'GSI', Constantinople, 17 Oct. 1922, in Brock to Admiralty, 19 Oct. 1922, ADM 137/1778.
64. SIS Report No.877, 18 Sept. 1922, WO 106/1503; Note of telephone message between Tyrrell and Curzon, 6.40 pm, 22 Sept. 1922, FO 800/157; record of telephone conversation between Lloyd George and Hankey, 4.30 pm, 22 Sept. 1922, CAB 21/241.
65. Curzon to Hardinge, 16 Sept. 1922, FO 800/157.
66. Osborne minute, 19 Sept. 1922, FO 371/7889/9444.
67. 'Draft Minutes', Conference of Ministers, 11 am, 19 Sept. 1922, FO 371/7892.
68. 'Draft Minutes', Conference of Ministers, 5 pm, 18 Sept. 1922, FO 371/7890.
69. *DBFP*, Series I, XVIII, p.46.
70. Harington to War Office (No.1222), 27 Sept. 1922, FO 371/7896.
71. SIS Report No.888, 23 Sept. 1922, Harington to WO (No.2368), 23 Sept. 1922, both FO 371/7894; Harington telegram to WO, 20 Sept. 1922, FO 371/7891; SIS Report No.903, 29 Sept. 1922, WO 106/1507; SIS Report No.888, 23 Sept. 1922, FO 371/7894; Harington (No.2368), 23 Sept. 1922, Harington (No.2509), FO 371/7897.
72. Nos.011123-4, No.011126, No.011139, all HW 12/38.
73. Minute by Osborne, 25 Sept. 1922, E 9793, FO 371/7893; No.011141, 23 Sept. 1922, HW 12/38.
74. No.011209, HW 12/38; Harington telegrams to WO (No.2284), 15 Sept. 1922; (No.2291), 17 Sept. 1922; FO 371/7889; Harington to WO (Nos.2402, 2422), 24 Sept. 1922; (No.2368), 23 Sept. 1922, FO 371/7894.
75. Harington to WO (No.2509), 29 Sept. 1922, FO 371/7897; Harington to WO (No.2462), 26–27 Sept. 1922, FO 371/7895; Harington to WO (No.2460), 27 Sept. 1922, FO 371/7896.
76. No.011123, HW 12/38.
77. Harington to WO (No.2385), 22 Sept. 1922, FO 371/7894.
78. SIS Section Ia to Oliphant, CX/1205, 20 Sept. 1922, FO 371/7891.
79. SIS report No.887, 22 Sept. 1922, WO 106/1504.
80. Harington to WO (No.2373), FO 371/7894.
81. M.I.2.b. memorandum, 27 Sept. 1922, WO 106/1504; Harington to WO (No.2464), 26 Sept. 1922, FO 371/7896.
82. Rumbold to FO (No.474), 'Private and Secret', 28 Sept. 1922, WO 106/1441.
83. SIS Reports No.907, 30 Sept. 1922, CX6/436, 28 Sept. 1922, CX6/871, 28 Sept. 1922, CX/1203, 30 Sept. 1922, all WO 106/1507; SIS Section Ia to Oliphant, CX/1205, 20 Sept. 1922, FO 371/7891, British Military Attache, Tehran, to GOC Iraq (No.56), 30 Sept. 1922, WO 106/1441; British Mission, Warsaw to WO (No.570), 29 Sept. 1922, WO 106/1507.
84. SIS Report No.892, 25 Sept. 1922, WO 106/1507, SIS CXG.433, 23 Sept. 1922, FO 371/7893.
85. SIS Section la to Oliphant 12 Sept. 1922, SIS Report No.866, 14 Sept. 1922, both FO 371/7889; Harington to WO (No.2295), 18 Sept. 1922, WO 106/1503; SIS Report No.869, 14 Sept. 1922, FO 371/7887. Such reports continued for the next 10 days – see SIS No.881, 21 Sept. 1922, WO 106/1507; SIS No.895, 26 Sept. 1922, WO 106/1504.
86. *DBFP*, Series I, XVIII, pp.60–61, 84.
87. Osborne minute, 25 Sept. 1922, FO 371/7893/9793.
88. Osborne minute, 28 Sept. 1922, FO 371/7896/10197.
89. Osborne minute, 26 Sept. 1922, with Curzon marginal note, nd, FO 371/7894/9914; GHQ Constantinople to WO, 25 Sept. 1922 (No.2421), FO 371/7894/9939.

90. Rumbold to mother, 20 Sept. 1922, Rumbold Dep. 30.
91. Harington telegram to War Office (No.2420), 24 Sept. 1922, FO 371/7895; Harington to WO (No.2368), 23 Sept. 1922, FO 371/7894.
92. Harington to WO (No.2414), 24 Sept. 1922, FO 371/7895.
93. Harington telegram to Shuttleworth (No.MH3), 24 Oct. 1922, Harington to WO (No.2427), 24 Sept. 1922, FO 371/7895.
94. Harington to Brock, 30 Sept. 1922, ADM 137/2498.
95. Brock to Admiralty (No.472), 10 Oct. 1922, FO 371/7902; 85th Infantry Brigade War Diary, Chanak, Order No.12, 11 Oct. 1922, WO 95/4964; Harington memorandum, 11 Oct. 1922, WO 32/5743.
96. Hankey memorandum, 'Ultimatum to the Turks', 30 Oct. 1922, CAB 21/241. Cf. Curzon to Rumbold (No.959), 29 Oct. 1922, FO 371/7896/10261; Conference of Ministers, 29 Sept. 1922, FO 371/7898, Cabinet, 30 Sept. 1922, CAB 23/31; *DBFP*, Series IA, XVIII, p.118.
97. Combined Staffs Paper No.3, 29 Sept. 1922, WO 106/1441.
98. Rumbold to FO (No.466), 27 Sept. 1922; (No.480), 28 Sept. 1922, both FO 371/7895.
99. Harington to WO (No.2486), 28 Sept. 1922, WO 106/1441.
100. No.011234, No.011276, HW 12/39.
101. Harington to WO (No.2516), 29 Sept. 1922, FO 371/7897.
102. Harington to WO (Nos.2514, 2519), both 29 Sept. 1922, FO 371/7899; GHQ Constantinople to WO (No.G12), 30 Sept. 1922, Harington to WO (No.2506), 28 Sept. 1922, both FO 371/7899/10491; Harington to WO (No.2493), 29 Sept. 1922, WO 106/1441; Harington to WO (No.1222), 27 Sept. 1922; (No.1223), 28 Sept. 1922; (No.2485), 28 Sept. 1922, all FO 371/7896; 28th Division HQ War Diary, Harington to Marden (No.2498), 28 Sept. 1922, Marden to Harington, 1300, 29 Sept. 1922, all WO 95/4964; Darforce to Harington, 27 Sept. 1922, WO 95/4961; GHQ Constantinople to WO, 30 Sept. 1922, Harington to WO (No.2514), 29 Sept. 1922, FO 371/7899
103. Nos.011251–2, Nos.011257–8, HW 12/39.
104. No.011200, No.011228, both HW 12/38; No.011245, HW 12/39.
105. SIS Report No.903, 29 Sept. 1922, FO 371/7899/10516; SIS Misc.18/1, 29 Sept. 1922, FO 371/7899/10515.
106. Edmonds minute, 10 Oct. 1922, FO 371/7902/10892.

The British Official Mind and the Lausanne Conference, 1922–23

ERIK GOLDSTEIN

The First World War and its aftermath saw Britain, briefly, become the predominant power in the Aegean. Through the occupation of Constantinople, the creation of an Army of the Black Sea, maritime supremacy, and a close relationship with Greece Britain attempted to achieve predominant control over one of the world's strategic maritime lines of communication, the Straits and the Aegean. The core of Britain's traditional interests lay with the Suez Canal and the bordering lands, but its aspirations of in this period were greater. As the Australian prime minister, Billy Hughes, exclaimed, 'We are like so many Alexanders. What other world's have we to conquer?'[1] Brtain's aspirations became tightly tied to those of Greece and its leader, Eleftherios Venizelos. When his regime collapsed, Britain maintained a tenuous attempt to retain its regional position, an effort which finally led to the debacle of the Chanak crisis. It was in the wake of this failed effort to impose British hegemony upon the Aegean world that London attempted to salvage something of its aspirations at the Lausanne Conference of 1922–23.

There were four phases in Britain's efforts to deal with the collapse of the Ottoman Empire: the first was the attempt to utilize Greece as its regional proxy which lasted from the establishment of the Venizelos government in 1917 until his fall in 1920; the second phase ran through the defeat of the Greek forces by Kemal in 1922; the third was a brief period which culminated in the Chanak crisis of late 1922; and the final phase culminated in the negotiated settlement at Lausanne in 1923.

As Britain contemplated the post-war world order during 1917–18, a preference emerged for the creation of a greater Greece.[2] Britain had wide ambitions as a victorious end to the war drew ever nearer, but it was clear that in some regions Britain's position would benefit from useful regional allies. For the eastern Mediterranean

Greece appeared to be a suitable candidate as a regional proxy that would fill some of the void left by the imminent collapse of the Ottoman Empire.

Even before the war the British prime minister, H.H. Asquith, had considered Venizelos to be 'the most capable man in Eastern Europe'.[3] Lord Riddell, one of Lloyd George's closest confidants, rated him as one of the six greatest men in the world, ranking with Woodrow Wilson, Lloyd George, Clemenceau, Marshal Foch, and General Botha.[4] When Allen Leeper of the Foreign Office's Political Intelligence Department received an invitation to dine with Venizelos during the Paris Peace Conference, he wrote excitedly to his brother, 'I've at last got Veniselos's autograph'.[5] Lloyd George dined with Venizelos during the Paris Peace Conference and, after one such encounter, Lloyd George's secretary noted: 'The two have a great admiration for each other, & D[avid] [Lloyd George] is trying to get Smyrna for the Greeks.'[6]

Greece had enjoyed good relations with Britain since the formation of a pro-Allied government under Venizelos and the dispatch into exile of King Constantine, who was viewed by the Allies as pro-German. Venizelos had brought Greece into the war on the Allied side and the Venizelos government hoped that the Allies would support the final achievement of the *Megalia Idea* (the Great Idea) – the return to Greek rule of its historic irredenta. Indeed, there was great fear as to future events if Venizelos were toppled. Harold Nicolson, of the Foreign Office's Political Intelligence Department, warned in March 1919, during the growing crisis between the Allies over the future of Anatolia, that any failure by Venizelos to save the unredeemed Greeks could lead to his fall: 'I need not elaborate the disastrous effects which any weakening of M. Venizelos' position would have upon Greece itself and general Entente interests in the Eastern Mediterranean.'[7] There were those who warned of pinning too much on the fate of one individual. Admiral de Roebuck at Constantinople observed: 'I cannot help wondering if the game is worth the candle. I should wonder, even if M. Veniselos were immortal; he is not immortal, but ephemeral, and he is not only ephemeral, but as regards Greece, a phenomenon.'[8]

During the meetings of the Allied leaders at Paris during the first part of 1919 Venizelos was able to obtain strong support for Greek ambitions. When Italy looked ready to pre-empt any settlement on the territorial fate of the Ottoman Empire by occupying southwest Anatolia, it was agreed to allow Greek forces to land at the key port of Smyrna, which they did under British naval protection. This landing sparked a Turkish Nationalist upsurge that, in turn, posed a dangerous threat to British plans.

Greece was seen by many observers as Britain's Trojan horse. By the summer of 1920 the United States High Commissioner at Constantinople, Admiral Mark Bristol, reported that 'the whole question in the Near East appears to be one in which England and Greece are combining to divide up the spoils of territorial and commercial advantage. ... The British are leaving the Greeks to do their fighting'.[9]

The idea of having in Greece a strong regional proxy was suddenly disrupted by an unanticipated sequence of events. On 25 October 1920, King Alexander, who had replaced his father on the throne, died as a result of a bite from a pet monkey. Three weeks later, on 15 November, to general surprise, Venizelos lost the general election. On 5 December, in a plebiscite, the Greek voters, despite Allied warnings, voted for the restoration of King Constantine. One British diplomat expressed astonishment to the British high commissioner at Constantinople, Sir Horace Rumbold: 'What an extraordinary thing Venizelos having been beat to a frazzle in his elections. Will Tino now return to Athens!! I imagine that a reversal of Greek policy will complicate your situation most disagreeably, for apparently you have little but the Greeks between you and the Kemalists.'[10] Lord Curzon, the foreign secretary, observed of these events: 'when elections took place, to the stupefaction of the world, Veniselos was hopelessly defeated and the king reappeared upon the scene'.[11] Winston Churchill later observed that 'the return of Constantine dissolved all Allied loyalties to Greece and cancelled all but legal obligations'.[12]

The restored government of King Constantine enjoyed no Allied support. France rapidly moved to build bridges to the Turkish nationalists, the newly emerging force in the region. In Britain for a considerable period many hoped for the rapid return of Venizelos and, therefore, to maintain something of the *status quo* in the meantime.[13] The key was to retain control of Constantinople.

The fall of the Venizelos government in Greece in 1920 eviscerated British interest in Greece as a regional ally and, from that stage onwards, British policy in the Near East was in disarray. The rise of a popular Turkish nationalist movement under Mustapha Kemal, later surnamed Atatürk, the victor of the Battle of Galipoli, posed the chief threat to British interests. Britain had little use for the decayed government of the Sultan, which led to its precarious existence under the eyes of the watchful Allied occupation force at Constantinople. As the First World War drew to a close it was thought that the Sultan might be moved to a small Turkish state in Anatolia, perhaps with Greece gaining control of what was once the seat of the Byzantine Empire, long a Greek dream. Now Britain was forced to try to use the Sultan and his government as the one force with some political legitimacy to counter Kemal and the Nationalists. Rumbold advised from Constantinople that: 'We are *not* pledged in any way to exert ourselves to maintain the Sultan of the throne. At the same time I am of the opinion that it is in our interest that he should remain, unless and until his position becomes wholly untenable.'[14] Rumbold's assessment was based on a combination of both local conditions and the wider impact of being seen to be responsible for the overthrow of a ruler who was also the Caliph.

The Greek landing at Smyrna acted as the catalyst for a Turkish nationalist movement, determined to prevent the dismemberment of the Turkish portions of the Ottoman Empire. In September 1919 a Nationalist Congress met at Sivas and issued a declaration of the unity of Turkish territory. A National Pact was agreed which enunciated six points; self-determination, the security of Constantinople, the opening of the Straits, minority rights, and the abolition of the hated capitulations. In elections for the Constantinople parliament the following month the nationalists won and, in January 1920, the National Pact was affirmed by the parliament.

Constantinople had been occupied, on behalf of the Allies, on 13 November 1918 by Lieutenant-General Sir Henry Wilson; the bulk of the troops under his command were British. By 17 December, General Milne, the commander of the Allied Army of the Black Sea, had moved his headquarters to the city as well.[15] Other Allied forces soon followed, though the British position was always preeminent. In an effort to stop the Nationalists the Allies decided in February 1920 that the Sultan's government could remain in the city and that therefore it would remain the capital. There was, however, little confidence in the immediate abilities of this regime and, therefore, on 12 March General Milne was ordered to officially occupy Constantinople, which was accomplished without opposition on 16 March. The Ottoman Ministry of War, the Admiralty, and other departments were placed under Allied control, with the military effectively coming under British supervision. Several hostile Ottoman ministers were deported to Malta. The Nationalists responded by establishing a provisional government at Ankara with Kemal as its leader. One of the National government's first acts was to make a military agreement with Soviet Russia, further increasing the level of Allied distrust of the Nationalists. It would take years for the illusion that Kemal was in some way a Soviet stooge or fellow traveller to dissipate in official circles in London.

The Allies, seeking to conclude the last of the peace treaties, in the summer of 1920, finally presented the treaty to the representatives of the Sultan's government. On 10 August 1920 the Treaty of Sèvres was signed. By its terms Turkey renounced all claim to non-Turkish territory. Smyrna and its hinterland would be placed under Greek administration for five years, after which a plebiscite as to its future would be held. Italy's control of the Dodecanese islands was confirmed, the remainder to the Aegean islands passed to Greece. Armenian independence was recognized. The Nationalist government denounced the treaty and the Constantinople government never dared to ratify the settlement.

The change of regime in Athens and the wholesale replacement of Venizelist officers with Royalist ones, combined with what was in effect an Allied financial boycott of Greece, seriously weakened Greek capabilities. As Greek forces moved to make effective their control of the Smyrna hinterland, they encountered the Turkish nationalist forces. At the pivotal Battle of the Sakaria river in August–September 1921 Greek forces were defeated and began an orderly retreat that soon became a rout. At the end of September King Constantine abdicated in favour of his son George, who was viewed with equal suspicion by the Allied powers. Real power, though, passed to a military junta.

France, assessing the total reversal of fortune in the regions now moved more rapidly to establish good relations with Kemal. On 20 October 1921, the French representative Henri Franklin-Bouillon, a figure widely disliked by British officials, concluded an agreement with the Nationalists. Allied cooperation in the region now collapsed. Italy had already been alienated in 1919 by the failure of its partners to find it suitable territorial rewards. Britain now stood as the only power blocking Kemal from Constantinople and Turkish unification. During the first half of 1922 Curzon, on behalf of the British government, attempted to broker a settlement not only between the rival Turkish governments, but also between Greece and Turkey. Greece remained buoyed, to some extent, by Lloyd George's ambivalent support. Though Lloyd George was unhappy with the current Greek regime, he had no time for the Turks. This led the Greeks, in July, to hope that they might be allowed to regain the initiative. In July they moved troops from Smyrna to Thrace in the hope that they would be allowed to move on Constantinople. The Allies, however, blocked this plan. Within weeks the Nationalist forces had launched a new offensive and the Greek forces unexpectedly and utterly collapsed. The road to Constantinople now lay open for the Nationalist forces, with only one obstacle in the way.

There was at Chanak (Chanakkale) a small British force, which was seen as the key to control of the Straits, now effectively in British hands. Rumbold commented from Constantinople on the 'importance of in no way reducing the forces concentrated by His Majesty's Government in this part of the world pending the meeting of the conference'.[16] Only a comparatively small British force now barred the Nationalists from Constantinople.

In September 1922 the Greek revolution, which overthrew Constantine, gave renewed hope to Lloyd George, who commented: 'The Greek Revolution has changed the situation. I think it just possible God may take a hand. It looks like it.'[17] Many in the Cabinet were willing to support military engagement, if necessary, among them Lloyd George, Churchill, and Austen Chamberlain. The General Staff, however, was convinced that this would result in defeat. When the idea was proposed that a conference be held with the Nationalists at Smyrna Curzon observed that, 'As to a conference at Smyrna, not even Nero held a symposium amid the smoking ruins of Rome and I do not see the delegates emerging from their several bathing machines on the shore'.[18] The association of Churchill with the hawks came as little surprise, leading Hardinge, the ambassador at Paris, to comment: 'he always advocates expeditions and military operations which end in failure.'[19]

Britain turned to its Allies and the Dominions for support in the defence of the Dardanelles, but elicited none. It briefly looked as if war would occur but, diplomacy pre-empted military force and a temporary agreement was signed at Mudania on 11 October which opened the way for Turkey to negotiate a new peace treaty to replace that agreed at Sevres in 1920. Lord Crawford, a senior conservative politician, noted at the time: 'The Mudania Pact is signed. I think we owe all credit to Curzon and Rumbold.'[20] Hardinge could not fail to chortle at the triumph of professional diplomacy over the machinations of Lloyd George's political secretariat, commenting to Curzon: 'it is most satisfactory seeing the F.O. coming to its own again and I trust that the Garden City will now have its wings clipped.'[21]

The Chanak incident precipitated the downfall of the Lloyd George coalition and the formation of a new, Conservative, government under Bonar Law, with Lord Curzon retaining the Foreign Office, on 23 October 1922. London was not the only capital to witness a change of government. In Greece, the king was deposed on 27 September, six of his ministers shot, and a military controlled government established. In Constantinople, Sultan Mohammed VI was deposed and the Sultanate abolished on 1 November.

It seems probable that the end of the Ottoman sultanate was precipitated by the Allied invitation to the Turkish Nationalists to participate in a peace conference. The Ottoman Grand Vizier approached Kemal with the proposal that they send a joint delegation. This led the Turkish National Grand Assembly to vote for the abolition of the sultanate, though retaining a member of the family in the office of caliph. Kemal had no intention of allowing the Allies to play off two Turkish governments.[22] The Ottomans had captured Constantinople under the great Sultan Mohammed II, the Conqueror. The last Sultan left on 17 November 1922, escorted by the British commander, General Harington, followed by a British ambulance carrying his luggage.²³ The same day delegations began to arrive at Lausanne to renegotiate the Treaty of Sèvres. As the American observer noted of the Turkish delegation, the Turks 'are coming, not hat in hand, but with a victorious army behind them. That makes a lot of difference'.²⁴

There was a generally consistent, and negative, view of the Turks in British officialdom, a view that had been prevalent for some decades. William Gladstone, who fought a notable election campaign focusing on reports of Turkish atrocities in Bulgaria, had demanded that the Turks be driven, bag and baggage, from Europe.²⁵ During the war, Arnold Toynbee, then employed in the Foreign Office, produced a book entitled *The Murderous Tyranny of the Turks*.²⁶ He subsequently became the official who prepared the British negotiating brief on the fate of the Ottoman Empire. Sir Eyre Crowe, soon to be permanent under-secretary at the Foreign Office, argued in January 1919 that the Turks should be ousted from Europe, observing that: 'The policy of allowing the Turk to remain in Europe is so contrary to our most important interests and so certain to involve the continuance of all the abomination associated with the Turks.'²⁷ It had been widely expected that the Turks would be displaced from Europe, including their capital at Constantinople, and that a much diminished Sultan would rule from a city in Anatolia.

The surprising success of Kemal and his followers overturned those hopes, but not the general attitude towards the Turks. Allen Leeper, one of the British delegation, observed on the eve of the conference: 'The Turks are so completely unsatisfactory to negotiate with, that I am not hopeful about the result. It is a terrible tragedy that, owing to French treachery, we have to allow them back into Europe at all.'²⁸ It is perhaps worth noting that Leeper was married to the niece of General Sir Ian Hamilton, the British commander at the Battle of Galipoli. Once the conference got under way Leeper did not alter his views but commented that 'The Turks are worse than even so anti-Turk a person as myself c[oul]d. have prophesied'.²⁹

The idea of holding a conference to resolve the complicated situation was not new. In May, Curzon had already considered convening a conference of the Sevres signatories to find some way out of the muddle.³⁰ Most British officials were deeply suspicious of the intentions of both France and Italy and when, in early September, the latter proposed a mediation conference to be held a Venice, Britain balked. It had no desire to have Italy in control of the agenda.[31] Curzon was sensitive to the recent precedent of the Paris Peace Conference of 1919 when what was intended to be a preliminary gathering metamorphosed into a full peace conference. Curzon was convinced that Italy's real object was 'that the preliminary Conference at Venice is to be converted into the final Peace Conference *held under the auspices of Italy*'.[32] Italy was not seen as a friendly power when it came to the eastern Mediterranean.

As the crisis escalated, the necessity of a conference became evident. On 15 September the Cabinet met and agreed that a conference should be held at an early date to discuss a Near East peace settlement, involving all interested parties. The Cabinet remained averse to the Italian proposal of Venice but indicated a willingness to accept a French offer of Paris, should such a proposal be made.[33] For a while the idea was even mooted of holding separate conferences, one on the peace settlement at Lausanne and a parallel one at Geneva on the Straits. Perhaps in the wake of the multi-faceted 1921–22 Washington conference, the idea of parallel conferences on related subjects was about to become the vogue but, in the end, this was found impracticable.[34]

After much discussion, Lausanne was selected as the venue. The site was chosen as it was on the direct line of the Orient Express from Constantinople (unlike Geneva), possessed good hotel accommodation, and was the seat of 1912 Turkish–Italian peace conference. Geneva was ruled out as it was the seat of League, which might make it unacceptable to the United States and Soviet governments both of which had ignored the League.[35]

The British High Commissioner at Constantinople attended the conference, observing that,

> The fact is that there has never been a conference like this before. The other peace conferences have been held in the capital or one of the towns of one of the principal countries concerned. Therefore the Prime Minister of the country or his deputy is ipso facto Chairman of the conference. He may be efficient or otherwise, but one knows with whom one is dealing. In this neutral country there are three Presidents of the

Conference and it is not possible for the British President to get a real move on his foreign colleagues or to run their commissions and sub-commissions himself. The result is that we are the helpless victims of their unbusinesslike and dilatory proceedings.[36]

Curzon, however, would find a solution to this problem.

One concern in London was that there might be a general election, just about the time of the peace conference, which might prevent Curzon from representing Britain.[37] If that were to happen, Britain, for the first time in years, would be represented only by career diplomats. In the end, Curzon was able to attend the first phase of the Lausanne conference, which ended in deadlock; in the second phase, it was indeed the career diplomats who finally achieved a settlement.

Opinions on who should be represented at the Near East Peace conference varied. As the topics would include not only the peace settlement with Turkey but the issue of the Straits as well, the Black Sea states would have to be allowed to be present. Curzon, though, was depressed at the idea of allowing either Russia or Bulgaria to participate: 'I shudder at a Conference in which all these people will interfere.'[38] A few days after the Cabinet agreed to a conference the Americans were approached, informally, to see if there was any chance of a United States representative taking part.[39] Clearly, Britain was hoping to get some less hostile states to participate. As events transpired, it was the United States observer delegation that caused great frustration for the British.

There was general agreement in London that the Dominions should not be present. Crowe commented: 'Are we to repeat the pandemonium of the Paris Peace Conference? I sincerely trust that we shall be spared the presence of any Dominion Representatives, except for the purpose of final signature.' This was a view with which the Foreign Secretary concurred.[40] Curzon was concerned that what he considered to be the illogical precedent of the Paris Peace Conference of 1919 would become established practice:

> No amount of sophistication can get us over the fundamentally contradictory principles underlying the arrangements then insisted upon. We at one moment maintain the position that the

British Empire, as also its foreign policy is one; at another moment we claim a separate and entirely independent position for each Dominion in the important sphere of foreign policy represented by the League of Nations. The arrangement is as difficult to defend in theory as it is difficult to work in practice.[41]

There may have been a lingering animus in London at the cool response the Dominions had given to London's request for support during the Chanak crisis. The Australian prime minister, Billy Hughes, in a vituperative message commented: ' We are to go on in the same bad old way. No part was taken by us in making Treaty of Sèvres.'[42]

One of the ongoing concerns for Britain in making peace in the Near East was any possible impact on the large Muslim population in its empire. Lloyd George undoubtedly startled his colleagues at the Paris Peace Conference when he once announced that he sat there as the representative of 'the greatest Mohammedan power'.[43] The British Empire's Muslim population was estimated to be 80 million, a position that had been further enhanced by its recent acquisitions in the Middle East. One reason that Britain had been so reluctant to dispense with the sultan in the period immediately after the occupation of Constantinople was his concurrent position as the Caliph-ul-Islam. The India Office and the Government of India were especially sensitive to the potential political popularity of the Khilifat movement within India.[44] Even when the Royal Navy took the last Sultan away, they chose the ship *HMS Malaya*, the only Royal Navy vessel ever paid for by a predominantly Muslim colony. After Kemal's success at Chanak, Rumbold cabled to Curzon from Constantinople his concern that Kemal's victory 'will have stimulated Moslems all over the world and even have raised the question of Islam versus Christianity'.[45] After the signing of the Mudania armistice, Rumbold commented that 'His Majesty's Government is being attacked in the rear by the combination of forces represented by labour, the "Daily Mail" and the politicians who imagine that the way to placate Islam is to yield on every point to a militant Turkey'.[46] He further warned from Constantinople that some of the Kemalists sought to establish 'Turkey in a position of hegemony in a great Islamic combine. For these Great Britain not only is, but will remain, the enemy. They desire nothing less than collapse of our position, first in Mesopotamia, then in the East generally'.[47]

When the issue of Dominions' representation at Lausanne was being discussed, the India Office made a plea to be allowed two representatives in order to be seen to be 're-asserting by action the supreme interest Britain, as the greatest Mohamedan power, has in Moslems'.[48] Admittedly, the response from within the Foreign Office was that there was no need for the added inconvenience of an Indian delegation.[49]

On the eve of the conference there came the surprise of the abolition of the sultanate and the consolidation of the Turkish government in the hands of the Nationalists. Some consideration was given to extracting what residual value there was from the deposed Sultan. Such senior Foreign Office officials as Curzon, Crowe, and Lindsay all supported giving asylum to the deposed ruler. Lindsay thought such a move might vindicate Britain in Islamic eyes, and Crowe thought serious consideration should be given to allowing him to live in India, as a counter-weight to the Khilafat movement.[50]

The Viceroy, Lord Reading, however, advised that there was no public support for the deposed Sultan-Caliph, who was seen as no more than a tool of the Allied occupation. Reading saw no way to make use of the deposed ruler and recommended standing aloof from his fate.[51] Crowe was astounded by this response: 'The viceroy's telegram is a revelation of the cynicism with which the Indian pro-Islam agitation is worked and utilized by the Govt. of India. To unprejudiced eyes it seems almost a scandal that H.M.G. should have to listen to such advice.'[52] The Sultan initially went to Malta, causing a concerned Foreign Office to ask the British High Commission at Constantinople if they thought he would be able to afford his accommodation. The commission's sage advice was that it would be impolitic to charge him until his final fate was known.[53]

A topic of discussion among British officials was the future status of the British diplomatic mission to Turkey, once peace was concluded. Historically Constantinople had ranked as an embassy, but given the much diminished nature of Turkish power there was discussion that the temporary High Commission be downgraded at peace to a legation. Nevile Henderson, the acting high commissioner, warned this would only cause resentment: 'Constantinople will be the seat of the Caliphate and as the greatest Moslem Power I should not have thought that it was in our interests to reduce the importance of the Mission here.'[54]

The possibility of American participation, if not as participatory delegates then at least as observers, was considered desirable, and the Americans were sounded out on the issue.[55] As events transpired, one of the main irritants in Anglo-American relations would be the American high commissioner at Constantinople, Admiral Mark Bristol, who also served as the chief American observer at Lausanne. Among the Allied high commissioners he was in a unique position as he was also commander of the US Naval Detachment in Turkish Waters. Bristol was viewed, correctly, by British officials as being anti-British. At the height of the Chanak crisis, when it was thought that the British High Commission would have to be evacuated from Constantinople and its functions left to a protecting power, Crowe advised against entrusting this role to the United States, as had been done when Britain and the Ottoman Empire had gone to war in 1914.

> I feel great reluctance to agree to suggestion that British interests should be confided to the preposterous Admiral Bristol. If the U.S. Representative were a person less hostile to Great Britain and less petty in his personal feelings, it would of course be the most desirable course to entrust the care of our interests to the United States.[56]

Even Grew observed of him that 'He is very pro-Turk and very anti-British'.[57] Grew also noted: 'Curzon is obviously anxious. He asks for our cooperation. Is fearful of Admiral Bristol's influence on a delicate situation.'[58] The issue of Bristol's precedence though continued to complicate matters. As soon as he arrived he replaced Grew as the senior American, as he ranked as an ambassador. The difficulty was that the Allied states were also represented at Lausanne by their high commissioners, and as at Constantinople they still refused to accept his as dean of the diplomatic corps: 'The present situation, therefore, is that no one can safely invite Bristol to dinner with any of the other Allied High Commissioners.'[59]

At the conference the matter arose of how to seat the American delegation; it had not been at war with the Ottoman empire, and had been aloof in many post-war international gatherings. When the British were informed that the Americans wished to be seated as equals, Harold Nicolson responded: 'Hooray, that simplifies things a lot. We rather feared that as "observers" you would want to sit away from the conference table and have one all to yourselves – sort of like children coming down from the nursery.'[60]

Anglo-American relations during the conference were often facilitated at the junior level. Two of Curzon's staff, Harold Nicolson and Allen Leeper, were old friends of the American diplomat Joseph Grew. They often met and dined together and in the process facilitated matters. The overall perception of the United States, perhaps exaggerated due to its personification in the form of Admiral Bristol, remained negative. Rumbold observed during a lull in the negotiations: 'The Americans make one sick. They talk big to one's face and pretend to help one and then go behind one's back.'[61] Grew felt the hostility of the British and noted in his diary that he was surprised that one of the first problems that presented itself was establishing friendly relations with the British delegation. He concluded this was due to Curzon's incorrect impression that the United States was pro-Turkish. During the second phase of the negotiations, despite all efforts at fraternization, Rumbold only called upon Grew once, despite their also being old colleagues, while the French and Italians continually visited. Grew considered himself an anglophile but he was clearly irked that Rumbold never consulted him or discussed his own opinions or shared information.[62]

When the conference collapsed and efforts were being made to resuscitate it, the Americans made a goodwill gesture to help ease the non-military situation. This led one Foreign Office official to remark that 'the general attitude of the U.S. towards European problems is that of a man standing on the bank of a river & offering advice on swimming to a drowning man'.[63]

Anglo-French relations in the Eastern Mediterranean had become strained even prior to the signing of the Mudros armistice in 1918. At the end of 1920 at a Cabinet meeting (though this was not minuted) Lloyd George observed that 'in Constantinople, Athens and elsewhere it had become almost a fixed habit of the French after agreeing on a common policy with us to go behind our backs and alledge [sic] that we were responsible for all the unpleasant features of that policy'.[64] This sense of frustration with France runs throughout this period and into the final peace negotiations. By the time of the Lausanne Conference Anglo-French relations were abysmal. At the centre of British unhappiness with France was its premier, Raymond Poincaré. Curzon in particular enjoyed notably bad relations with the French leader. He advised the new British ambassador at Paris, Lord Crewe, that Poincaré was a 'rather disagreeable & a bad-tempered man – and does things that no gentleman would attempt'.[65] In this view he was not alone. Lord Stamfordham, writing on behalf of the king, in response to the report of the normally francophile Sir William Tyrrell, observed 'it is evident that in Poincaré we have the one serious stumbling block in achieving a satisfactory settlement with France'.[66] Allen Leeper, one of the Foreign Office staff to accompany Curzon, called the French premier 'that detestable little liar & cad'.[67]

Greece unquestionably benefited from being represented by Venizelos, to whom the Athens government had turned in desperation to represent them in the negotiations. He earned the respect of all who observed him. Rumbold wrote that 'Monsieur Venizelos fights his battle with great skill and volubility and always has an answer ready to meet Turkish arguments'.[68] Grew noted in his diary: 'Venizelos' personality is so attractive and his manner so forceful and convincing that one is always impressed when he talks. He is undoubtedly the outstanding figure of the conference.'[69] Rumbold, however, was one of the few not dazzled by the Greek statesman, commenting that he profoundly distrusted him.[70]

The Turkish delegation was led by Ismet Pasha (later surnamed Inönü), one of the Nationalist generals. The Turkish delegation did not seem to inspire confidence. Grew considered: 'They have no apparent skill or experience of peace conferences, and I must say they have a good deal of my sympathy.'[71] A month later he noted: 'I do not attach too much importance to what the Turks say after a good dinner. I am told that Ismet, under the warming effects of good champagne, has three times told Lord Curzon that the British could keep Mosul.'[72] But for all their seeming incompetence, Rumbold was led to complain: 'it is exasperating to think that a small country like

Turkey, with only seven million inhabitants, should be giving so much trouble to the biggest countries in the world. The Turks ought to be seen and not heard!'[73] In fact, the Turkish delegation did possess some tactical skill, as Rumbold admitted: 'It is clear to us here, though it has not been apparent to Lord C., that the Turks will temporise until they see whether the Reparations Conference produces a split between the French and ourselves.'[74] Indeed, such tactics did prove successful; Grew, in critiquing the failure of the first phase of the conference, concluded: 'I believe that the element that contributed most to the failure of the Conference was the defection of the French; they broke the solid front, gave the Turks new strength and encouragement and ruined the chances of a successful outcome. The responsibility is theirs.'[75]

Mussolini, newly installed in power, attended the opening of the conference. Curzon's assessment of him was that he was 'no statesman', and he observed that the Italian leader was always asking the British delegation for suggestions, 'because he has not the slightest idea of what to ask himself'.[76] Leadership of the Italian delegation was left to Marchese Garroni, of whom the British were deeply suspicious. The Italian high commissioner at Constantinople, he had intended to sail aboard an Italian ship from the city, but as it pulled out of dock it collided with a Spanish warship and instead he was forced to take a more tedious rail journey.[77] Once the conference convened, relations did not improve, with Rumbold complaining that 'the Italians periodically blackmail us'.[78]

Soviet Russia was likewise represented. Rumbold did not care for their chief delegate, the Soviet commissar for foreign affairs, 'Chicherin's first appearance was interesting, but we are all tired of his thin, high-pitched and raping voice. Many of the Russians look awful ruffians.'[79]

Normally a conference is presided over by a representative of the host country. The president of the Swiss Federal Council did indeed open the conference on 20 November 1922, but Switzerland had always made it clear that it would not preside, though it was happy to facilitate matters by providing an acceptable venue. Britain, France, and Italy had agreed prior to the opening of the conference that the chair would rotate between themselves, as the organizing powers. Poincaré and Mussolini attended the ceremonial opening but left the following day. This provided Curzon with the opportunity to seize the chair, informing his fellow delegates that as the senior representative of the organizing powers he would hold the chair. Using his position, Curzon promptly organized the conference into three working committees on territorial matters, capitulations, and financial and economic matters. He proposed that he would chair the first, Garroni the second, and Barrère the third. This was the first and only plenary session of the conference. Curzon in a remarkable diplomatic coup had seized the chair for himself, then appointed himself chair of the most important sub-committee, and then prevented further debate about his actions by not again convening a plenary session. In fact, most of the activity of the conference surrounded Curzon's committee, which met 26 times, while Garroni's met only five, and Barère's six times. It was a busy conference, nonetheless, leading Grew to confide to his diary: 'This is a busy life, almost as busy as Paris during the big Peace Conference.'[80]

Harold Nicolson, who attended the conference and who has left the most luminous account of its proceedings, wrote in admiration of Curzon's virtuosity. 'Curzon displayed unrivalled technical capacity. He so arranged the time-table that the subjects in which the Turks were in a weak position should be taken first: whereas the subjects in which they were in a strong position or could hope for Russian support were postponed.'[81] Curzon may have enjoyed high politics and the manoeuvring that allowed him his coup, but the detail of negotiation bored him. He told Crowe: 'I do not much care for the technical aspect of negotiation. But I think it is an obligation of honour.'[82] He had aspired to the prime ministership not long before and was frustrated with the selection of Bonar Law to fill that office. He vented his frustration to Lord Crewe: 'I am afraid that his ignorance of the proceedings, not merely of Conference, but of diplomacy in general, led him to precipitate matters in a manner which was both unnecessary and unwise.'[83]

As the conference moved towards collapse at the end of January, the Army asked for permission to evacuate British forces from Constantinople to Galipoli once news was received that Turkey had not accepted the Allies' terms.[84] Curzon, when consulted, vehemently opposed any such move as being detrimental to British interests and the ability ultimately to make a peace with Turkey. Maurice Hankey, the Cabinet secretary, was dismayed by this attitude which flew in the face of all military advice. He was aware of the plethora of problems facing the country, the crumbling entente, the danger to British forces at Mosul, the volatile situation in Egypt, combined with the economic difficulties at home.

The breakdown of the conference coincided with greater crises in international relations. On 11 January 1923 French forces occupied the Ruhr over the German default on its reparations payments. The Lausanne negotiations had now reached that natural stage in difficult peace talks when a break is useful for all sides and a useful cause for disruption is found. In this instance, the future of the capitulations provided grounds for suspending talks and allowing all parties a respite and an opportunity for direct consultations at home. The conference was adjourned on 4 February. The final hours of the first phase of the Lausanne conference were, nonetheless, worthy of a thriller with final *demarches* and, ultimately, with the Orient Express being held at the station for an extra half hour before Curzon finally boarded, with all essentials agreed but the psychological moment for signature not yet ready.[85]

Grew, as an active observer of the conference, placed some of the blame for collapse upon Curzon, but put most of the blame upon France. Noting that Curzon had 'assumed the attitude of a Viceroy whereas, as a matter of fact, he was nothing but an equal', Grew goes on to observe, however, 'I believe that the element that contributed most to the failure of the Conference was the defection of the French; they broke the solid front, gave the Turks new strength and encouragement and ruined the chances of a successful outcome. The responsibility is theirs ... the harm had already been done by Poincaré in Paris'.[86] Curzon returned to London and when it proved possible to restart the negotiations he was occupied with other matters. During the second session of the Lausanne conference Rumbold headed the British delegation.

In the end a treaty was negotiated, with Turkey succeeding in regaining control of Eastern Thrace, Smyrna, and the strategically important Aegean islands of Imbros and Tenedos. The idea of establishing an independent Armenia, carved out of eastern Turkey was dropped. The treaty of Sèvres had envisaged a Turkey under

Allied tutelage but, as a post-conference report observed, the Lausanne settlement 'leaves the Turks masters in their own house'.[87] The Treaty of Lausanne was signed on 24 July 1923, ratified on 24 August, and the last British troops left Constantinople on 2 October. Rumbold had at least succeeded in seeing a settlement agreed. When the treaty was discussed in parliament he was amazed to see Curzon presenting it as a triumph and 'disgusted' to see Curzon take all the credit, commenting that 'Curzon is a man who accepts the cream brought to him by someone and kicks the man who brought it'.[88]

For Britain the Lausanne negotiations were a way by which it might extricate itself from an impossible position with as little damage to British power and prestige as possible. The showmanship of Curzon and the doggedness of Rumbold were needed to project a sense that Britain was still the primary arbiter of the Aegean world. In aspects of the negotiations Britain did achieve important objectives, especially a formula which would ultimately leave it in control of the oilfields of Mosul. This would ultimately be used to demonstrate British success in the final settlement. In the Aegean sphere, however, which had initially been the primary focus of British interests, there was only the public projection of a diplomatic success to cover the reality of Britain's failed bid for Aegean hegemony. Rumbold was realistic about what had really been achieved at Lausanne. On writing to the king of the settlement Rumbold was frank: 'We cannot nor do we pretend that the instrument we have just negotiated is a glorious one. It is anything but that. Still, given the circumstances in which we have had to negotiate with the Turks, I think that we have obtained the least unsatisfactory terms possible.'[89] Britain may have won the war, but ultimately in the Lausanne settlement it did not quite win the peace it had sought.

NOTES

1. Imperial Conference, 2nd meeting, 21 June 1921. Minutes of the Conference are in RG25/2279/file S/6/1, National Archives of Canada, Ottawa (hereinafter cited as NAC). Minutes of the Imperial Conference are also in CAB 32/2, and Notes of Informal Talks in CAB 32/4, Cabinet Papers, Public Record Office, Kew, London.
2. E. Goldstein, 'Great Britain and Greater Greece', *Historical Journal*, 32/2 (1989), pp.339–56. See also M.L. Smith, *Ionian Vision: Greece in Asia Minor, 1919–1922* (London, 1973).

3. Asquith to Venetia Stanley, 11 Aug. 1914. M. and E. Brock (eds.), *H.H. Asquith: Letters to Venetia Stanley* (Oxford, 1982), p.165.
4. Lord Riddell, *Lord Riddell's Diary of the Peace Conference and After, 1918–1923* (London, 1933), pp.6–7.
5. A.W.A. Leeper to RWA Leeper, 19 May 1919. A.W.A. Leeper Papers, now at Chruchill College, Cambridge.
6. A.J.P. Taylor (ed.), *Lloyd George: A Diary, by Frances Stevenson* (London, 1971), p.183, entry for 8 May 1919.
7. FO 608/37/92/1/1/4392. Minute by Nicolson to Crowe, 15 March 1919. Foreign Office Papers, Public Record Office, London.
8. Admiral de Roebuck to Curzon, 9 March 1920. *Documents on British Foreign Policy, 1919–1939* (London 1963), 1st series, vol.13, p.18.
9. Bristol Diary, 'Report on Operations for Week Ending 4 July 1920', 4 July 1920. Bristol Papers, Library of Congress, Washington, DC.
10. Rumbold 28, Percy Loraine (Warsaw) to Rumbold, 17 Nov. 1920. Rumbold Papers, Bodleian Library, Oxford.
11. CAB 32/2, Imperial Cabinet, 4th mtg., 22 June 1921.
12. W. Churchill, *The Great War* (London, 1934), vol. 3, p.1559.
13. *DBFP*, 1st series, vol.12, p.439.
14. Rumbold 29, Rumbold to Curzon, 10 Dec. 1921.
15. This designation was not officially adopted until 13 May 1919.
16. FO 371/7306/E11502/27/44, Rumbold to Curzon, 17 Oct. 1922.
17. Lloyd George to Margaret Lloyd George, 28 Sept. 1922. K. Morgan (ed.), *Lloyd George: Family Letters, 1885–1936* (Cardiff, 1973), p.196.
18. Hardinge 45, Curzon to Hardinge, 1 Oct. 1922. Hardinge of Penshurst Papers, University Library, Cambridge.
19. Hardinge 45, Hardinge to Curzon, 2 Oct. 1922.
20. J. Vincent (ed.), *The Crawford Papers: The Journals of David Lindsay Twenty-Seventh Earl of Crawford and Tenth Earl of Balcarres 1871-1940 During the Years 1892 to 1940* (Manchester, 1984), p.450, entry for 12 Oct. 1922.
21. Hardinge 45, Hardinge to Curzon, 11 Oct. 1922.
22. On the end of the sultanate see A.L. Macfie, *The End of the Ottoman Empire, 1908–1923* (London, 1998), pp.197–207.
23. Bristol Diary, 17 Nov. 1922.
24. Grew Diary 20, Grew to M. Perry (sister), 13 Nov. 1922. Grew Diary, Houghton Library, Harvard University.
25. Gladstone to the House of Commons, 7 May 1877. On this issue see also R. Shannon, *Gladstone and the Bulgarian Agitation* (Hassocks, 1975).
26. A. Toynbee, *The Murderous Tyranny of the Turks* (London and New York, 1917) with a preface by Viscount Bryce.
27. FO 608/52/120/1/3/316. Minute by Crowe, 22 Jan. 1919.
28. AWA Leeper to his father (Alexander Leeper), 14 Nov. 1922.
29. AWA Leeper to his father (Alexander Leeper), 23 Jan. 1923.
30. FO 800/386/Tu/22/4, AWA Leeper to Vansittart, 4 May 1922.
31. FO 371/7886/E9137/27/44, de Martino to Curzon, 10 Sept. 1922.
32. FO 371/7886/E9137/27/44, minute by Curzon, 10 Sept. 1922.
33. FO 371/7891/E9674/27/44.
34. FO 371/7904/E11262/27/44; FO 371/7905/E11291/27/44.
35. FO 371/7904/E11262/27/44, Hardinge (Paris) to FO, 12 Oct. 1922.
36. Rumbold 30, Rumbold (Lausanne) to N. Henderson (Constantinople), 16 Jan. 1923.

37. Bland 9/2, Crowe to Bland, 17 Oct. 1922. Bland Papers, Churchill College, Cambridge.
38. FO 371/7903/E11084/27/44, minute by Curzon 26 Sept. 1922.
39. *FRUS, 1923* vol.II, p.879, Dulles to Phillips, 19 Sept. 1922.
40. FO 371/7902/E10888/27/44, minute by Crowe, 12 Oct. 1922.
41. FO 371/7907/E12276/27/44, memorandum by Curzon, 'Dominion Representation at Lausanne', 6 Nov. 1922.
42. FO 371/7909/E12275/27/44, Hughes (PM Australia) to Colonial Secretary, 2 Nov. 1922.
43. *Foreign Relations of the United States: Paris Peace Conference*, vol.5, p.756.
44. Gail Minault, *The Khilafat Movement: Religous Sybolism and Political Mobilization in India* (New York, 1982).
45. FO 371/7886/E9444/27/44, Rumbold to Curzon, 18 Sept. 1922.
46. FO 371/7306/E11502/27/44, Rumbold to Curzon, 17 Oct. 1922.
47. FO 371/7306/E11502/27/44, Rumbold to Curzon, 17 Oct. 1922.
48. FO 371/7909/E12236/27/44, cable from viceroy, 5 Nov. 1922.
49. FO 371/7913/E12771/27/44, minute by Lindsay, 16 Nov. 1922.
50. FO 371/7910/E12293/27/44, 6 Nov. 1922.
51. FO 371/7913/E12699/27/44, 10 Nov. 1922.
52. FO 371/7911/E12455/27/44, minute by Crowe, 11 Nov. 1922.
53. Rumbold 30, N. Henderson to Rumbold, 29 Nov. 1922.
54. Rumbold 30, N. Henderson to Rumbold, 19 Dec. 1922.
55. *FRUS, 1922*, vol.II, pp.881–2, Harvey (London) to State Dept., 12 Oct. 1922; FO 371/7903/E11066/27/44, Curzon to Geddes (Washington), 13 Oct. 1922.
56. FO 371/7900/E10700/27/44, minute by Crowe, 8 Oct. 1922.
57. Grew Diary 22, 22 Jan. 1923.
58. Grew Diary 20, 24 Nov. 1922.
59. Grew Diary 20, 2 Dec. 1922.
60. Grew Diary 20, 20 Nov. 1922.
61. Rumbold 31, Rumbold to Oliphant, 2 April 1923.
62. Grew Diary 22, 2 Sept. 1922.
63. FO 371/9064/E1525/1/44, minute by Osborne, 7 Feb. 1923.
64. HNKY 1/5, diary, 31 Dec. 1920. Hankey Papers, Churchill College, Cambridge.
65. Crewe C/12, Curzon (Lausanne) to Crewe, 25 Dec. 1922. Crewe Papers, University Library, Cambridge.
66. FO 800/386/Fr/22/2, Stamfordham to Crowe, 13 Nov. 1922.
67. AWA Leeper to his father, 14 Nov. 1922.
68. Rumbold 30, Rumbold to Stamfordham, 10 Dec. 1922.
69. Grew Diary 20, 24 Nov. 1922.
70. Rumbold 30, Rumbold to N. Henderson, 23 Jan. 1923.
71. Grew Diary 20, 22 Nov. 1922.
72. Grew Diary 20, 21–31 Dec. 1922.
73. Rumbold 30, Rumbold to Harington (Cple), 29 Dec. 1922.
74. Rumbold 30, Rumbold to Henderson, 5 Dec. 1922.
75. Grew Diary 22, 4 Feb. 1923.
76. FO 371/7919/E14422/2//44, minute by Curzon, 21 Dec. 1922.
77. Bristol Diary, 16 Nov. 1922.
78. Rumbold 30, Rumbold to N. Henderson, 5 Dec. 1922.
79. Rumbold 30, Rumbold to N. Henderson, 12 Dec. 1922.
80. Grew Diary 20, 23 Nov. 1922.

81. H. Nicolson, *Curzon: The Last Phase, 1919–1925, A Study in Post-War Diplomacy* (London, 1937), pp.292–3.
82. FO 800/ME/22/2, Curzon to Crowe, 17 Dec. 1922.
83. Crewe C/12, Curzon (Lausanne) to Crewe, 5 Jan. 1923.
84. CAB 23/45, Cabinet meeting 30 Jan. 1923.
85. R. Langhorne, 'The Treaty of Lausanne (1923) and the Recognition of Modern Turkey: The International Context', in *Atatürk Türkiiye'sinde (1923–1983) Dis Politika Sempozyumu* (Istanbul, 1984), pp.101–24
86. Grew Diary 22, 4 Feb. 1923.
87. FO 371/9083/E6330/1/44, 'Treaty of Sèvres and Treaty of Lausanne', 16 June 1923.
88. Rumbold 32, Rumbold to Henderson, 29 Feb. 1924.
89. Rumbold 31, Rumbold to George V, 16 July 1923.

Austen Chamberlain and the Continental Balance of Power: Strategy, Stability, and the League of Nations, 1924–29

B.J.C. McKERCHER

> For we cannot afford to see France crushed, to have Germany or an eventual Russo-German combination supreme on the Continent, or to allow any great military power to dominate the Low Countries.
>
> Chamberlain, January 1925[1]

As foreign secretary from November 1924 to June 1929, Austen Chamberlain dominated British foreign policy. Central to his diplomatic strategy was the maintenance of the European balance of power and, in this circumstance, pursuit of a leadership role for Britain within the League of Nations. The foundation upon which Chamberlain based his European strategy lay with his determination to have Britain play the vital role of stabilizing relations between France and Germany, whose mutual antipathy after the Great War, compounded by the severity of the Treaty of Versailles, threatened continental security. By October 1925, his work bore fruit with the conclusion of the Locarno agreements, the most important of which was a British guarantee of the Franco-German border.[2] For the remainder of his tenure at the Foreign Office, Chamberlain used Locarno – Germany's membership in the League was part of that settlement – as the diplomatic mechanism to underwrite his strategic conception of the balance of power. Yet, despite the renaissance of historical analysis since the mid-1980s concerning Chamberlain's time as foreign secretary, there has been virtually no consideration of his strategic ideas in the making and execution of British foreign policy.³ Indeed, the most recent – and unhelpful – examination of his service as foreign secretary is distinguished by this failure.⁴ Appreciating that Austen Chamberlain defended Britain's external position in the latter half of the 1920s with a consistent strategic vision has two benefits: it fills a major historiographical lacuna at an important moment in the evolution of inter-war Britain; and, flowing from this appreciation, some of the serious criticisms of his diplomatic record – the success of 1925 not only forced him to support the Locarno system unflinchingly, it gave his diplomacy an inflexible quality; it undermined the efficacy of the League; and it constituted 'a false dawn' because its promise was not realized⁵ – can be shown to be wide of the mark.

Chamberlain became foreign secretary after a 30-year political career that had seen him hold several major Cabinet posts and the leadership of the Unionist Party. His career had foundered in October 1922 when he lost that leadership by not containing a rebellion of Unionist backbenchers and junior ministers who opposed continuing in a coalition government led by the Liberal, David Lloyd George. After two years in the political wilderness, Chamberlain was invited by the new party leader, Stanley Baldwin, to join a newly elected Conservative government as foreign secretary – the party had shed the 'Unionist' label and returned to its original name. His selection as foreign secretary had as much to do with Baldwin's recognition of his ministerial talent as with elementary political reasons touching the unity of the Conservative Party. Still, the fact remains that Chamberlain had a nearly impregnable position in the Cabinet and party after November 1924 and, with this base, endeavoured to rebuild his reputation.⁶ For Chamberlain, although Britain stood as the only world power in the 1920s and faced global foreign policy problems deriving from the defence of its empire and the honouring of widespread treaty commitments, the European question remained the most important. A continental equilibrium remained essential when Britain faced crucial strategic problems in Europe that threatened both its security and the stability needed for its post-war revival. In this context, because almost all of the European Powers belonged to the League, British support for the international organization became the leitmotif of Chamberlain's diplomatic strategy.

Chamberlain never served as foreign secretary before November 1924.[7] But as a professional politician with long experience in or near the Cabinet – he received his first ministerial position, civil lord of the admiralty, in 1895 – his career had provided him with much insight and some experience of British external policies. As a consequence, he had a strategic vision of essential British interests and their maintenance and defence. He had been chancellor of the exchequer twice (1903–5, 1919–21), Indian secretary (1915–17), minister without portfolio and chairman of the post-war Economic Defence and Development Committee (1918–19), and Lord Privy Seal (1921–22). In these positions, and during time on the opposition benches, he dealt often with the issues of national security, imperial defence, war- and peace-making policy, and paying for capable armed forces.[8] In 1902, following the Boer War, he had been a member of the ministry that created the Committee of Imperial Defence (CID) to coordinate foreign and defence policies and, subsequently when in office, helped guide its counsels. As a senior member of the opposition in 1914, he had an influential role during the July crisis in pushing the Cabinet to declare war on Germany – for reasons tied clearly to maintaining the European balance.[9] And, of course, it almost goes without saying that he had familiarity with intergovernmental negotiation and working with foreign statesmen and diplomatists.[10] Perhaps more important in this regard, life within the Unionist-Conservative Party, long distinguished by cutthroat political machinations in which he had been bloodied more than once, gave Chamberlain an on-going education in the intricacies of *realpolitik* – of identifying threats, finding and keeping allies, and using available resources to protect and extend his interests.[11]

Given his new responsibilities in 1924, he arrived at the Foreign Office with a strategic view of Britain's essential external interests. His father, Joseph, had been an arch-imperialist – perhaps the arch-imperialist – in the late Victorian and Edwardian periods. Austen shared his father's beliefs about the Empire being the *sine qua non* of Britain's status as the only global power; in fact, Joseph sent his son to Cambridge university to study under Sir John Seely, the historian of the British Empire. And Sir Halford Mackinder, the seminal geopolitical strategic philosopher, had been one of Joseph

Chamberlain's advisers and speech-writers. Even after Joseph's political eclipse – he had a stroke in 1906 and died in 1914 – Austen long supported a system of imperial preference to strengthen the Empire when the so-called 'White' dominions began asserting their independence. Moreover, earlier, in the 1890s, he, his father, and his brother, Neville, gave tangible expression to their beliefs by investing heavily, though ultimately unsuccessfully, in a West Indian hemp plantation.[12] Then, when the Irish rebellion broke out in 1919, Austen played a crucial role as a senior minister in seeking to resolve the crisis and keep independent Ireland within the emerging Commonwealth.[13] At the same time, because Britain was an island nation with a maritime empire, and via his Admiralty experience, Austen understood the importance of the Royal Navy as both the lynch-pin of imperial defence and the guardian of the vital seaborne lines of communication essential for Britain's economic survival. This appreciation derived not only from a grasp of the grand strategic role of the Royal Navy in projecting power; it also obtained from his appreciation of what can be called the minutiae of navalism, everything from maintaining the infrastructure of overseas bases to ensuring the welfare of sailors to make them better fighters.[14]

But to a large degree, and despite filial piety towards his father's imperial beliefs, Chamberlain always saw European stability as fundamental for British security; and, importantly, he had a greater first-hand knowledge of the continent than any British foreign secretary for at least half a century.[15] As a young man in 1885–87 living in France and Germany to study and learn languages – he came to speak fluent French and passable German – he was exposed to the swirl of European politics. His experiences at that time, including meetings with statesmen as diverse as Georges Clemençeau and Otto von Bismarck, confirmed for him the importance to Britain of liberal democratic France as a counterweight to authoritarian and aggressive Germany. As he recorded in October 1887 after attending lectures by the German nationalist historian, Heinrich Treitschke:

> Treitschke has opened to me a new side of the German character – narrow-minded, proud, intolerant Prussian

chauvinism. And the worst of it is that he is forming a school. ... I fear my generation of Germans, and those a little younger will be far more high-handed and will presume far more on the victories of '66 and '70 than those who won them.[16]

In 1899 Joseph Chamberlain, then the colonial secretary, and a clutch of influential Unionist ministers supported an effort to conclude an Anglo-German alliance as a means to contain Russian ambitions in China; it came to nought because the German price was too high: British support of German interests in Europe, including the Balkans.[17] Although welcoming the search for an ally, Austen seems to have been less sanguine about this initiative than his father; for him, a French connection gave Britain greater security. As he told Count Metternich, the German ambassador to Britain, a few years later:

> Ever since I have known English politics – say since the early 'eighties – there has been a real desire among the masses of our people for a good understanding with France, partly no doubt because they wished to see an end put to the secular rivalry and distrust between these two great nations facing each other across twenty miles of sea; partly because they thought there was a closer communion of ideas between these two great liberal nations than between ourselves and any other.[18]

This attitude animated Chamberlain during the 1914 July Crisis, when he argued forcefully for British involvement in a continental war in alliance with France and Russia against Germany. In the immediate aftermath of the Great War, as Lloyd George's government sought means to ensure Western European stability, Chamberlain encouraged an Anglo-French alliance to restrain a revanchist Germany.[19] What Chamberlain believed – and argued consistently during his entire political career when considering British strategic interests – was that Britain was ultimately a European power. The security of the home islands had always to be the first consideration. In what might be considered his valedictory address as foreign secretary, a speech to the Royal Institute of International Affairs (RIIA) in February 1930, he laid out his views on this subject.[20] In warfare, he observed, 'whilst tactics vary, the principles of strategy remain unaltered. Are there not some strategic principles which govern the course of British foreign policy and to which English parties and English ministers pay a real if only an instinctive obedience?' Before answering his question, Chamberlain first argued that in the post-Great War period, two 'circumstances' had changed British diplomatic tactics: 'rapid communication both of ideas and persons' and 'the constitutional development of the British Empire'. The first circumstance meant that 'no part of the world is now isolated either physically or morally from the rest'. The second signified that within the Empire, Britain was 'only one among many voices, *primus inter pares* it may be, but no longer alone'. Hence, the tactical milieu in which British diplomatists had to function had altered significantly from that before 1914; and in this context, the League had importance: 'It is not merely a sense of the appalling horrors of modern war which has driven the world to seek protection from it in the League of Nations; it is the growing perception that our interests are so inter-woven that the victors suffer only less than the vanquished and that even the neutral is involved in the common disaster to mankind.'

From these observations flowed the answer to his question. Changing circumstances and the introduction of new elements like the League did not enervate the immutable strategic prescription to maintain the security of the British home islands: the European balance of power.[21] In Chamberlain's estimation, from the mid-eighteenth century onwards, British leaders had consistently though not always successfully pursued the balance to maintain peace on the continent:

> Nothing, therefore, has occurred to release us from the necessity of maintaining a watchful interest in continental affairs. On the contrary, positive engagements now reinforce and extend our old interests, and in those positive engagements arising from the [League] Covenant the share of the Dominions is the same as our own.

Isolation from continental affairs portended danger. As he observed about the late 1890s, when his father and other ministers considered a German alliance: 'With Germany unfriendly, France embittered, Italy uncertain and Russia hostile, we were indeed isolated, and even though the loyalty and support of the Colonies made that isolation splendid it did not render it safe.' The strategic response involved reliance on the balance. In holding this belief, Chamberlain was not alone. He was one of a new generation of British leaders at the turn of the century who believed that Britain's security resided in finding allies and friends both to defend the Empire and maintain the continental balance of power – he was a member of the Unionist ministry that concluded the 1902 Anglo-Japanese alliance and the 1904 entente with France.[22] As he informed Lord Crewe, the British ambassador at Paris, soon after becoming foreign secretary,[23] Britain should be the 'honest broker' in continental affairs. But as he also reminded the RIIA five years later, post-war international politics differed markedly from those before 1914. The cost of that struggle in blood and treasure had been high and must not be made again. Whilst some contemporary writers were arguing that in earlier times peace was 'a kind of by-product' from successful pursuit of the balance, Chamberlain saw clearly that after 1918 the 'problem of statesmanship is to reconcile peace with security and to maintain our sovereign independence without recourse to war'. Concerning Europe, his tenure as foreign secretary had been based upon reconciling peace and security on the continent via active pursuit of the balance.

At the moment of Chamberlain's selection as foreign secretary, Europe lacked political stability. The reason devolved from what might best be termed a Franco-German 'Cold War' that had at its heart a French strategy after 1919 to keep post-war Germany weakened and ensure French primacy on the continent.[24] Paris' instrument to achieve this goal lay in the strict enforcement of the Treaty of Versailles, chiefly those provisions forcing Germany to disarm and compelling it to pay heavy reparations. In January 1923, when the depression-plagued German government defaulted on reparations payments, the French and their Belgian ally sent troops to occupy Germany's industrial heartland, the Ruhr Valley. They intended to seize the Ruhr's production in lieu of reparations, a stratagem with the double merit of enfeebling Germany further. This action proved a major diplomatic defeat for France. With its economy in shambles, Weimar Germany's fragile government confronted domestic extremism from left and right. Seeing

European recovery tied to Germany's economic renewal – for Britain necessary to rekindle trade and the United States to recover its war debts – London and Washington used their considerable financial strength to undermine French policy; the franc's solvency could be undercut by gold reserves held by the British and American central banks. Anglo-American intervention produced the Dawes Committee, an international group of bankers that devised methods to bring about German recovery: annual reparations on a fixed scale, political control of the German economy through a series of commissions, and a reorganized German central bank, supported by an American loan, to stabilize the mark.[25]

For the British, Germany' economic revival constituted only one-half the means to achieve European stability; the other half lay in finding a regime of political security, a matter equally important to Paris and Berlin. As the Dawes Committee deliberated, two British governments sought vainly to find such a regime. In office till January 1924, Baldwin's first government proposed the Draft Treaty of Mutual Assistance. Its signatories were to commit to desist from wars of aggression, empower the League Council to apportion national peace-making responsibilities, foster regional security agreements, and, respecting the latter, confine military obligations to those against aggressors on the same continent.[26] The short-lived minority Labour ministry led by James Ramsay MacDonald, in power from January to October 1924, rejected the Conservative initiative. MacDonald's Cabinet calculated that the Draft Treaty would place a heavy burden on the RN in the wider world, and that any regional agreement concerning Europe not only echoed the pre-1914 alliances, it could weaken Britain because of Dominion reluctance to enforce British commitments. MacDonald's government countered with the 'Geneva Protocol', a three-part undertaking by which League members would arbitrate all international disputes, disarm by agreement, and pledge mutual support in the event of unprovoked aggression anywhere in the world.[27] Before it could get achieve the Protocol, MacDonald's ministry surrendered office to Baldwin's second government.

Chamberlain thus inherited the problem of finding a means to achieve European political security. Recognizing the demanding tasks of being foreign secretary – as a world power, Britain confronted diplomatic problems in every area of the globe – he dedicated himself to learning quickly as much as he could about the problems confronting British diplomacy and the administration of the Foreign Office.[28] Working with the Foreign Office permanent under-secretary (PUS), Sir Eyre Crowe, Chamberlain received a range of departmental memoranda, information from British embassies and consulates, and briefings concerning the major international issues confronting Britain. The most important dealt with the Franco-German question, specifically with the Dawes Plan, the issue of German disarmament, and the continuing Ruhr occupation;[29] and in these submissions lay consideration of the wider strategic problem of finding a way to bring stability to the continent. Given that Crowe had been the author of the famous 1907 Foreign Office memorandum on the nature of the European balance of power – and given that he had used his influence after he became PUS in 1920 to promote those who shared his strategic vision to senior Foreign Office positions and embassies abroad[30] – the information funnelled to Chamberlain about Europe put the problem in terms of Britain finding means to establish a balance on the continent. The information was also to a degree critical of Germany. On both points, Chamberlain needed no persuading.

Chamberlain's subsequent role in the efforts of the second Baldwin government to bring stability to continental Europe is well known.[31] Given his long-held views about France and Germany, he initially saw Berlin's policies as the reason for continental instability. For instance, an immediate difficulty concerned ending by January 1925 the Allied occupation of the Rhineland region centred on Cologne; this action was mandated in 1919 as long as Germany lived up to its obligations imposed by the peace settlement. But the Germans were violating the disarmament provisions of Treaty of Versailles, something that caused Chamberlain in late December to exclaim: the 'Germans have played the fool as usual about Cologne'.[32] Similarly Chamberlain looked to improve Anglo-French relations, which had been damaged by post-war territorial squabbles in the Near East and by the Ruhr occupation. He stood, he wrote to Crewe in the New Year, as 'the most pro-French member of the Government';[33] and he used a meeting in Paris on 5 December 1924 with Edouard Herriot, the French premier, to foster greater Anglo-French trust.[34]

However, Chamberlain was a realist. The second Baldwin government's policy concerning Europe centred on its handling of the on-going search for security. At a CID meeting on 4 December, the leading members of the new Cabinet agreed that they could not support the Protocol.[35] Their difficulty was finding an alternative policy. Chamberlain thus returned to his earlier view about an Anglo-French alliance; it could maintain the continental equilibrium by giving Britain a means to restrain France from dangerous undertakings like the Ruhr occupation.[36] His colleagues were divided. On one hand, Winston Churchill, the chancellor of the exchequer, reckoned that Britain should remain aloof from continental affairs; on the other, Robert, Viscount Cecil of Chelwood, the chancellor of the Duchy of Lancaster and a member of the League of Nations Union (LNU) who had earlier supported the Protocol, wanted a firm British commitment to the League goals of disarmament and arbitration.[37] Chamberlain's realism came to the fore when he realized that an Anglo-French alliance did not have the backing of Baldwin's Cabinet and would also serve to antagonize Berlin. Thus, when in January 1925 the German foreign minister, Gustav Stresemann, proposed an Anglo-Franco-German Pact to guarantee the inviolability of the Franco-German border as defined by the Treaty of Versailles, Chamberlain jumped on it as the means by which Britain could maintain the balance between France and Germany.

Stresemann's proposal initiated nine months of twisted diplomacy that, on 16 October 1925, produced the Locarno treaty and a workable system of European security based on Great Power cooperation. In this process, Chamberlain played the pivotal role by, first, getting the Baldwin Cabinet to support the 'Rhineland Pact' and then removing Franco-German points of contention. In essence, Locarno brought a system of security to Europe because Britain agreed in partnership with Italy to guarantee the Franco-German border. And by his willingness to have Italy as a co-guarantor of the 'Treaty of Mutual Guarantee', Chamberlain ensured that the four European Great Powers on the League Council would share joint responsibility for continental security. 'What I pride myself upon', he told his sister after returning from Locarno, 'is that I secured the

Eastern settlement & that I have taught Germany or at least her wisest statesmen that her security lies in our friendship with France not in dividing France & us.'[38] Chamberlain received tangible rewards for his efforts in 1925: the Garter and the Nobel Peace Prize. Less tangibly but more important, his Locarno success cemented his control over British foreign policy for the remainder of the second Baldwin government. This point is important. For Chamberlain, Locarno was not the end of a political process; it was the fashioning of a political instrument by which he could use British power to ensure security on the continent.

After Locarno, continental security resided in the willingness of the Germans and French to work with one another over disarmament whilst achieving a financial *modus vivendi*. Paris and Berlin naturally continued to seek advantages for themselves in their national policies – just as London did. But there were limits to which the continental powers could go before they would upset the balance. Through the agency of Chamberlain's Foreign Office, Britain helped set those limits. The result was that for the remainder of the second Baldwin government – it surrendered office in June 1929 – and for a year afterward, the system of security built at Locarno initiated a five-year highwater mark in international politics: Franco-German animosities were superceded by a cooperative spirit – uneasy, but cooperative; Germany joined the League as an acknowledged Great Power with a permanent seat on the Council; the League established a Commission to prepare for a World Disarmament Conference; the success of Dawes saw increased American loans flow into Germany and, from Germany, regular reparations payments to the former Allies; modified by the Powers, proposals submitted by a new international financial committee chaired by another American, Owen Young, rationalized reparations payments; and negotiations began that ended the Allied occupation of the Rhineland.[39] On all of these issues, Chamberlain and his Foreign Office advisors pursued for Britain 'the honest broker' status that reduced Franco-German friction and provided a improved political atmosphere in which post-war European revival could be nurtured.

Chamberlain, therefore, worked with Briand and Stresemann – and, when necessary, Benito Mussolini, the Italian dictator – to maintain a continental equilibrium and sustain that political atmosphere. Admittedly, things did not always run smoothly. Occasional setbacks occurred, particularly in the Disarmament Preparatory Commission in 1928; but these problems always proved temporary because Chamberlain's diplomatic strategy allowed for British influence to nurture dialogue, negotiation, and compromise. Quite simply, there were no 'Ruhr crises' in the latter half of the 1920s – nothing even approaching the severity of that crisis; and the reason derived from Chamberlain's success in using British influence to maintain the balance of power. In this context, it is instructive to understand how Chamberlain perceived the balance after taking office in November 1924 – the discipline of new political office melding with his earlier experience with external policy; how he understood Britain's self-appointed role as 'the honest broker'; and how he used that role after Locarno, especially through the medium of the League, to foster continental security. Not only does exploring these three issues allow for a long-needed appreciation of his strategic ideas, it shows how some criticisms of his diplomatic record are hollow.

Chamberlain's strategic ideas crystallized after January 1925 when he called a meeting of senior Foreign Office officials to examine the issue of European security.[40] An important memorandum that reached his desk came from the historical advisor, Sir James Headlam-Morley.[41] Prefacing an historical analysis of European security with Palmerston's famous comment that 'We have no eternal allies and no perpetual enemies, our interests are eternal, and those interests it is our duty to follow', Headlam-Morley argued that since at least the Congress of Vienna, Britain had pursued policy to ensure a continental-wide balance. Thus, the post-1918 Eastern European 'successor states', where the old Habsburg, Hohenzollern, and Romanov borderlands intersected, had now to be considered and helped as much as Germany and France to ensure peace. But Germany remained the key. Just as there had been a conscious effort by Lord Castlereagh, the British foreign secretary in 1814–15, to allow for the emergence of a Concert of Europe that included a France cleansed of aggressiveness, Headlam-Morley held that the same process had occurred at Paris in 1919 to allow Germany eventually to take its rightful place as a Great Power. 'Germany of the present day', he observed, 'or Germany of any near future is not even the Germany of 1870.' Allowing that 'German ambitions need not alarm us so long as we see to it that Germany is confined within her present limits', the Germany of 1925 was a state with which Britain could do business.

Chamberlain's assessment of Headlam-Morley's analysis contended that:

> I draw a far sharper distinction than he between the nature of our interests in the West & East of Europe & between the character of the influence or intervention which we should seek to exercise in these two spheres. I would say broadly that in Western Europe we are all a partner; that, comparatively speaking, in Eastern Europe, our rôle should be rather that of a disinterested amicus curiae. Our safety in certain circumstances is bound up with that of France or Belgium or Holland. If this be secured, I do not believe that it is bound up with Roumania for example; &, if I rightly apprehend him, I could not contemplate linking our fortunes so closely with the Eastern States as he would do.[42]

Chamberlain saw the security of the entire subcontinent devolving from stability in its western reaches; and it was in this region that British 'influence or intervention' should be brought to bear. Eastern European states on their own were in no position to imperil continental security; hence, Britain need not make commitments there. Even Russia would pose no threat if Germany was secure in the West. Russia was weak, 'an imponderable factor, curiously enough as frightened of other people as other people are of her'. Whilst Chamberlain still talked of British security being 'bound up with that of France or Belgium or Holland', Germany now had a pivotal position in the emerging constellation of European power: 'the more ambitious peacemakers of Versailles when they framed the Covenant, still left a gap which only a new Concert of Europe can fill. For this reason, amongst others, & because their very hesitation shows that the Germans recognize the full implications of the step, I should rejoice to see Germany join the League & take her seat at the Council.'

Chamberlain's comments show the evolution of his strategic thinking after just a few months in office and as the Cabinet searched for a regime of European security to replace the Protocol. Whereas originally supporting an Anglo-French alliance as the best means to ensure the balance – surmising that Germany posed the threat – he now concluded that Britain could have more influence in continental affairs by brokering between Paris and Berlin. Looking to the future, or at least the future after the Rhineland pact was concluded, he saw that the League, following German membership, would provide the mechanism by which Britain could balance between France and Germany. Significantly, perhaps reflecting Mackinder's influence, Chamberlain showed decided objectivity in assessing the strengths of the continental powers – his description of 'Russia', for instance, lacked the adjective 'Bolshevik', and he reckoned that this state was so weak that it would be unable to threaten the continental balance for some time; if Germany found friends in the West, potential Russian threats would be pushed even further into the future. Therefore, Chamberlain's strategy to ensure British security entailed active involvement in continental affairs, an element of his thinking since at least the mid-1890s; however, his long-held view about an Anglo-French alliance as a means of achieving stability was impossible to sustain by 1925 because of domestic and dominion opposition and because such an agreement would needlessly antagonize Germany;[43] hence, a multilateral Rhineland pact tied to the League constituted the best means to maintain the continental equilibrium. Chamberlain's concept of the balance was narrowly defined – not continent-wide but limited to the Franco-German border. But it was a realistic conception. A Romanian–Hungarian border dispute would not provoke a major European crisis in 1925 or for the foreseeable future thereafter; a Franco-German one would. British efforts, consequently, needed to focus on Western Europe where the four Great Powers – Britain, France, Germany, and Italy – would be committed by treaty; and of course, along with Japan, these powers comprised the permanent members of the League Council. And for problems confronting Europe outside of the Franco-German border, the League could be used as a political instrument to ensure stability.

Close and constant contact by the Great Powers' representatives at Geneva would permit major problems to be addressed and means of settlement discovered. In Chamberlain's conception, the permanent European members of the League Council had decided importance in ensuring stability. In the aftermath of the final Locarno negotiations, Chamberlain wrote:

> I was called to face a situation comparable to that which faced Castlereagh after the fall of Napoleon. I had to face it without having been, as he was, the representative of my country in the years which won victory for the Allies & without any of his acquired prestige & little, very little, of his personal knowledge of & intercourse with foreign rulers.[44]

But Chamberlain grasped strategic principles – and he conjoined this knowledge with historical lessons about success in Britain's continental policies. During the negotiation of what became Locarno, the historian, Charles Webster, published a study of Castlereagh's foreign policy.[45] As Chamberlain told his sister: 'I came into office with clear ideas of what must be done & with confidence I knew how & how only it could be done. A little later Webster's "Castlereagh's foreign policy" was published & I found that I had been talking Castlereagh (adapted to the XX century) without knowing it.' In essence, Chamberlain had decided that the European Great Powers, including Germany, had to work together in a new Concert of Europe within the confines of the League. In doing so – and Chamberlain can be taken at his word – he showed that 'instinctive obedience' he later explained to the RIIA about the 'strategic principles which govern the course of British foreign policy'. Privately, he was more direct: 'And I like to think that there is a continuity of British foreign policy; I am grateful that I can feel that I have justified my father's belief in me & repaid the care he gave to my training, & I am proud to feel that as the foreign minister of a great nation I have restored confidence in our word & won back our old influence.' The 'old influence' was his determination use British strength to mediate amongst the continental Great Powers, chiefly, France and Germany and, when the issue concerned it, Italy.[46]

This issue brings up the questions of the 'honest broker' and the League. Until Chamberlain became foreign secretary, League policy was controlled by other politically powerful ministers with interest in the international organization. Moreover, British delegations always included members of public lobby groups like the LNU.⁴⁷ Crowe and other senior Foreign Office officials chafed at this situation.⁴⁸ At the League Assembly in September 1924, the result was that Gilbert Murray, a delegation member, an Oxford don, and leader of the LNU, pressed the Greek representative to support a British initiative. Murray had no authority for this action; and it produced unwanted strain in Anglo-Greek relations. On becoming foreign secretary, Chamberlain accepted immediately the political necessity of having British foreign policy speak with one voice. Within a week, he won an intra-Cabinet fight with Cecil, who wanted to control Britain's League policy.⁴⁹ Within a month, he attended his first League Council, ostensibly to consider the security question, but just as much to show the representatives of other Powers that he controlled League policy and to establish personal contact with other diplomatists. In this context, this visit proved fruitful. As Chamberlain told Cecil's brother, the Marquess of Salisbury, 'I must make it clear that there is only one foreign policy and only one authorized exponent of it'.⁵⁰

There would be, moreover, a single strategy upon which that policy would be based. By mid-March 1925, in a Foreign Office minute, Chamberlain outlined his strategic approach to policy development. At the tactical level, he posited: 'Great Britain has it in her power at this moment to bring peace to Europe. To achieve this end two things are indispensable: 1. that we should remove or allay French fears. 2. that we should bring Germany back into the concert of Europe.'⁵¹ Whilst both objectives were 'vital', '[n]either by itself will suffice & the first is needed to allow of the second.' Uniting these intertwined tactics would be his strategic approach that exploited his acknowledged francophilia. Taking the line that 'Great Britain's part now is the same as in 1815 & *mutatis mutandis* Castlereagh's policy is the right one today', he told his Foreign Office advisors:

> My sympathies are French. If they were not, I should be less useful than I think I have been & can yet be. Unless I were known to be pro-French I could never get them to move on the lines of Cabinet policy & I could not afford to say or do as much to help Germany. But ... do not let [us,] ... because of our

strong French sympathies, tie ourselves to the defence of all the vagaries of French policy or allow our reason to be quenched in her fears. Unless we hold the balance & use our influence on both sides to the full, Europe will continue to stand en vedette till Armageddon breaks out again. Our business is to prevent that & because we are friends of France to prevent her from committing suicide under the influence of her fears.'

Here lay Chamberlain's understanding of Britain's self-appointed role as 'the honest broker'; within it, the League provided the means to hold the balance.

Thereafter, unless infirm, Chamberlain attended the four League Councils each year – in March, June, September, and December – and led the British delegation to the annual Autumn Assembly. At these venues, he met regularly with Briand and, after Germany joined the League in 1926, Stresemann. He also ensured regular contact with senior Italian delegates, as well as those of lesser powers. Working behind the scenes, at private meetings subsequently and derisively called 'Geneva tea parties' by critics like Cecil, Chamberlain, Briand, and Stresemann worked with these luminaries, as well senior League bureaucrats, to resolve European problems. But all progress in ensuring stability required providing France with security from German revanchism and by bringing Germany into the polity of nations. Chamberlain used the mechanism of the League to achieve this end. Hence, for the foreign secretary, the League did not exist as an end in itself. It existed as an arm of each power's, including Britain's, diplomatic arsenal; but it was a peaceful arm that, unlike before 1914, allowed for reasoned debate and the amelioration of potentially dangerous situations by allowing close and constant contact amongst diplomatists like him.

In a major speech on the subject of the League delivered at Glasgow University in December 1926, Chamberlain admitted that the organization could do many things through its manifold commissions and agencies like the Permanent Court of International Justice to facilitate the pursuit of peace and stability.[52] The League also had an important role in addressing a range of international social and economic problems. But at Glasgow, as he did every time he discussed the League, he did not hide his view that whilst all member states had roles in enforcing the Covenant, the Great Powers on the Council bore the greatest responsibilities because they had the ultimate political and military responsibility to ensure international peace and security. Yet, the League existed as a fact of international life; it had a crucial role to play in sustaining peace and security; and Chamberlain would do everything in his power to utiltize it to this end. As he told his ambassador at Constantinople just after the Glasgow speech; 'The League is; the League waxes in influence and authority. I can't conduct the foreign policy of this country without taking account of it as a hard fact; and that not only or mainly because of British public opinion.'[53] Equally important was the 'hard fact' that the League could not be ignored by Paris and Berlin – nor could it be ignored by the lesser powers.

A test for the three main Locarno powers came in the second half of 1927, when tensions between Poland and Lithuania threatened to escalate into a major crisis; the resolution of the problem also demonstrated Chamberlain's pursuit of the balance. Uneasy after 1918, relations between Poland and Lithuania worsened after the 1923 Polish annexation of the city of Vilna, the ancient capital of Lithuania, and its hinterland. The Lithuanian government immediately announced that, whilst it had no intention of retaking Vilna by force, it considered itself at war with Poland: but it was a peaceful war in that the Polish–Lithuanian border was sealed and all transit and commerce blocked. Irridentist tensions in Lithuania then simmered till September 1926, when Lithuania suddenly concluded a non-aggression pact with Russia.[54] Thereafter, the Polish government led by Marshal Josef Pilsudski worried about increasing warmth in Russo-Lithuanian relations – and the obvious block to its Baltic ambitions. The situation was not helped by troublesome German–Lithuanian relations, an echo of the Lithuanian annexation of the German-speaking port of Memel in 1923. As Sir Ronald Lindsay, the British ambassador, in reported February 1927:

> [Stresemann] was receiving reports of great expenditures by Poland on purchases of horses, munitions of war etc., and he said that rumours were reaching him that some arrangement was in contemplation by which Poland would obtain virtual protectorate over Lithuania. He wished you to know of his

absolute conviction that any such event would mean war to which it would be difficult to set limits.⁵⁵

Germany could not countenance a large Poland on its eastern flank.

The initial views of Chamberlain and his advisors suggested that although Paris was not supportive of Polish territorial aggrandisement, the French might be manoeuvring to strengthen their Polish ally politically in the region.⁵⁶ In 1926, despite French backing, Warsaw had suffered a major diplomatic defeat by failing to win a new non-permanent League Council seat then on offer – a Polish presence on this crucial body would strengthen the French once the Germans took their permanent seat promised at Locarno.⁵⁷ Chamberlain and the Foreign Office opposed the Polish candidacy because it would create a political imbalance at the centre of the League just as Germany officially re-entered the comity of nations; but showing political skill so as not to damage unduly Anglo-Polish relations, Chamberlain allowed lesser League members, chiefly anti-Polish Sweden, to block Warsaw's ambitions.

For the British, other issues intervened in the middle months of 1927 to shift their gaze from Eastern Europe – chiefly, naval disarmament talks at Geneva.⁵⁸ But by the autumn, Lithuanian–Polish tensions increased further when Pilsudski's government prepared for military action and demanded that Lithuania announce that there was no state of war with Poland.⁵⁹ The Lithuanian government refused because such a declaration could be understood as a renunciation of its claim to Vilna. The crisis reached the League Council in December 1927;⁶⁰ and despite residing in Eastern Europe, the problem for the British had a direct connection with Franco-German relations: Poland and France were formal allies; and German–Polish relations, always uneasy, could be damaged irreparably by further Polish aggrandisement on Germany's borders. The chance existed that Franco-German relations could sour, imperilling more important Great Power negotiations touching reparations and disarmament discussions under way in Geneva.⁶¹ Chamberlain reckoned that Pilsudski 'was mediating recourse to force' on the assumption that the British, French, and Germans could never agree on a unified point of view.⁶² In conformity with his strategic precept that Britain was a partner with France and Germany in maintaining the Western European balance, the foreign secretary used his skill to convince Briand and Stresemann to support a peaceful resolution via the League.[63] The unity of opinion of Paris and Berlin, supported by London, was imperative to ensure stability in Eastern Europe and, thereby, in the more important West.

Accordingly, on 10 December, after pronouncing that any state of war between Poland and Lithuania was abolished and prompted by the unified view of the three Locarno powers, the Council recommended that the two states begin negotiations to resolve their differences.[64] Admittedly, when the negotiations began in January 1928, the Lithuanians avoided them – they finally sat down with the Poles in March. The Lithuanians worried that the talks would be used to force an acceptance of the loss of Vilna. Still, the immediate problem had been resolved in December 1927; it had been resolved by the success of Chamberlain in getting his two Locarno partners to work together in the League Council; and, as a result, the continental balance did not wobble. Chamberlain observed privately immediately afterwards that: 'France, England & Germany have pulled well together (If anyone tells you Locarno is dead, tell them that they are talking nonsense) & while those three are invited I am not greatly afraid of a breach of the peace by anyone else.'[65] A permanent solution to the Polish–Lithuanian dispute would have been preferable to the short-term one that did emerge. Yet it follows that the powers rarely expected permanent solutions to nettled questions like those over frontiers in Eastern Europe. For that reason, the Locarno settlement had included those arbitration treaties concerning Germany's eastern borderlands. Whilst the Franco-German border was fixed, that of Germany with its eastern neighbours was flexible. In December 1927, Chamberlain's diplomacy showed how the effectiveness of his strategy of using Locarno and the League to maintain continental stability.

The enduring criticisms of Chamberlain's diplomacy contend that the success of 1925 forced him to support the Locarno system to such an extent that it gave his diplomacy an inflexible quality, that it undermined the efficacy of the League, and that it constituted 'a false dawn' because its promise was not realized. Part of the response to these criticisms is that Chamberlain took office in

November 1924 believing that Britain had to seize the initiative to bring about continental stability. Going back 40 years, his background and political experience lay at the base of this belief. But while Baldwin's Cabinet agreed that the Protocol was not a means by which Britain could involve itself on the continent, it divided over an alternative. Chamberlain would not be deflected from pursuing a diplomatic strategy of active involvement; and when his preference for an Anglo-French alliance fell by the wayside, the German proposal for a Rhineland pact offered a means by which Britain could influence continental affairs. 'I am much more of a "Européen" than most of my countrymen', he told Crowe's successor, Sir William Tyrrell in September 1927, 'for I have a clearer perception than they of the inextricable way in which our interests are bound up with every possibility of the European situation.'[66] Coupled with his unvarnished francophilia, which he used unblushingly as a lever in dealing with both Paris and Berlin, his willingness to make Britain the arbiter of European affairs led to Locarno and the confirmation of Britain as 'the honest broker' in the continental balance between France and Germany. And as an important corollary, Chamberlain seems to have understood that as stability returned to Europe, a stability fostered by reparations agreements, Locarno, and the Disarmament Conference, German economic and military power would grow to France's disadvantage. Locarno gave wise British statesmen a diplomatic mechanism to ensure that as German strength revived, it did so in a way that could be made supportive of resolving difficult problems by cooperation rather than force of arms.

Crucially, therefore, Locarno was not the end of Chamberlain's diplomatic odyssey; it was the beginning. Considering his strategic conception of what precisely Locarno could do and how the League tied into its operation meets his critics on all three points. No doubt exists that Chamberlain doggedly supported the Locarno system during his service as foreign secretary – and after. Yet, in considering the record of British foreign policy in the almost five years he served as foreign secretary, one is struck by the simple fact that not once in that period was Europe subjected to an equivalent of the Ruhr crisis that had the potential to undermine the new international order created by the Paris Peace Conference. The Versailles Treaty, especially, had imperfections, chiefly the transfers of territory and population, the establishment of a harsh reparations regime, and the forced disarmament of Germany when its neighbours, especially France and Poland, were not compelled to reduce their national armouries. However, in the five years before Chamberlain became foreign secretary, German resistance to Versailles, French determination to force German compliance as a means of keeping Germany perpetually weak, and the instability in Eastern Europe that resulted from French alliances with the successor states to obviate German irredentism threatened European stability. As the unsuccessful pursuit of the Draft Treaty and the Geneva Protocol demonstrated, the search for a system of continental security showed the importance of finding a means to bring about stability. Without stability – and French troops were still in the Ruhr in early 1925 – Europe would not be unable to revive economically, politically, or socially.

Believing firmly that Britain was a European power whose security could not come from isolation from the continent, he used the negotiations that led to Locarno and the treaty thereafter to ensure that major political earthquakes did not occur along the fault-line of Franco-German animosity. For the foreseeable future, his strategic thinking saw the danger to stability residing in Western Europe; as replete as it was with ethnic anger and territorial covetousness, Eastern Europe was not a region where Britain should or could make commitments. Eastern European problems could be resolved by British pressure in Paris, Berlin, and Geneva; and Russia was dormant and would remain so as long as Germany benefited from the Western orientation of its foreign policy. Maintaining the balance of power had long served as the best means to protect British interests. The alternatives like a complete reliance on League collective security or retreating within the Empire were pregnant with danger. Thus, while some policy failures in Europe can be ascribed to his diplomacy after October 1925, like that relating to disarmament in 1928, the successes must be accorded to him as well. As difficult as it sometimes was, Chamberlain's maintaining the balance via Locarno, inflexible though it might have been, gave Europe an unprecedented period of cooperation in the inter-war period.

And the League became the means by which Chamberlain pursued the balance. Chamberlain understood the criticism that pro-League politicians like Cecil and lobby groups like the LNU levelled at him. But the argument he made publicly at Glasgow in 1926 demonstrated the recognition that both he and the League functioned in a real world. And what was true of the British foreign secretary was also true for the German and French foreign ministers. The Great Powers on the Council bore the greatest responsibilities in enforcing the Covenant because they had the ultimate political and military responsibility to ensure international peace and security. The mechanism of the League allowed for close and constant contact amongst the foreign ministers of the Great Powers; it allowed them to meet the representatives of the lesser powers; and it allowed great and small powers alike to resolve issues. Chamberlain's diplomatic strategy required the League – as he also said privately in 1926, the 'League is; the League waxes in influence and authority'. Admittedly, the organization could not do everything; it had limitations. After Locarno, however, when Germany joined, it provided a venue for Chamberlain to broker between Briand and Stresemann. It also provided a mechanism by which the British, French, and Germans could force recalcitrant states like Lithuania and Poland to reconcile their differences, no matter how uneasy that reconciliation might be. On both counts, in Chamberlain's strategic conception, the League Council was akin to the post-1815 Concert of Europe. Just as the Concert proved crucial in bringing about European stability after the Napoleonic wars, the restructured League Council after 1925 could do the same for post-Great War Europe. Rather than undermining the League, Chamberlain's foreign policy provided it with an effective role in helping to maintain continental security after 1925. It was just that his conception of a 'Concert of Europe' within the Council ran counter to the internationalist sentiments of people like Cecil and Gilbert Murray, whereby each power's sovereignty should be lessened so as to promote international harmony. Of course, after 1925, Chamberlain's conception of the League and the European balance brought international stability; before 1925, the vision of the Cecils and Gilbert Murrays produced nothing effective.

Hence, was Locarno 'a false dawn' in international politics? High-level regular contact among the British, French, and German foreign ministers broke down within a year of Chamberlain leaving office in June 1929. Within four years, German irridentism took a new and aggressive path following the rise of Adolph Hitler to power; and, in March 1936, when Hitler's forces remilitarized the Rhineland in violation of Versailles and Britain and France did not respond, Locarno was officially dead. Chamberlain can be held responsible for the first of these problems. The 'Locarno tea parties' created a system of personal diplomacy in which all manner of important issues were discussed and settled in private by men who essentially were willing to work together. When Chamberlain left office, when Stresemann died suddenly in October 1929, and when Briand was eclipsed politically in the early 1930s, newer leaders did not have any formal structures within which to work. Yet, Locarno remained; and the ability of newer leaders in London to use it as the key element of Britain's continental strategy remained. That they chose not to do so has nothing to do with Austen Chamberlain.

However, in the period before he left office, Locarno did achieve a great deal. It brought stability to the continent for the first time in seven years. It allowed for Germany's revival as an accepted Great Power. It permitted a political atmosphere in which Franco-Belgian troops could be withdrawn from the Ruhr, in which the Young Committee could deliberate, and in which Allied troops could end the occupation of Germany. It also allowed the British, French, and Germans to work together within the League – and outside, if necessary – to ensure stability in other regions of the subcontinent. As indicated earlier, just as any setbacks in Europe between October 1925 and June 1929 can be ascribed to Chamberlain, the laurels for any successes must be accorded to him as well. It was his diplomatic strategy – maintaining the European balance by pursuing a leadership role for Britain in the League – that allowed for the stability of the latter half of the 1920s in Europe. The foundation upon which Chamberlain based his European strategy lay with his determination to have Britain play the vital role of 'honest broker' in stabilizing relations between France and Germany. He proved to be an able practitioner of the balance of power.

CHAMBERLAIN AND THE CONTINENTAL BALANCE OF POWER 231

NOTES

I would like to thank David Varey for assistance in preparing this article.

1. Minute, 4 Jan. 1925, Chamberlain, FO (Foreign Office Archives, Public Record Office, Kew) 371/11064/362/9.
2. The Locarno settlement comprised seven agreements and a diplomatic note: (i) Final Protocol of the Locarno Conference; Annex A. Treaty of Mutual Guarantee between Germany, Belgium, France, Great Britain and Italy; Annex B. Arbitration Convention between Germany and Belgium; Annex C. Arbitration Convention between Germany and France; Annex D. Arbitration Treaty between Germany and Poland; Annex F. Draft Collective Note to Germany regarding Article 16 of the Covenant of the League of Nations; (ii) Treaty Between France and Poland; (iii) Treaty Between France and Czechoslovakia. See Cmd.2525: *Final Protocol of the Locarno Conference, 1925 (and Annexes) Together With treaties between France and Poland and France and Czechoslovakia Locarno, October 16, 1925* (London, 1925).
3. Cf. D. Dutton, *Austen Chamberlain. Gentleman in Politics* (Bolton, 1985); G. Johnson, 'Lord D'Abernon, Austen Chamberlain and the Origin of the Treaty of Locarno', *Electronic Journal of International History* (www.ihrinfo.ac.uk/publications/ejihart2.html, 2000); E. Maisell, *The Foreign Office and Foreign Policy, 1919–1926* (Brighton, 1994); and the otherwise excellent commentary in R. Self (ed.), *The Austen Chamberlain Diary Letters: The Correspondence of Sir Austen Chamberlain with his Sisters, Hilda and Ida, 1916–1937* (Cambridge, 1995). And I must here include my own work in which, although implying that Chamberlain had an astute grasp of strategy, I did not provide in-depth analysis to show why he did so. See B.J.C. McKercher, *The Second Baldwin Government and the United States, 1924–1929: Attitudes and Diplomacy* (Cambridge, 1984), Chapter I and passim; idem, 'Austen Chamberlain's Control of British Foreign Policy, 1924–1929', *International History Review*, 6 (1984), pp.570–91.
4. R.S. Grayson, *Austen Chamberlain and the Commitment to Europe. British Foreign Policy 1924–29* (London, 1997), p.4; R.S. Grayson, 'Austen Chamberlain', in T.G. Otte (ed.), *The Makers of British Foreign Policy from Pitt to Thatcher* (Basingstoke, 2002), pp.150–72 is simply a summary of his book. It talks about 'phases' of Chamberlain's European policies; but phases and strategy are different issues.
5. Cf. Grayson, *Chamberlain*, p.281; Dutton, *Chamberlain*, p.259; F.P. Walters, *A History of the League of Nations*, Vol.I (Oxford/London/New York/Toronto, 1952), pp.342–6.
6. See McKercher, 'Chamberlain's Control'.
7. The next two paragraphs are based on Dutton, *Chamberlain*, pp.12–229; C. Petrie, *The Life and Letters of the Right Hon. Sir Austen Chamberlain*, Vol. I (London, 1939). Cf. A. Chamberlain, *Down the Years* (London, 1935). These paragraphs disagree profoundly with the argument that for Chamberlain before October 1922, 'there is no evidence of any distinctive or considered views on foreign policy': in Grayson, *Chamberlain*, p.4. Grayson has no grasp either of strategy or of strategic thinking and, consequently, no appreciation of Chamberlain's strategic beliefs.
8. For just the latter part of the Great War and the immediate period of peace, see the following examples: Chamberlain memorandum, 'Visit of French Delegate in Connection with British Man-Power Contribution' (GT 4756), 5 June 1918, CAB

(Cabinet Archives, Public Record Office, Kew) 24/53; Chamberlain memorandum, 'Calling Up Men for the Army' (GT 4974), 28 June 1918, CAB 24/55; Chamberlain memorandum, 2 Dec. 1918, CAB 21/123; Barstow (Treasury) minute to Chamberlain, 28 July 1919, T (Treasury Archives, Public Record Office, Kew) 1/12353; Chamberlain memorandum, 'The Future of the Supreme Economic Council' (CP 104), 11 Nov. 1919, CAB 24/93; Chamberlain note, 'International Financial Situation' (CP 597), 9 Feb. 1920, CAB 24/97; 'The Present Situation in Germany. Note by the Chancellor of the Exchequer on the Memorandum of the General Staff' (CP 671), 17 Feb. 1920, CAB 24/98; Chamberlain supplementary note, 'Our American Debt' (CP 2214A), 3 Dec. 1920, CAB 24/116.
9. On 2 August 1914, Chamberlain drafted a letter for the Unionist leadership to Herbert Asquith, the prime minister, that stated: 'We feel it our duty to declare that, in our opinion, any hesitation, in now supporting France and Russia, our intimate friends (with one of whom at least we have for years past concerted naval and military measures affecting gravely her own military and naval dispositions at this moment), would be fatal to the security of the United Kingdom; and we offer His Majesty's Government the assurance of the united support of the Opposition in all measures required by England's intervention in the war.' Quoted in Chamberlain, *Down the Years*, pp.95–6.
10. For instance, Chamberlain to Ida, 23 Dec. 1921, AC 5/1/221.
11. 'Why do any of us meddle with public work? It is all worry & disappointment & vexation whether if be District Councils or Cabinet councils or Prime Ministers or Ministers of Health': Chamberlain to Ida, 14 Jan. 1922, AC 5/1/224.
12. Dutton, *Chamberlain*, p.18.
13. Chamberlain to Hilda, his sister, 24 July, 31 Oct., 12 Dec. 1920, AC 5/1/170, 5/1/177, 5/1/183.
14. On the minutiae, see Petrie, *Chamberlain*, I, pp.73–6. On wider strategic issues, see his views during the 1909 House of Commons debates over new dreadnought construction contained in A. Chamberlain, *Politics from the Inside. An Epistolary Chronicle 1906–1914* (New Haven, CT, 1937), pp.162–9 passim.
15. See the insightful A. Chamberlain, *Seen In Passing* (London, 1937), which looks at Europe's cultural heritage.
16. Quoted in Chamberlain, *Down the Years*, pp.44–45. Cf. H. Hjelholt, *Treitschke und Schleswig-Holstein. Der Liberalismus und die Politik Bismarcks in der schleswig-holsteinischen Frage* (Munich/Berlin, 1929); I. Ludwig, *Treitschke und Frankreich* (Munich/Berlin, 1934).
17. I. Geiss, *German Foreign Policy, 1871–1914* (London, 1976), pp.86–689; C.J. Lowe, *The Reluctant Imperialists*, Vol.I: *British Foreign Policy 1878–1902* (London, 1967), pp.232–6.
18. From a conversation with Count Metternich, May 1908, quoted in Chamberlain, *Down the Years*, pp.54–5.
19. Chamberlain memorandum (CID 246-B), 28 June 1920, CAB 4/7.
20. Except where noted the rest of this paragraph and the next are based on A. Chamberlain, 'Great Britain as a European Power', *Journal of the Royal Institute of International Affairs* (hereafter *JRIIA*), 9 (1930), pp.180–88.
21. Cf. M.L. Roi and B.J.C. McKercher, '"Ideal" and "Punch-Bag": Conflicting Views of the Balance of Power and Their Influence on Interwar British Foreign Policy', *Diplomacy & Statecraft*, 12 (2001), pp.47–78.

CHAMBERLAIN AND THE CONTINENTAL BALANCE OF POWER   233

22. On the generational differences, see K.E. Neilson, *Britain and the Last Tsar: Anglo-Russian Relations, 1894–1917* (Oxford, 1996), Chapter 1.
23. Chamberlain to Crewe (British ambassador, Paris), 2 April 1925, Chamberlain MSS FO (Foreign Office Archives, Public Record Office, Kew) 800/258. Cf. Selby (Chamberlain's private secretary) to Phipps (*chargé*, British Embassy, Paris), 10 March 1925, Chamberlain MSS FO 800/257; Chamberlain to his wife, 3 Feb. 1926, AC 6/1/636.
24. See C. Baumgart, *Stresemann und England* (Cologne/Weimar/Vienna, 1996), pp.112–49; E.Y. O'Riordan, *Britain and the Ruhr Crisis* (Basingstoke, 2001); S.A. Schuker, *The End of French Predominance in Europe. The Financial Crisis of 1924 and the Adoption of the Dawes Plan* (Chapel Hill, 1976). Cf. J. Jacobson, 'Is There a New International History of the 1920s', *American Historical Review*, 88 (1983), pp.617–45.
25. M.P. Leffler, *The Elusive Quest. America's Pursuit of European Stability and French Security, 1919–1933* (Chapel Hill, 1979), pp.40–157; McDougall, *Rhineland Diplomacy*, pp.250–59; A. Orde, *British Policy and European Reconstruction after the First World War* (London, 1990), pp.227–65; Schuker, *French Predominance*, pp.98–108.
26. Cmd.2200; R. Cecil, 'The Draft Treaty of Mutual Assistance', *JRIIA*, 4 (1924), pp.45–82.
27. A. Henderson, *Labour and the Geneva Protocol* (London, 1925); P.J. Noel-Baker, *The Geneva Protocol for the Pacific Settlement of International Disputes* (London, 1925).
28. He told Sir Eric Drummond, the secretary-general of the League, that he needed some time to get first-hand knowledge of the issues. See Chamberlain minute, 4 Jan. 1925, FO 371/110647/3902.
29. Chamberlain took office on 6 Nov. 1924. For examples of initial materials prepared for him on various facets of the German question, see Central Department memoranda on 'The Evacuation of the Cologne Zone', 'Commercial Treaty with Germany', 'Entry of Germany into the League of Nations', 'Financial Questions between the Allies', 'German Disarmament', 'Current Events', all 7 Nov. 1924, all FO 371/9803/16848/37. These were supplemented by additional – and updated – materials over the next six weeks. For instance, Central Department 'Memorandum on the Evacuation of the Rhineland', 29 Nov. 1924, FO 371/9833/17469/4736. Also see Nicolson minute, 6 Nov. 1924, Crowe minute, 7 Nov. 1924, Chamberlain minute, 9 Nov. 1924, all FO 371/9803/16848/37. In his minute, Chamberlain wrote appreciatively: 'These and the other memoranda already seen by me are just what a new entrant like myself needs.'
30. See Crowe, 'Memorandum on the Present State of British Relations with France and Germany', 1 Jan. 1907, in G.P. Gooch and H. Temperley (eds.), *British Documents on the Origins of the War*, III (London, 1928), pp.397–420. On Crowe's efforts at promotion, cf. B.J.C McKercher, 'Old Diplomacy and New: The Foreign Office in the Interwar Period', in M.L. Dockrill and B.J.C. McKercher (eds.), *Diplomacy and World Power: Studies in British Foreign Policy, 1890–1951* (Cambridge: Cambridge University Press, 1996), pp.79–114.
31. Except where noted, the next two paragraphs are based on C. Baechler, *Gustave Stresemann (1878–1929). De l'impérialism à la sécurité collective* (Strasbourg, 1996), pp.583–650; C. Baumgart, *Stresemann und England* (Köln/Weimar/Wien,

1996), pp.179–219; Dutton, *Chamberlain*, pp.230–53; J.R. Ferris, *Men, Money, and Diplomacy: The Evolution of British Strategic Policy, 1919–26* (Ithaca, NY, 1989); J. Jacobson, *Locarno Diplomacy. Germany and the West 1925–1929* (Princeton, NJ, 1972), pp.12–26, 47–67; D. Johnson, 'Austen Chamberlain and the Locarno Agreements', *University of Birmingham Historical Journal*, 8 (1961), pp.62–81.
32. Chamberlain to Ida, 28 Dec. 1924, AC 5/1/343. On German violations, see Warburton (War Office) to Baxter (Foreign Office), 12 Nov. 1924, enclosing General Staff memorandum on 'Appreciation of the Probable Future Course of Action Respecting Military Control in Germany', 12 Nov. 1924, FO 371/9728/17183/9; Hurst (FO legal adviser) minute, 15 Dec. 1924 and Crowe minute, 16 Dec. 1924, both FO 371/9833/18489/4736; Creedy (War Office) to Foreign Office, Dec. 1924, Crowe and Chamberlain minutes, 24 Dec. 1924, both FO 371/ 833/19106/4736.
33. Chamberlain to Crewe, 20 Feb. 1925, AC 52/91.
34. 'Memorandum of a conversation between Mr. Chamberlain and M. Herriot', 5 Dec. 1924, CAB 21/289.
35. CID 190th meeting, 4 Dec. 1924, CAB 2/4.
36. His 5 Dec. 1924 conversation with Herriot provides a clue to his thinking: 'M. Herriot expressed himself very satisfied with the course of our interview ... and he again assured me of his earnest desire to work cordially with us in all parts of the world. I had myself earlier observed to him that national friendship could not be kept in watertight compartments, and that we could not really work cordially in Europe if our agents were quarrelling elsewhere.' In 'Memorandum of a conversation between Mr. Chamberlain and M. Herriot', 5 Dec. 1924, CAB 21/289.
37. Cf. Cecil to Hankey, 8 Dec. 1924, CAB 21/289; Churchill to Chamberlain, 23/25 Feb. 1925, with enclosure, Chamberlain FO 800/257.
38. Chamberlain to Ida, 31 Oct. 1925, AC 5/1/367.
39. Cf. D. Artaud, *La question des dettes interalliées et la reconstruction de l'Europe (1917–1929)* (Paris, 1978), pp.901–8; B. Kent, *The Spoils of War. The Politics, Economics, and Diplomacy of Reparations, 1918–1932* (Oxford, 1989), pp.287–321.
40. Chamberlain minute, 4 Jan. 1925, FO 371/11064/362/9. The decision to call the meeting came before receiving the German proposal. The meeting and a number of the memoranda received by Chamberlain came afterwards.
41. Headlam-Morley, 'Memorandum on the History of British Policy and the Geneva Protocol', 12 Feb. 1925, with Crowe minute, 18 Feb. 1925, FO 371/11064/1252/9. This paper later appeared in J. Headlam-Morley, *Studies in Diplomatic History* (London, 1930), pp.171–92.
42. Chamberlain minute, 21 Feb. 1925, FO 371/11064/1252/9.
43. Chamberlain to Ida, 1 March 1925, AC 5/1/347; Chamberlain to his wife, 10 March 1925, AC 6/1/600.
44. Chamberlain to Ida, 28 Nov. 1925, AC 5/1/370.
45. C.K. Webster, *The Foreign Policy of Castlereagh 1815–1822: Britain and the European Alliance* (London, 1925).
46. This notion informed the crucial Foreign Office submission to the Cabinet that supported Britain's role as guarantor of the Franco-German border. This memorandum flowed from that meeting of senior Foreign Office officials called by

Chamberlain in January. See Nicolson (FO Central Dept) memorandum on 'British Policy Considered in Relation to the European Situation', 20 Feb. 1925, FO 371/11064/1569/9. As Chamberlain's covering note, 19 Feb. 1925, ibid., pointed out to the Cabinet: 'A successful British foreign policy depends, first, on a clear appreciation of the facts of the situation with which we have to deal, and, secondly, on an equally clear conception of British interests and of their relation to the facts.'

47. See CC 47(24)4, 5 Aug. 1924, CAB 23/48.
48. For instance, Crowe minute, 2 Feb. 1924, FO 371/10574/841/841; Crowe minute, 28 June 1924, FO 371/10575/5509/3771; Orde (FO Western Dept) memorandum, 'Inclusion of a Treasury representative in the British delegation to the Assembly' – 11 Aug. 1924, FO 371/10575/ 6679/3474.
49. This dispute is traced in McKercher, 'Chamberlain's Control', pp.575–7.
50. Chamberlain to Salisbury, 2 Jan. 1925, Chamberlain MSS FO 800/257.
51. Chamberlain, minute, 19 March 1925, Chamberlain FO 371/10756/3539/3539. Grayson quotes a portion of this important minute – Grayson, 'Chamberlain', p.158 – but gets the citation wrong.
52. A. Chamberlain, *The League of Nations* (London, 1926).
53. Chamberlain to Clerk, 29 Dec. 1926, Chamberlain MSS FO 800/259.
54. See Mantoux (League of Nations Political Section) memorandum, 'Accord entre la Lituanie et l'U.R.S.S. le 28 Septembre 1926', 20 Oct. 1926, LNR (League of Nations Registered Files, League of Nations Archives, Palais des Nations, Geneva, Switzerland) 628/54812/544483.
55. Lindsay telegram (20) to FO, 6 Feb. 1927, FO 371/12539/512/61.
56. On early British views, see Chamberlain despatch (258) to Crewe, 27 Jan. 1927, FO 371/12539/357/61; Gregory (FO Northern Dept) memorandum, 26 Jan. 1927, initialled by Chamberlain, FO 371/12539/365/61.
57. This issue is analysed in McKercher, 'Chamberlain's Control'.
58. See D. Carlton, 'Great Britain and the Coolidge Naval Conference of 1927', *Political Science Quarterly*, 83 (1968), pp.573–98; C. Hall, *Britain, America, and Arms Control, 1921–37* (London, 1987), pp.36–58; McKercher, *Baldwin Government*, pp.65–76; D. Richardson, *The Evolution of British Disarmament Policy in the 1920s* (London, 1989), pp.119–39.
59. Cf. A.E. Senn, 'The Polish Lithuanian War Scare, 1927', *Journal of Central European Affairs*, 21 (1961), pp.267–84; idem, *The Great Powers, Lithuania, and the Vilna Question, 1920–1928* (Leyden, 1966). For a contemporary assessment, see L. Meriggi, *Il conflitto lituano-polacco e la questione di vilna* (Milan, 1930).
60. See Voldemaras (prime minister and foreign minister, Lithuania) to Drummond (secretary-general, League of Nations): LNR 629/62530/62530; 'Report of the Netherlands Representative' (on the Lithuanian–Polish dispute brought to the LoN Council under Art.11 of the Covenant), 10 Dec. 1927: LNR 629/63679/62530.
61. On reparations, see Jacobson, *Locarno Diplomacy*, pp.143–7; B. Kent, *The Spoils of War. The Politics, Economics, and Diplomacy of Reparations, 1918–1932* (Oxford, 1989), pp.272–3; M. Piesche, 'Die Rolle des Reparationsagenten Parker Gilbert während der Weimarer Republik (1924–1930)', *Jahrbuch für Geschichte*, 18 (1978), pp.135–69. Cf. Cmd. 2263; 'Reports of the Expert Committees Appointed by the Reparation Commission (1924)', *Allied Powers Reparations Commission* (University Publications of America), Reel 1; 'The Experts' Plan for Reparations Payments (1927)', 'Report of the Agent-General for Reparations Payments (10 Dec. 1927)',

both ibid., Reel 2. On disarmament, see B.J.C. McKercher, 'Of Horns and Teeth: The Preparatory Commission and the World Disarmament Conference, 1926–1934', in B.J.C. McKercher (ed.), *Arms Limitation and Disarmament, 1899–1939: Restraints on War* (New York, 1992), esp. pp.177–8.
62. Chamberlain to Ida, 12 Dec. 1927, AC 5/1/440.
63. Cf. Chamberlain to Crewe (33), 4 Nov. 1927, Chamberlain, 'Record of a conversation with Stresemann', 12 Dec. 1927, Chamberlain to Lindsay, 16 Dec. 1927, all in *DBFP*, Series 1A, Vol.IV: *Europe and Security Questions 1927–28* (London, 1971), pp.78–9, 180–83, 192–3.
64. 'At that session [in Dec. 1927] the Council adopted a resolution noting that a state of peace existed between Poland and Lithuania, and, amongst other things, urging the two Governments to reach a good understanding by direct negotiations'. In 'Report on the Fiftieth Session of the League of Nations', 4–9 June 1928, FO 411/8.
65. Chamberlain to Ida, 12 Dec. 1927, AC 5/1/440.
66. Chamberlain to Tyrrell, 19 Sept. 1927, Chamberlain MSS FO 800/261.

The British Government and the Sale of Arms to the Lesser European Powers, 1936–39

GLYN STONE

Hitherto, the tendency amongst historians of British defence and rearmament policies in the 1930s has been to concentrate on strategic policy[1] or on Treasury and other constraints on the extent and pace of British rearmament[2] which have been used to defend or justify appeasement against its critics. In addition, other historians have written, normally critically, about the performance of the armaments industries in rearming the United Kingdom and helping it to prepare for war.[3] However, there has been little or nothing written on an important aspect of defence and rearmament in the period, namely, the sale of arms abroad which had a political as well as a commercial dimension. As a preliminary attempt to examine this neglected area, this discussion will focus on government policy and attitudes with regard to the sale of arms abroad, notably to European countries and on the attitudes and responses of the single most important arms producer in the United Kingdom during the period under review, that is, Vickers-Armstrong. The examination will include specific references to arms negotiations between the British authorities and potential European allies and customers, including Portugal, Turkey, Greece, Yugoslavia, Romania, and Poland.

The decision by Stanley Baldwin's government in 1935 to begin an extensive rearmament programme was bound to make increasingly heavy demands on the British armaments industry; and on occasions (ironically) the government would be compelled, much to the annoyance of British armaments manufacturers, to purchase military equipment from abroad, for example, Swedish Bofors guns and Czech Bren machine guns.[4] During 1936–37 an increasing number of requests came from European and Dominion governments for the provision of British arms; the government was faced with the dilemma of losing political goodwill abroad, to the consternation of the Foreign Office, or of denuding the stocks of its own armed forces, which were already grossly inadequate, to the consternation of the service departments.

The question whether to give priority to the British defence programme and to discourage the acceptance of orders by United Kingdom firms for the supply of arms to foreign countries was discussed at length by the Defence Policy and Requirements Committee (DPR) on 8 October 1936. Ministers were presented with a Foreign Office memorandum detailing 'a formidable list of foreign countries desirous of placing orders in this country for the supply of their armaments requirements'. While the Foreign Office recognized 'the essential necessity of placing our own arms requirements in the matter of defence reorganization before every other consideration', it also stressed the importance for armaments manufacturers of maintaining exports to retain foreign markets for the period following the completion of Britain's own rearmament programme. However, as serious as the situation might be for the British arms industry, its political consequences were a matter of even greater concern:

> Loss of trade in one direction may conceivably be made good in others. But the prestige and influence with her allies and other friendly foreign countries which His Majesty's Government can enjoy through the satisfaction of their legitimate requests for assistance in carrying out defence requirements cannot be maintained by other means, in the event of those countries finding themselves unable to obtain their requirements in this country and being compelled to place their orders elsewhere.[5]

According to the Foreign Office, chief among those countries that had already begun to place orders in Britain or those which were likely to do so in future were the allies or prospective British allies, namely, Iraq, Egypt, and Portugal. Next in immediate importance came the requirements of Turkey, Greece, Afghanistan, and Persia. These powers, the Foreign Office believed, were most liable, failing satisfaction in Britain, to turn to Germany or Italy for their needs.

The Foreign Office also observed that the Netherlands, Baltic States, and Finland were all disposed to place orders with Britain; and that more distant countries, such as those in South America, and Siam might with encouragement become 'useful clients'. It seemed a matter of certainty to the Foreign Office that unless the country were able to fulfil the requirements of the more important of the 'prospective clients', a considerable price would be paid for failure.[6]

The chairman of the DPR, Sir Thomas Inskip, minister for co-ordination of defence, reminded his colleagues on 8 October that they had previously agreed that they would inform him when the service departments considered foreign orders might interfere with Britain's rearmament programme; he would then deal with the question in consultation with the service ministries and the Board of Trade. He complained that this decision appeared to have been overlooked.[7] The secretary of state for air, Lord Swinton, denied that the service departments, in particular his own, were making no effort to meet foreign arms orders; and he asserted that even the Foreign Office 'from time to time' had stressed the necessity for the early completion of the home rearmament programme. Sir Samuel Hoare, the first lord of the admiralty, stressed the 'immense advantage which had accrued to the Admiralty in allowing British firms to accept foreign orders' which had been 'a very important means of keeping armament firms in existence'. It was also important to retain foreign arms orders for political reasons. He drew attention to the different situation that might have ensued had Turkish armament in the Dardanelles been supplied by the United Kingdom prior to 1914: 'we should then have known the precise extent of their armament supply.' Following further discussion, the DPR concluded that it was essential to continue arms exports to foreign countries; and, in cases where there was a conflict between home defence requirements and supplying foreign arms orders, it reaffirmed the existing procedure subject, at the suggestion of the chancellor of the exchequer, Neville Chamberlain, to the inclusion of the Foreign Office.[8]

While it had been agreed at the highest level that it was important not to discourage foreign arms orders, there remained uncertainty about the attitude to be adopted by British missions abroad to assist British firms in obtaining contracts to supply armaments to foreign countries. Eventually, in July 1937, having taken advice from the DPR, the Foreign Office issued a circular telegram to all United Kingdom missions emphasizing the significance of encouraging foreign arms orders notwithstanding the considerable demands of home defence:

> Commercially both the short view and the long view interests of this country require that the United Kingdom should enjoy the maximum volume of export trade that it can handle. Foreign markets are more easily lost than recovered when lost; and a policy under which potential foreign purchasers would be, in effect, invited for some time to come to look elsewhere than to the United Kingdom to obtain for their defence forces armaments or ancillary stores which they were unable to produce for themselves would be prejudicial to the political and permanent economic interests of this country.[9]

Despite these clearly stated intentions, the service departments were not prepared to sanction the release of scarce equipment in all cases, especially when the requests were for the most up-to-date weapons. It was to sort out priorities that the Committee of Imperial Defence (CID) set up a sub-committee in October 1937 – the Sub-Committee on Armament Orders from Foreign Countries, an interdepartmental committee consisting of representatives from the Foreign Office, War Office, Air Ministry, Admiralty and Board of Trade. The sub-committee was chaired by Sir Arthur Robinson and its terms of reference were: 'To consider cases of demands from Foreign Countries for armaments and munitions of war concerning more than one Government Department, in which difficulties arose either on financial grounds or in regard to supply.'[10] This committee was eventually replaced in June 1939 by a more extensive one that included additional representatives from the Treasury, the Export Credits Guarantee Department, and the Industrial Intelligence Centre (IIC). Robinson continued as chairman of this new body, the Allied Demands Committee, and Sir Edward Bridges, the cabinet secretary, acted as deputy chairman. Its terms of reference emphasized the committee's role in examining and reporting on demands from allied countries in the light of the ascertained supply position and having regard to all other factors – political, strategic and financial. The committee was also authorized, in case of urgency, to report directly to the Cabinet or to an ad hoc meeting of ministers.[11]

The dilemma for the government was brought home during the crucial defence appraisal and review which took place during the last months of 1937. In a December 1937 paper for his Cabinet colleagues, entitled 'Defence Expenditure in Future Years', Inskip emphasized the vital importance of preparing a long war strategy that included the maintenance of economic stability as the fourth arm of defence and of Britain's reputation as a politically stable country with formidable powers of resistance. He also acknowledged that the level of British rearmament was a crucial reinforcement of Britain's international position:

> Not only must we be strong enough to withstand a knock-out blow, but we must be seen to be strong. So long as our armaments are believed to be below the level of safety, our all important influence for the maintenance of peace will suffer, and we shall be liable to successive rebuffs which will reduce that influence still further. Indeed, so far as there have been any improvements in the international situation within recent times, it is largely due to our rearmament. In the interests of peace we cannot afford that an impression should grow up that we are relaxing our efforts.[12]

The service departments remained convinced that the urgent and increasing foreign demand for arms would imperil the level of safety determined by Inskip. Yet, during the same defence review, the chiefs of staff (COS) had argued that as long as Britain's naval, military, and air forces remained insufficient to meet their defensive commitments – which extended from Western Europe, through the Mediterranean to the Far East – it was imperative from the point of imperial defence to take any political or international action which would reduce the number of potential enemies and to gain the support of potential allies.[13] As subsequent events were to demonstrate, one price of gaining the support of potential allies was the supply of modern arms from British stocks. In responding to the COS' paper, the foreign secretary, Anthony Eden, had stressed the need 'to draw into closer relationship with us all those smaller states whose assistance in time of war would not be negligible, but whose support to the other side might be disastrous'. In this connection, Eden made reference to Portugal, Greece, Turkey, Yugoslavia, Romania, and Poland.[14] It was precisely these countries that would make increasingly heavy demands on Britain's supply of arms during 1938–39 (with demands from the Dominions, India, Egypt, and China).

At the same time, British authorities were only too aware of Germany's willingness and ability to supply arms to the smaller European powers to gain political and diplomatic advantage. In February 1938, the IIC emphasized the tremendous benefit that the Germans derived from the mass production of armaments, on an unprecedented scale, in terms of relatively lower prices and the capacity to supply. It also stressed the role of the Reich government in providing special facilities and encouraging manufacturers and dealers to sell abroad. Germany did not confine its interest to short term, commercially sound transactions only, but deliberately exploited its ability to export armaments as part of a general political policy that in the long run might also prove commercially profitable.

> She has derived full benefit from establishing herself in an expanding market and has been prepared to force an entry into that market even at some initial loss: realizing that in the case of armaments, more perhaps than of any other commodity, a type once adopted by a foreign Power almost certainly ensures repeat orders.[15]

The contents of the IIC memorandum created considerable concern in the Foreign Office to the extent that the new foreign secretary, Lord Halifax, insisted that it be placed before the CID. He revealed the depth of his concern to Inskip in late April 1938. As a result of intelligence reports, he now understood how it was that Germany, 'without the resources we possess, and while engaged on a programme of rearmament hitherto greatly in excess of our own', could simultaneously export armaments in the open market and to the Spanish nationalist forces in the Spanish Civil War. These exports were far in excess of 'anything we are able to accomplish even when the markets open to us include the Dominions, which in certain cases are pressing us for urgent delivery'. For the Foreign Office:

> the inability to export arms in adequate quantities to friendly and potentially friendly countries involves, to my mind, a very real risk that those countries will either be drawn both commercially and politically into the German orbit, or, if they are not, will prove to be inadequately armed at a time when well-equipped allies may be essential to our own safety.

Halifax was insistent that the contrast between German and British armaments output was a source of considerable disquiet. It rendered the satisfactory conduct of foreign affairs a matter of extreme difficulty not least because 'our political influence is now, and is likely to remain largely dependent upon the relation between our armed strength and Germany's'.[16]

At Foreign Office behest, the IIC memorandum was placed before the CID at the end of April 1938. Subsequent discussion in this committee and at Cabinet confirmed that it was not possible to imitate the German system of mass production in its entirety, based as it was 'on the method and organisation of the totalitarian state'.[17] Consideration of the issue centred on the feasibility of adopting or adapting some of the methods of German industry to achieve a greater measure of war preparedness in the United Kingdom and to improve the position of the export trade.[18] With reference to this trade, further attention was drawn at a CID meeting on 12 May 1938 to the German potential for affording long-term credits to importing countries – seven years in the case of Afghanistan and five years in the cases of Bulgaria and Greece. It was also becoming increasingly clear that Berlin paid much more attention to the quantitative than to the qualitative aspect, believing that 'large numbers would always defeat smaller numbers despite any technical superiority of the latter'. It was further pointed out that Great Britain's arms exports in 1937 amounted to £8.2 million as compared to £18 million for Germany – excluding warships on both sides.[19]

At the end of July, Inskip was instructed to consult with the relevant departments; but progress on arms exports was very slow, probably because of the growing Czech crisis. In November 1938, following a meeting of the CID on 20 October, the COS finally produced a review of the relative strategic importance of potential foreign customers. Determining strategic importance was based on, first, the value of the military facilities that these powers could afford to Britain in war and, second, the need to deny such facilities to an enemy. Belgium and Holland were equally placed as the first priority because of their geographical significance in relation to the defence of the United Kingdom itself. With the Suez Canal, Egypt ranked second because it was considered to have very high strategic importance for the defence of the Empire, 'even should we find ourselves at war with Germany, Italy and Japan with no British fleet in the Mediterranean'. Portugal and Turkey were rated equal third: the former had high strategic value for Atlantic defence, particularly if Gibraltar was denied to Britain by hostile action from Spain; with the latter considered essential in countering Italy in the eastern Mediterranean, there was every incentive to prevent a repeat of the Turkish–German alliance of the First World War. Situated fourth, Iraq had value in contributing to the protection of British imperial communications and oil interests in the Middle East, including those of Iran; a hostile Iraq would threaten those interests. Greece was ranked fifth in view of its importance as a source of valuable naval and air facilities in a war against Italy that would assist British forces in their control of the Aegean Sea and the central Mediterranean; it was important that these facilities be denied to Germany and Italy and that Greece not fall under their influence.

Saudi Arabia was placed sixth. Its territory flanked both British sea communications through the Red Sea and Persian Gulf and the overland route via Iraq; and it was also recognized that an unfriendly Saudi Arabia could foment Arab unrest throughout the Middle East. In ranking Afghanistan seventh, the COS acknowledged its strategic significance in the long term as a buffer state between the Soviet Union and India. They considered Yugoslavia eighth in importance via its relation to the Adriatic and the need to deny facilities there to a naval power hostile to Britain. It was also recognized that the attitude of Yugoslavia in war would have repercussions on Greece, Romania, and possibly Turkey; and for this reason an alliance or benevolent neutrality would be to Britain's advantage. Romania occupied ninth place in recognition of its strategic importance in denying oil and wheat supplies to Germany and Italy; and it was particularly important that it should not pass under German domination since this would give Germany access to the East and to the Black Sea via the Danube. Bulgaria was ranked tenth given its Black Sea coast and the fact that it barred the route to the Bosphorus. Hungary was placed eleventh, and last, because it had no direct strategic concern to Britain.[20]

At the beginning of December 1938, the CID approved the COS assessment of potential customers. This followed a discussion in which Sir Warren Fisher, the Treasury permanent under-secretary, conceded ground to those ministers such as Hoare, now the home secretary, and Sir Kingsley Wood, the secretary of state for air, who were anxious to meet the requirements of these lesser powers.[21] Despite Treasury reservations, Inskip was invited in consultation with the three service ministers and their advisors to examine 'the practicability of increasing manufacturing capacity for certain armaments with a view to building up a greater war potential while placing the Government in a position to supply foreign countries'.[22] The subsequent investigation revealed that the principal items requiring consideration were aircraft, anti-aircraft guns and artillery equipment, and armour. While the position in the short term was reasonably optimistic in relation to aircraft, and then only in relation to existing models which were becoming obsolete, like the Blenheim and Battle bombers and the Gladiator fighter, that for anti-aircraft guns and artillery was far from promising since these could only be supplied from new capacity still in the development stage. As Inskip noted:

> It is obvious ... that our present capacity is insufficient to meet our own authorised programme as recently enlarged, and that it will take periods varying from one and a half to two years before any new capacity now laid down can be brought into production. It must be remembered that our existing manufacturing resources are now working to full capacity; and that in a period approaching two years, a proportion of our resources will be released on completion of our present programmes. It follows, therefore, that capacity will be released for foreign orders so soon, or almost as soon, as any

new capacity specially created for this purpose only, could come into production.[23]

While there was little that could be done in the short term in meeting the demand of foreign countries, the government was prepared to provide financial assistance under a new Exports Credit Act to a number of countries up to £10 million. This change in government policy was a triumph for the Foreign Office position on arms exports. At a CID meeting on 17 November 1938, Halifax, supported by other ministers including Hoare, Leslie Hore Belisha, the secretary of state for war, Lord Stanhope, the first lord of the admiralty, and the Australian foreign minister, Stanley Bruce, succeeded in overcoming the reservations of the president of the Board of Trade, Oliver Stanley, to extending credits with certain foreign countries even if such transactions could not be justified commercially.[24] Following the meeting and after further consultation by the Treasury, Foreign Office and Board of Trade, China was allocated £3 million, Greece £2 million, Portugal, Egypt and Romania £1 million, Iraq £500,000, Afghanistan £250,000, Iran and Saudi Arabia £250,000; £1 million was to be kept in reserve. Turkey had previously been granted export credits up to £6 million.[25]

It was recognized in government circles that the COS review of the order of priority had been based on strategic considerations only. Accordingly in February 1939, on behalf of the Foreign Arms Orders Committee, the Foreign Office drew up a separate list based on political consideration – which was accepted by the committee. Whereas Egypt had been placed second in order of strategic priority by the COS, it was elevated to first place by the Foreign Office on political grounds. Iraq was promoted to second; Belgium was relegated to third; Portugal to fourth; and Turkey to fifth place. Greece remained in sixth. The Netherlands was transferred to seventh place followed by Romania eighth, Yugoslavia ninth, and Afghanistan tenth. Placed eleventh on the COS list, Bulgaria was relegated to seventeenth by the Foreign Office; Hungary was omitted completely because of German influence in Budapest. Ironically, in view of events which were to materialize shortly, Poland was placed twenty-sixth in order of priority in a group that included South American countries and the Soviet Union.[26]

Following the German occupation of Prague in March 1939, the British government was faced with rapidly escalating requests for armaments from a growing number of European powers – most significantly, France, Poland, Greece, and Romania – while Turkey and Portugal continued to make heavy demands. For example, Kingsley Wood announced at a CID meeting on 20 April 1939 that the Air Ministry had received a demand for 450 aircraft from Romania and 250 aircraft from Poland. In all cases, the conclusion was the same: the material demanded could be released only at the expense of Britain's own requirements. Although the CID invited the service departments 'to continue to make every effort to meet the demands for armaments from foreign countries who are allies or potential allies of this country', it was obvious that a firm order of priority would have to be established.[27]

A revised list had been drawn up prior to the meeting on 20 April by the Foreign Office; it included both political and strategic considerations. In this revised list, Egypt was assigned first place, with Iraq second, followed in order of preference by Belgium, Portugal, Turkey, Greece, Netherlands, Romania, Poland, Yugoslavia, and Afghanistan.[28] In the light of developments in European diplomacy over the next two months, and purely on political grounds, extensive amendments were made by the Foreign Office during June 1939: Poland was promoted to first place, Egypt second, Turkey third, and Romania fourth. Iraq was demoted to fifth place and Portugal to sixth, followed in order of preference by Greece, Belgium, Yugoslavia, Bulgaria, and the Netherlands. The promotion of Poland to first place by the Foreign Office was based on the conviction that without British and French assistance, Poland's resistance in the 'undeclared war of nerves and attrition' that was taking place would inevitably collapse with disastrous results for the policy of 'encouraging resistance to aggression among Germany's eastern neighbours'. The Foreign Office held that Germany appeared to be counting on such a collapse within two or three months, and only 'a considerable measure of financial and material support from France and Great Britain' could save Poland from ultimate surrender. Egypt was placed second because its good will was vital to British interests in the Mediterranean; and Cairo's confidence in Britain's ability to protect Egypt exercised a decisive effect upon the whole British position in the Middle East. As an essential link in the non-aggression front, Turkey held third place, partly because it had still to be induced 'to give assurances to Greece and Romania such as would automatically bring her into the war if our guarantees to those countries became operative'. Romania occupied the fourth rank because the COS had decided that its participation in the war was desirable, and it was, accordingly, necessary to strengthen Bucharest's will to resist. In this connection, the importance of Romanian oil needed no emphasis; its geographical position at the mouth of the Danube and at the junction of Poland, the Soviet Union, and the Balkan States was most significant. In making Iraq fifth, the Foreign Office was influenced not only by existing treaty obligations; Britain needed to retain Iraqi goodwill, vital to the Empire in war, which was also of 'the greatest importance in peacetime to our whole position in the Middle East – all the more so in view of the state of unrest in Palestine'. Portugal remained sixth because its 'recent reaffirmation of fidelity to the [Anglo-Portuguese] alliance' required tangible recognition if the intensive propaganda of Germany and Italy was to be held in check. Finally, the Foreign Office placed Greece seventh because of its susceptibility to Italian attack in war and German pressure in peace. However unlikely, Greece's defection would have a disastrous impact on Turkey's attitude, nullifying attempts being made to strengthen the Balkan entente and encourage Yugoslavia to resist German pressure.[29]

In terms strictly of financial assistance, Halifax advised Cabinet on 21 June to consider a modified version of the Foreign Office memorandum:

> These four countries – Poland, Turkey, Greece and Roumania – he would place in the first category. The second category would consist of Portugal, Egypt and Iraq – countries allied to us but less immediately threatened. The third category would consist of countries such as Yugoslavia and Bulgaria and perhaps Spain, which were wavering between the Rome-Berlin axis and the democratic countries, but which might turn in the right direction if given suitable help. The fourth category would include Afghanistan and Saudi Arabia – countries which

were unlikely to join the enemy, but which for various reasons, we might wish to support.[30]

In addition to these political evaluations, strategic considerations were also fully explored during the first part of July 1939 by the deputy chiefs of staff (DCOS) who, having established a 'rough general order of priority', for the first time included a priority order for the three separate categories of land (including anti-aircraft), sea and air armaments. In arriving at this final order of priority, the DCOS took into account the essential factors of the broad strategy of the conduct of war, the fighting value of the forces of the particular countries, and the value of a country to Great Britain in so far as it could deny facilities to the enemy.[31]

In the DCOS evaluation, France was placed first because it was anticipated that it would bear the main burden of defence against both Germany and Italy. It was admitted that in the Mediterranean, the Atlantic and the Far East, France was Britain's chief ally. Belgium came second in importance because even if it attempted to maintain strict neutrality, the possibility could not be overlooked that Germany would violate that neutrality to gain strategic advantage; and, strategically, Belgium's geographical position was vital to both Britain and France. The DCOS, however, rated neither the strength nor military value of the Belgian Air Force and advised against directing aircraft to Belgium that could be more usefully employed by other potential allies. In placing Egypt third, the DCOS emphasized that its security, and with it control of the Suez Canal and communications in the Middle East, was of high strategic importance. Without such security, it would be 'almost impossible to maintain sea communications with Turkey and other Balkan countries whose cooperation in an eastern front was so necessary'. Despite the fact that the DCOS considered the value of the Egyptian forces to be low, they regarded Egypt as being in 'a special position' in view of Britain's special commitments and as 'taking the same priority as British territory'. Turkey was allocated fourth place on the grounds that the Allied position in the Mediterranean would be considerably strengthened from the outset of hostilities by its intervention as an ally. Considered to be the most powerful member of the Balkan entente, Turkey as a belligerent was in a position to control the Dardanelles and, thereby, increase pressure on Italy. Moreover, the free passage of Allied troops – including Russia if it intervened – through the Dardanelles was assured. Next to France, in the opinion of the DCOS, Turkey was potentially Britain's most valuable military ally in Europe.

Since Poland had by far the largest and best equipped army, it was the key power in Eastern Europe; and the DCOS were accordingly prepared to place it high on the list. However, if it proved possible to supply Poland from Russia, they were quite prepared to relegate it from fifth to a lower position owing to the difficulty of delivering supplies in war. If Russian supplies were not forthcoming, it would be desirable in view of the shortage of equipment for France to supply Poland rather than the United Kingdom. In placing Holland sixth, the DCOS were mindful that in view of Belgium's neutralist tendencies, it was most improbable that a German advance could be delayed or held in eastern Belgium or Holland; accordingly, equipment designed for use in Holland – land and air armaments – should not receive a high degree of priority. But despite its evident desire to remain neutral, Holland received high priority in respect of the naval requirements for its forces in the Far East where Dutch possessions were considered of great strategic importance in any struggle with Japan. Portugal held the seventh position because, in the event of Gibraltar being denied to Britain by hostile action from pro-Axis Franco Spain, British use of Portuguese bases (notably Lisbon and the Azores and Cape Verde islands) and their denial to a potential enemy was essential. The DCOS concluded that it was of high strategic importance to Britain that Portugal should be able to defend itself from invasion by Spain and from seaborne and air attack. Yet Portugal was not placed higher because of the low military value of its armed forces.

Finally, of the remaining European powers, Bulgaria was surprisingly placed eighth. The DCOS considered its assistance as essential in helping Romania resist German aggression and in binding Yugoslavia to the other Balkan powers. Greece was placed tenth despite its strategic significance for British forces in the eastern Mediterranean. Romania was placed a lowly eleventh – despite its significant geographical position, without which there could be no continuous Eastern Front – because the DCOS were unimpressed by the 'low fighting value of her forces'. They thought it preferable that the Soviet Union should supply Romania with its requirements. Yugoslavia was placed twelfth because the DCOS did not believe there was much chance of it being on Britain's and France's side in war; while Hungary was considered so much under Germany's domination that it was not worth providing it with any arms.

Between 1936 and 1939, despite the massive increase in weapons production, British arms firms sold precious few of their products abroad. Although they had Foreign Office support, these firms failed to persuade the service departments to release equipment, essentially the latest models, for export. This was a source of great disappointment, not least for Vickers-Armstrong, the largest of all the firms in the British armaments industry.

Before the government's rearmament programme, Vickers had been sustained by foreign arms orders that had enabled research to be carried out and skilled manpower, albeit in limited numbers, retained. The company's six-monthly reports for 1936 reveal their frustration at the constraints imposed on arms sales abroad. The first of these, written by General Sir Noel Birch, noted:

> With the exception of a set-back in 1931, the years of the financial crisis, our foreign business has been gradually and steadily increasing during the past six years. We now have up-to-date models and the advantage of having carried out costly and intensive research and I feel certain that but for the pressure of Government orders, and in spite of Germany having entered the foreign market, our business this year would have increased and probably have gone on increasing.

In addition, he complained, business with Bulgaria, Greece, and China had been abandoned because these countries were not prepared to accept the terms of delivery that envisaged a long waiting period. In his second six-monthly report, Birch lamented having to turn down custom for land armaments worth over £1 million; and he warned that 'next year unless the political situation changes foreign trade is bound to decline. Germany in particular is taking full advantage of the situation'.[32] The situation had not improved by the summer of 1937 when Birch reported that, while Vickers had taken foreign arms orders worth £380,000, it had to turn down 'good foreign business prospects' to the amount of approximately £1 million with the company's foreign rivals taking full advantage of the situation.[33] By the end of 1937, foreign arms orders had increased to £763,000, which accounted for approximately one-eighth of all the company's orders, including home defence. Moreover, in his second six-monthly report for 1937, Birch estimated that the value of prospective foreign business they had been unable to undertake because of the demands of home defence amounted to 'practically' £3 million.[34]

The British government sympathized and acknowledged the value of arms exports during the lean years for the armaments manufacturers before 1935; but the service departments remained largely intransigent. They remained unimpressed when Vickers argued that the sale of arms to friendly countries could directly benefit the armed services in times of emergency: the weapons produced could be immediately requisitioned. Birch put this argument to the permanent undersecretary at the Foreign Office, Sir Robert Vansittart, in May 1937 in the context of a Portuguese order for anti-aircraft guns:

> If the War Office allows us to make the anti-aircraft guns now under consideration for Portugal and war breaks out in the meantime, the War Office will have up-to-date Guns declared to be the best gun in Europe by at least nine countries, and to accompany their Army into the field. ... Surely we should not allow our Army to go into the field without protection from the best gun in Europe which we can have made at other people's expense.[35]

Although Vansittart declared himself to be impressed, he admitted that he was in the hands of the War Office, and they were less impressed. They were also unimpressed by Vickers' claims that unless they received foreign orders, they would be unable to take advantage of the export market once the government's defence programme was completed to the clear detriment of their shareholders. Indeed, the War Office went as far in July 1936 as to seek to prohibit Vickers from taking any more orders from abroad. To say the least, the company was mortified:

> Should the decision be allowed to stand the future of Vickers after the rush will be seriously affected and the money spent and the work done in establishing foreign markets will to a great extent have been wasted. The shareholders also, many of whom are of small means, who have stood by the firm in lean times, must eventually sustain a financial loss. From the War Office point of view, unless we receive foreign orders at the cessation of the rush, industrial mobilization will suffer. Some of the markets we now hold will be lost for all time; others will be hard to regain.[36]

While Vickers prevented such prohibition by appealing to Article 49 of the government's White Paper of March 1936, which stated that normal business was not to be interfered with, it made little difference owing to the continuing refusal of the War Office and the Air Ministry to sanction most of the orders. The Admiralty was a little more forthcoming.

As far as Vickers was concerned, there was no improvement in the position before the outbreak of war in September 1939. Indeed, during August, they were confronted with a new directive requiring foreign and Dominion governments to direct their initial enquiries to the service departments rather than to the arms firms. The result would be that some enquiries would be rejected, in some cases the service departments would undertake to supply from their stocks, and, in others, enquiries would be passed on to the armaments firms. Sir Charles Craven, chairman of Vickers, complained bitterly to Admiral Lord Chatfield, Inskips' successor as minister for co-ordination of defence, and rehearsed once more all of their arguments:

> if we had not secured ... foreign orders when British orders were not forthcoming, it would not have been possible for us to retain the services of our skilled staff and maintain our plants in that degree of efficiency which has enabled us to bear our share ... of the heavy and urgent burden created by the British Government's Re-armament Programme. I submit therefore that our foreign armaments orders have been in the National Interest, and that it would be regrettable if the proposed new procedure ... was of so complete and permanent

a nature as to disturb our direct relations with foreign governments and so prejudice our chances of obtaining foreign contracts as soon as circumstances permit on the resumption of normal export trading, a matter of such vital importance to this country.[37]

Craven's expressed hope that normal trading procedures would be temporary was shared by Chatfield, but the outbreak of the Second World War one month later dashed any prospects that this would be the case.

It was quite natural for armaments firms to wish to take advantage of the opportunities which the deteriorating political situation in Europe after 1937 offered in regard to a rapid expansion of their export trade; it was quite another matter for the government, and the service departments in particular, to acquiesce. The Foreign Office, however, took a different view. It sought to encourage the Cabinet and the service departments to adopt a broader perspective while acknowledging the two most important priorities of defence following the reappraisal of December 1937: the protection of the United Kingdom against attack and the preservation of trade routes on which the country depended for essential imports of food and raw materials.[38] After the *Anschluss* of March 1938, and even more so following the German occupation of Prague in March 1939, several smaller European powers sought closer ties with Britain. In these circumstances, the Foreign Office recognized that one of the touchstones of Britain's capacity 'to draw into closer relationship with us those smaller states whose assistance in time of war would not be negligible, but whose support to the other side might be disastrous' was the ability to supply their armaments requirements which were increasingly substantial. Aware of the intense competition of Germany and faced with the intransigence of the service departments, which refused to denude their stocks of modern weapons or allow the armaments firms to set aside anything other than a token part of their future production for export purposes, the Foreign Office struggled to salvage what it could of its relations with the smaller European powers. In the event, its endeavours proved more successful in the case of the flanking powers of Portugal and Turkey than they did with the central and southeastern European states, notably Poland, Romania, Yugoslavia, and Greece.

Britain's 'oldest ally', Portugal, was the first European power to make a request for substantial British weapons during the rearmament period after 1935. Confronted by competition from both Nazi Germany and fascist Italy between the beginning of the Spanish Civil War in July 1936 and the outbreak of a general European war in September 1939, British authorities were able to persuade the quasi-fascist regime of Antonio Oliveira Salazar to seriously consider purchasing British arms. These comprised modern fighter aircraft, mobile 3.7 inch anti-aircraft guns, submarines, motor torpedo boats, and a coastal defence system for the port of Lisbon based on a plan drawn up by Major-General Frederick Barron, inspector of defences at the War Office. The detailed specifications for Barron's Plan included 9.2 inch guns, 6 pounder twin equipment, 40 mm Bofor equipment, static anti-aircraft equipment, and anti-aircraft searchlights. The securing of these orders by the British government owed much to the presence and advice of a British military mission which visited Portugal for several months during 1938.[39] Still, it proved extremely difficult to fulfil these orders in view of the United Kingdom's own considerable defence requirements on land, sea, and air, and despite the repeated urgings of the Foreign Office. As late as July 1939, Halifax urged Chatfield to give preferential treatment to Portugal on the grounds that its full cooperation in time of war was essential, that accordingly it was necessary to ensure it would be a useful ally, and, particularly, that it would contribute to ensuring Franco Spain withheld help from the Axis Powers. The foreign secretary was adamant that 'the political and strategic importance of securing the three policy objectives must be allowed equal weight with the claim of the military advisers'. With specific reference to Portugal's anti-aircraft requirements, he insisted that from the political point of view, Portugal had first claim over all other foreign and dominion countries.[40] Halifax's strong appeal barely moved the military authorities, and the outbreak of war a month later reinforced their intransigence.[41] Failure to supply Portugal's demands for modern armaments did not prove fatal to Anglo-Portuguese relations before September 1939. Despite advantages that Germany and Italy possessed in terms of their ability to supply Portuguese needs, Salazar did not sign any substantial contracts for artillery, aircraft, or naval vessels other than with Italy for mountain artillery.

The improvement in Anglo-Turkish relations following the Abyssinian crisis and the Montreux Straits Conference resulted in a trickle of Turkish arms orders which, by 1938, had become a flood. Constantly mindful of the fact that Germany, 'by establishing a close association and predominant position with the Turkish Army' before 1914, had secured Turkey's military support when the First World War came, the British government was only too willing to place a very high priority on Turkish arms demands.[42] Indeed, in May 1938, Turkey was granted extraordinary credit amounting to £6 million to purchase arms in the United Kingdom. By July, almost £3.6 million had been earmarked for Turkey's naval programme, including the purchase of four destroyers, four submarines, and two minelayers, £200,000 for the purchase of 18 Blenheim bombers, and £700,000 for coastal defence equipment. The remainder had still to be finalized. Meanwhile, at the end of June 1939, ministers had agreed to extend further credits to the Turkish government amounting to £10 million, contingent on the signing of a political agreement to reinforce the Anglo-Turkish declaration of May 1939.[43] It was anticipated that the Turks would wish to utilize part of the £10 million – between £3 and £4 million – to construct armament factories within Turkey itself. According to a memorandum by Desmond Morton of the IIC, the total Turkish output of armaments would only suffice to meet war expenditure of between one and three Turkish divisions; and the position regarding Turkish naval and air armaments was no better. Plant capacity was retarded by the lack of skilled or even semi-skilled labour and indigenous raw materials, most of which would have to be imported.[44] Meanwhile, in the short term, the Turkish armed forces were heavily dependent on the import of arms from Britain and France following the deterioration in Turco-German relations after the Anglo-Turkish declaration. The Allied Demands Committee, at its meeting on 18 July, estimated that when other outstanding contracts had been completed, there would be about £400,000 available from the original £6 million credits. It agreed that the Air Ministry should be authorized to send 14 Hurricane fighters and ancillary equipment to Turkey.[45]

While, almost exceptionally, the military authorities in London were wholly in favour of the despatch of war material to Turkey, the Treasury was reticent about permitting any further deliveries before the political agreement was signed. Sir John Simon, the chancellor of the exchequer, had stressed on 28 June that he did not want the government to drift into the position 'where we would be offering credits and still more credits as an inducement to the Turks to sign'.[46] Having heard at first hand the views of General Charles Huntziger, a senior French officer who had prepared a draft Anglo-French–Turkish convention after a visit to Ankara, the DCOS advised on 3 August that irrespective of the conclusion of the political agreement, the service departments should be instructed to despatch at once a token consignment of the armaments allocated to the Turks. The Turkish president, Ismet Inönü, who had succeeded Kemal Attatürk in November 1938, had spoken emphatically to Huntziger on this point. The general thought there was a real danger that 'unless we give the Turks early tangible proof of our intentions to fill, in some measure, the gap in their defences which the cessation of the supply of German equipment has entailed, we shall lose all the ground which we have recently gained'.[47] Chatfield, endorsed the DCOS report and urged Halifax to approve an immediate shipment of arms to Turkey.[48]

Final authorization of the shipment of arms to Turkey continued to be withheld, however, because of the delay in reaching a political agreement and also because final Anglo-Turkish discussions on the offer of the £10 million credit had not been held.[49] The delay was a source of considerable anxiety to British military authorities. The DCOS advised Chatfield that it was essential to avoid a complete impasse, in which 'the Turks decline to sign the guarantee agreement until deliveries have begun, while we refuse to begin deliveries till the guarantee agreement is signed'. Such an impasse would, the DCOS suggested, be extremely serious. They believed 'it to be not impossible the result may even be to throw them [the Turks] into the arms of Germany, with results upon the whole structure of our anti-aggression front which it would be redundant to elaborate'.[50] Acting on this advice, Chatfield prodded Halifax again to find a way through the impasse:

In view of the critical situation at the moment, I attach particular importance to Turkey's immediate requirements being sent forthwith while the Mediterranean route is still available. It seems, therefore a question as to whether we are to give way to Turkey's unreasonableness in our higher strategic interests. It is undoubtedly almost as important to arm the Turks as to arm ourselves as they are our most solid ally.[51]

While the foreign secretary persuaded the Treasury to drop the pre-condition of a political agreement, he failed to convince Simon and his advisers to do likewise with regard to the credit agreement. The shipment of arms continued to be delayed on grounds of constitutional propriety. Halifax had argued strongly that the despatch of war materiel to Turkey was not only a military precaution of the first importance from Britain's point of view but also 'a psychological gesture of urgent importance from the point of view of Turkish morale and their faith in our capacity and willingness to help them'.[52] He had further stressed that during the next few weeks or months, the country would be living in what were 'practically war conditions'. In these circumstances, the principle should be adopted that where the despatch of war material was urgently necessary on political grounds, 'it should not be held up owing to the absence of duly concluded credit agreements or other difficulties of a similar kind. The time had come when 'we cannot allow purely constitutional difficulties to stand in the way of political necessities'.[53]

Having stood firm on their insistence that no arms could be shipped to Turkey until the conclusion of a credit agreement, the Treasury caved in on 25 August, one week before the outbreak of war. No doubt influenced by the personal visit from Hore-Belisha on 24 August, Simon's conversion was probably a response to the conclusion of the Nazi–Soviet Non-Aggression Pact the day before.[54] At the end of August 1939, arrangements were completed for the despatch of war material to Turkey: four 3.7 inch anti-aircraft guns and their ammunition and equipment (tractors, searchlights, sound locators), the first of 24 to be delivered during the next few months; five light tanks; 15 Hurricane fighters; ten Blenheim bombers, 25 Avro-Ansons; and 500 mines, 200 torpedoes, and 350 depth-charges.[55]

Whilst during the late 1930s Greece occupied a less significant place in British strategic and political priorities than either Turkey or Portugal, policy-makers in London wished to achieve an improvement in Anglo-Greek relations. It was, therefore, somewhat disquieting to discover in the aftermath of the Munich settlement that despite his pro-British sentiments, King George of Greece was feeling 'personally hurt by the absence of tangible evidence that His Majesty's Government was interested in his country'.[56] At the same time, the Greek prime minister and dictator, General John Metaxas, revealed that the tangible evidence of this interest was British assistance in rearming the Greek armed forces. The British ambassador at Athens, Sir Sydney Waterlow, surmised that British inactivity in this matter would result in Greece being 'obliged definitely to accept the German embrace'. Waterlow's belief was confirmed by a high official Greek source.[57] At the end of the year, in response to a Greek request for 12 Spitfire fighters, the Air Ministry offered to release 12 Blenheims and 12 Battle aircraft. Athens insisted on Spitfires, threatening that if delivery were deferred, the order would go to Germany.[58]

Following this unpromising start, the service attachés in Athens discussed Greek armament requirements with Metaxas, who stressed that his country's defence plans were based on a Mediterranean war in which Italy would be hostile and Greece would be on Britain's side.[59] It transpired that Greek arms requirements from the United Kingdom would focus on the navy and air force, since Metaxas hoped to obtain most of the war materiel for the Greek army from France, then arranging £3 million of credits.[60] By this time Greece had been included among the countries to be offered credit, amounting to £2 million, under the new export guarantee legislation. However, its demands far exceeded this amount and included an 18,000-ton cruiser with ten-inch guns, four or more modern destroyers, 15 anti-aircraft guns, 24 Spitfires in addition to the dozen ordered previously, and 38 Blenheims – though the Greek chief of the air staff, Colonel Gazis, preferred Wellingtons or Hampdens.[61] British military authorities quickly concluded that it was essential to scale down and reprioritize Greek arms requirements, especially following the German takeover of Czechoslovakia in March 1939. The COS recommended that the

Greeks should be advised to make provision for a force of fighters, another of bombers, anti-aircraft guns, coast defence guns, trawlers for use as minesweepers, and anti-submarine vessels. The armaments would be generally of a defensive character, appropriate since it was unlikely in the opening stages of war that Greece would embark on offensive operations. The COS confirmed that the proposed armaments would fit in with Britain's strategic requirements; there was no mention of an 18,000-ton cruiser.[62]

Metaxas' government accepted the chiefs' advice but continued to insist on the delivery of Spitfires when offered the alternative of Hurricanes.[63] As with other powers, the acceleration of Britain's own rearmament programme made delays in arms exports to Greece inevitable, despite the insistent requests from Athens and the support of the Foreign Office for early delivery.[64] By the outbreak of war in September 1939, not a single Spitfire nor any anti-aircraft guns for coastal defence had been delivered to the Greek government; and in view of Italy's non-belligerency at this stage, Greece would continue to occupy a less elevated place in Britain's strategic and political priorities.

Like Greece, Yugoslavia did not rank highly in British strategic and political priorities in the late 1930s; but with the reorientation of British policy during March–April 1939, it occupied a position of greater significance. After the *Anschluss*, Yugoslavia was the only southeastern European power whose frontiers were common with both Germany and Italy, and the events in Czechoslovakia and Albania during March–April 1939 had left it dangerously exposed. As a result, the Yugoslav government rejected any possibility of a British guarantee though, as Sir Ronald Campbell, British ambassador at Belgrade, reported, Yugoslavia would remain neutral if war came and would resist any violation of its neutrality.[65] It was recognized in the Foreign Office that in the prevailing circumstances, it was unlikely that the Yugoslav government would openly declare its intentions; the Foreign Office anticipated, however, that Belgrade would be under pressure from the Axis Powers to join the Anti-Comintern Pact and leave the League of Nations. Sir Alexander Cadogan, Vansittart's successor at the Foreign Office, learnt on 5 May from the French ambassador, Charles Corbin, that in view of Yugoslavia's 'delicate position', Paris felt that no 'definite démarche' could 'at present usefully be made in Belgrade'. Moreover, the French government believed that if any communication were made to the Yugoslav government concerning its attitude and action in the event of hostilities, it would 'be likely to retort with the enquiry as to the intentions of the Western Powers' which in the circumstances might 'be rather embarrassing to answer'.[66]

One source of embarrassment would be the incapacity of the British and French to supply arms to Yugoslavia. In April 1939, Morton advised that as Czechoslovakia with its massive arms industry had been absorbed into the Third Reich, Germany and Italy were the only places where considerable quantities of heavy guns and artillery might be bought 'off the peg'; moreover, the capacity to manufacture and deliver quickly was for practical purposes confined to Germany. He added that 'even if we or any other nation on our side were willing to accept orders for these armaments, delivery would be delayed for a very long time indeed'.[67] In January–February 1939, the British government had received an enquiry from Yugoslav authorities concerning the supply of 120 anti-aircraft guns and equipment; it was clear from the outset that such an order would seriously disrupt Britain's own rearmament programme.[68]

Whilst refusing to be associated openly with British efforts to construct an anti-aggression front in Eastern Europe during the early summer of 1939, Belgrade followed up its initial enquiries and appealed to the British to assist in repairing 'the backward state of Yugoslav armaments' by supplying arms even 'at the cost of some sacrifices', particularly aircraft, anti-aircraft and anti-tank guns.[69] The British response was to provide a credit of £1 million for economic assistance and a further credit of £500,000 for military purchases, to consider the supply of 24 Hurricanes, and to rule out the provision of anti-aircraft and anti-tank guns within the foreseeable future. Campbell's warning that unless the British government gave the Yugoslavs some encouragement, they would 'cease any longer to look to us for help with consequences that might be far reaching' was understood in London. But in terms of British priorities, Yugoslavia ranked below Poland, Romania, Turkey, Greece, and Portugal.[70] By the end of July, even the provision of 24 Hurricanes was no longer feasible. All the Air Ministry could offer was 12 Hurricanes by December, with the possibility of more sometime in 1940.[71] When, on 22 August 1939, the Foreign Office received an appeal from Paul, the Yugoslav prince regent, for assistance in securing defensive armaments, especially anti-tank and anti-aircraft guns, the response was entirely negative. As justification for this decision, the War Office cited existing commitments to supply Turkey and Greece with anti-aircraft and anti-tank guns. Accordingly, the embassy at Belgrade was informed that in 'all circumstances it would be clearly misleading to encourage the Yugoslav government, towards whom unlike Turkey and Greece we have no specific obligation, to hope for early delivery'. At the same time, the hope was expressed that the French government might be able to supply Yugoslavia with a number of anti-tank guns.[72]

Before 1939, preferring to purchase its requirements from France, Czechoslovakia, Germany, and Italy, Romania scarcely figured as a customer of the British arms industry. But, as with Yugoslavia, the events of March–April 1939 transformed the position with the British guarantee to Romania. Within days of the British declaration, Bucharest presented a formidable list of requirements, including 250 bombers, 200 fighters, two destroyers, three high-speed motor torpedo boats, and two submarines.[73] Nonetheless, and despite Romania's elevation in the list of priority countries for British arms, there was no prospect of meeting its requirements. Halifax warned Grigore Gafencu, the Romanian foreign minister, of this situation when the latter visited London on 24 April. The foreign secretary doubted 'with the best will in the world' whether 'we could immediately give Romania anything nearly approaching all that she wanted'.[74] This was particularly the case in that the Romanians declined to take Battles in place of Blenheims and Gladiators in place of Hurricanes and Spitfires. Eventually, and following strong representations by the Foreign Office, the Air Ministry was persuaded to provide immediately 40 short-nosed Blenheims and a token delivery of four Hurricanes.

The offer of four Hurricanes was received with incredulity by the Romanian Legation in London; so much so that the minister, Virgil Tilea, felt unable to communicate it to his government. Meanwhile, in Bucharest, the government was disappointed that the £5 million credit provided by the British under the Anglo-Romanian Protocol of 11 May had been treated as a commercial transaction and not as a political loan.[75] In early July, acting on the personal instructions of King Carol, Tilea urged Halifax to meet Romania's requirements immediately and without delay. As a result, the Air Ministry made the four Hurricanes available immediately, with the possibility of releasing an additional eight later in the year; under increased pressure, it subsequently sent all 12 Hurricanes.[76] The 40 short-nosed Blenheims were also released for immediate delivery. The extremely limited provision of British aircraft – and the inability of the Admiralty to meet Romanian demands for naval vessels, other than the supply of three Vosper motor torpedo boats – were not calculated to advance British prestige. Nor could it improve Romania's confidence to resist Axis pressure, especially as the Germans chose in the summer of 1939 deliberately to curtail arms exports to Bucharest.[77]

Of all the European countries requiring arms from Britain in the late 1930s, Poland had the most advanced armaments industry; but, according to the British Embassy in Warsaw, it 'still had a long way to go' before it could 'be considered armed and equipped in accordance with the standards of a first class European Power'.[78] The IIC was even less impressed. In a report produced in May 1939, it estimated that the capacity of Polish industry under the most favourable conditions was sufficient only to maintain about ten divisions or less in active operations, judged by Western Front standards, and to deliver aircraft at a negligible rate. In addition, Poland's difficulties had been compounded by the loss of Bohemia and Moravia to the Third Reich since, along with France, Czechoslovakia had been its main supplier of armaments.[79] Notwithstanding the British guarantee to Poland of 31 March 1939 and its rapid rise in the priority list of British customers requiring arms, Polish deficiencies would not be repaired by British arms exports. British military authorities concluded that only Soviet Russia could supply the quantities of armaments required to equip the Polish forces fully.[80] The British ambassador in Poland, Sir Howard Kennard, was of the same opinion. He surmised that the Poles would have realized in the course of the Anglo-Polish staff conversations, held in Warsaw during the last week of May, that 'we shall not be able to help them directly in a military sense', by which he meant that 'though we might draw away from Poland powerful German forces, we should not be able to send them ships, aeroplanes, men or munitions'.[81]

The Poles recognized their precarious position only too well and looked to find considerable support from their new British ally in terms of a loan in excess of £60 million, repayable over 40 years, and consisting of £24 million to invest in Poland's industrial infrastructure, £15 million for defence material, and £24 million cash.[82] The British government could see its way to lending only £8 million to cover the cost of supplying immediately 100 Battles and 14 Hurricanes, industrial equipment, excluding machine tools, and raw materials including copper and nickel.[83] In addition, it was prepared to consider the provision of a cash loan of £5 million provided the French government made an equivalent contribution. Despite Foreign Office representations and COS arguments that it was essential to provide financial support to make up for Britain's inability to provide direct military assistance, the Treasury was adamant that the cash loan should not exceed £5 million. It also objected in principle to providing cash to Poland to spend on the open market.[84] The Foreign Office recognized that limited British support would be badly received by their Polish ally. In early July, Halifax endeavoured without much success to reassure the Polish ambassador, Count Edward Raczynski, that 'the modesty of the credits granted to Poland' was the result of Britain's need to maintain its reserve economic strength for an inevitable long war.[85] He might have added even if, meanwhile, Poland was defeated.

Further delay in the loan negotiations held up the consignment of war materiel to Poland until early August 1939. The first consignment, including aircraft, was to leave on 8 August. Continued delay, a result partly of Treasury objections, meant that it did not leave until late August, with Constanza, Romania as its destination for transit to Poland; by that time, the Nazi–Soviet Pact had sealed Poland's fate. The consignment consisted of 14 Hurricanes, one Spitfire, 600 tons of bombs, and 112 Browning machine guns (for fighters), but it never reached Poland. Instead it was diverted to Instanbul and given to the Turks.[86]

In the contemporary world, the arms trade forms a sizeable part of the global economy. The mid-1930s witnessed a significant expansion of this trade with the growing demand in Europe and elsewhere for British, French, and German war material. The British experience indicates the supremacy of military over commercial considerations and financial over political ones. Arms companies, such as Vickers, appealed in vain at the determination of the service departments to give absolute priority to domestic rearmament, while the political and diplomatic imperatives identified by the Foreign Office likewise had to take second place to the realities of British defence priorities as outlined in Inskip's memorandum of late 1937. Similarly, when the COS sought to compensate countries such as Poland for their inability to satisfy their own arms requirements with financial incentives, the Treasury intervened to set limitations. The allocation of credits under the export guarantee legislation of 1939 went only a short way to meeting the requirements of potential European allies such as Poland, Romania, Greece, and Yugoslavia; and even the Turks, who received the most aid, believed that British credit arrangements were insubstantial for their needs.

The Foreign Office recognized the need to convert the lesser European powers to its side and much energy was expended in the late 1930s seeking to persuade the military authorities and the Treasury to go as far as possible in meeting requirements. At the same time, Halifax and his officials recognized the arguments that Britain's own defence needs must have priority, and that a too generous allocation of credits and loans would undermine the financial side of the long war strategy that was so vital to Britain's continuation as a Great Power. The problem lay in the effect that severely limited support would have on the perception of the lesser powers concerning the military and financial realities behind British diplomacy; not the least was whether seeking accommodation with Britain was a better alternative than coming to terms with the ambitions of the Axis powers. Certainly, for Portugal, Greece, Romania, Yugoslavia, and Turkey, the latter was an option to consider seriously, at least before the Nazi–Soviet Pact. It is difficult to escape the conclusion that the British government in the late 1930s, in terms of its arms sales policies, failed to inspire erstwhile and actual Allies with sufficient confidence to commit themselves.

NOTES

1. See, for example, N.H. Gibbs, *Grand Strategy Vol I: Rearmament Policy* (London, 1976); M. Howard, *The Continental Commitment: British Defence Policy in the Era of the Two World Wars* (London, 1972); S. Roskill, *Naval Policy between the Wars II: The Period of Reluctant Rearmament, 1930–1939* (London, 1976); B. Bond, *British Military Policy between the World Wars* (Oxford, 1980); M. Smith, *British Air Strategy between the Wars* (Oxford, 1984).
2. For example, G. Peden, *British Rearmament and the Treasury, 1932–1939* (Edinburgh, 1979); R.P. Shay, Jr., *British Rearmament in the Thirties: Politics and Profit* (Princeton, NJ, 1977); J. Ruggiero, *Neville Chamberlain and British Rearmament: Pride, Prejudice and Politics* (Westport, CT, 1999); R.A.C. Parker, 'British Rearmament 1936–1939: Treasury, Trade Unions and Skilled Labour', *English Historical Review*, 96 (1981); F. Coghlan, 'Armaments, Economic Policy and Appeasement: Background to British Foreign Policy, 1931–1937', *History*, 57 (1972).
3. For example, M.M. Postan, *History of the Second World War: British War Production* (London, 1952); C. Barnett, *The Audit of War: The Illusion and Reality of Britain as a Great Nation* (London, 1986); P. Fearon, 'Aircraft Manufacturing', in N. Buxton and D.H. Aldcroft (eds.), *British Industry between the Wars: Instability and Industrial Development* (London, 1979); G.A. Stone, 'Rearmament, War and the Performance of the Bristol Aeroplane Company, 1935–1945', in C.E. Harvey and J. Press (eds.), *Studies in the Business History of Bristol* (Bristol, 1988).
4. Consider, for example, the government's decision to order Bren guns from Czechoslovakia during 1937 which evoked a bitter response from Vickers who had hoped that their own Vickers-Berthier machine gun would be preferred. See *Vickers' Papers*, K620 (microfilm). The company's papers are located at the Library of the University of Cambridge.
5. Vansittart memorandum (DPR 122), 29 Sept. 1936, CAB 16/140.
6. Ibid.
7. For the decision see DPR (DR) 25th meeting, 23 July 1936, CAB 16/136. See also the unpublished papers of Lord Weir, WEIR 17/2.
8. DPR (DR) 27th Meeting, 8 Oct. 1936, CAB 16/136.
9. Foreign Office Circular, 'Supply of Armaments to Foreign Countries', 24 July 1937, FO 371/21274/12964/902.
10. CID Sub-Committee on Armament Orders from Foreign Countries, 'Composition and Terms of Reference' (FAO 1), CAB 16/187.
11. 'Membership and Terms of Reference of the Allied Demands Sub-Committee of the Committee of Imperial Defence' (AD1), 20 June 1939, CAB 16/219.
12. 'Defence Expenditure in Future Years: Interim Report by the Minister for Co-ordination of Defence' (CP 316(37)), Dec. 1937, CAB 24/273.
13. For the COS memorandum see *DBFP*, 2nd Series, 19, no. 316, pp.501–13.
14. Ibid., no. 348, 578.
15. 'Note by Minister for Co-ordination of Defence: Germany – Export of Armaments' (CP 117(38)), 2 May 1938, CAB 24/276.
16. Halifax to Inskip (CP 117(38)), 17 April 1938, CAB 24/276.
17. Ibid.
18. CID 322nd and 330th meetings, 12 May 1938 and 21 July 1938, CAB 2/7; and CC 24(38), 18 May 1938, CAB 23/93.

THE BRITISH GOVERNMENT AND THE SALE OF ARMS 267

19. CID 322nd meeting, 12 May 1938, CAB 2/7.
20. 'Relative Strategic Importance of Countries requiring Arms from the United Kingdom' (CID 1488-B (COS)), 28 Nov. 1938, CAB 16/187.
21. Fisher had stated emphatically that the Treasury view was that the government should concentrate primarily on its own programme regarding the employment of both material and financial resources. The Treasury was opposed to a policy of dissipating the country's strength which 'would result from an attempt to cater for the full requirements of foreign countries'. CID 340th meeting, 1 Dec. 1938, CAB 2/8.
22. Ibid.
23. 'Minister for Co-ordination of Defence: the increase of manufacturing capacity for certain armaments to build up a greater war potential and to meet foreign orders' (CP 289(38)), 19 Dec. 1938, CAB 24/281.
24. CID 338th meeting, 17 Nov. 1938, CAB 2/8. See also Board of Trade memorandum circulated with a note by the secretary of the CID (CID 1480-B), General H.L. Ismay, 5 Nov. 1938, CAB4/28; president of the Board of Trade memorandum (CP 277(38)), 5 Dec. 1938, CAB24/281; CC 58(38) 7 Dec. 1938, CAB 23/93.
25. 'Export Credits Legislation: Memorandum by the Secretary of State for Foreign Affairs' (CP 1(39)), 28 Dec. 1938, CAB 24/282; CC 1(39), 18 Jan. 1939, CAB 23/93. See also CID 338th meeting, 17 Nov. 1938, CAB2/8; 'Memorandum by the Minister for Co-ordination of Defence' (CP 260(38)), 6 Dec. 1938, CAB24/281.
26. 'Order of Priority of Countries Requiring Armaments from the United Kingdom: Memorandum by the Chairman of the Sub-Committee on Armament Orders from Foreign Countries' (CID 1530-B), 23 Feb. 1939, CAB 4/29.
27. CID 353rd meeting, 20 April 1939, CAB 2/8.
28. 'Order of Priority for Countries requiring Armaments from the United Kingdom: Memorandum by the Foreign Office' (CID 1547-B), 18 April 1939, CAB 4/29.
29. 'Note by the Secretary: Memorandum by the Foreign Office – Political Importance of Foreign Countries requiring assistance from the United Kingdom' (AD 4), 20 June 1939, CAB 16/219.
30. CC 33(39), 21 June 1939, CAB 23/100.
31. 'Relative Strategic Importance of Countries requiring assistance from the United Kingdom: report of the Deputy Chiefs of Staff Sub-Committee' (AD 28 and DCOS 110), 17 July 1939, CAB 16/219.
32. Vickers' Papers, K611 (microfilm).
33. Ibid.
34. Ibid.
35. Birch to Vansittart, 20 May 1937; Birch to Sir Charles Craven (chairman Vickers Armstrong), 21 May 1937, ibid.
36. Unsigned memorandum, 'Vickers Foreign Sales of Military Armaments', 23 July 1936, Vickers' Papers, K619.
37. Craven to Chatfield, 1 Aug. 1939, Chatfield to Craven, 8 Aug. 1939, Vickers' Papers 532, 863.
38. CC 46(37), CC 49(37), both CAB 23/90; CP 316(37), CAB 273.
39. For details of the British military mission to Portugal during 1938 see G. Stone, *The Oldest Ally: Britain and the Portuguese Connection, 1936–1941* (Woodbridge, 1994), pp.62–73.
40. 2nd meeting Allied Demands Committee, 18 July 1939, CAB 16/219; Foreign Office memorandum, 'Arms Requirements of Portugal and Yugoslavia' (AD 22), both CAB

16/219; Halifax to Chatfield, 31 July 1939, FO 371/24064/11368/160.
41. Admiralty to Foreign Office, 5 Oct. 1939, FO 371/23161/15840/13834; Halifax to Churchill (first lord of the Admiralty), 14 Oct. 1939, FO 371/23161/17167/13834; Halifax to Selby (British ambassador, Lisbon), 3 Nov. 1939, FO 371/23161/17167/13834.
42. For the First World War precedent concerning Turkish support for the central powers, see Vansittart memorandum (DPR 122), Sept. 1936. CAB16/140.
43. Baggallay (Foreign Office) to Playfair (Treasury), 14 July 1939, FO 371/23294/4995/143.
44. 'Summary and Appreciation of CID Paper No. J.I.C. 126', 25 July 1939. FO 371/23294/5207/143.
45. Playfair to Bowker (Foreign Office), 1 Aug. 1939, FO 371/23294/5421/143.
46. Baggallay to Playfair, 14 July 1939, FO 371/23294/4995/143.
47. 'Anglo-Turkish Staff Conversations: Anglo-French-Turkish Military Convention' (DCOS 159), FO 371/23925. See also Sir Hugh Knatchbull-Hugessen (British ambassador, Angora) to Halifax, 30 July 1939, FO 371/23925/5482/143.
48. Chatfield to Halifax, 4 Aug. 1939. FO 371/23295/5530/143. The prime minister, Neville Chamberlain, approved the DCOS report *in toto* subject to the approval of his senior ministerial colleagues; Cornwall Jones to Baggallay, 9 Aug. 1939. FO 371/23925/5605/143.
49. FO to Knatchbull-Hugessen, 12 Aug. 1939, FO 371/23295/5668/143.
50. Admiral Tom Phillips to Chatfield, 15 Aug. 1939, ibid.
51. Chatfield to Halifax, 15 August 1939, FO 371/23295/5774/143. See also Phillips to Baggallay, 14 Aug. 1939, FO 371/23295/5752/143.
52. In this connection, the director of operations at the War Office, General Sir Henry Pownall, informed Sir Lancelot Oliphant, assistant undersecretary at the Foreign Office, that the Turkish military attaché had been to see General Albert Lelong, the French military attaché, and 'inveighed with considerable violence against the British attitude towards the supply of war material for Turkey. He compared the British attitude most unfavourably with the French since France had already despatched a considerable amount of war materiel to Turkey whereas, so far, we had done nothing except discuss methods of payment'. Pownall to Oliphant, 19 Aug. 1939, FO 371/23295/5917/143.
53. Halifax to Simon, 18 Aug. 1939, FO 371/23295/5868/143; Simon to Halifax, 23 Aug. 1939, FO 371/23295/5933/143.
54. Baggallay minute, 25 August 1939, FO 371/23295/5933/143; FO to Knatchbull-Hugessen, 25 Aug. 1939, FO 371/23295/5929/143.
55. 4th meeting Allied Demands Committee, 10 Aug. 1939, CAB 16/219; 'Foreign Office memorandum: Despatch of War Material to Turkey', 11 Aug. 1939. FO 371/23295/5638/143; FO to Knatchbull-Hugessen, 28 Aug. 1939, FO 371/23295/6029/143.
56. Waterlow (British ambassador, Athens) to FO, 12 Oct. 1938, with Cadogan (permanent undersecretary) and Mounsey (assistant undersecretary) minutes, both 17 Oct. 1938, all FO 371/22357/8187/134.
57. Waterlow to FO, 16 Oct. 1938, 'Enclosure to Annex in Chiefs of Staff Memorandum: Supply of Armaments to Greece', 31 March 1939, FO 371/23760/2233/31.
58. FO to Waterlow, 23 Dec. 1938, FO 371/22357/10070/134; Waterlow to FO, 30 Dec. 1938, FO 371/22357/10349/134.

THE BRITISH GOVERNMENT AND THE SALE OF ARMS 269

59. Waterlow to FO, 26 Jan. 1939, FO 371/23760/642/31.
60. Waterlow to FO, 28 Jan. 1939, FO 371/23760/673/31; Waterlow to Halifax, 25 Jan. 1939, FO 371/23760/734/31.
61. 'Annexes A, B, and C in Foreign Office to Secretary CID' (FAO 18), 6 Feb. 1939, CAB16/187.
62. 'Extract from the minutes of the 284th meeting of the Chiefs of Staff Sub-Committee', 27 March 1939, FO 371/23760/1207/31.
63. Waterlow to FO, 31 March 1939, FO 371/23760/2209/31.
64. See, for example, an appeal from Metaxas in mid-August 1939 for the British to expedite delivery of 16 4.5 inch anti-aircraft guns required for coastal defence. Ingram (FO) to undersecretary of state (WO), 15 Aug. 1939, FO 371/23762/6381/31.
65. 'Foreign Office Note for use by the Secretary of State at the Cabinet Meeting on 26 April 1939: Yugoslavia', 25 April 1939, FO 371/23884/3310/409; Campbell to Foreign Office, 26 April 1939, FO 371/23884/3348/409. Sir Noel Charles, the British chargé d'affaires at Rome, reported that Galeazzo Ciano, the Italian foreign minister, had warned the Yugoslav foreign minister, Aleksandar Cincar-Marcovic, that 'acceptance of a guarantee from Great Britain would offend the spirit of the 1937 Italo-Yugoslav agreements and compromise the foundations of Italo-Yugoslav friendship': Charles to FO, 25 April 1939, FO 371/23884/3372/409.
66. Halifax to Phipps (British ambassador, Paris), 11 May 1939, FO 371/23884/3768/409/98.
67. Morton to Nicholls (Foreign Office), 14 April 1939, FO 371/23884/3010/409.
68. See WO to FO, 10 Jan. 1939, FO 371/23879/308/173; WO to FO, 30 Jan. 1939, FO 371/23879/522/173; Admiralty to FO, 3 Feb. 1939, FO to Admiralty, 6 Feb. 1939, both FO 371/23879/836/173.
69. Campbell to FO, 12 May 1939, FO 371/23884/3993/409.
70. Campbell to Halifax, 17 June 1939, Campbell to FO, 18 June 1939, FO to Campbell, 26 June 1939, all FO 371/23879/4947/173.
71. Kingsley Wood to Halifax, 19 July 1939, FO 371/23879/5862/173.
72. Shone (chargé d'affaires, Bled), 22 Aug. 1939, WO to FO, 27 Aug. 1939, FO to Campbell, 28 Aug. 1939, all FO 371/23879/6692/6897/173.
73. Nicholls minute, 11 April 1939, FO 371/23853/2616/1928.
74. 'Extract from Record of Conversation with the Romanian Foreign Minister in London', 24 April 1939, FO 371/23853/3272/1928.
75. Ingram minute, 27 June 1939, FO 371/23853/5249/1928; Leslie Burgin (minister of supply), 'Memorandum of an interview with the Roumanian Minister', 27 June 1939, FO 371/23853/5529/1928.
76. Halifax to Hoare (minister, Bucharest), 5 July 1939, FO 371/23853/5496/1928; FO to British Legation, Bucharest, 14 July 1939, FO 371/23853/5568/1928; 'Allied Demands Sub-Committee: Supply of Aircraft to Roumania' (AD 46), 2 Aug. 1939, CAB 16/219.
77. See 'Foreign Office Note of Telephone Conversation with Air Ministry', 31 Aug. 1939, FO 371/23854/7031/1928.
78. 'Poland: Annual [Embassy] Report, 1938', FO 371/23142/522/522/55.
79. 'Industrial Intelligence Centre Memorandum: Poland – Armament Supply in War', 14 May 1939, FO 371/23145/7664/1110.
80. 'Report of United Kingdom Delegation on Anglo-Polish Staff Conversations (23–30 May 1939)' (COS 927), 12 June 1939, FO 371/23129/9510/427.

81. Kennard to Cadogan, 31 May 1939, FO 371/23145/8057/1110.
82. Ashton-Gwatkin (head, FO Economic Department) note, 'Requests of Polish Government for Credits', 20 June 1939, FO 371/23145/8361/1110.
83. Aide-mémoire, 1 July 1939, FO 371/23145/9244/1110.
84. Aide-mémoire to French government, 29 June 1939, FO 371/23145/9128/1110; Leith Ross (economic adviser to the Cabinet) memorandum, 30 June 1939, FO 371/23145/9194/1110; Sargent (assistant undersecretary, FO), minute, 30 June 1939, FO 371/23145/9244/1110. Then see Admiral Cunningham to Cadogan, 5 May 1939, FO 371/23144/6997/1110; General Lord Gort to Cadogan, 6 May 1939, FO 371/23144/6998/1110; Air Marshal Newall to Cadogan, 8 May 1939, FO 371/2314/1110.
85. Halifax to Norton (chargé d'affaires, Warsaw), 3 July 1939, FO 371/23145/9297/1110.
86. 'Allied Demands Committee: Diversion of Arms shipped for Poland' (AD(39)24), FO 371/23147/15171/1110.

Invading Europe: The British Army and its Preparations for the Normandy Campaign, 1942–44

DAVID FRENCH

The ability of the British army to generate and sustain fighting power during the Normandy campaign has attracted a good deal of criticism. The morale of British troops committed to the campaign has been reckoned to be fragile; some of their equipment was inferior to that of the Wehrmacht; they had not been prepared to fight in the kind of terrain they encountered in the Normandy bocage; and several of their senior officers were found wanting.[1] However, generals in their memoirs, and historians in their post-war studies have devoted little attention to the preparations that the army undertook to prepare itself for the campaign before the landing. Montgomery wrote a mere two pages on it.[2] His chief of staff, Freddie de Guingand, and his operations officer, David Belchem, did not mention it at all in their own accounts of the campaign.[3] Historians of the divisions that spent four long years in Britain between Dunkirk and D-Day usually wrote only a few token pages on pre-invasion training before passing on to examine the more exciting doings of their division in north-west Europe.[4] The official British historian of the campaign merely wrote of 'months of individual and combined training'.[5]

It is only recently that historians have begun to look at the preparations of the army for the campaign. A pioneer in this respect is the Canadian historian, J.A. English, who analyzed the preparations of the Canadian formations committed to Overlord.[6] A younger generation of British historians, notably Steven Hart and Tim Harrison-Place, have now begun to examine the preparations of the British components of 21st Army Group.[7] And elsewhere the present author has analyzed the morale of the British divisions committed to Montgomery's command.[8] The purpose of this article is to take these investigations a step further and examine three crucial issues that had a direct bearing on the combat capability of the 2nd British Army in Normandy. It will examine how that army was created from formations drawn from both Home Forces and 8th Army and analyze how those formations were trained in the UK before entering combat. It will consider how senior commanders were selected to lead the army. And, finally, it will show how each of these issues had a significant influence on the combat capability of British troops in Normandy.

The 2nd British Army, that formed the main British contribution to the ground forces committed to Operation Overlord, was created by detaching formations that had hitherto been part of Home Forces and attaching to them formations brought home from the Mediterranean. The process leading to its creation was a long and tortuous one. From September 1939 the British army had prepared to fulfil two quite different missions. Preparing for a major assault landing on a hostile shore did not figure in either of them. In the winter of 1939/40 the War Office was busy creating an army of up to 55 field force divisions that would be capable, by late 1941 at the earliest, of mounting a major offensive on the Western Front. While a handful of regular divisions represented the British military presence in France, the burden of creating this force fell upon a hastily expanded Territorial Army. These plans were undermined by the fall of France in the summer of 1940. For the next two years, although a handful of divisions were despatched to North Africa, the bulk of the army was configured as a home defence force, preparing to repulse a major German invasion of the United Kingdom.[9]

This had major implications for the ability of the army to mount a cross-Channel invasion. Between the wars the Territorial Army was a shop-window force. On paper at least it was strong in 'teeth' units, but it lacked the corps, army, and lines of communication units it needed to operate effectively overseas. This problem was made even worse when the Chamberlain government decided to double its paper strength on the eve of war. In September 1939 the War Office was determined to rectify these faults. It would create a balanced army with a sufficiency of logistics and support units so that it could operate overseas far from its home base. But one of the first acts of the Churchill government in the summer of 1940 was to abandon this policy. In June 1940, the War Cabinet and the War Office took two decisions that had a profound impact on the army's ability to despatch a significant force overseas. The War Cabinet decided to raise no fewer than 120 new infantry battalions. Following the Dunkirk evacuation, volunteers were pouring into the army and the government had to respond by organizing them. As rifles were almost the only weapons available, they perforce had to be organized into infantry battalions. Initially the new battalions were formed into infantry training groups but in October 1940 these were transformed into brigades and then, in February 1941 into nine improvised 'County' divisions.[10] Impressive on paper, but equipped on a much lower scale than field force formations, they were only capable of holding static defences on the coast.[11] Second, on 17 June 1940 the CIGS ordered that no further base or lines of communication units were to be raised and that those not needed for home defence were to be disbanded.[12] Operating in the UK, Home Forces could rely instead upon civilian facilities for much of its maintenance and communications.

By 1941 the army possessed a superfluity of infantry divisions and a growing number of armoured divisions. What it could not do was despatch a large army overseas. Not only were most divisions still lacking vital equipment, but the army as a whole lacked the supply and transport units to enable an overseas expeditionary force to sustain itself. Divisions in Home Forces had a 'divisional slice' – that is, a manpower allocation that included their own personnel plus personnel allocated to support them at corps and army level and on the lines of communication – of about 25,000 men.[13] Divisions operating overseas needed a significantly higher manpower 'slice' of between 36,500 to 39,000 men.[14] By the spring of 1941 the Royal Army Ordnance Corps (RAOC) and Royal Army Service Corps (RASC) already needed another 200,000 men. These numbers could not be made good by increasing the rate of call-up. In March 1941, the War Cabinet issued the Army Scales Directive, which decreed that the army had already reached its manpower ceiling.[15] Although the ceiling was raised a little in the course of the war, this meant that henceforth gaps in the order of battle could only be filled by converting existing units to perform new roles.[16]

It was only in late 1941, when the onset of autumnal weather temporarily removed the possibility of an invasion, and when the production of new equipment had got properly under way, that the War Office could begin to take the first steps to create a better balanced army. It disbanded the 'County' divisions and transformed their infantry units into other arms of the service. Most of the battalions available for conversion were transformed into 'teeth' rather than 'tail' units, being used to form new armoured regiments, army tank battalions, artillery units, and the British cadre of new formations being created in India. Or they were broken up and used as drafts to replace casualties.[17] At the same time, in order to give effect to Churchill's insistence that the army economize its demands for manpower and equipment in a way consistent with its prime role to repel an invasion of the United Kingdom, the War Office converted nine infantry divisions (the 15th, 38th, 45th, 47th, 48th, 54th, 55th, 76th, and 77th) into lower establishment divisions. They differed from the ten remaining higher establishment divisions (the 1st, 3rd, 4th, 43rd, 44th, 46th, 51st, 52nd, 53rd, and 56th) in that they had only two rather than three field artillery regiments, were without a machine gun battalion or a reconnaissance regiment, were allocated fewer engineers and possessed only a single RASC company compared to three in a higher establishment division.[18] Although they were better equipped than the 'County' divisions to perform a semi-static role in the UK, they were not sufficiently well equipped or mobile to form part of an overseas expeditionary force.

Throughout this period the provision of lines of communication and base units remained a low priority. In late 1941 and early 1942 the War Office had plans to raise just enough for an expeditionary force of no more than four divisions.[19] In October 1941, far from agreeing to create more of them, Churchill had insisted that they be combed out to provide more men for the teeth arms.[20] David Margesson, the secretary of state for war, agreed, informing the prime minister that divisions in the UK were given only just enough transport to carry out their immediate operational tasks. He also hoped to reduce the manpower allotted to rearward services by merging the Royal Army Service Corps and Royal Army Ordnance Corp's repair organizations into a new service, which eventually became the Royal Electrical and Mechanical Engineers (REME).[21]

The result of this wholesale reorganization was that when GHQ Home Forces carried out a staff study in May 1942, they discovered that it might just be possible to despatch an expeditionary force of six divisions overseas but doing so would tax the available lines of communication units and require large-scale adjustments in the layout of forces remaining in the UK. Sending a larger force of up to 24 divisions in the near future was impossible. Even after all lines of communication and headquarters units had been mobilized to support them, there would still have been a shortage of 12,000 transport personnel, 15,000 signallers, 37,000 RASC personnel, 11,000 medical staff, and 24,000 ordnance personnel. The only way to find these men would be by reorganizing and retraining existing units. That would take some months and a decision to act would have to be taken immediately if they were to be ready by the spring of 1943.[22] No decision was taken. Until the autumn of 1942 the threat of an invasion persisted. As long as it did, Sir Bernard Paget, who had replaced Sir Alan Brooke as commander-in-chief of Home Forces in December 1941, insisted that the existing, defensive structure of Home Forces had to remain unchanged. It was not until 18 December 1942 that the chiefs of staff informed the War Office that, as in their estimation a sea or airborne invasion was highly unlikely in 1943, it was now safe to begin reorganizing forces in the UK on an offensive basis.[23]

Historians who have claimed that the British army could have mounted an invasion of Europe in 1943 have mistaken men under arms and numbers of divisions in the order of battle for a field army capable of mounting mobile operations overseas.[24] Even if all of the other elements necessary for a successful invasion of Europe had been present, a second front on anything more than a very small scale was logistically impossible in 1943. This was apparent even before the chiefs of staff and War Cabinet agreed that Sledgehammer, a landing in strength on the French coast, should not be mounted as the Germans, who were still fighting fiercely in Russia, had not been sufficiently demoralized to guarantee its success. On 8 July 1942, therefore, Churchill informed Roosevelt that the best way to relieve Russia would be to mount a smaller operation, Gymnast, subsequently re-christened Torch – the invasion of French North Africa.[25] The headquarters of 1st Army, the British contribution to the operation, was activated on 10 July. It was only with considerable difficulty that the 675 administrative and support units needed to sustain the mere six divisions it was allocated could be found.[26]

Once they had been mobilized, the cupboard was bare. Home Forces now had no mobile army HQ and very few lines of communication units.[27] 'The whole situation', admitted Lieutenant-General J.G. Swayne, the chief of the general staff, Home Forces, 'is at present chaotic and needs clarifying.' What it did have once 1st Army had gone abroad was (including Canadian troops) six corps HQs, eight infantry divisions, and six armoured divisions on the higher establishment. They could be supported by ten independent infantry brigades, five army tank brigades, two armoured brigades and a third forming, and 95 infantry battalions deployed guarding airfields or vulnerable points. There were also nine lower establishment divisions at home.[28]

On paper this was a formidable force. In reality, a great deal of work was necessary before another expeditionary force could be sent overseas. In August 1942 Swaynne had written that 'At least six months would be required before any target date for SLEDGEHAMMER or ROUND-UP to convert the necessary base and L. of C. units for a B.E.F.'[29] It was only in January 1943 that planning began for Home Forces to split itself into two separate organizations, a smaller Home Forces largely concerned with training drafts and guarding against small raids, and the new expeditionary force.[30] In January the formations earmarked for the expeditionary force contained only 123,000 men. They required another 300,000 men to bring them up to full strength and the War Office therefore ordered the wholesale conversion of units to begin.[31] Government control of manpower was now so tight – in December 1942 two divisions had actually been disbanded in the Middle East to provide drafts – that everything had to be done within the army's existing manpower ceiling. Plans were not finalized until March 1943 and the division between the new, smaller, Home Forces and the 21st Army Group did not take place until mid-May.[32]

In January 1943 Paget had estimated that the complete expeditionary force, an army and three corps headquarters, 11 British divisions, and five Canadian divisions, would not be ready until August.[33] Even that could only be achieved by allocating 94,000

British personnel to the 1st Canadian Army to make good its deficiencies in rearward services.[34] Five months later, in the face of continuing manpower shortages, and the need to earmark more formations than anticipated for operations in North Africa and for Operation Huskey – the invasion of Sicily – it was clear that even this was optimistic. By August it was estimated that the War Office would barely be able muster enough GHQ, line of communication and army troops to support five divisions. The complete expeditionary force would not be ready until April 1944.[35]

The amalgamation of 'green' divisions from Home Forces with veteran formations from the Mediterranean to form the 2nd British Army was not inevitable. It came about partly as a result of a suggestion from Montgomery and partly as a result of a political decision taken by Churchill. Montgomery set great store on the value of battlefield experience. In March 1942, he had identified the lack of it as the greatest weakness of Home Forces, writing that:

> We suffer from a very grave disadvantage in this country in that we lack day-to-day experience of modern battle fighting, and those of us who have commanded units and formations in battle in this war are few in number. Very few of our soldiers have any idea of the conditions of the modern battle. Our enemies know this very well and will hope to profit from it.[36]

In September 1943, he suggested to Brooke a way in which this deficiency could a least in part be made good. He wanted the corps troops of XXX Corps and its two infantry divisions, 50th (Northumbrian) and 51st (Highland) divisions, to be shipped home in their entirety from the Mediterranean.

> It seems to me that if you get home to the UK the Corps HQ, the Corps Artillery, and the two Divisions of the Corps, *and you keep the whole party together in England as a Corps*, then you will have a Corps which has taken part in every type of fighting, which is a superb team, and which would be a model for the whole Army in England to study. To break up such a weapon would be a thousand pities. To have such an experienced fighting Corps would be worth untold gold when it comes to a cross-Channel venture. I am sure you would agree that it is not

necessarily the "big battalions" that give success in war; it is the best weapon, properly wielded, even if it is relatively small.[37]

Churchill's intervention came two months later. By November 1943 the War Office had earmarked a dozen divisions to Overlord. Churchill did not think that was enough. The Americans were committing 15 divisions in the initial stages of the operation and the prime minister insisted that, for political reasons, the British had to match them. 'We have carried the recent trouble entirely by mentioning that we had preponderance on the battlefront', he wrote to Sir P.J. Grigg, the secretary of state for war. 'We ought to have at least equality in this other critical task.'[38] Montgomery's suggestion was therefore accepted, and a third division, the highly experienced 7th Armoured Division, was also transported to Britain.

The performance of these three divisions in Normandy suggests that Montgomery had misread their capabilities. A secret War Office report prepared on the eve of D-Day confided: 'There is complete confidence throughout the army at home in the success of the invasion operations which are believed to be impending, though most soldiers seem to be well aware that they are not likely to be a "walk-over". This confidence has been increased by appointment of new senior commanders.'[39] But there is also evidence that the willingness of soldiers to participate in the landing varied, often according to the experience of particular units and formations. Soldiers returning from the Mediterranean, where they had already seen much frontline service, were far less enthusiastic about taking part in the forthcoming operation than 'green' troops. The consequences of this soon became apparent in Normandy, when all three veteran divisions experienced serious morale problems. When it arrived in Britain from the Mediterranean, 50th (Northumbrian) Division was earmarked as one of the follow-up formations for the invasion. As a result of Eisenhower's and Montgomery's decision to widen the landing from a three- to a five-division front, it found itself propelled into the role of an assault division. The division's historian noted that: 'This was a compliment to the fighting qualities of the Division in the past two years, but it occasioned no general rejoicing. Experience enabled officers and men to appreciate all it meant, and it was, in general, with a sober and dogged determination that all faced up to what lay ahead.'⁴⁰ In fact, there were many indications that morale was fragile in the division before the landing and that it worsened as the campaign continued.⁴¹ In November 1944 the shortage of drafts gave Montgomery an excuse to send the division home in skeleton form. 'The decisive argument' for doing this, according to Grigg, 'is that the Division is battle weary and can no longer be counted on for an offensive role.'⁴²

The 51st (Highland) Division suffered from many of the same problems that bedevilled the 50th (Northumbrian). In mid-July Montgomery and the division's corps and army commanders agreed that: '51 Division is at present not (repeat not) battle worthy. It does not (not) fight with determination and has failed in every operation it has been given to do. It cannot (cannot) fight the Germans successfully.'⁴³ Similarly, after the Goodwood operation in July 1944, Lieutenant-General Sir Richard O'Connor described the performance of 7th Armoured Division as 'rather disappointing'.⁴⁴ In mid-June it had already experienced a major setback at Villers Bocage, when it had lost almost an entire armoured regiment. After another failure in early August to capture the village of Aunay as part of Operation Bluecoat, the commander of 2nd British Army, Sir Miles Dempsey, concluded that 'in recent operations in NORMANDY it has failed to show the necessary dash, and has been far too slow in coming into action'.⁴⁵ The performance of these three veteran divisions in Normandy must cast doubt upon Montgomery's prediction that XXX Corps did indeed represent 'the best weapon'.

Fragile morale was not the only reason for the lacklustre performance of the veteran divisions of 2nd British Army in Normandy. Inappropriate training was probably equally important. British military doctrine decreed that senior officers were responsible for training the subordinates they would actually lead in battle. The headquarters of 2nd Army began to form at Cowley barracks, Oxford, in May 1943, although it was some months before it was complete. It was responsible for the training of I, VIII, and XIII Corps. The HQ of 21st Army Group, responsible for commanding both 2nd British Army and 1st Canadian Army, was activated at Wentworth in July.⁴⁶ By 1943, the British army had learnt by bitter experience the need for realistic large-scale training. In January of that year, in the course of making a successful bid to requisition

100,000 acres of the Yorkshire Wolds as a training area for armoured formations, an Army Council committee noted:

> the experience of the present war showed the absolute interdependence of training and high morale. We could not afford to take risks with inadequate training, pitted as we were against an enemy as strong as was Germany. The campaigns in Malaya and the Middle East had illustrated the absolute need for the highest possible training of our troops and, if and when British armoured formations re-entered the Continent, they would be committed to battle with the enemy practically from the moment of landing.[47]

Sir Bernard Paget, its first commander, laid down the pattern of training for all formations in 21st Army Group. In April 1943 he decided that divisions earmarked to form part of 2nd British Army should be trained according to whether they were assault divisions or follow-up formations.[48] Henceforth, large-scale training exercises took three forms. All formations took part in exercises to practise the complex logistical arrangements that had to be got right if the troops and all of their impedimenta were to arrive in France at the right time and the right place. Thus, in September 1943 Exercise Harlequin was held to practise passing troops through their concentration areas, through their assembly and transit areas and to their points of embarkation. And at the end of April 1944 Exercise Cropper III took place to practise ferry control.[49]

Assault formations were practised in making beach-landings and rehearsed the manifold problems of getting ashore and establishing a beachhead. The original assault plan called for a landing on a front of only three divisions, and the task of securing the initial British lodgement was given to formations in I Corps. Thus, 3rd Infantry Division, which had not seen active service since Dunkirk, spent the period from the summer of 1943 to March 1944 practising assault landings at Burghead Bay on the Moray Firth.[50] Each of 50th (Northumbrian) Division's brigades spent two weeks training with the special armoured assault vehicles of 79th Armoured Division. This was followed by a period at the Combined Operations Training Centre at Invarrary to practise landing operations and finally the division did a period of collective combined training in Dorset with the Royal Navy and Royal Air Force.[51] Every month between January and March 1944 the assault divisions carried out two large-scale exercises.[52] Between 24 April and 4 May these culminated in the last major pre-invasion exercise, Fabius. All of the British, Canadian, and American divisions earmarked for the assault landing embarked on their landing craft and practised landing at Slapton Sands, Hayling Island, Bracklesham Bay, and Littlehampton.[53] The upshot was that the divisions earmarked to carry out the initial landing were thoroughly trained to perform that role.

The exact roles of the follow-up divisions in VIII and XII Corps could not be predicted with any exactitude because it was difficult to foretell the precise configuration of the initial lodgement ahead of time.[54] But in general terms it was possible to predict the types of operations they could expect to undertake after the bridgehead had been secured. VIII Corps trained across the Yorkshire Wolds and XII Corps in Kent. In late September and early October 1943, for example, VIII Corps (Guards Armoured, 15th Scottish, and 6th Guards Tank Brigade) took part in Exercise Blackcock in North Yorkshire. They practised a nighttime breakout from a bridgehead followed by daylight exploitation by an armoured division.[55] This exercise only lasted for a week, but in February 1944 the Corps took part in Operation Eagle, a fortnight-long exercise during which they practised river crossings, gapping minefields, vehicle recovery, and battlefield supply.[56] Between these large-scale exercises units took part in their own programmes of unit and sub-unit training.[57] Units and formations that had trained together before D-Day operated well together in Normandy. This was evidenced by the cooperation between 6th Guards Tank Brigade and 15th (Scottish) Division. They had trained together for a year in 1942–43 when the Guards' tanks were part of the 15th Division.[58] Together, these exercises represented probably the most extensive and thorough training programme the British army in the UK had ever undertaken.

However, there remained four significant shortcomings in the training of 2nd British Army. At the unit level, when Montgomery returned from Italy in early 1944 he learnt that commanding officers of battle-experienced units were reluctant to send their junior officers and NCOs to schools in Britain because 'they say the teaching is not in accordance with what goes on in battle'. Many COs believed that

'Battle School trainees are so often "wooden" in their action and so often try to apply a manoeuvre which they have previously seen to totally unsuited situations and ground'.[59]

Second, with only one exception, no formation actually practised operations in the kind of close country that they encountered in the Normandy bocage. The large-scale exercises VIII Corps mounted, for example, took place across the open countryside of the Yorkshire Wolds, which, like the open and flat fields of Norfolk where 7th Armoured Division trained, were very different from the bocage. Before their troops actually encountered it, British planners simply did not understand the nature of the terrain they would encounter inland from the beaches or how it would constrict their operations. 21st Army Group's planning staff recognized that 'the area will not be an easy one for forces to advance through rapidly in the face of determined resistance', but also believed that 'it will likewise be most difficult for the enemy to prevent a slow and steady advance by infiltration'.[60] Montgomery expected that, after only a brief period of fighting in the bocage his tanks would break out into the plains of northern France.[61] One of the main reasons why the attempt by 7th Armoured Division to seize Tilly-sur-Seulles and push vigorously inland failed was because its tanks and infantry had not trained together 'in country similar to the area of proposed operations'.[62] The only exception to this was 43rd (Wessex) Division. It performed comparatively well in Normandy partly because by chance its main training area in England, around Folkestone in Kent, strongly resembled the small, hedge-lined fields of the bocage.

Third, among assault divisions too much emphasis was placed on the training in how to overcome the expected fierce German resistance on the beaches and too little on how to conduct the fighting inland.[63] Complacency had characterized the attitude of 50th (Northumbrian) Division towards training for some time. After the occupation of Sicily the division congratulated itself that, despite its inability to get behind and cut off the German rearguards that had opposed it, the division did not require any special training in operating in closed country.[64] An observer with the division in Normandy reported after the landing: 'There was also perhaps a feeling amongst a large number of men that having landed they had achieved their object, and there was time for a cigarette (and even a brew up) rather than getting on with the task of knocking out the enemy defences and pushing inland.'[65] It seems likely that there was also a lack of commitment to really serious training amongst some units of the veteran divisions. 7th Armoured Division, destined to be a follow-up division in XXX Corps, was highly experienced. Many of its members looked upon taking part in the cross-Channel invasion with little enthusiasm. The division's historians captured the relaxed attitude of the division to pre-invasion training when he wrote: 'For most of us this period of training was agreeable enough. We were not overworked and had considerably greater opportunities for leave and recreation than those which the home army were accustomed.'[66]

Finally, there was also an important defect in how the British organized their armoured formations. In the desert by late 1942, 8th Army had learnt that tanks should be concentrated, and that armoured divisions should not be broken up and deployed piecemeal. Although they accepted that the division had to have a whole lorried infantry brigade, they remained committed to the idea that the two brigades should fight separate, albeit coordinated actions. The tanks' role was to forge ahead when the terrain was suitable, destroying the enemy's armoured and unarmoured forces and dislocating his lines of communication by deep penetrations or flank attacks. The role of the infantry brigade was to cover the advance of the tanks in enclosed country, to mop up and hold ground taken by the tanks, and to form a secure pivot around which the armour could manoeuvre. The role of the divisional artillery was to neutralize or destroy hostile anti-tank guns to enable the tanks to advance unhindered. To help them do so, by late 1942 most armoured divisions had a regiment of self-propelled guns attached to its armoured brigade. In the close country of Tunisia and Italy the two brigades usually tried to work together, one advancing close behind the other. Combined attacks by both the armoured and lorried infantry brigades were deprecated because they required exceptional coordination and left the divisional commander without any reserves.[67] However, in September 1943 the enclosed country of southern Italy compelled 7th Armoured Division to depart from this prescription for a short time. Advancing from Salerno, the division improvised an advanced guard of a squadron of tanks, a lorried infantry company, and a battery of self-propelled artillery, followed closely by the remainder of the lorried infantry brigade and the divisional artillery. For three days the advanced guard fought its way forward along a handful of narrow roads and 'plenty of cover on each side in the form of built up areas or thick orchards'.[68]

Despite that experience the division seems not to have been prepared for the similar conditions it encountered in the Normandy bocage in June 1944. This was partly because its corps commander, Gerald Bucknall, taking his lead from 21st Army Group's planning staff, did not envisage a prolonged period of fighting in the bocage. It was also because its divisional commander's request that one company of each of his lorried infantry battalions be mounted in armoured half-tracks so that they could match the pace of advance of his tanks was refused. It took the defeat of 22nd Armoured Brigade at Villers Bocage and the abortive advance of the armoured divisions of VIII Corps during Operation Goodwood in July before senior commanders recognized that tanks and infantry had to operate on a far more intimate basis if they were to overcome the kind of dense anti-tank defences the Germans could prepare in northwest Europe.[69] Their willingness to change tactics in the middle of the campaign was symptomatic of how the army finally overcame the problems of fighting in the bocage. But because of faulty pre-invasion training, it took time and suffered casualties before it did so.

In late 1943 it was apparent that the invasion of France would mark the culmination of Britain's military effort and senior officers were intensely anxious to be part of it. In July 1943, Paget was appointed to command 21st Army Group and Sir Kenneth Anderson to command 2nd British Army. Both appointees were little more than caretakers. After the war Montgomery dismissed the possibility that Paget might have commanded the British forces earmarked for the landing out of hand. Paget had excelled as a troop trainer, but his combat experience since 1939 had been limited to a few days during the Norwegian campaign in 1940.[70] In Tunisia, where he had commanded 1st British Army, Anderson had developed a reputation for being 'difficult to get on with at times'.[71] This by itself would not have precluded him from another field command, for much the same was said about Montgomery. But his handling of the German offensive at Kasserine had caused Churchill to doubt his ability and, by the end of February 1943, his immediate superior, Sir Harold

Alexander, had concluded that commanding an army 'is beyond his ceiling'.⁷² In January 1944, both incumbents stepped aside. Paget went to the Middle East as the new GOC-in-C, and Anderson, after Brooke 'had so kindly but firmly shattered my hopes and dreams', was sent to East Africa.⁷³

By September 1943, Churchill and Brooke had already considered Montgomery to command 21st Army Group, although both were to waiver a little before making the final decision in December.⁷⁴ Eisenhower, the overall Allied commander, would have preferred Alexander. Churchill toyed with the same idea, but plumped for Montgomery on the grounds that the 'War Cabinet consider that the public confidence will be better sustained by the inclusion of the well known and famous name of Montgomery and I agree with them as the operations will be to many people heart shaking'.⁷⁵ Alexander remained in Italy in command of all the Allied armies operating in that theatre.

However, the fact that he was to command 21st Army Group did not mean that Montgomery had a free hand to appoint his own subordinates. At the War Office, Brooke, as president of the Senior Officer's Selection Board, had the final say in recommending senior appointments to commands in 21st Army Group to the secretary of state for war and the prime minister. He was not without advice. In May 1943, for example, at the end of the Tunisian campaign, Alexander had recommended that three of his corps commanders, Richard McCreery, Brian Horrocks, and John Crocker, should return to England to take commands of corps earmarked for the second front.⁷⁶ Montgomery had equally definite, but different ideas. In September 1943 he recommended that Oliver Leese, then commanding XXX Corps under him should be given command of VIII Corps in England and that Gerald Bucknall, then commanding a division in 8th Army, should succeed Leese in command of XXX Corps.⁷⁷ In June 1943, Bucknall had been commanding I Corps in Scotland when it began to plan and train to carry out the initial assault across the Channel.⁷⁸ He then dropped down a rank to gain field experience as a divisional commander in Sicily to fit him to command a corps in action.⁷⁹

However, by late December, when he knew that he would command 21st Army Group, Montgomery had decided that he wanted Leese and another of his corps commanders, Miles Dempsey, to command the 2nd British and 1st Canadian Armies respectively. In December 1942 Dempsey had taken command of XIII Corps in North Africa and led it throughout the invasion of Sicily. Montgomery reported favourably on him, and his experience in successfully planning and executing a major combined operation obviously stood him in good stead when the time came to appoint the new army commander. Montgomery dismissed Harry Crerar, the Canadian officer earmarked to command 1st Canadian Army, as, 'quite unfit to command an Army in the field at present; he has much to learn and he will have many shocks before he has learnt it properly'.[80] He recommended that when he relinquished command of 8th Army, command of it should devolve upon Sir Richard O'Connor. O'Connor had gained an outstanding reputation as a master of mobile warfare in late 1940 when his Western Desert Force had defeated the Italian 10th Army in North Africa. However, in 1941 he was captured by a German patrol and incarcerated in an Italian POW camp until he escaped in 1943. Montgomery would undoubtedly have liked Horrocks to command one of his corps. But Horrocks had been badly wounded in North Africa and by November 1943 his doctors believed that it would take him at least another six months to recover.[81] Montgomery had also been impressed in Sicily by the work of Guy Simmonds, the young Canadian commander of 1st Canadian Division, and recommended that he be sent back to England to command II Canadian Corps for the invasion.[82]

But Brooke was unwilling, or in some cases unable, to meet all of Montgomery's wishes. Brooke did allocate him two of his choices as corps commanders. Simmonds was given II Canadian Corps and Bucknall commanded XXX Corps. Dempsey was given command of an army, but it was 2nd British Army. By 1944 it was politically impossible for the British War Office to place a British general in command of a major Canadian formation, and Crerar stayed where he was.[83] It was a measure of Brooke's high opinion of his capabilities that, after interviewing him personally to discover how he had been affected by his three years of incarceration, he gave O'Connor command of VIII Corps despite Montgomery's protests.[84] Oliver Leese was posted to command 8th Army. Alexander's recommendation in favour of Crocker seems to have weighed heavily with Brooke, for after he recovered from a wound he had suffered at the end of the Tunisian campaign, he was appointed to command of I Corps, which was earmarked as part of 1st Canadian Army. He gave command of XII Corps to Neil Ritchie. Ritchie had commanded 8th Army for a brief period in the first half of 1942, but Auchinleck had dismissed him following the fall of Tobruk and he returned to England. For most soldiers that would have spelt the end of their active career, but Ritchie was a protégé of Brooke's. The CIGS felt that he had been unfairly treated and that Auchinleck had promoted him above his ceiling, and now gave him a second chance.

Below the level of corps commander, and once he had taken command of 21st Army Group, Montgomery lost little time in trying to replace inexperienced commanders and staff officers, or experienced men he thought were not competent, with men who had proven themselves serving under him in North Africa and Italy. At the HQ of 21st Army Group this meant a clear-out of senior staff officers and their replacement by men like Freddie de Guingand and David Belchem who had served with him in 8th Army.[85] In Belchem's opinion, 'This greatly facilitated getting down to work, since we knew one another well'.[86] He was content to allow two of the commanders of the three veteran divisions he had brought back from Italy, Major-General D.C. Bullen-Smith – 51st (Highland) Division) – and Major-General G.W.J. Erskine (7th Armoured Division), to remain in post. The third, Major-General S.C. Kirkman – 50th (Northumbrian) Division – remained in Italy but was promoted to command a corps. Between late November 1943 and March 1944 two of the five commanders of the 'green' infantry divisions were replaced, as was the divisional commander, armoured brigade commander, commander Royal Artillery and GSO1 of 11th Armoured Division.[87] The GSO1 of the Guards Armoured Division and the Brigade Majors of 5th Guards Armoured Brigade and 6th Guard Tank Brigade were all replaced by experienced officers from the Mediterranean shortly before D-Day.[88] The 59th Division lost its divisional commander (Major-General W.P.A. Bradshaw) and two of its three infantry brigadiers between December 1943 and March 1944. The new divisional commander, Major-General L.O. Lynne, had successfully commanded an infantry brigade in Tunisia and Italy.

In 49th Division, the divisional commander remained, but one of his brigadiers was replaced by an experienced brigade commander from 50th (Northumbrian) Division.[89] Major-General W.H.C. Ramsden had commanded 3rd Division, earmarked as one of the assault divisions since December 1942. But he had fallen foul of Montgomery shortly after he had taken command of 8th Army, and he had sent him home. A similar fate befell him in December 1943, when he was replaced by Major-General T.G. Rennie, who had impressed Montgomery when he served with 51st (Highland) Division in North Africa.

In one case, Montgomery wanted to dismiss a commander before he had even had the opportunity to fail. In February 1944 he tried to engineer the dismissal of Sir Alan Adair from the command of the Guards Armoured Division. By October 1943 Crocker, himself a Royal Tank Regiment officer, was concerned that Adair's division 'tends to follow the Guards pattern too much, and not enough the tank idea'.[90] On 19 February 1944 Dempsey wrote to Adair's corps commander, O'Connor, that Montgomery believed that 'the G[uar]ds Arm[oure]d div.[ision] needs a lot of improving to get them ready for battle, and that Adair lacks the drive to get them right; and also lacks the drive to lead them in battle. I hope you are prepared to say this in your report'.[91] But O'Connor refused to submit an adverse efficiency report on him on the grounds that, having only just taken command of the corps, he could not yet judge Adair's abilities. Senior officers of the Brigade of Guards, like Sir Arthur Smith, the major-general commanding the Brigade of Guards, also rallied to his support.[92] Adair remained and O'Connor did not regret his decision, describing him in August 1944 as 'a tower of strength'.[93]

With the benefit of hindsight, the wisdom of some of these decisions was questionable. Montgomery did not change his mind about Crerar's unsuitability to command the 1st Canadian Army. In July he admitted to Brooke that he was trying to keep him out of the line for as long as possible and felt that, once he did take command, he had to be careful to only 'give him tasks within his capabilities'.[94] Within days of taking command he had fallen out with Crocker, one of his corps commanders, and Montgomery had to intervene to try to compose their quarrel.[95] Experience in Normandy led Dempsey to conclude that Montgomery's doubts about O'Connor were justified and that by 1944

O'Connor had lost some of the drive that he had possessed in 1940.[96] Even Montgomery accepted that he had made mistakes in some of his appointments. In August 1944, he relieved Bucknall from the command of XXX Corps, ostensibly because of the failure of his corps to press forward sufficiently vigorously during Operation Bluecoat. 'Pete' Pyman, Bucknall's brigadier-general staff, agreed that the charge was justified, writing after the event that although he had done well on D-Day, 'the open warfare was not nearly so much up his street. He kept getting out of position'.[97] Montgomery described Bucknall as being meticulous and careful in everything he did 'but he is nearly always 24 hours too late, and the enemy profits thereby'. In recommending his supercession, he added: 'I admit, frankly, that I made a mistake in appointing him.'[98] Montgomery simultaneously relieved Erskine from command of the 7th Armoured Division.[99] Like the 51st (Highland) Division, whose commander he had already relieved, the Desert Rats seemed to be unwilling to close with the enemy in the way Montgomery thought necessary and he laid the responsibility for that squarely on their commanders.[100]

The army that landed in Normandy in June 1944 – whatever its alleged faults – was a very different and very much more battle-worthy organization than the army that was expelled ignominiously from France in May and June 1940. Between the Dunkirk evacuation and D-Day the British army experienced a military renascence. However, as the Normandy campaign showed, the transformation was not complete, and it still had certain shortcomings.

The war correspondent Alexander Clifford noted distinct variations in the performance of different divisions in Normandy. In his opinion, the three divisions brought back from the Mediterranean, where they had seen extensive service in North Africa, Sicily, and Italy, 7th Armoured, 50th (Northumbrian) and 51st (Highland) Divisions, did not perform as well as three 'green' divisions, 11th Armoured, 15th (Scottish), and 43rd (Wessex) Divisions, which came to the battle without their extensive experience.[101] Similar rumours must have reached London, for in the middle of the breakout from Normandy, Churchill asked for a report on the combat capability of the veteran and 'green' divisions of 21st Army Group. Montgomery's reply confirmed Clifford's conclusions. On 2 September he wrote:

Generally it can be said that the veteran Divisions were best on D Day and for the first few weeks but that the UK trained divisions then caught them up and are now the best. You will remember that in January last I took a number of senior officers from the experienced divisions and posted them across the UK divisions. This paid a very good dividend and these officers taught battle technique and procedure to the UK divisions. Divisions that have been fighting for three years are now getting tired. The best divisions in 21 Army Group are now the UK divisions like 15 43 49 53 11 Armd Gds Armd and NOT repeat NOT divisions like 50 51 and 7 Arms.[102]

In contrast to the performance of the veteran divisions, 'green' formations, proved themselves to be reliable. That was partly because the morale of their members was, on the whole, more stable. By contrast, many of the officers and men of the veteran divisions were war-weary even before they landed in Normandy. It also owed much to the fact that the training the 'green' divisions received in the UK as follow-up formations was in general better suited for the role they had to perform than the training of the veteran 8th Army Divisions that made the first breech in Hitler's Atlantic Wall. The latter had trained to carry out an assault landing. But thereafter senior officers seem to have assumed that their previous combat experience would carry them through the next phase of the battle without requiring them to do any special training for the peculiar conditions they would encounter or the particular operations they would undertake in France.

In the light of the British army's chronic manpower problems in 1944, and Churchill's insistence that in the opening stages of the campaign at least the British had to have numerical equality with the Americans, it was unrealistic to expect that experienced formations from the Mediterranean would not be committed to the Normandy campaign. However, the way in which they were committed was not inevitable. Major-General G.P. Roberts, who commanded the inexperienced 11th Armoured Division, suggested after the war that the combat capability of the army might have been considerably improved had Montgomery's policy of posting experienced staff officers and commanders to 'green' formations been carried a stage further and some of the veteran divisions been broken up entirely and used as cadres to provide a greater leavening of experienced personnel for divisions going into combat for the first time.[103] But, given Montgomery's insistence that the veteran formations of XXX Corps had to be kept intact, that was never seriously considered.

NOTES

1. See, for example, C. d'Este, 'The British Army and the Challenge of War 1939-45', in D. Chandler and I. Beckett (eds.), *The Oxford Illustrated History of the British Army* (Oxford, 1994), pp.298-9
2. Field Marshal Viscount Montgomery of Alamein, *Normandy to the Baltic* (London, 1946), pp.36-7.
3. Major-General D. Belchem, *Victory in Normandy* (London, 1981); Major-General Sir F. de Guingand, *Operation Victory* (London, 1947).
4. See, for example, Lieutenant-General H.G. Martin, *The History of the Fifteenth Scottish Division 1939-45* (Edinburgh, 1948), pp.1-29; N. Scarfe, *Assault Division. A History of the 3rd Division from the Invasion of Normandy to the surrender of Germany* (London, 1947), pp.30-60; Brigadier C.N. Barclay, *The History of the 53rd (Welsh) Division in the Second World War* (London, 1956), pp.1-58.
5. Major L.F. Ellis, *Victory in the West*, Vol.1: *The Battle for Normandy* (London, 1962), p.133.
6. J.A. English, *The Canadian Army and the Normandy Campaign. A Study in the Failure in High Command* (New York, 1991).
7. S.A. Hart, *Montgomery and 'Colossal Cracks'. The 21st Army Group in Northwest Europe, 1944-45* (Westport, CT, 2000); T. Harrison Place, 'Tactical Doctrine and Training in the Infantry and Armoured Arms of the British Home Army, 1940-44' (unpublished Ph.D. thesis, Leeds University, 1997); idem, 'Lionel Wigram, Battle Drill, and the British Army in the Second World War', *War in History*, 7 (2000), pp.442-62.
8. D. French, '"Tommy is no Soldier": The Morale of the Second British Army in Normandy', *Journal of Strategic Studies*, 19 (1996), pp.154-78.
9. D. French, *Raising Churchill's Army. The British Army and the War Against Germany, 1919-45* (Oxford, 2000), pp.184-9.
10. Minutes of the Army Council, 6 Aug. 1940; PRO WO 260/41; DSD to C-in-C Home Forces, 30 Sept. 1940, WO 163/48/ACM(AE)15.
11. DSD to Brooke (C-in-C Home Forces), 15 Feb. 1941, WO 260/43.
12. Re-organization of the army from 3 Aug. to 25 Dec. 1940, WO 193/221.
13. DSD to DCIGS, 18 July 1942, WO 193/230.
14. Minutes of the commander in chief's conference held at GHQ, 14 May 1942, WO 205/1c.
15. Churchill, 'Directive by the Minister of Defence', 6 March 1941, PREM 3/55/1.
16. Director General of Army Requirements, 'Revision of the Basis on which Army Requirements are Calculated' (ECAC Paper 13), 6 March 1941, WO 163/84; DSD to General Staff directors, 13 March 1941, WO 193/979.
17. Margesson [secretary of state for war] to Churchill, 2 Oct. 1941; PRO WO 216/1; DSD to Brooke, 11 Nov. 1941, WO 260/43; DSD to DMO&P, GHQ Home Forces, DMT, DAFV, 1 Sept. 1941, WO 193/979; Margesson to Churchill, 2 Oct. 1941, WO

216/1; Readjustment of units and personnel for Stage II in implementation of FFC-36. Minutes of a meeting held 20 Oct. 1941, WO 193/979; DSD to Brooke, 27 Oct. 1941, WO 260/43.
18. DSD to Brooke, 11 Nov. 1941, WO 260/4223.
19. DSD to Brooke, 18 Nov. 1941, WO 260/43; DSD to Brooke, 11 Feb. 1942, and 'Minutes of a meeting held on 26 January 1942 to consider the organization of the Expeditionary Force', both WO 193/230; Margesson to Churchill, 2 Oct. 1941, WO 216/1
20. Churchill to Margesson, 15 Sept. 1941, WO 259/74; Churchill to CIGS and Margesson, 1 Oct. 1941, WO 216/1.
21. Margesson to Brooke, 2 Oct. 1941, WO 216/1.
22. DDSD(O), Home Forces, to G(OPs) Home Forces, 'Numerical estimate of forces for continental operations', 13 May 1942, WO 199/453.
23. Franklyn Committee, 'Terms of Reference' (ECAC/M(43)7), 12 Feb. 1943, WO 163/90.
24. J. Grigg, *1943. The Victory that Never Was* (London, 1980), 214.
25. W.S. Churchill, *The Second World War*, Vol. IV: *Hinge of Fate* (London, 1951), pp.391–2, 404; W.F. Kimball (ed.), *Churchill and Roosevelt. The Complete Correspondence*. Vol.1. *Alliance Emerging* (Princeton, NJ, 1984), pp.520–21; AG1A to Commander, Expeditionary Force, 8 July 1942, WO 193/230.
26. 'Formation of forces for major operations on the continent, June–July 1943. Minutes of a conference', 4 July 1943, WO 199/435; DSD to GHQ Home Forces, 3 Aug. 1942, WO 260/16.
27. Swayne to Paget, 19 Aug. 1942, WO 199/451.
28. DSD to DCIGS, 18 July 1942, WO 193/230.
29. Swayne to Paget, 19 Aug. 1942, WO 199/451.
30. 'Minutes of a meeting held in room 220, War Office, at 3pm Tuesday, 5th January 1943, to consider the build-up of forces for offensive operations', 12 Jan. 1943, WO 199/461.
31. Ibid.; DSD to GHQ, Home Forces, 12 Jan. 1943, WO 260/17.
32. 'Minutes of 100th & 108th meeting of the ECAC' (ECAC No.100), 5 March, 30 April 1943, WO 163/90.
33. Paget to PUS, War Office, 15 Jan. 1943, WO 199/461.
34. 'Note on the present position regarding build-up of the B.E.F.', 25 March 1943, WO 193/101.
35. 'Note on a meeting held at the War Office to consider a draft paper Review of Manpower 1943, 27 April 1943', 'Minutes of a meeting held in room 220 War Office, at 11:00 hrs 12 May 1943 to discuss the War Establishment for GHQ, BEF', both WO 199/461.
36. 'Army Commander's Personal Memorandum No. 2', 21 March 1942, WO 199/2623.
37. Montgomery to Brooke, 29 Sept. 1943, Alanbrooke MSS 6/2/23.
38. Churchill to Grigg, 6 Nov. 1943, WO 259/77.
39. 'War Office Committee on Morale in the Army. Eighth Quarterly Report, Nov. 1943–Jan. 1944' (AC/G(44)22), 23 May 1944, WO 163/53.
40. E.W. Clay, *The Path of the 50th. The Story of the 50th (Northumbrian) Division in the Second World War 1939–45* (Aldershot, 1950), p.228.
41. French, '"Tommy is no Soldier"', pp.154–78.
42. Grigg to Churchill, 3 Nov. 1944, WO 216/101.
43. Montgomery to CIGS, 15 July 1944, CAB 106/1066.
44. O'Connor to Harding, 18 July 1944, O'Connor MSS 5/3/37.
45. Dempsey to Montgomery, 3 Aug. 1944, Montgomery MSS BLM 119/15.
46. Director of Staff Duties to C-in-C, 21st Army Group, 22 June 1943, WO 260/17.

47. 'Papers and Minutes of the Proceedings of the Executive Committee of the Army Council', 29 Jan. 1943, WO 163/90/94.
48. 'Minutes of the C-in-C's Conference held at GHQ', 28 April 1943, WO 201/1c.
49. War Office, *Training in the Army* (London, 1961), p.196. A copy is retained in WO 277/36.
50. Scarfe, *Assault Division*, pp.30–53.
51. Clay, *The Path of the 50th*, pp.22–9.
52. Head Quarters, Second British Army, *An Account of the Operations of Second British Army in Europe, 1944–45* (Germany, 1945), p.6. A copy is retained in Pyman MSS 4/42.
53. 'Training policy', G(Operations) Home Forces to MGGS, Home Forces, 4 May 1944, WO 199/1226.
54. 'With the Scottish Division in the Battle of Normandy', nd, MacMillan MSS DS/MISC/15.
55. Colonel A.W. Heap, 'Narrative of Exercise BLACKCOCK, 28 September to 2 October 1943', WO 199/1388.
56. Captain the Earl of Rosse and Colonel E.R. Hill, *The Story of the Guards Armoured Division* (London, 1956), p.26; Anonymous, *Taurus Pursuant. A History of the 11th Armoured Division* (Germany, 1945), pp.9–10.
57. See, for example, the war diary of 6th Duke of Wellington's Regiment, 'War Diary, 6th Duke of Wellington's Regiment, Jan.–May 1944', WO 166/15096.
58. 'Notes for Lecture to Gds Trg. Battalion Pirbright. No.1. 1948', Verney MSS I/3.
59. 'School of Infantry. Infantry Training Conference April 1944. Points raised by delegates. Agenda for Discussion to be held at 1415hrs 23 April 1944', WO 204/1895.
60. GHQ 21 Army Group (G Plans), 'Appreciation on possible developments of operations to secure a lodgement area. Operation Overlord', 7 May 1944, WO 205/118.
61. M. Carver, *Out of Step. The Memoirs of Field Marshal Lord Carver* (London 1989), p.180.
62. 'Notes from Theatres of War. Report by Captain L.C. Coleman, AIF', 3 Oct. 1944, WO 232/21.
63. Carver to Liddell Hart, nd, Liddell Hart MSS 1/153/20.
64. 'Notes on operations – Sicily. Extract from reports on the operations of a Division in Sicily', 17 Aug. 1943, WO 201/527.
65. 'News and Views on Training', 10 Dec. 1944, WO 204/7580.
66. Anonymous, *A Short History of the 7th Armoured Division. June 1943 to July 1945* (Germany, 1945), p.23.
67. War Office, *Military Training Pamphlet*, No.2: *The Offensive* (London, 1943), a copy is retained in LHCMA 15/8/176.; idem, *Military Training Pamphlet*, No.41: *The Tactical Handling of the Armoured Division and its Components* (London, 1943), a copy is retained in WO 232/41; Brigadier L.G. Whistler, 'The Lorried Infantry Brigade. Its Functions and Difficulties', 20 Aug. 1943, WO 204/7592; Lieutenant-General K. Anderson to AFHQ, 16 June 1943, WO 232/14; Carver, *Out of Step*, p.165.
68. 'Part I. Seaborne Operations and Beach Organisation', nd [but circa Oct. 1943, WO 201/527; Major-General G.W.J. Erskine, '7th Armoured Division. Report on Operations', 20 Nov. 1943, WO 232/17.
69. O'Connor to Nairne, nd (but circa 1970–72), O'Connor MSS 1/5; Brigadier W.R.N. Hinde, '22 Arm[oured] B[riga]de op[eration]s', 6–15 June 1944, Liddell Hart MSS 15/4/18; 'Reports on the Fighting in Normandy 1944. Immediate Report No. 4', 11 June 1944, CAB 106/963.

70. 'Interview with Field Marshal Montgomery at Islington Mill on 22 September 1969', Liddell Hart Mss 1/269/192b
71. Brooke to Anderson, 23 Dec. 1942, Brooke to Anderson, 21 Dec. 1942, both Alanbrooke MSS 6/2/53.
72. Churchill to Alexander, 23 Feb. 1943, Alexander to Brooke, 27 Feb. 1943, both Alanbrooke MSS 6/2/17.
73. Anderson to Brooke, 21 Jan. 1944, Brooke MSS 6/2/54.
74. Churchill to Attlee, 2 Sept. 1943, WO 259/41; D. Fraser, *Alanbrooke* (London, 1982), pp.374–5.
75. Kimball, *Churchill and Roosevelt*, p.627
76. Alexander to Brooke, 19 May 1943, Alanbrooke MSS 6/2/17.
77. Montgomery to Nye, 11 Sept. 1943, Alanbrooke MSS 6/2/23.
78. 'Notes for History. Talks at I Corps HQ, 9–10 June 1943', Liddell Hart MSS 11/1943/36.
79. Montgomery to Bucknall, 12 Aug. 1943, Bucknall MSS 80/33/1/folder 4; CIGS to PM, 14 Jan. 1944, PREM 3/336/2.
80. Montgomery to Brooke, 28 Dec. 1943, Alanbrooke MSS 6/2/23.
81. Brooke to Mountbatten, 5 Nov. 1943, Alanbrooke MSS 6/2/52.
82. Montgomery to Brooke, 28 Dec. 1943, Alanbrooke MSS 6/2/23.
83. CIGS to Churchill, 12 Jan. 1944, PREM 3/336/2.
84. O'Connor to Major Nairne, 1971, O'Connor MSS 8; 'Notes for History. Talk with Evetts', 15 June 1944, Liddell Hart MSS 11/1944/36.
85. N. Hamilton, *Monty. Master of the Battlefield 1942–44* (London, 1983), pp.527–9.
86. Major-General D. Belchem, *All in the Day's March* (London, 1978), p.179.
87. Anonymous, *Taurus Pursuant*, p.10.
88. Lieutenant General Sir A. Smith to O'Connor, 8 Feb. 1944, O'Connor MSS 5/2/1A.
89. Clay, *The Path of the 50th*, p.228.
90. Liddell Hart, 'Notes for History. Talk with JC[rocker]', 10 Oct. 1943, Liddell Hart MSS 11/1943/64.
91. Dempsey to O'Connor, 19 Feb. 1944, O'Connor MSS 5/4/4.
92. Smith to O'Connor, 11 Feb. 1944, O'Connor MSS 5/4/4; O'Connor to Nairne, nd (but *circa* Feb. 1971), O'Connor MSS 8.
93. O'Connor to Loyd, 17 Aug. 1944, O'Connor MSS 5/3/37.
94. Montgomery to Brooke, 14 July 1944, Montgomery to Brooke, 7 July 1944, both Alanbrooke MSS 6/2/27.
95. Montgomery to Crerar, 26 July 1944, Alanbrooke MSS 6/2/28.
96. 'Notes of a talk with General Sir Miles Dempsey, 4 Nov. 1968, RLEW 7/7.
97. General Sir H.E. Pyman, *Call to Arms* (London, 1971), p.74.
98. Montgomery, 'Report on Lt. Gen. Bucknall', 2 Aug. 1944, BLM 119/14.
99. Montgomery to CIGS, 2 Aug. 1944, CAB 106/1066.
100. Montgomery to CIGS, 15 July 1944, CAB 106/1060.
101. 'Notes for History. Alexander Clifford, 22 May 1945', Liddell Hart mss 11/1945/8.
102. Montgomery to VCIGS, 2 Sept. 1944, BLM 115/29.
103. Major-General G.P.B. Roberts, *From the Desert to the Baltic* (London, 1987), p.168.

Killing the MLF? The Wilson Government and Nuclear Sharing in Europe, 1964–66

JOHN W. YOUNG

In reviewing the early months of his administration in January 1965, Harold Wilson claimed one major foreign success: 'Apart from anything else we have killed the MLF.'[1] The MLF, or Multilateral Force, was a scheme to create a jointly owned nuclear force for European defence among certain NATO members. This study examines Wilson's claim, in the light of numerous other problems that faced the MLF, and places a particular emphasis on British relations with the United States and West Germany. It will be seen that the most significant step taken by Labour was to launch a counter-initiative, the Atlantic Nuclear Force (ANF), which itself never came to fruition. In asking whether Wilson's government 'killed' the MLF, it is essential to discuss the origins and fate of the alternative proposal. In contrast to earlier works, the following will argue that the essential element of the MLF – a mixed-manned surface fleet – remained a testing problem in the debate over European defence until April 1966, well after Wilson's claim to have 'killed' the project. Paradoxically, however, he does deserve credit for helping end the project and pave the way for a European security situation based around East–West détente, non-proliferation and a system of NATO nuclear consultation.

The MLF was founded on the belief that Western Europeans wanted greater influence over nuclear weapons policy. In particular, although nuclear arms were available for Germany's defence, the United States kept physical control of the warheads and the Bonn government – in contrast to London and Paris – owned no such weapons. Yet, by 1960, Germany felt threatened by new Soviet Medium-Range Ballistic Missiles (MRBMs). There were understandable concerns about giving Germany access to nuclear arms after the world wars, but NATO's supreme commander, Lauris Norstad, spoke in November of turning the alliance into a nuclear power in its own right, with 'multilateral' control over MRBMs. Under President John F. Kennedy, the MLF developed as a way to achieve several aims. It would answer demands from non-nuclear members to share in shaping NATO nuclear policy, but without possessing such weapons themselves. It might absorb the independent deterrents of Britain and France, so contributing to non-proliferation. Then, when it became clear that General Charles De Gaulle would retain France's deterrent, it was seen as a way to prevent Paris outbidding Washington for Bonn's cooperation on nuclear questions. Since it would be providing the actual weapons, Washington privately intended to retain veto power over MLF decisions. But, partly to meet French criticisms that the Force was an example of United States domination, Washington did not publicly rule out the possibility of a 'European' nuclear force emerging in future. Vital to MLF plans by 1963 was a mixed-manned surface fleet of 25 ships armed with Polaris missiles. This was preferable to land-based MRBMs because it would be truly international, not based on the national territory of particular members.[2] However, the MLF faced considerable problems. Apart from French opposition, difficulties surrounded its financial cost, command system and military effectiveness. Furthermore, the Soviet Union felt it gave Germany 'a finger on the nuclear trigger' and refused to negotiate a global non-proliferation treaty while this remained a possibility. Actually, Germany was bound by earlier agreements not to *manufacture* nuclear weapons, but it could *deploy* weapons supplied by other countries. American State Department officials, foremost Under-Secretary George Ball, argued that Germans would inevitably want access to such weapons in due course and that it was best to pre-empt this by creating a multilateral system, through which Germany could influence nuclear policy without having a 'national' deterrent.[3]

London's attitude was another problem. The British recognized that, if the MLF absorbed their national deterrent, it would reduce Britain's level of importance in the Western Alliance, but they were reluctant to offend Washington, especially after Kennedy agreed, at the 1962 Nassau summit, to supply them with Polaris missiles.

Conservative premier, Harold Macmillan, made a commitment at Nassau to a multilateral force, but only in an ambiguous communiqué. He hoped only to commit Britain's deterrent on the same basis as its conventional forces were committed to NATO: reserving the right to withdraw should 'supreme national interests' be at stake. The Ministry of Defence (MOD) always disliked the MLF, claiming that it was unnecessary for European defence, would accelerate the arms race and prove a manpower burden. It argued a surface fleet would be vulnerable to attack and, being armed with Polaris missiles, could trigger a strategic nuclear exchange if used to respond to Soviet MRBMs. Defence Secretary Peter Thorneycroft called it 'the biggest piece of nonsense that anyone had ever dreamt up'. But the Foreign Office feared that outright opposition would alienate Washington and Bonn, reduce British influence in the Alliance, and, perhaps, lead to a German–American special relationship.[4] In 1964, Britain submitted proposals for a nuclear force comprised of land-based missiles and tactical aircraft in Europe; Britain's Polaris submarines would thereby be excluded, but the force could have a mixed-manned element and the Conservatives agreed to participate in a mixed-manning exercise. But, in Washington in April, the foreign secretary, 'Rab' Butler, warned that the forthcoming British election made it impossible to finalize policy on the MLF.[5]

Labour's position was wrapped up in the party's debate over the nuclear deterrent. In 1960, the annual conference had dramatically voted in favour of unilateral nuclear disarmament; but the party leader, Hugh Gaitskell, successfully fought back the following year. Unity was then rebuilt around the position that Britain would not replace its existing deterrent, the V-bomber force. Under Labour, it seemed, Britain would remain in NATO and accept the need for nuclear defence, but not purchase Polaris.[6] Denis Healey, Labour's defence spokesman, described the MLF as 'a Heath Robinson contraption', and Labour seemed likely to oppose that, too.[7] Labour's election manifesto, however, was ambiguous on these points. It criticized the wastefulness of nuclear arms and the danger of proliferation; it also argued that the British deterrent could not be used independently of the United States. Yet it only promised: 'We shall propose the renegotiation of the Nassau agreement'; and whilst stating that 'We ... oppose the current American proposal for a new mixed-manned nuclear surface fleet', it did not rule out other forms of nuclear sharing. In fact, in February, when challenged in the Commons, Healey refused to say whether Labour would cancel Polaris.[8] Also significant were remarks by Wilson, in March, to American Defense Secretary Robert McNamara: while Labour was committed to renegotiate Nassau, electoral considerations might lead it not to abandon nuclear arms, but to integrate them into a common force other than MLF. Wilson knew the Americans ideally wished to end the British nuclear deterrent, but he also knew the deterrent 'had an emotional appeal to the man in the pub'.[9]

Germany's position was of great importance to Britain. In 1963, Foreign Minister Gerhard Schroeder told Labour's foreign affairs spokesman, Patrick Gordon Walker, that Bonn was strongly committed to the MLF, though he admitted that some Germans were interested in a nuclear deal with France.[10] The 'Gaullists' in Bonn included ex-Chancellor Konrad Adenauer, who had little liking for his successor, the more 'Atlanticist' Ludwig Erhard. In spring 1964, Erhard rejected an approach from France for closer defence cooperation.[11] Around the same time, in Washington, President Lyndon Johnson and his advisers agreed to press on quickly with the MLF and told Erhard that Germany's support of this aim was vital. This may have encouraged Erhard on a course that, as Labour entered office, created grave suspicions of German intentions.[12] On 2 October 1964, he wrote to Johnson, suggesting they make an early start in drafting an MLF agreement on a bilateral, United States–German basis. Erhard was aware of the delicacy of this suggestion, which makes it difficult to understand why he made it public on 6 October. It stirred immediate suspicion among other countries and even within Germany itself.[13] It could hardly have been worse timed from the viewpoint of Anglo-German relations. As Healey explained later that month, he was keen to work with Bonn, but Erhard's initiative seemed an attempt to establish a preeminent position with Washington.[14] Gordon Walker, too, believed 'We must at all costs avoid a US alliance with Germany over our heads', which was one reason he disliked the MLF.[15] Furthermore, Erhard's gaffe sparked an intensification of French attacks on the MLF project, in turn provoking an increasing divide between the 'Gaullists' and 'Atlanticists' in Bonn.[16]

On becoming defence secretary in October 1964, Healey found 'the British Naval and Air Staffs ... deeply hostile to the MLF'. A leading critic was the chief of defence staff, Earl Mountbatten of Burma, who 'considered it the greatest piece of military nonsense I had come across in fifty years'. Another critic was the MOD's chief scientific adviser, Solly Zuckerman, who argued that the MLF would 'slow down the process of détente' with Moscow, represented nuclear proliferation, and might not even satisfy German nuclear ambitions.[17] Yet, largely because of the need to work with America and Germany, the Foreign Office believed Britain must be positive. Even before Erhard made the fact public, the Foreign Office feared Washington and Bonn 'have decided in the last analysis, to go ahead without us' and that it would damage Britain's interests not to cooperate.[18] The importance of the United States to Britain hardly needed stating. But Wilson's private secretary, Oliver Wright, wrote that 'our relationship with the United States depends on a close and friendly relationship with Germany', because Washington saw Germany as essential to Western defence. Frank Roberts, the ambassador to Germany, even argued it was in British interests to achieve an MLF quickly, because this would strengthen Erhard's position against the Gaullists in Bonn. From Paris, Pierson Dixon emphasized that a negative policy on MLF helped de Gaulle's ambitions of disrupting NATO.[19] Other key ambassadors, such as Lord Harlech in Washington and Evelyn Shuckburgh at NATO headquarters, were exasperated with MOD attitudes. Harlech even wrote that MOD comments on the superfluity of the MLF to Western nuclear defence could equally be applied to the British deterrent that the MOD was so determined to maintain.[20] Given such strong views, an attempt to reconcile Foreign Office and MOD views in a memorandum for incoming ministers proved impossible.[21]

There were actually plenty of ideas about how the new government might fulfil its policies on non-proliferation, the renegotiation of Nassau, and opposition to the MLF, while keeping close to Washington and Bonn. The Conservative proposals for a land and aircraft-based force were still being studied at NATO headquarters, by an MLF Working Group of interested states, although Wilson made clear Labour was not committed to them.[22] The

Foreign Office was concerned that any new British initiative would look like a time-wasting exercise, but some believed it possible to produce a scheme that would be attractive to Washington and Bonn. For months Shuckburgh had been pressing a scheme whereby the United States and Britain would commit nationally controlled nuclear forces to NATO, alongside the MLF, but subject them to majority voting as a concession to other members; and in October, Roberts pointed out that the German defence minister, Kai-Uwe von Hassel, had long since suggested putting Britain's Polaris submarines in the MLF. Most remarkable, in view of later developments, was a conversation between two middle-ranking diplomats, the British Embassy's Kenneth Scott and the State Department's Henry Owen, on the eve of Wilson's electoral victory. Speculating on Labour's likely tactics, they foresaw a possible name change for the MLF, greater emphasis on non-proliferation, and, so as to 'renegotiate' Nassau, the commitment of Polaris submarines to a NATO force.[23]

A decision taken early in the new government was that Britain would retain Polaris. Wilson's memoirs say this was because it 'was clear that production of the submarines was well past the point of no return'. In fact, it would have been possible to cancel Polaris at limited cost; Healey confirms there were contingency plans to convert them for conventional use.[24] It was probably the ambition of continuing a Great Power role, the desire to influence United States nuclear thinking, and the relatively low financial expenditure that led to the retention, as well as the narrowness, of Labour's election victory – by only a handful of seats.[25] It is also essential to recognize, however, that the decision was inextricably tied to the MLF controversy. Wilson, Gordon Walker, and Healey first discussed Polaris in an ad hoc committee, referred to as MISC 16, whose record suggests there was little discussion of the motives for keeping Polaris beyond the need to contribute to the ANF, already being developed as Britain's alternative to the MLF. Furthermore, the 11 November meeting was only part of a process, following from early diplomatic exchanges with the Americans and leading to a full-scale defence review and talks with Britain's NATO allies.[26]

Accounts of the ANF usually credit the plan to Healey.[27] But Wilson boasted at the time that he thought of the key element in his bath during the election. This was that Britain would commit its strategic weapons to a joint force for as long as it lasted, abandoning the Nassau condition of withdrawal to meet 'supreme national interests'. Such a concession would appear significant: by limiting Britain's 'independent' nuclear capability it would please those who wanted to end this; and it would bring Britain nearer to equality of status with Germany. Wilson broached the idea with Alasdair Hetherington, editor of the *Guardian*, on 22 October and that evening revealed it to Gordon Walker. It was the latter, however, who claimed to develop many other features of the ANF, including its name, the proposal for an inter-governmental authority to control it, and the argument it should have its own commander. Gordon Walker insisted: 'There were no Ministerial discussions about what I was to say – I developed the notion on my own initiative', building on 'Wilson's basic idea'.[28] An outline plan was presented by the foreign secretary in late October in Washington, where he intended gaining time and exploring possibilities. He spoke of subsuming the MLF in a broader ANF, which might contain British V-bombers and Polaris submarines, plus an equivalent contribution of United States submarines. Britain would be outside the mixed-manned element and would retain some independent nuclear capability outside the NATO area. Particular emphasis was laid on the need to have an American and a British veto over the use of the force, to prevent it being seen as proliferation. But the key change from Conservative schemes was that Britain's 'contribution would be committed absolutely so long as the Alliance lasted'. The secretary of state, Dean Rusk, and Ball expressed scepticism about the appeal of the ANF to Bonn, especially Britain's absence from the surface fleet. But the national security adviser, McGeorge Bundy, himself sceptical about the MLF, felt 'the first signs are better than we feared before the election'. The Americans agreed to put off detailed talks until a visit by the prime minister in December.[29]

Following the Washington talks, British officials worked on the detailed scheme that went before MISC 16 on 11 November. Apart from the elements explained to the Americans, other features of London's thinking are noteworthy. First, whilst Britain would initially oppose participation in a mixed-manned force, it might eventually concede a limited role in this. Second, it was hoped that, in return for ending the independent status of the deterrent, Britain could win concessions like the reduction of costly British conventional commitments in NATO, a point about which the Treasury was particularly keen. Significantly, however, the officials' paper believed the ANF would be no more acceptable to the Soviets than the MLF; and, whilst it was hoped to give the Germans real influence over nuclear policy, 'we can never offer them equal nuclear status'.[30] The chiefs of staff were predictably concerned about withdrawing the 'supreme national interests' clause but, meeting on 10 November, they discussed a way of minimizing the significance of this issue: even if Polaris were internationalized, Britain could keep an effective veto by being the country that possessed the codes needed for firing the nuclear weapons.[31] This fits Saki Dockrill's conclusion that 'the ANF was supposed to abandon the British "independent" nuclear deterrent, but at the same time keep British nuclear weapons under Britain's control'. Wilson certainly seems to have wanted to keep communications with the Polaris submarines in British hands so that, despite the commitment to the ANF and the end of the 'supreme national interests' clause, they could actually have been taken back into national control fairly easily. It was always intended that the submarines would revert to British control if NATO came to an end.[32]

The Germans were given an outline of British thinking when Gordon Walker visited Bonn in mid-November and were predictably anxious to retain a surface fleet with British membership. After all, a mixed-manned element was the only way the Germans could share in a nuclear force on a basis acceptable to other governments and wanted it to be treated seriously. However, Bonn was now less keen on pushing for an early MLF agreement due to the criticisms from France that Erhard had recently stirred up.[33] The ANF was next discussed during a defence review at the prime minister's country retreat, Chequers, on 21–22 November. Gordon Walker outlined the ANF and said further study would be made to devise a mixed-manned element which was *not* a surface fleet and did not add to the size of the Western nuclear arsenal. The ANF would have its own commander, partly because the force would be armed with strategic weapons (not theatre ones) and partly to circumvent a French veto through NATO. The non-nuclear members of the alliance, including Germany, would be represented on the authority controlling the

ANF and could have a veto (either individually or collectively) over its use. Through the authority, they would also be able to discuss nuclear policy and provide political guidance to the ANF commander, who would work closely with NATO. But, importantly, these non-nuclear countries would commit themselves not to acquire nuclear weapons, which meant that Germany would be unable either to own or control them. French membership was actually considered unlikely, but it was vital to offer this so that de Gaulle could not claim to have been excluded. America, Britain, and (if a member) France as powers that already possessed nuclear weapons would definitely be granted a power of veto over ANF actions. In return for 'internationalizing' the nuclear deterrent, the British still had hopes of securing reductions in the country's conventional defence spending in Europe. They also hoped to win a greater say in global nuclear planning from Washington. The ANF was therefore a complex, carefully conceived proposal, designed to offer concessions to the non-nuclear members of NATO and, on the surface, to end Britain's 'independent' nuclear status, while replacing the MLF and advancing non-proliferation. It was clearly geared to maintaining particular British interests but could not be dismissed as mere time-wasting. In briefing Wilson for the weekend, Burke Trend warned that the ANF would not solve every problem: in particular, the Soviets and French were likely to see it as similar the MLF. Yet the ANF seems to have been accepted by the meeting without controversy.[34]

The day after the review, Wilson publicly criticized the MLF and upset both the Americans and Germans when he said it 'adds nothing to Western strength, is likely to cause a dissipation within the alliance and may add to the difficulties of Western agreement'. Although Wilson spoke in the heat of parliamentary debate, the German press saw this as contradictory to the British line in diplomatic contacts.[35] The United States ambassador at London, David Bruce, dissuaded Ball from issuing a counter-statement, but Rusk and Bundy forcefully complained to Harlech. The United States embassy reported that during the debate, with the exception of the small Liberal Party, 'no-one had really kind word for MLF in present form' and that 'even Labour's front-bench showed little enthusiasm for the ANF. Significantly, Wilson did concede that 'as long as the American veto remains', the MLF did not imply 'additional fingers on the trigger'. The danger, rather, was that the MLF might develop a system of majority voting, which would in future allow other European countries to take decisions on weapons use.[36] The prime minister continued to refer to this danger, despite repeated American assurances that it was actually unreal.[37] The Chequers debate was reported to the full Cabinet on 26 November and with it, in effect, the decision to retain Polaris. This created remarkably little difficulty. The diaries of one minister, Richard Crossman, simply suggest bemusement. As one account puts it, the new government 'conjured away the idea of an independent nuclear deterrent with the ANF' and in the process 'abandoned its opposition to nuclear weapons'.[38]

There is some debate about how seriously leading ministers took the ANF. Healey's memoirs declare that it sank 'without trace, because nobody wanted it'. Wilson's official biographer is similarly blunt, arguing that, since 'the British had only advanced it as a device to frustrate the formation of the MLF', the ANF 'soon perished'; while Zuckerman later wrote that if 'the ANF seemed to be a gimmick designed to get rid of the MLF, it certainly succeeded in its purpose'.[39] But it has long been appreciated that the ANF had a positive aim – internationalizing the British nuclear deterrent – and a negative one – replacing the MLF. Dick Taverne, Healey's parliamentary private secretary in 1964, thought that 'Denis would have accepted the ANF proposal if it had come of'.[40] Andrew Pierre, a former American embassy official in London, wrote at length about the ANF, treating it as a serious proposal and noting that Britain did not properly turn against it until late 1965. Such a positive view has recently been restated with a particular emphasis on the way the ANF fulfilled Britain's aim of non-proliferation.[41] The archives reveal, among other points, that Gordon Walker considered the ANF 'our major foreign policy initiative'.[42] Clearly, therefore, the ANF was a serious proposal at first: having launched it, London would have had to sign up if others had promptly done so. But it always had flaws and commanded little real support beyond the Foreign Office, so that it was willingly scuttled once it encountered difficulties. The ANF fitted British needs well in late 1964, offering the chance to undermine the MLF and renegotiate

Nassau, without either alienating the Americans and Germans or scrapping Polaris. It had to appear serious in order to achieve this. A vital consideration is that, at this juncture, Britain could not foresee pressures for nuclear sharing receding quickly. As originally conceived, ANF also promised to contribute positively to such aims as non-proliferation, the reduction of defence spending, and greater influence over United States nuclear policy. But the last two aims fell by the wayside quickly when it became clear that Washington did not value Britain's supposed 'concessions' that highly. Also, as officials predicted, France and the USSR saw nothing attractive in it, so that it did nothing to help non-proliferation. Furthermore, as will be seen below, Britain remained under pressure to join a mixed-manned surface fleet and the MLF took rather longer to sink than most accounts allow.

Having devised the ANF, the main problem was to convince the United States it was serious. American support was vital if Germany was also to be won over. Wilson later claimed: 'President Johnson was pressing the MLF with even more fervour than President Kennedy, though his enthusiasm was the result of fanatical pressures from his top officials, particularly ... Ball ... and ... Rostow'. The former proved the most dogged supporter of the MLF in 1964–65; the latter, as Chairman of the State Department's Policy Planning Council, had warned that the British election could prove 'a major turning point ... in the future of Europe' because the fate of the MLF might decide whether NATO disintegrated. Wilson's memoirs also emphasize the pressure he was put under to agree to the MLF ahead of meeting Johnson. Bruce urged this, as did Richard Neustadt (special assistant for the MLF), and Ball, who were sent to London to smooth the way for the summit.[43] Neustadt told the prime minister on 25 November that there could be severe Anglo-American differences if the British did not take seriously the idea of a mixed-manned surface fleet. Five days later, Ball met Wilson and said that the basic objectives of MLF must be kept intact.[44] During the Neustadt visit, the British proposed to replace the MLF surface fleet with a mixed-manned force of Minuteman missiles that, since these missiles already existed, would not escalate the arms race. But the idea had no appeal in Washington: it might provoke problems with Congress and 'if difficulties sailing with foreigners trouble the

Earl of Burma, he should consider same problem living underground next to a megaton'.[45] Thus Wilson went to Washington expecting to be pressed hard on MLF. Nonetheless, before departing, he told Hetherington, that 'time was on our side and against the Americans. We were not in a hurry for an agreement'. A German election was due in September 1965 and, if there were no early agreement on the MLF, the whole issue might have to be deferred for many months.[46]

In fact, as many accounts of the MLF show, there were already considerable doubts about the MLF in Washington. At a meeting on 31 October, for example, Ball was keen to proceed with project quickly; but Bundy was again sceptical, more open to delay, and less obsessed by the need to satisfy Germany. He was concerned, too, at the way MLF advocates alienated France and Britain, and he wanted policy to be controlled from the White House.[47] In mid-November, via his deputy Chester Cooper, Bundy indirectly contacted Healey to say the pro-MLF group in Washington was losing influence and that Johnson's position was flexible.[48] Then, on 25 November, he declared: 'I am reaching the conclusion that the US should now arrange to let the MLF sink out of sight.' French opposition, the need to advance non-proliferation, and possible congressional opposition all figured in Bundy's list of reasons but, first of all, he put a 'deeply reluctant' Britain.[49] Hope for the British was also provided by developments in Bonn, where de Gaulle's intensified attacks on the MLF provoked ever greater arguments in the CDU and led Erhard to favour delaying the project. Oliver Wright considered this 'an excellent thing from our point of view'.[50]

With his advisers Johnson was evasive as to the precise line he would take at the summit, probably because he was seeking some elusive consensus position. He said he would not 'have a showdown' on the MLF but wanted to press Wilson to work with Germany.[51] In an initial meeting between the two on 7 December, the president was again confusing. He offered advice on how Britain could join the mixed-manned force but Wilson was astounded his anti-German feelings – 'much worse than anything on the Labour backbenches'.[52] As the *Sunday Mirror* correspondent, Anthony Shrimsley, wrote in a well-informed contemporary account, Wilson's tactics were designed to change United States policy 'not by condemning the MLF but by side-stepping it', with the ANF portrayed as an improved version of nuclear cooperation. In the main plenary on 7 December, the British highlighted the difficulties with the MLF and asked the Americans to study a detailed memorandum on the ANF.[53] But, as Wilson sidestepped the MLF, so Johnson avoided a definite decision on the ANF. Instead, after a long discussion with his advisers on the morning of 8 December, he approved a memorandum that agreed the British proposal should be considered by NATO allies. It would only do so, however, alongside the MLF. The president found certain aspects of the ANF appealing: it would internationalize the British deterrent while preventing a German 'finger on the trigger'; but he was reluctant to commit himself before knowing the reaction of European governments. During the plenary session that followed, the Americans said they had not abandoned previous policy altogether and that they still saw a mixed-manned surface fleet, with British participation, as desirable. The essential point was that America would not particularly push either project – putting the onus on Britain and Germany to find a way forward.[54]

Wilson's retrospective interpretation of these events was that 'we had won the day', and other British accounts frequently claim they had indeed killed the MLF.[55] There is much in favour of this view. Without firm American support, and with a complex alternative now on the table, it would be even more difficult to make progress on the original project. Instead of rejecting the ANF, the Americans had accepted it as a possible way forward. Healey referred to the events of 8 December as 'Ball's last stand'.[56] Furthermore, Johnson's new instructions about Atlantic nuclear defence, issued to United States officials on 17 December, made clear that while the United States still favoured a multilateral agreement of some sort, it would not force the issue on Europe. The pro-MLF group in the State Department had clearly been restrained.[57] It has been rightly pointed out that Wilson does not deserve all the credit for this; he 'had been pushing at an open door in Washington'.[58] Indeed, many American accounts, while agreeing that the December summit spelt the end of MLF, argue that its demise was primarily due to doubts in Washington.[59] But Bundy, though wanting Johnson to take the credit for the summit outcome, said it was the Wilson visit that that had forced the American rethink. Equally important, in both British and American accounts, two essential points are largely ignored. First, as well as criticizing the MLF, the British had put forward their own scheme, the ANF. A proper account needs to consider the fate of this scheme. Second, many writers end the story of the MLF in December 1964 only with the benefit of hindsight, exaggerating the extent to which Johnson had made a 'decision' about the MLF and playing down the fact that the issue would still be alive months later. Britain might no longer face joint United States–German pressure to enter the MLF, but neither would Germany face joint Anglo-American pressure to enter the ANF. Furthermore, Bundy emphasized, in a message to London, that Wilson should not be too critical of the MLF in public and that the ANF should include a mixed-manned surface fleet. A kind of MLF/ANF fusion was therefore a possibility. Certainly the MLF, though wounded, was not yet dead and Wilson still had to face negotiations on the ANF with Bonn.[60]

When Wilson reported to the Cabinet on 11 December, he admitted the idea of a mixed-manned surface fleet was still on the table but emphasized United States readiness to consider the ANF. He also predicted that the September German elections would prevent progress for much of 1965.[61] An opportunity to explain the ANF to the Germans came that same day, when Wilson met Schroder, who still wanted British membership of a mixed-manned fleet but agreed to study British ideas.[62] In his speech to Labour's annual conference in Brighton, Wilson made much of the internationalization of the nuclear deterrent, and he rounded off his successes on 17 December with a convincing display against the opposition on nuclear issues in the Commons.[63] Small wonder that the following day Hetherington found the prime minister 'very cheerful and confident', saying he had had a wonderful fortnight and was hopeful of winning Erhard over to the ANF. Gordon Walker was equally ebullient, telling Wilson that Britain was 'in a greatly improved diplomatic position' on nuclear issues compared to October, partly thanks to growing United States and German uncertainty, but 'largely thanks to the initiative of our own proposals'.[64] If anything, the situation continued to improve. The ANF plan was outlined to interested allies – principally the Italians and Dutch – during the Atlantic Council meeting of mid-December, and the possibility was raised of a conference being convened in late

January. But this quickly became bogged down in procedural arguments, a situation that suited London. As Gordon Walker wrote on 23 December: 'Our general position should be that we ... want an early decision. In fact I think that it would pay us if things drag on a bit, perhaps until the German elections. But it must look as if others, not we, are dragging our feet'. The same day, fulfilling this two-faced policy, he wired the embassy in Washington asking them to 'impress on the [US] that we are eager to reach the earliest possible conclusion'.[65] There were, however, continuing divisions within Whitehall. The MOD still disliked any British contribution to a surface fleet, whilst the Treasury now had doubts about the ANF, partly because the initiative was obviously not going to lead to cuts in conventional defence spending. But the Cabinet Office feared that the MOD's opposition to a surface fleet was still weakening Britain's negotiating position.[66]

In a remarkable misreading of the evidence at this point, one account has argued that Johnson favoured the ANF but 'transferred the responsibility for fashioning [it]' to the Labour government, that the British pressed for a prompt agreement upon it, and that to 'counter the British proposals, Bonn sought delay'.[67] In fact, as seen above, the British were quite happy with the delays; Erhard was obliged to avoid a decision primarily because of the upcoming elections in Germany; and, if anyone, it was the Americans who still urged progress, without being wedded to either the ANF or MLF. Harold Caccia, the permanent under-secretary of the Foreign Office, even told Bruce that the British were relaxed about MLF since, with American pressure having eased and with German elections due, no meaningful discussions were likely until late in the year. This is not to say that the Foreign Office wanted the ANF to fade from view. Gordon Walker believed it would 'pay us to have some delay' because 'it is good to have time for people here to get used to the idea of ANF and also to see that it would be much better to have this than nothing'. He even expressed concern that the Americans would abandon the scheme and promised himself: 'I will press hard, sometime this year, to get the ANF accepted. It *is* the only real solution for the German problem.' Wilson took a different approach, however. In conversation with Hetherington, the premier was happy that he could blame the Germans and their elections for delaying a nuclear force. He declared that the MLF was dead, that it was 'the ANF or nothing', and that it could be dropped if Germany could be persuaded to sign a non-proliferation treaty. It is not a remark that suggests Wilson had any deep commitment to the ANF.[68]

In Bonn the atmosphere was rather different. Schroder was pessimistic, complaining that Washington had lost interest in the MLF, a view Erhard shared and which clearly shows that the German leaders still wanted a 'hardware' solution. Even Bundy was upset at their reading of United States policy and at British claims that 'we have adopted their view. This of course is not the case'. Rusk wrote to Schroder insisting that the aims of American policy remained the same, even if tactics had changed, and stating – highly significantly – that 'in our view the ANF proposals can leave room for the MLF substantially as it was initially conceived'. A message also was sent to Gordon Walker, urging Anglo-German progress.[69] Then, at a press conference on 16 January, Johnson said that the United States still favoured a mixed-manned fleet, a statement that publicly recommitted his administration to support it. It is difficult to reconcile all this with the view that the president had decisively killed the MLF in December.[70] A few days later the Germans sent a memorandum to London setting out their initial response to the ANF. Predictably, they wanted it to retain certain of the features of the MLF, not least a surface fleet with British participation. But they also hoped that all elements of the Force might in due course be mixed-manned. They wanted the ANF to be under NATO's supreme commander, for the sake of effectiveness and doubted the value of a non-proliferation undertaking outside a global context. Despite such criticisms, the British were surprised the Germans had replied so soon and were pleased that they accepted the overall aims of the plan, the general desirability of non-proliferation, and a reduced size of surface fleet.[71] The Cabinet Office even feared that the Germans wanted to proceed quickly, a development 'obviously not without its political embarrassments for the [British] Government at the present time'.[72] In fact Erhard had definitely concluded that, to prevent the issue provoking discord during the elections, it would be better not to press nuclear sharing at present.[73]

At this point, a key pro-ANF figure disappeared from the scene: on 21 January, Gordon Walker, who had already lost one seat in the general election, lost a by-election designed to bring him back to the Commons. He immediately resigned. His successor, Michael Stewart, adhered to the Foreign Office line of favouring the ANF but, possibly, lacked his predecessor's personal commitment as an originator of the scheme. Six weeks later, Gordon Walker was in America, blaming the United States for failing to push the ANF and arguing that bilateral Anglo-German talks would achieve nothing.[74] Wilson and Erhard had met face-to-face on 30 January, when Winston Churchill's funeral brought the chancellor to London, but deliberately avoided controversy. Wilson emphasized that France was welcome to join the ANF, which need not be seen as anti-Gaullist, and Erhard declared that Bonn had no desire for national control over nuclear arms.[75] Yet even the prospect of German access to nuclear weapons via a multilateral arrangement continued to cause problems. Labour was committed to pursue a global non-proliferation treaty (NPT), and work on drafting such a document was well under way in the Foreign Office, directed by the minister for disarmament, Lord Chalfont.[76] The desire to achieve an NPT had been strengthened in October by the first Chinese atomic test and worries that, in response, India would now develop a nuclear weapon. But a key problem with ANF was that, as officials had predicted, the Kremlin saw it as no better than the MLF. The Soviet premier, Alexei Kosygin, wrote to Wilson on 6 January, saying that the ANF would still mean German participation in nuclear policy and so amounted to proliferation.[77] Throughout 1965, despite British arguments to the contrary, the Soviets repeated that an NPT was incompatible with the ANF.[78]

In early March, the Conservatives' Peter Thorneycroft attacked the ANF as insincere, declaring the 'only engagement which this nuclear force has ever been in was to sink the MLF and that was apparently successful'.[79] In Washington, the State Department remained keen on nuclear sharing, but Johnson accepted that little would happen before the German elections; and Bundy again took a negative view of nuclear sharing, arguing that it would be better to give 'thought to other possibilities for nuclear co-ordination within the Alliance which may be more modest'.[80] After the United States efforts to achieve progress in January, there was thus a return to the position of leaving matters to London and Bonn, with Johnson failing to resolve the differences within his administration. A Wilson–Erhard summit was held in Bonn on 6–9 March, but, as Wilson told Johnson afterwards, 'it soon became very clear that ... Erhard was not going to have anything to do with nuclear matters this side of the German elections'. It was agreed that official talks should be held via a working group at NATO headquarters in Paris. This same forum had discussed the MLF in the past and was more welcome to the Germans than the British. Then again, it was a low-profile location where, as Shuckburgh argued, talks could be conducted 'quietly', away from the press.[81] Yet Shuckburgh now doubted the wisdom of pursuing talks at all. Having spent two years discussing the MLF without result, he was reluctant to repeat the process with an alternative scheme. He felt Britain was setting itself up for arguments with France, disagreements with Bonn, and eventual failure. In response, Whitehall officials tried to make his job as easy as possible, confident that for several months there would be little pressure to make substantial concessions. All Shuckburgh had to do in the talks, which opened between interested powers on 5 May, was defend the existing ANF proposal and explore possibilities without commitment.[82]

Meanwhile, the MLF and ANF continued to be undermined by developments on other fronts. Of particular importance were the NPT negotiations and the idea of exploring a 'software' solution to NATO's nuclear problems, concentrating on consultation. On 8 March Chalfont had met the head of the United States Arms Control and Disarmament Agency, William Foster, to discuss the British draft NPT. He found the Americans very critical, partly because the draft seemed to rule out a future 'European' nuclear force. Stewart discussed the issue with Rusk on 22 March, which only confirmed the differences, and the Americans opposed the tabling of the British draft in the UN-sponsored disarmament talks.[83] Then in Cabinet, Barbara Castle, the radical minister of overseas development, raised the other problem in the way of Britain's NPT policy: Soviet opposition to the ANF.[84] For a time, the Foreign Office continued to hope that it might be possible to devise an NPT that also allowed for the creation of the ANF. The British had always been adamant that the ANF was non-disseminatory by its very construction.[85] But by early July there were serious differences, not only with the Americans and Soviets, but also the Germans, who responded to Britain's latest draft NPT – the first that Bonn had seen – with strong criticisms: they wanted the MLF/ANF issue resolved before an NPT was signed and to leave open the possibility of a 'European' nuclear force.[86] The Americans sympathized with German concerns and did not want the British to press their draft.[87] Indeed, on 22 July Rusk sent a forceful telegram to Stewart warning of the danger of Western divisions, which the Soviets would exploit. The United States had doubts about how seriously the Soviets wanted an NPT anyway.[88] When, in August 1965, the British refused to co-sponsor an American draft NPT for the United Nations Disarmament Conference, their differences became publicly obvious.[89] By then, the Foreign Office, hitherto most sympathetic to nuclear sharing, had begun to contemplate the abandonment of ANF to secure the NPT. In July John Barnes, head of the Western Organisations Department, rejected the notion: 'Apart from the fact that the ANF was the Government's first major initiative in foreign affairs, its abandonment would cause sharp offence to the Americans and Germans.' By October the option was being studied more seriously.[90]

By then, a potential alternative way forward had opened up for NATO nuclear cooperation, which made the idea of abandoning the ANF seem realistic. During the debate over a nuclear force in 1960–64, it was always understood that the issue of weapons ownership rested alongside that of planning for their use. It had even been recognized that a system of consultation might be a substitute for the MLF: Gordon Walker had suggested this to the Italian government in February 1964.[91] Only in May 1965 did NATO discussions properly focus on consultation, however, when McNamara proposed a 'select committee' to look at an expanded alliance role in nuclear planning. The idea was very different to nuclear sharing, although McNamara was at pains to say that the two ideas were not mutually exclusive.[92] Together with the NPT situation, McNamara's proposal appears to have caused a significant shift in favour of extricating Britain from the nuclear sharing imbroglio altogether, though it was difficult to drop the ANF, partly because this was a British initiative and partly because United States and German feelings still had to be considered. In

Cabinet in late September, Stewart conceded that the ANF stood in the way of an NPT, adding that the Germans 'might therefore have to be satisfied with machinery for closer consultation on nuclear matters instead of a collective nuclear force'. Summing up, Wilson underlined the point that the ANF might prove stillborn and stressed the possibilities of East–West detente.[93] Three weeks later Stewart discussed the issue with Rusk in Washington and, while insisting that Britain was still committed to the ANF, underlined the way it complicated the non-proliferation talks. Chalfont, who accompanied him, went further and said the NPT was more vital than a NATO force.[94] The current state of debate in the British camp was explained by one official as follows: 'Chalfont was convinced that the ANF should be dropped in favour of a (NPT), while … Stewart, though sympathetic, was hard pressed by important proponents of the ANF to overcome such an attitude. Meanwhile, the UK is maintaining an appearance of continued support for the ANF.'[95]

But public statements by Stewart in Washington, to the effect that Britain was not necessarily tied to its original ANF plan, led to press speculation that Britain was losing interest in the scheme, reports which the Foreign Office was at pains to deny.[96] This came at a delicate moment because, with Erhard victorious in his elections, his government was free to revitalize its campaign for nuclear sharing; and, as Barnes warned, 'if the impression gains ground that the ANF is dead, the Germans, far from being content with consultative arrangements only, may go back to the MLF'.[97]

Wilson's memoirs, in common with so many other accounts, treat the MLF as a dead issue after December 1964, except for the briefest mention of a visit from Rusk and McNamara 11 months later, when there was 'a last attempt to revive the ghost'.[98] In fact, for several weeks, it seemed the situation had returned to that of 11 months earlier. In Washington, following Erhard's victory, there were renewed differences between Bundy and the State Department. Ball was ready to be 'quite ruthless', finally hoping to end the British nuclear deterrent and provide Germany with nuclear equality. But Bundy hoped that a planned visit from the chancellor to Washington in December could lay the MLF to rest.[99] On the British side, Frank Roberts shared the State Department's belief that Germany still wanted nuclear sharing, a point confirmed by the German ambassador to London, Herbert Blankenhorn.[100] When Schroder and Stewart held talks in mid-November, the former still expressed a preference for an MLF-style body, and Stewart had to conclude that there was 'a clear gap' between them.[101] But Wilson took a similar view to Bundy. In Cabinet on 7 December 1965, he insisted the 'MLF was dead' and appeared happy that the ANF, too, was unlikely to see the light of day. Instead, there should be 'more consultation and less hardware'. On 16 December, however, when Wilson visited Washington, he found it expedient to say that the ANF was still on the table, even if he also said that he preferred a 'software' solution.[102]

A few days after the Wilson visit, Erhard and Schroder arrived in Washington and, as the State Department predicted, renewed their pressure for a 'hardware' solution. Erhard put a memorandum before Johnson showing that the Germans were ready to talk on the basis of the ANF, though only if amended, for example to allow for the mixed-manning of Polaris submarines. It was fortunate for Wilson that his own summit with Johnson had taken place before Erhard's; otherwise, the president might have put the prime minister under immediate pressure to accept the German ideas.[103] As it was, both Johnson and Erhard sent Wilson a copy of the German paper, the president commenting that there should be a serious response to it. But by now Wilson was determined to do nothing. He made his scepticism about a hardware solution clear to Johnson and Erhard in two cleverly worded telegrams of 5 January, promising to study the German memorandum whilst hoping that progress would continue on McNamara's scheme for consultative machinery.[104] After that Johnson, as indecisive as he had ever been on the problem, simply failed to follow it up. Bruce noted that 'The President is said to have become so preoccupied over Vietnam and other problems that he has not given further attention to' nuclear sharing.[105] In late January, Rusk again urged Johnson to push the British towards a collective nuclear arrangement but, yet again, Bundy successfully spoke against this proposal.[106] On the British side, whilst Roberts remained concerned not to dash German hopes of a hardware solution, the Foreign Office now firmly hoped that Bonn would be happy with consultative arrangements.[107] Johnson did write to Wilson on 20

February, saying it was still essential to protect Germany's interests in a non-proliferation treaty. But that same day Wilson told Hetherington that since the German elections had held up progress for so long it was only fair that the election in Britain, held in March, should cause similar delays. 'We're pregnant now', he declared.[108] In mid-February, when Erhard suggested talks at the foreign ministers' level on NATO nuclear issues, Wilson instructed officials not to hurry in drafting a reply.[109]

Shortly, another event occurred to aid Wilson in his efforts to bury nuclear sharing. De Gaulle's announcement, on 7 March, that he was pulling France out of NATO's integrated command structure provoked several months of crisis in the alliance and made it desirable to close off other potentially divisive debates, not least that surrounding the MLF/ANF. Ironically, only a few days before the general's move, Wilson had bluntly declared himself 'totally opposed' to any 'hardware' arrangement with Germany in discussion with the American ambassador to the UN, Arthur Goldberg – records of which were kept specially restricted in Whitehall.[110] Soon Wilson tried to exploit De Gaulle's 'rogue elephant tactics' by arguing that it was time to emphasize détente and persuade Germany to alter its policy on nuclear weapons. He wrote to Johnson at length on 29 March urging that the Germans should be content with consultation.[111] Yet still the issue would not die and Labour's clear election victory on 31 March removed Wilson's best justification for delay. Indeed, Rusk urged Johnson on 11 April that tripartite talks with Germany and Britain on nuclear sharing could now begin, arguing: 'The British have been playing a game. They have been for abandoning their independent nuclear weapon in principle, but against it in practice. ... They have advanced the ANF ... then backed away from their own proposal.'[112] This echoed a complaint of Schroder's to Stewart a few weeks before, that the British had lost interest in the ANF just as the Germans wished to take it up.[113] A potentially significant fact was that Bundy's resignation as national security adviser, especially when he was replaced by MLF 'fanatic' Walt Rostow. One Downing Street adviser professed 'grave worry', fearing this would lead to the revival of ANF/MLF. 'I share your anxieties', replied Wilson. 'But we will play it our way.'[114] Rostow did write to Johnson on 17 April about the need for America to pressurize Britain and Germany on a nuclear deal.[115] Furthermore, as the Foreign Office knew, the Americans continued to study the possibility of a NATO nuclear force for some time afterwards, hoping to hold tripartite Anglo-US–German talks on it. Johnson was still apparently unwilling to rule out concessions to Erhard on the issue. Given the continuing United States and German interest in a 'hardware' solution, the Foreign Office felt unable to press its NATO allies decisively to rule out the option, despite continuing pressure from Chalfont to do just that in the interests of the NPT talks.[116]

Nonetheless, Wilson was increasingly confident that talks on a nuclear force were likely to be deferred until the NATO crisis was resolved. He said as much to the Cabinet in mid-May.[117] Sure enough, when he met Erhard a few weeks later, the need to take a common approach to NATO's problems was paramount and the issue of nuclear sharing was avoided, although Schroder told Stewart that the 'hardware' option should remain open.[118] In fact, German pressure for nuclear sharing seems to have eased from mid-March onward, when Blankenhorn told the British that support for it in Bonn was limited to Schroder and a few others. However, only in September 1966, in Washington, did Erhard finally concede that 'Nobody was expecting a "hardware solution" any longer'.[119] Meanwhile, talks on a 'software' solution had proceeded and, in December 1966, the North Atlantic Council agreed to create a Nuclear Defence Affairs Committee to discuss nuclear planning, under which was a Nuclear Planning Group, including America, Britain and Germany as well as the United States and Britain. An NPT was signed in 1968.

Franz-Josef Strauss, one of Germany's 'Gaullists', once remarked that the ANF was 'the only fleet that had not been created that torpedoed another fleet that had not sailed'.[120] It is a quip that suggests, as Wilson claimed, that Labour had done most to 'kill' the MLF. But it can equally be argued that America's reluctance to press the project was the real cause of its demise; or that French opposition, linked to 'Gaullist' elements in Bonn, was the most significant culprit. Easier still to defend is the case that the MLF died because of a combination of factors, some stretching back long before Labour took office, and others merely fortuitous, such as the timing of the German and British elections. It was always a complicated proposal, touching on delicate questions and subject to negotiations between several states with differing interests. Those who advocated it certainly seem to have overestimated the German determination to achieve a 'hardware' solution to the problem of NATO control of nuclear weapons.[121] It would be a mistake, however, to brush aside Wilson's claim of having 'killed the MLF'. It may have been much more drawn out in its death throes than many accounts suggest, but Labour's early determination to replace it with an alternative, the ANF, proved highly significant. This was difficult to criticize as a spoiling tactic because it was carefully put together, fitting established Labour criticisms of Conservative nuclear policy. It seemed to offer an end to the independent British nuclear deterrent and a way for other NATO members to share in nuclear planning. It led the Americans to reconsider their attitude towards the MLF ahead of Wilson's December 1964 visit and opened the prospect of complicated discussion when Germany was approaching an election. 'If Harold Wilson had not come to Washington, it is hard to say when ... Johnson would have gotten around to grappling with the thorny issue of MLF'.[122] Had Labour failed to develop an alternative to the MLF, Ball would have found it easier to argue that Johnson should adhere to its established policy and Erhard's government would not have been made the prime public defender of such a controversial project at a delicate point in German political life.

Whether the British genuinely wanted the ANF to succeed is, of course, a different issue to whether they used it to kill the MLF. The latter undoubtedly seems true; the former is debateable. The ANF fitted Labour's existing priorities, such as abandoning MLF, ending the independent status of the nuclear deterrent, preserving good relations with Washington and Bonn, and improving East–West relations. Initially it does seem to have been a serious proposal. Gordon Walker certainly hoped it would come to fruition and, having been responsible for it, London could not easily abandon it. However, as it sank alongside the MLF, there is little evidence that anyone in London mourned the ANF, and the fact is that by about October 1965, British aims either were not helped by it – the case with defence cuts – or could be achieved without it – such as providing non-nuclear NATO members with a say in nuclear planning. The way it clashed with the aim of achieving an NPT was particularly significant, causing a haemorrhage of support from the ANF in the Foreign Office, where previously its greatest support had been. Also important was that Wilson could neutralize the nuclear issue in domestic terms. 'One of the more remarkable features of the parliament was the almost total disappearance of the independent nuclear deterrent as an issue between the parties.'[123] This may not have had a profound impact on his overwhelming 1966 election victory, but neither can he be said to have made any serious errors on the nuclear front during his first administration. Set against his narrow majority in 1964, United States and German support for the MLF at that time, and Labour's divisions on nuclear questions when in opposition, it was no mean achievement to retain Britain's deterrent and help kill the multilateral project without provoking strain in the Atlantic Alliance or political controversies at home.

NOTES

I am grateful to the British Academy for providing a grant to support the archival research that led to this chapter.

1. B. Castle, *The Castle Diaries, 1964–70* (London, 1984), p.4.
2. On MLF generally, see D. Schwartz, *NATO's Nuclear Dilemmas* (Washington, 1983), Chapter 5; P. Winand, *Eisenhower, Kennedy and the United States of Europe* (New York, 1993), pp.203–43, 315–23, 332–50; J. Steinbruner, *The Cybernetic Theory of Decision* (Princeton, NJ, 1974), pp.285–310; H. Haftendorn, *NATO and the Nuclear Revolution* (Oxford, 1996), pp.126–45; C. Bluth, *Britain, Germany and Western Nuclear Strategy* (Oxford, 1995), Chapter 3.
3. See G. Ball, *The Past has Another Pattern* (New York, 1982), pp.261–62; J. Stromseth, *The Origins of Flexible Response* (London, 1988), pp.79–82.
4. D. Murray, *Kennedy, Macmillan and Nuclear Weapons* (London, 1999), Chapters 5–7, quote from 124; J. Baylis, *Ambiguity and Deterrence* (Oxford, 1995), pp.320–31.
5. *FRUS 1964*, Vol.13, pp.7, 41–3.
6. C. Ponting, *Breach of Promise* (London, 1989), pp.86–7.
7. D. Healey, *The Time of My Life* (London, 1989), pp.245, 304.
8. Labour Party, *The New Britain* (London, 1964), available at www.fisby.co.uk; *HC Debs*, 5th Series, Vol. 690, Col.480.
9. Quoted in P. Ziegler, *Wilson: The Authorised Life* (London, 1993), p.208.
10. R. Pearce (ed.), *Patrick Gordon Walker: Political Diaries* (London, 1991), pp.284–5.
11. Stromseth, *Origins*, pp.82–3; B. Heuser, *Nuclear Mentalities* (London, 1998), pp.112–13; idem, *NATO, Britain, France and the FRG* (London, 1999), pp.154–6.
12. *FRUS 1964*, Vol.13, pp.35–9, and see 59–60.
13. Bonn to FO, 9 Oct., PREM 13/25; *AAP, 1964*, Vol.II (Munich, 1996), Docs 263, 281; *FRUS*

1964, Vol.13, pp.78–9, and see 80–83; P. Hammond, *LBJ and the Presidential Management of Foreign Relations* (Austin, TX, 1992), pp.121–3.
14. 'Record of Meeting of 23 October', 26 Oct., PREM 13/25.
15. Diary memorandum of August, Pearce, *Gordon Walker Diaries*, pp.299–300.
16. Some accounts have blamed France's anti-MLF stance on Labour's ANF: S. Schrafstetter and S. Twigge, 'Trick or Truth? The British ANF Proposal, West Germany and US Non-Proliferation Policy', *Diplomacy & Statecraft*, 11 (2000), pp.170–71; Bluth, *Nuclear Strategy*, pp.100–101 (but n.124 suggests Bluth is confused). French officials began the campaign as Labour entered office: Bonn to FO, 16 Oct. 1964, Paris to FO, 23 Oct. 1964, both PREM 13/25; Dixon to Barnes, 9 Oct. 1964, FO371/179030/365; *AAP, 1964*, Vol.II, Docs.296, 297.
17. Healey, *Time*, p.304; P. Ziegler (ed.), *From Shore to Shore: The Diaries of Earl Mountbatten of Burma 1953–79* (London, 1979), p.104; Zuckerman to Wilson, 1 Dec. 1964, and Zuckerman memorandum, 9 Nov. 1964, both PREM 13/103.
18. SC(64)39(Final), 25 Sept. 1964, FO371/177829/6; also see brief for Caccia (FO permanent under-secretary), 14 Oct. 1964, FO371/179031/383.
19. Wright to Wilson, 24 Oct. 1964; PREM 13/343; Bonn to FO, 21 Oct. 1964, PREM 13/25; Dixon to Hood, 13 Oct. 1964, FO371/179030/369.
20. Harlech to Caccia, 1 Oct. 1964, Shuckburgh to Hood (No.364), 9 Oct. 1964, both FO371/179030/357.
21. See especially OPD(O)(64)2, 23 Oct. 1964, CAB 148/40; COS(64)63, 27 Oct. 1964, Item 5, DEFE 4/176.
22. Wright to Bridges, 2 Nov. 1964, PREM 13/25.
23. Barnes minute and memorandum, 14 Oct. 1964, FO371/179030/373; Bonn to FO, 21 Oct. 1964, PREM 13/25; Scott to Barnes, 12 Oct. 1964, FO371/179030/370.
24. H. Wilson, *Labour Government, 1964–1970. A Personal Record* (London, 1971), p.40; L. Freedman, *Britain and Nuclear Weapons* (London, 1980), pp.31–2; Healey, *Time*, p.302; and the discussion in P. Hennessy, *Cabinet* (London, 1986), pp.145–7.
25. See Ponting, *Breach*, pp.87–9.
26. MISC 16/1 (11 Nov. 1964), CAB 130/212; Trend to Wilson, 10 Nov. 1964, PREM 13/26; MISC 11/2 (9 Nov. 1964), CAB 21/6047.
27. For example, Bluth, *Nuclear Strategy*, pp.99–100; Schrafstetter and Twigge, 'Trick or Truth', p.168.
28. Diary Memorandum, 26 Dec. 1964, Gordon Walker FO 800/951; Records of Meetings, 22 Oct. 1964, 19 Nov. 1964, Hetherington Papers, London School of Economics 7/16 and 20. Schrafstetter and Twigge, 'Trick or Truth', pp.168–9, wrongly claim the 'supreme national interests' clause was retained in ANF.
29. Records of Meetings, 26–27 Oct., PREM 13/25; *FRUS 1964*, Vol.13, pp.93–5; Bundy memorandum to Johnson, 26 Oct. 1964, Johnson Papers National Security File (NSF), Country File, UK, Box 213.
30. MISC 16/1 (11 Nov. 1964), CAB 130/212; MISC 11/2(Final), 9 Nov. 1964, and Laskey to Trend, 5 Nov. 1964, both CAB 21/6047; Dodd to Clarke *et al.*, 19 Nov. 1964, T 225/2569.
31. Secretary's Standard File entries for COS(65)65, 3 Nov. 1964, informal meeting, 5 Nov. 1964, COS(65)67, 10 Nov. 1964, all DEFE 32/9; and see A. Pierre, *Nuclear Politics* (Oxford, 1972), pp.278–9.
32. S. Dockrill, 'Britain's Power and Influence: The Wilson Government's Defence Debate at Chequers in Nov. 1964', *Diplomacy & Statecraft*, 11 (2000), p.230; Records of Meetings, 26 Nov. 1964, 4, 18 Dec. 1964, all Hetherington Papers; see FO800/951, diary memorandum, 1 Jan. 1965, Gordon Walker FO 800/951 for evidence that Gordon Walker intended to keep virtual British control of the Polaris submarines.

THE WILSON GOVERNMENT AND NUCLEAR SHARING   321

33. Record of Gordon Walker–Schroder meeting, 16 Nov. 1964, PREM 13/343; *AAP, 1964*, Vol.II, Doc. 334; C. Hoppe, *Zwischen Teilhabe und Mitsprache: die Nuklearfrage in der Allianzpolitik Deutschlands 1959–66* (Baden-Baden, 1993), pp.214–19.
34. MISC 17/3, 21 Nov. 1964, MISC 17/4, 22 Nov. 1964, both CAB 130/213; Trend to Wilson, 19 Nov. 1964, PREM 13/18; Pierre, *Politics*, pp.278–9; Dockrill, 'Power and Influence', pp.229–32. For explanations of features of the ANF, see memorandum, 7 Dec. 1964, PREM 13/104.
35. Bonn to FO telegrams, 25 Nov. 1964, PREM 13/25; Hadow minute, 26 Nov. 1964, Bonn to FO (527), 27 Nov. 1964, both FO371/179034/524; *AAP, 1964*, Vol.II, Docs.362, 372.
36. *HC Debs*, 5th Series, Vol.720, Cols.942–45, 1032–34; Washington to FO, 23 and 25 Nov. 1964, PREM 13/26; David Bruce diary, 23 Nov. 1964; London to State, 24 Nov. 1964, *The Lyndon B. Johnson, National Security Files, Western Europe*, Vol.II: *United Kingdom* (microfilms, Frederick, MD, 1993).
37. For example, New York to FO, 29 Nov. 1964, PREM 13/27.
38. CC11(64)5, 26 Nov. 1964, CAB 128/39; R. Crossman, *The Diaries of a Cabinet Minister*, Vol.I: *1964–6* (London, 1975), p.73; A. Morgan, *Harold Wilson* (London, 1992), p.271.
39. Healey, *Time*, pp.304–5; Ziegler, *Wilson*, p.209; S. Zuckerman, *Monkeys, Men and Missiles* (London, 1988), p.375.
40. Stromseth, *Origins*, p.84; G. Williams and B. Reed, *Denis Healey and the Policies of Power* (London, 1971), p.173.
41. Pierre, *Politics*, pp.276–83; Schrafstetter and Twigge, 'Trick or Truth', pp.161–84.
42. Diary memorandum, 26 Dec. 1964, Gordon Walker FO 800/951.
43. Wilson, *Government*, pp.43, 46; Rostow to Rusk, 12 Oct. 1964, Johnson NSF, Subject File, Box 23.
44. *FRUS 1964*, Vol.13, pp.120, 126–32; record of meeting, dated 27 Nov. 1964, PREM 13/103; record of meeting and draft telegram, 30 Nov. 1964, PREM 13/27.
45. Note for 'DJM' (Maitland), 1 Dec. 1964, PREM 13/108; State to London (Bundy to Ball), 29 Nov. 1964, *The Lyndon B. Johnson, National Security Files, Western Europe*, Vol.II.
46. Record of meeting, 4 Dec. 1964, Hetherington 8/18.
47. *FRUS 1964*, Vol.13, pp.95–6, 103–7.
48. Healey to Gordon Walker, 16 Nov., PREM 13/25. For confirmation that Cooper was Bundy's 'emissary', see Hardman to Healey, 18 Nov. 1964, DEFE/33.
49. *FRUS 1964*, Vol.13, pp.121–2.
50. Bluth, *Nuclear Strategy*, pp.101–3; Wright to Wilson, 9 Nov. 1964, PREM 13/25; Bonn to FO, 12 Nov. 1964, and Wright's handwritten minute thereon, PREM 13/343.
51. *FRUS 1964*, Vol.13, pp.133–4; memoranda of conversations on 5 and 6 Dec. 1964 (both dated 6 Dec.), Johnson NSF, Country File, UK, Box 214; Hammond, *LBJ*, pp.128–32; P. Geyelin, *Lyndon B. Johnson and the World* (London, 1966), pp.168–73.
52. Note for the record, 7 Dec. 1964, PREM 13/103; *FRUS 1964*, Vol.13, pp.137–9.
53. A. Shrimsley, *The First Hundred Days of Harold Wilson* (London, 1965), pp.99–100; record of meeting, 7 Dec. 1964, and annexed memorandum, PREM 13/104.
54. Records of meetings, 8 Dec. 1964, with American memorandum, PREM 13/104; memorandum of conversation (Johnson and advisers) on 8 Dec., (dated 10 Dec. 1964), Johnson NSF, Country File, UK, Box 214; *FRUS 1964*, Vol.13, pp.146–56.
55. Wilson, *Government*, p.50; Shrimsley, *Hundred Days*, p.102; Castle, *Diaries*, p.xv; Williams and Bruce, *Healey*, pp.174–5; E. Short, *Whip to Wilson* (London, 1989), p.97.
56. Healey, *Time*, p.305; Wilson, *Government*, p.50.
57. *FRUS 1964*, Vol.13, pp.165–7; Stromseth, *Origins*, p.85; Geyelin, *Johnson*, pp.175–6.
58. Morgan, *Wilson*, p.271.
59. For example: Geyelin, *Johnson*, Chapter 7, the earliest account and earliest example of

exaggerating Johnson's decisiveness on the issue; G. Seaborg, *Stemming the Tide* (Lexington, KY, 1987), Chapter 12; T. Schwartz, 'Lyndon Johnson and Europe', in H.W. Brands (ed.), *The Foreign Policies of Lyndon Johnson* (College Station, TX, 1999), pp.45–7; Steinbruner, *Cybernetic Theory*, pp.285–310.

60. *FRUS 1964*, Vol.13, pp.156–60; FO to Washington, 15 Dec., PREM 13/104; Bundy to Johnson, 16 Dec. 1964, *Special Assistant* (microfilms), p.xx.
61. CC 14(64)2, 11 Dec., CAB 128/39.
62. Record of meeting, 11 Dec. 1964, FO to Paris, 12 Dec., and see record of Healey–Hassel meeting, 14 Dec. 1964, all PREM 13/27; *AAP, 1964*, Vol.II, Docs.381–4.
63. Labour Party, *Report of the Sixty-Third Annual Conference, 12–13 December 1964* (London, 1965), pp.114–16; *HC Debs*, 5th Series, Vol.704, Cols.691–704; Crossman, *Diaries*, p.105.
64. Record of meeting, 18 Dec. 1964, Hetherington 8/15; Paris to FO, 15 Dec. 1964, PREM 13/27.
65. Paris to FO, 16 Dec. 1964, PREM 13/27; UK Delegation NATO to FO, 19 Dec. 1964, Gordon Walker to Wilson, Callaghan, and Healey, 23 Dec. 1964, FO to Washington, 23 Dec. 1964, all PREM 13/219.
66. Dodd to Lester, 22 Dec. 1964, Clarke to Armstrong, 31 Dec. 1964, both T 225/2569; Laskey to Trend, 3 Dec. 1964, Rogers to Trend, 4 Dec. 1964, both CAB 21/6047.
67. Schrafstetter and Twigge, 'Trick or Truth', pp.172–4.
68. Bruce diary, 8 Jan.; diary memorandum, 1 Jan. 1965, Gordon Walker FO 800/951; record of meeting with Wilson, 11 Jan. 1965, Hetherington Papers, 8/12.
69. *FRUS 1964*, Vol.13, pp.169–74; Bundy to Johnson, 12 Jan. 1965, and Rusk to Walker, 14 Jan. 1965, Johnson NSF, Subject File, Box 25; *AAP, 1965*, Vol.I, Docs.3, 15, 17. On German attitudes, see Haftendorn, *NATO*, pp.140–41; Hoppe, *Nuklearfrage*, pp.222–6, 237–43; A. Schertz, *Die Deutschlandpolitik Kennedys und Johnsons* (Cologne, 1992), pp.287–90.
70. *Public Papers of the Presidents of the United States, Lyndon B. Johnson, 1965*, Book I (Washington, 1966), pp.57–59; Geyelin, *Johnson*, pp.177–8.
71. Bonn to FO, 18 Jan. 1965, with German memorandum, PREM 13/219; Le Hardy to PS, 19 Jan. 1965, DEFE 25/34; *AAP, 1965*, Vol.I, Docs.20, 21.
72. Laskey to Rogers and Trend, 22 Jan. 1965, Rogers to Trend, 25 Jan. 1965, both CAB 21/6047.
73. *FRUS 1964*, Vol.13, pp.175–9.
74. Ibid., pp.188–9.
75. Record of meeting, 30 Jan. 1965, PREM 13/174.
76. On Labour's approach to NPT, see J.P.G. Freeman, *Britain's Nuclear Arms Control Policy in the Context of Anglo-American Relations, 1957–68* (London, 1986), pp.196–208.
77. Kosygin to Wilson, 6 Jan. 1965, PREM 13/219.
78. Schrafstetter and Twigge, 'Trick or Truth', pp.177–8 argue that the British wanted to prevent German possession of nuclear weapons because such weapons were 'a potent symbol in the pecking order of European states'; but they cite no British sources to support this claim. The archives repeatedly show that the British were concerned about Soviet reaction to a German nuclear capability. For example, records of Stewart–Gromyko and Wilson–Gromyko meetings, 17–18 March 1965, PREM 13/603; records of meetings with Soviet officials, 21 July 1965 and 4 Oct. 1965, PREM 13/220; records of Stewart-Gromyko meetings, 30 Nov. 1965, 2 Dec. 1965, PREM 13/805.
79. *HC Debs*, 5th Series, Vol.707, Cols.1330–32, 1362–65.
80. *FRUS 1964*, Vol.13, pp.187–88.
81. Shuckburgh to Hood, 19 Jan. 1965, FO 371/184406/60; records of meetings of 7–9 March

THE WILSON GOVERNMENT AND NUCLEAR SHARING 323

1965, PREM 13/329; *AAP, 1965*, Vol.I, Docs.116, 122; *FRUS 1964*, Vol.13, pp.190–91; H. Osterheld, *Aussenpolitik unter Bundeskanzler Ludwig Erhard* (Frankfurt, 1992), p.176.
82. UK Delegation NATO to FO, 15 March 1965, PREM 13/220; OPD(O)(ANF)(65)2(Final), 20 April 1965, CAB 146/48.
83. Record of meeting, 8 March 1965, FO371/181387/45; *FRUS 1965*, Vol.11, pp.193–6.
84. Castle, *Diaries*, p.26; CC 19(65)2, 30 March 1965, CAB 128/39.
85. PREM 13/532 and FO 371/181388 *passim*.
86. Stark to Street, 21 June 1965, FO 371/181388/91; Bonn to FO, 5 July 1965, FO 371/181388/97. On German policy, see Bluth, *Nuclear Strategy*, pp.161–3; Hoppe, *Nuklearfrage*, pp.261–73.
87. Washington to FO, 20 July 1965, Bonn to FO, 20 July 1965, FO371/181389/120; and see *AAP, 1965*, Vol. II, Doc.296.
88. *FRUS 1965*, Vol.11, pp.225–32.
89. Information telegram, 14 Aug. 1965, 371/181391/192; Geneva to FO (203), 17 Aug. 1965, 371/181391/203; Geneva to FO (215), 19 Aug. 1965, all FO 371/181391/215; *FRUS 1965*, Vol.11, pp.233–5; Freeman, *Arms Control Policy*, pp.209–21.
90. Barnes minute, 20 July 1965, FO 371/184413/296; brief for Chalfont, nd (but early Oct. 1965), FO371/181392/263.
91. Pearce, *Gordon Walker Diaries*, p.295.
92. Bluth, *Nuclear Strategy*, pp.180–85; P. Buteux, *The Politics of Nuclear Consultation in NATO* (Cambridge, 1983), pp.37–44; Hoppe, *Nuklearfrage*, pp.250–61.
93. CC 49(65)3, 23 Sept. 1965, CAB 128/39.
94. Record of meeting, 12 Oct. 1965, PREM 12/220; dinner meeting, 11 Oct. 1965, FO 371/184415/378.
95. Evidence from the Lyndon Baines Johnson Library, quoted in Freeman, *Arms Control*, p.219.
96. FO to Bonn (372), 19 Oct. 1965, FO 371/184415/364; FO to Bonn, 20 Oct. 1965, FO 371/184415/372; Roberts to Gore Booth (374), 18 Oct. 1965, all FO 371/184415/374.
97. Barnes minute, 30 Oct. 1965, FO 371/184415/367.
98. Wilson, *Government*, p.184; and record of meeting, 26 Nov. 1965, PREM 13/805.
99. *FRUS 1964*, Vol.13, pp.243–7, 261–2; *FRUS 1965*, Vol.11, p.264; Rostow–Ball telephone conversation, 22 Oct. 1965, Ball Papers Box 1; note and memorandum, Ball to Bundy, Rusk, and McNamara, 27 Oct. 1965, Johnson NSF, Agency File, Box 39.
100. Bonn to FO, 8 Oct. 1965, FO to Bonn, 27 Oct. 1965, both PREM 13/220; H. Blankenhorn, *Verstandnis und Verstandigung* (Frankfurt, 1980), p.495.
101. Records of meetings, 19 Nov. 1965, PREM 13/927; *AAP, 1965*, Vol.III, Doc.423; Blankenhorn, *Verstandnis*, p.497.
102. Castle, *Diaries*, p.75; record of plenary, 16 Dec. 1965, PREM 13/686.
103. *AAP, 1966*, Vol.III, Docs.466, 469; G.C. McGhee, *At the Creation of a New Germany: From Adenauer to Brandt* (New Haven, CT, 1989), pp.183–6; Osterheld, *Aussenpolitik*, pp.268–9. Schrafsteeter and Twigge, 'Trick or Truth', p.176 reverse the order of visits and erroneously claim nuclear sharing was not discussed.
104. PREM 13/805. Erhard to Wilson, 22 Dec. 1965, Johnson to Wilson, 23 Dec. 1965, and replies, 5 Jan. 1966, PREM 13/805; but see, FO brief (British objections to Erhard's memorandum) for Stewart, nd, FO 371/190663/19.
105. Bruce diary, p.12 (including quote) Jan. 1966, 15 Jan. 1966, 3 Feb. 1966; *FRUS 1966*, Vol.13, pp.300–301.
106. Bundy to Johnson, 28 Jan. 1966, and annexed draft letter, Johnson White House Central File, Confidential File, Box 44, 'Foreign Affairs 1966' folder.
107. For example, Roberts to Gore-Booth, 26 Jan. 1966, FO 371/190664/27; Thomas minute, 23 Feb. 1966, FO 371/190664/29.

108. *FRUS 1965*, Vol.13, pp.316–18; record of meeting, 20 Jan. 1966, Hetherington Papers 11/4.
109. Erhard to Wilson, 5 Feb. 1966 (delivered on 16 February), Wright to Maclehose, 16 March 1966, PREM 13/805.
110. Unsigned letter to Maclehose, 4 March 1966, PREM 13/1273.
111. Wilson to Johnson, 21, 29 March 1966, both PREM 13/1043.
112. *FRUS 1966*, Vol.13, pp.363–5.
113. Record of meeting, 16 March 1966, PREM 13/927.
114. Balogh to Wilson, 25 April 1966, with Wilson minute, PREM 13/3094.
115. *FRUS 1966*, Vol.13, pp.370–72.
116. Beeley to Gore-Booth, 4 April 1966, Barnes minute, 6 April 1966, both FO 371/190665/67; Dean to Gore-Booth, 6 April 1966, FO 371/190665/69; Thomson minute, 6 May 1966, FO 371/190665/64. On the US studies, *FRUS 1966*, Vol.13, pp.374–5, 396–8, 402–3, 417–19, 433–4.
117. CC 24(66)2, 12 May 1965, CAB 128/41.
118. Wilson to Johnson, 27 May 1966, PREM 13/2559; record of Stewart–Schroder meeting, 24 May 1966 PREM 13/933; Osterheld, *Aussenpolitik*, pp.316–19.
119. Samuel minute, 17 March 1966, FO 371/190665/56; FRUS 1966, Vol.13, p.472.
120. P. Ziegler, *Mountbatten* (London, 1985), p.597.
121. Ball, *Another Pattern*, p.274 admits this.
122. Geyelin, *Johnson*, p.167.
123. D.E. Butler and A. King, *The British General Election of 1966* (London, 1966), p.7n,

Abstracts

Power and Stability in British Foreign Policy, 1865–1965, *by Erik Goldstein and B.J.C. McKercher*

Even before 1865, it was an axiom that British foreign policy was designed and pursued to ensure international stability. Stability not only gave security to the British Isles and to its global Empire; it minimized disruptions to trade and commerce – the life-blood of 'Great' Britain. In the century after 1865, the pursuit of international stability remained at the heart of diplomatic initiatives supported by capable armed forces and a strong economy. The grand strategy by which successive British governments endeavoured to achieve these national and imperial ends involved the maintenance of a balance of power – both in Europe and in the wider world where the protection of British interests in the form of prestige, markets, strategic outposts, and lines of communication preoccupied cabinets, the Foreign Office, the service ministries, other departments of state, and, sometimes, public opinion. In one sense, there were a number of individual balances of power – in Western Europe, in the western and eastern Mediterranean, in the Western Hemisphere, in South Asia, and in the Far East and Pacific Ocean. In the British diplomatic parlance of the late nineteenth and early twentieth centuries, these balances were represented as 'questions', like the 'Eastern Question'; and the answers to these questions combined in the minds of those responsible for British foreign policy as representing a global balance of power. In this context, the European balance of power had decided importance because any continental disequilibrium could imperil the security of the home islands, the centre of the Empire, and the well-being of Britain's people and economy.

British Power and Stability: The Historical Record, *by Zara Steiner*

This article provides an overview of British foreign policy and the European balance of power from the late nineteenth century to the early Cold War. British attitudes towards the Continent, like those of the continental Powers toward Britain, are bound to remain ambivalent. When looking back to the history of these complex relations, two main readings stand out. The first is that Britain's attempts to underwrite European stability from Waterloo to the present day left the country exhausted and stripped of its Empire. The other reading perceives in these costly efforts a successful preservation of British integrity and independence. What allowed, for many years, the country to have the luxury of choices with regard to its relations with Europe was the underlying security of the home islands and the existence of a vast Empire overseas. Examining in broad brush strokes the idea and practice of the balance as Britain's international position altered in the half century or so before 1950, the case is made that whatever the reading of these complex relations, the British were always 'reluctant Europeans'.

Power, Sovereignty, and the Great Republic: Anglo-American Diplomatic Relations in the Era of the Civil War, *by Brian Holden Reid*

Historians have tended to view the American Civil War (1861–65) as a milestone in Anglo-American relations. It marked the transfer of dominance from Great Britain to the United States in the Western Hemisphere. As Great Britain backed the losing side, overwhelming American power brought about a British withdrawal. This article argues that this is a very oversimplified interpretation of their relations in this period. Britain did not intervene in the Civil War because it was not good policy; throughout the British relied on deterrence because, save for the war years, American power could not be translated into military power. The British secured most of their policy objectives thanks to a combination of prudent and conciliatory conduct, and a desire to avoid war, but also due to calm resolution that belied belligerent and sometimes outlandish public statements. British leaders have often been criticized for hypocrisy and double standards, but such criticisms seem unfair. Their belief that the Civil War was futile resulted from a humanitarian desire to halt the killing. It should be remembered that although the nineteenth century witnessed many local conflicts, great wars seem to have disappeared. It therefore appeared to be a laudable objective to attempt to arbitrate in what turned out to be the greatest war after 1815. It is also important to recall that Europeans were less interested in this conflict than the Americans themselves, and that preoccupation with affairs closer to home led to hasty and erroneous judgements.

'Almost a Law of Nature'? Sir Edward Grey, the Foreign Office, and the Balance of Power in Europe, 1905–12, *by T.G. Otte*

This article considers the concept of the balance of power as it was applied by the British Foreign Office before the First World War, focusing on 1905–12. The place of the balance of power in British thinking is discussed, focusing on the ideas of the small number of individuals that shaped British foreign policy in this period. The balance of power in the years before the war was a product of more than the military balance sheet but also of the diplomatic dynamics.

'Après la Guerre finit, Soldat anglais partit': Anglo-French Relations 1918–25, *by Alan Sharp and Keith Jeffery*

This article examines a number of issues of British foreign policy during the making of the First World War Peace Settlements from the armistice to the Locarno Pact, utilizing in particular the work of Michael Dockrill as a starting point. Particular attention is given to British relations, especially the tensions, with France, Germany, and the United States. A link is drawn in the conclusion to the decisions made during 1918–25 and the consequences regarding the Second World War.

'Far Too Dangerous a Gamble'? British Intelligence and Policy during the Chanak Crisis, September–October 1922, *by John R. Ferris*

In considering the role of intelligence in the events that culminated in the 1922 Chanak crisis, particular attention is given to the extent to which intelligence assessments of Turkish Nationalist troop strengths influenced British decisions. Key political figures included Lloyd George, Lord Curzon, Winston Chuchill, and Austen Chamberlain, as well as military officers such as General Harington and Admiral Brock, and the diplomat Sir Horace Rumbold. It concludes that the final armistice, signed at Mudania, met British objectives, but only after running too high a risk.

The British Official Mind and the Lausanne Conference, 1922–23, by Erik Goldstein

From the collapse of the Ottoman empire in 1918 until the Lausanne Conference in 1923 Britain attempted to establish itself as the dominant power in the Aegean, largely in order to control its strengths. This would see the British occupation of Constantinople, the collapse of Allied cooperation, the Chanak crisis, and the final resolution at Lausanne.

Austen Chamberlain and the Continental Balance of Power: Strategy, Stability, and the League of Nations, 1924–29, by B.J.C. McKercher

As foreign secretary from November 1924 to June 1929, Austen Chamberlain dominated British foreign policy. Central to his diplomatic strategy was the maintenance of the European balance of power and, in this circumstance, pursuit of a leadership role for Britain within the League of Nations. The foundation upon which Chamberlain based his European strategy lay with his determination to have Britain play the vital role of stabilizing relations between France and Germany, whose mutual antipathy after the Great War, compounded by the severity of the Treaty of Versailles, threatened continental security. By October 1925, his work bore fruit with the conclusion of the Locarno agreements. For the remainder of his tenure at the Foreign Office, Chamberlain used Locarno – and Germany's membership in the League that was part of that settlement – as the diplomatic mechanism to underwrite his strategic conception of the balance of power. This article addresses the neglected issue of the strategic base of Chamberlain's European policy and addresses three criticisms of his record as foreign secretary.

The British Government and the Sale of Arms to the Lesser European Powers, 1936–39, by Glyn Stone

This article considers sales of British arms in the prelude to the Second World War, during the end of last Baldwin government, and the Chamberlain government, which had political as well as commercial motivations. Particular attention is paid to the leading British arms manufacturer, Vickers-Armstrong, and sales to Portugal, Turkey, Greece,

Yugoslavia, Romania, and Poland. There was often a concern that a failure to procure British arms would lead countries to turn to Germany and Italy. The interest in meeting these requests often conflicted with growing domestic defence needs for the same equipment. The conclusion is drawn that Britain ultimately failed to inspire potential allies with sufficient confidence to commit themselves to Britain.

Invading Europe: The British Army and its Preparations for the Normandy Campaign, 1942–44, by David French

The combat capability of 2nd British Army during the Normandy campaign has been much deprecated. This article tries to shed new light on these criticisms by examining three neglected aspects of the army's preparations for the campaign. It examines how the army was created from formations drawn from both Home Forces and 8th Army; it explores how its formations were trained in Britain before D-Day; it considers how senior commanders were selected to lead the army; and finally it demonstrates how athese issues had a significant influence on the combat capability of British troops in Normandy.

Killing the MLF? The Wilson Government and Nuclear Sharing in Europe, 1946–66, by John W. Young

This article investigates the claim of Britain's prime minister, Harold Wilson, to have 'killed' the Multilateral Force, an attempt to bring about nuclear sharing within NATO and answer the supposed German desire for equality of status. Earlier accounts have often seen the Multilateral Force as being abandoned, largely thanks to shifts in American policy, in late 1964. The case argued here is that the proposal continued to tax the alliance well into 1966, that important elements in the American and German governments continued to support it and that the British do deserve some credit for bringing the whole idea to an end. In particular the launch of an alternative proposal (the 'Atlantic Nuclear Force'), Wilson's readiness to argue with Washington and Bonn, and the exploitation of French withdrawal from NATO in 1966 proved important, even if British opposition was only one of several factors working against nuclear sharing. In the process he was also able to neutralise the dangers posed to him in the domestic political sphere by the debate over nuclear weapons.

Notes on Contributors

John Ferris is Professor of History, University of Calgary. He has written widely in intelligence, military, diplomatic and strategic history. His publications include *Men, Money, and Diplomacy: The Evolution of British Strategic Policy, 1919–26* (1989) and *British Army and Signals Intelligence during the First World War* (co-editor, 1992).

David French is Professor of Modern British History, University College, London. He is the author of three books on British strategy during the First World War. His most recent book, *Raising Churchill's Army: The British Army and the War against Germany, 1919–1945* (2000) was awarded the Arthur Goodzeit Prize for 2000 by the New York Military Affairs Symposium. He is currently writing a study of 'The Regimental System and British Military Culture, c.1870–1970'.

Erik Goldstein is Professor of International Relations, Boston University. He was previously Professor of International History, University of Birmingham. His most recent books are *The Munich Crisis: New Interpretations and the Road to World War II* (co-editor, 1999), *Guide to International Relations and Diplomacy* (co-editor, 2002), and *The First World War Peace Settlements, 1919–1925* (2002). He is also the editor of the Cass series, 'Diplomats and Diplomacy'.

Keith Jeffery is Professor of Modern History at the University of Ulster. Among his publications are *The British Army and the Crisis of Empire, 1918–1922* (1984), *A Military History of Ireland* (with Thomas Bartlett, 1997), and *Ireland and the Great War* (2000), the *1998 Lees Knowles Lectures*, which he delivered at the University of Cambridge. He is currently working on aspects of twentieth-century British imperial history and a biography of Field Marshal Sir Henry Wilson (1864–1922).

Brian McKercher is Professor and Chair, War Studies, Royal Military College of Canada. Among his publications are *The Second Baldwin Government and the United States, 1924–1929: Attitudes and*

Diplomacy (1984), *Esme Howard. A Diplomatic Biography* (1989) and *Transition of Power: Britain's Loss of Global Preeminence to the United States, 1930–1945* (1998). His co-edited books include (with M.L. Dockrill) *Diplomacy and World Power: Studies in British Foreign Policy, 1890–1951* (1996).

T.G. Otte is a Senior Lecturer in International History, the University of the West of England, Bristol. He is the editor of *The Makers of British Foreign Policy: From Pitt to Thatcher* (2002), *Personalities, War, and Diplomacy: Essays in International History* (with Constantine A. Pagedas, 1997), and *Military Intervention: From Gunboat Diplomacy to Humanitarian Intervention* (1995). He has just finished a monograph on Britain, the Great Powers, and the China Question, 1894–1905. He is a regular contributor to *The Times Literary Supplement*, and is also Reviews Editor of *Diplomacy & Statecraft*.

Brian Holden Reid is Professor of American History and Military Institutions and Head of the Department of War Studies, Kings College, London. From 1987 to 1997 he was seconded by the Department to the Staff College, Camberley, where he served as Resident Historian. He was the first civilian to serve on the Directing Staff for over a century, and helped set up the Higher Command and Staff Course for senior officers. Among his publications are *J.F.C. Fuller: Military Thinker* (1987), *Studies in British Military Thought: Debates with Fuller and Liddell Hart* (1996), *The Origins of the American Civil War* (1996), and *The American Civil War and the Wars of the Industrial Revolution* (1999). He is currently engaged in writing a new history of the American Civil War and hopes to complete the trilogy eventually with a book on the war's impact.

Alan Sharp is Professor of International Studies and Head of the School of History and International Affairs at the University of Ulster. His major research interests are in British foreign policy after the First World War, with a particular focus on Lord Curzon's tenure of the Foreign Office and the career of James Headlam-Morley. His most recent book is a set of essays jointly edited with Professor Glyn Stone, *Anglo-French Relations in the Twentieth Century: Rivalry and Cooperation* (2000).

Zara Steiner is an Emeritus Fellow, New Hall, Cambridge. Her most recent work (co-authored with Keith Neilson) is a revised edition of *Britain and the Origins of the First World War* (2003).

Glyn Stone is Professor in International History, University of the West of England, Bristol. His research focuses on Anglo-French and Anglo-Portuguese relations before, during and after the Second World War and has a particular interest in the international politics of the Spanish Civil War (1936–39). His publications include *The Oldest Ally: Britain and the Portuguese Connection, 1936–1941* (1994).

John Young is Professor of History, University of Nottingham. His publications include *Winston Churchill's Last Campaign: Britain and the Cold War 1951–5* (1996), *Britain and the World in the Twentieth Century, 1895–1997* (1997), *Britain and European Unity, 1929–99* (2000), and the forthcoming *World Politics since 1945: An International History* (co-authored with Dr C. John Kent).

Bibliography

PRIMARY SOURCES

Public Record Office, London
Cabinet Papers
Command Papers
Foreign Office Papers
Treasury Papers

Manuscript Collections
Alanbrooke, Lord: Liddell Hart Centre for Military Archives, King's College, London
Asquith of Oxford, Lord: Bodleian Library, Oxford
Attlee, Clement: Bodleian Library, Oxford
Balfour, Arthur: Add MSS Series, British Library, London
Ball, George: Lyndon Johnson Library, Austin, Texas
Bertie of Thames, Lord: Add MSS Series, British Library, London
Bristol, Mark: Library of Congress, Washington
Bruce, David: Virginia Historical Society, Richmond, Virginia
Campbell-Bannerman, Sir Henry: MSS Series, British Library, London
Cartwright, Sir Fairfax: C(A) Series Northamptonshire Country Record Office]
Chamberlain, Sir Austen: FO 800 Series, Public Record Office and AC Series, University Library, University of Birmingham, Birmingham
Crewe, Lord: University Library, Cambridge
Cromer, Lord: FO 633 Series, Public Record Office
Crowe, Sir Eyre: Bodleian Library, Oxford
Curzon of Kedleston, Earl: India Office Records and Library, British Library, London
de Bunsen, Sir Maurice: Bodleian Library, Oxford
Domvile, Barry: Domvile Series, National Maritime Museum, Greenwich
Fisher, W.W.: FHR Series, National Maritime Museum, Greenwich
Fisher, H.A.L.: Bodleian Library, Oxford
Gordon-Walker, Patrick: FO 800 Series, Public Record Office
Grew, Joseph: Houghton Library, Harvard University
Hankey, Sir Maurice: Churchill College, Cambridge
Hardinge of Penshurst, Lord: FO 800 Series, Public Record Office
Headlam-Morley, Sir James: Churchill College, Cambridge
Hetherington, Alasdair: British Library of Economic and Political Science, London
Johnson, Lyndon Baines: National Security Files Series and White House Central File Series, Lyndon Johnson Library, Austin
League of Nations Archives, Palais des Nations, Geneva, Switzerland
Leeper, A.W.A.: Churchill College, Cambridge.
Lincoln, Robert Todd: Library of Congress, Washington
Lloyd George of Dwyfor, Earl: House of Lords Record Office, London
Maurice, Sir Frederick: Liddell Hart Centre for Military Archives, King's College, London
Montgomery of Alamein, Lord: Imperial War Museum, London
O'Connor, Sir Richard.: Liddell Hart Centre for Military Archives, King's College, London
Rennell of Rodd, Lord; Bodleian Library, Oxford
Ripon, Lord: Add MSS Series, British Library, London
Rumbold, Sir Horace: Bodleian Library, Oxford

Spender, Hugh: Add MSS Series, British Library, London
Spring-Rice, Sir Cecil: Churchill College Archive Centre, Cambridge
Wilson, Sir Henry: Imperial War Museum, London

Government
Anonymous. *Un Livre Noir: Diplomatie d'avant-guerre d'aprés les documents des Archives Russes, Novembre 1910-Juillet 1914*, Vol.II (Paris, s.a.)
Bittner, L. et al., eds. *Österreich-Ungarns Aussenpolitik, 1908–1914: Diplomatische Aktenstücke*, 9 vols. (Vienna, 1930)
Department of State [United States]. *Diplomatic Correspondence, 1861* (Washington, DC, 1862)
Diplomatic Correspondence, 1862, Part 1 (Washington, DC, 1862)
Diplomatic Correspondence, 1863, Part 1 (Washington, DC, 1864)
Diplomatic Correspondence, 1865, Part 1 (Washington, DC, 1866)
Foreign Relations of the United States, 1922, Vol.II (Washington, DC, 1938)
de Siebert, B., ed. *Entente Diplomacy and the World: Matrix of the History of Europe* (London, 1920)
Foreign Ministry [Germany]. *Akten zur Auswartigen Politik der Bundesrepublik Deutschland, 1964*, 2 vols. (Munich, 1996)
Akten zur Auswartigen Politik der Bundesrepublik Deutschland, 1964, 3 vols. (Munich, 1996)
Foreign Office [Great Britain]. *Documents on British Foreign Policy* (London, on-going)
Gooch, G.P. and H.W.V. Temperley, eds. *British Documents on the Origins of the War, 1898–1914* (London, 1928)
Schwertfeger, B., ed. *Die Belgischen Dokumente zur Vorgeschichte des Weltkrieges, 1885–1914* 8 vols. (Berlin, 1925)

Diaries and Correspondence
Brock, Michael and Eleanor, eds. *H.H. Asquith: Letters to Venetia Stanley* (Oxford, 1982)
Buckle, G.E., ed. *The Letters of Queen Victoria*, 3rd Series, Vol.I (London, 1928)
Cambon, H., ed. *Paul Cambon: Correspondance, 1870-1924*, Vol.II (Paris, 1940)
Castle, B. *The Castle Diaries 1964–70* (London, 1984)
de Siebert, B., ed. *Graf Benckendorffs Diplomatischer Schriftwechsel, 1907–1912*, 2 vols. (Berlin, new edn., 1928)
Dilks, D., ed. *The Diaries of Sir Alexander Cadogan, 1938–1945* (London, 1971)
Fellner, F., ed. *Schicksalsjahre Österreichs, 1908–1919: Das politische Tagebuch Josef Redlichs*, Vol.I (Graz, 1954)
Gilbert, M., ed. *Winston S. Churchill*, Vol.IV: *Companion*, Part 2: *July 1919–March 1921* (London, 1972)
Gooch, G.P., ed. *The Later Correspondence of Lord John Russell, 1840–1878*, Vol.II (1885)
Grant, A.R.C. and C. Combe, eds. *Lord Rosebery's North American Journal, 1873* (1967)
Howard, C.H.D., ed. *The Diary of Sir Edward Goschen* (London, 1980)
Izvolsky, H., ed. *Au Service de la Russie: Alexandre Iswolsky, Correspondance Diplomatique, 1906–1911*, Vol.I (Paris, 1937)
Jaeckh, E. ed. *Kiderlen-Wächter, der Staatsmann und Mensch: Briefwechsel und Nachlass*, 2 vols. (Stuttgart, 1924)
Jeffery, K., ed. *The Military Correspondence of Field Marshal Sir Henry Wilson 1918–1922* (London, 1985)
Kessel, E., ed. *Generalfeldmarschall Graf Alfred von Schlieffen: Briefe* (Göttingen, 1958)
Kimball, W.F., ed. *Churchill and Roosevelt. The Complete Correspondence.* Vol.1. *Alliance Emerging* (Princeton, 1984)
Lincoln A. *Collected Works*, ed. R.P. Basler, Vols.4 and 8 (New Brunswick, 1953)
Morgan, Kennneth, ed. *Lloyd George: Family Letters, 1885–1936* (Cardiff, 1973)

Morris, A.J.A., ed. *The Letters of Lt.Col. Charles à Court Repington, 1903–1918* (Stroud, 1999)
Pearce, R., ed. *Patrick Gordon Walker: Political Diaries* (London, 1991)
Peball, K., ed. *Conrad von Hötzendorff: Private Aufzeichnungen* (Vienna, 1977)
Petrie, C. *The Life and Letters of the Right Hon. Sir Austen Chamberlain*, Vol.I (London, 1939)
Public Papers of the Presidents of the United States: Lyndon B. Johnson, 1965, Vol.I (Washington, 1966)
Riddell, Lord. *Lord Riddell's Diary of the Peace conference and After, 1918–1923* (London, 1933)
Self, R., ed. *The Austen Chamberlain Diary Letters: The Correspondence of Sir Austen Chamberlain with his Sisters, Hilda and Ida, 1916–1937* (Cambridge, 1995)
Simon, J.Y., ed. *The Papers of Ulysses S. Grant*, Vol.15 (Edwardsville, 1969)
Stevenson, Frances. *Lloyd George: A Diary, by Frances Stevenson*, ed. A.J.P. Taylor (London, 1971)
Wank, S., ed. *Aus dem Nachlass Aehrenthal: Briefe und Dokumente ... 1885–1912*, 2 vols. (Graz, 1994)
Vincent, John, ed. *The Crawford Papers: The Journals of David Lindsay Twenty-Seventh Earl of Crawford and Tenth Earl of Balcarres 1871–1940 during the Years 1892 to 1940* (Manchester, 1984)
Walters, E., ed. 'Unpublished Documents: Aehrenthal's Attempt to Re-Group the European Powers', *Slavonic and East European History*, 30/73(1951)
Ziegler, P., ed. *From Shore to Shore: the diaries of Earl Mountbatten of Burma 1953-79* (London, 1979)

Books
Adams, E.D. *Great Britain and the American Civil War*, Vol.I (New York, 1925)
Alexander, C. *Ironside's Line: The Definitive Guide to the General Headquarters Line Planned for Great Britain in Response to the Threat of German Invasion, 1940–42*, vol.2 (Storrington, 1999)
Allain, J.-C. *Joseph Caillaux*, Vol.I (Paris, 1978)
Allen, H.C. *The Anglo-American Relationship Since 1783* (London, 1959)
Andrew, C.M. and A.S. Kanya-Forster. *France Overseas: The Great War and the Climax of French Imperial Expansion* (1981)
Angelow, J. *Kalkül und Prestige: Der Zweibund am Vorabend des Ersten Weltkriegs* (Cologne, Vienna, 2000)
Anonymous. *A Short History of the 7th Armoured Division. June 1943 to July 1945* (Germany [No city or publisher shown], 1945)
Anonymous. *Taurus Pursuant. A History of the 11th Armoured Division* (Germany [No city or publisher shown], 1945)
Artaud, D. *La question des dettes interalliées et la reconstruction de l'Europe (1917–1929)* (Paris, 1978)
Arthur, P. *Special Relationships: Britain, Ireland and the Northern Ireland Problem* (Belfast, 2001)
Baechler, C. *Gustave Stresemann (1878–1929) De l'impérialism a la sécurité collective* (Strasbourg, 1996)
Ball, G. *The Past has Another Pattern* (New York, 1982)
Barclay, C.N. *The History of the 53rd (Welsh) Division in the Second World War* (London, 1956)
Barker, E., *et al. Why We Are At War: Great Britain's Case* (Oxford, 3rd rev. edn. 1914)
Barlow, I.C. *The Agadir Crisis* (Durham, NC, 1940)
Barnett, C. *The Audit of War: The Illusion and Reality of Britain as a Great Nation* (London, 1986)

Barraclough, G. *From Agadir to Armageddon: Anatomy of a Crisis* (London, 1982)
Bartlett, C.J. *The Long Retreat* (London, 1972)
Baumgart, C. *Stresemann und England* (Cologne/Weimar/Vienna, 1996)
Baylis, J. *Ambiguity and Deterrence* (Oxford, 1995)
Beesely, E.S. *Queen Elizabeth* (London, 1892)
Belchem, Major-General D. *All in the Day's March* (London, 1978)
Belchem, Major-General D. *Victory in Normandy* (London, 1981)
Bemis, S.F. *A Diplomatic History of the United States* (New York, 5th edn., 1936)
Bialer, U. *The Shadow of the Bomber: The Fear of Air Attack in British Politics, 1932-1939* (London, 1980)
Bley, H. *Bebel und die Strategie der Kriegsverhütung, 1904–1913: Eine Studie über Bebels Geheimkontakte mit der britischen Rgeierung* (Göttingen, 1975)
Bluth, C. *Britain, Germany and Western Nuclear Strategy* (Oxford, 1995)
Bond, B. *British Military Policy between the World Wars* (Oxford, 1980)
Bourne, K. *The Balance of Power in North America, 1815–1908* (London, 1967)
Boyle, A. *Trenchard: Man of Vision* (London, 1962)
Bridge, F.R. *The Hapsburg Monarchy among the Great Powers, 1815–1918* (Oxford, 1990)
Bright, J. and J.E.T. Rogers, eds. *Speeches on Questions and Public Policy By Richard Cobden*, Vol.II (London, 1870)
Brogan, B. *The Longman History of the United States* (London, 1985)
Bülow, B. Von. *Denkwürdignkeiten*, Vol.I (Berlin, 1930)
Burrows, M. *The History of the Foreign Policy of Great Britain*, rev. edition (Edinburgh, 1897)
Buteux, P. *The Politics of Nuclear Consultation in NATO* (Cambridge, 1983)
Butler, D.E. and A. King. *The British General Election of 1966* (London, 1966)
Butterfield, H. *History and Human Relations* (London, 1951)
Carver, M. *Out of Step. The Memoirs of Field Marshal Lord Carver* (London 1989)
Chamberlain, A. *Down the Years* (London, 1935)
Chamberlain, A. *The League of Nations* (London, 1926)
Chamberlain, A. *Politics from the Inside. An Epistolary Chronicle 1906–1914* (New Haven, CT, 1937)
Chamberlain, A. *Seen In Passing* (London, 1937)
Charmley, J. *Splendid Isolation? Britain and the Balance of Power, 1874-1914* (London, 1999)
Churchill, R.S. *Lord Derby: King of Lancashire* (London, 1959)
Churchill, W.S. *The Great War* (London, 1934)
Churchill, W.S. *The Second World War*, Vol.IV: *Hinge of Fate* (London, 1951)
Clarke, J. *British Diplomacy and Foreign Policy, 1782–1865: The National Interest* (London, 1984)
Clay, E.W. *The Path of the 50th. The Story of the 50th (Northumbrian) Division in the Second World War 1939–45* (Aldershot, 1950)
Clemenceau, G. *Grandeur and Misery of Victory* (London, 1930)
Connell-Smith, G. *The United States and Latin America: An Historical Analysis of Inter-American Relations* (London, 1974)
Conrad von Hötzendorff, Field Marshal. *Aus meiner Dienstzeit, 1906–1918* (Vienna, 1923)
Cook, A. *The Alabama Claims: American Politics and Anglo-American Relations, 1865–1872* (Ithaca, 1975)
Crossman, R. *The Diaries of a Cabinet Minister*, Vol.I: *1964–6* (London, 1975)
Crowe, S.E. and E. Corp. *Our Ablest Public Servant: Sir Eyre Crowe 1864–1925* (Braunton, 1993)
Curtius, F., ed. *Memoirs of Prince Chlodwig of Hohenlohe-Schillingsfürst*, Vol.II (London, 1906)

D'Abernon, Lord. *An Ambassador of Peace*, Vol.II (London, 1929)
Dakin, D. *The Greek Struggle in Macedonia, 1897–1913* (Thessalonika, 1993)
Decleva, E. *Da Adua a Sarajevo: La politica estera italiana e la Francia, 1896–1914* (Bari, 1971)
Dehio, L. *The Precarious Balance: The Politics of Power in Europe, 1494–1945* (London, 1963)
Dilks, D. *Curzon in India*, Vol.1 (London, 1969)
Dockrill, M.L. *British Defence since 1945* (Oxford, 1988)
Dockrill, M.L. and J.D. Goold. *Peace Without Promise: Britain and the Peace Conferences 1919–1923* (London, 1981)
Dockrill, M.L. *British Establishment Perspectives on France, 1936–1940* (Basingstoke, 1999)
Dockrill, M.L. and B.J.C. McKercher, eds. *Diplomacy and World Power: Studies in British Foreign Policy, 1890–1951* (Cambridge, 1996)
Duroselle, J.-B. *Clemenceau* (Paris, 1988)
Dutton, D. *Austen Chamberlain. Gentleman in Politics* (Bolton, 1985)
Egremont, M. *Under Two Flags: The Life of Major General Sir Edward Spears* (London, 1997)
Ellis, L.F. *Victory in the West*, Vol.1: *The Battle for Normandy* (London, 1962)
English, J.A. *The Canadian Army and the Normandy Campaign. A Study in the Failure in High Command* (New York, 1991)
Fejtö, F. *Requiem pour un empire défunt: Histoire de la destruction de l'Austriche-Hongrie* (Paris, 1993)
Ferris, J.R., ed. *The British Army and Signals Intelligence During the First World War* (London, 1992)
Ferris, J.R. *The Evolution of British Strategic Policy, 1919–1926* (Basingstoke, 1989)
Ferris, J.R. *Men, Money, and Diplomacy: The Evolution of British Strategic Policy, 1919–26* (Ithaca, 1989)
Förster, S. *Der doppelte Militarismus: Die deutsche Heeresrüstungspolitik zwischen Status-Quo-Sicherung und Aggression, 1890–1913* (Stuttgart, 1985)
Fraser, D. *Alanbrooke* (London, 1982)
Freedman, L. *Britain and Nuclear Weapons* (London, 1980)
Freeman, J.P.G. *Britain's Nuclear Arms Control Policy in the Context of Anglo-American Relations, 1957–68* (Lonndon, 1986)
French, D. *Raising Churchill's Army: The British Army and the War against Germany 1919–1945* (Oxford, 2000)
Geiss, I. *German Foreign Policy, 1871–1914* (London, 1976)
Gerlach, M. *British Liberalism and the United States: Political and Social Thought in the Late Victorian Age* (London, 2001)
Gibbs, N.H. *Grand Strategy* Vol.I: *Rearmament Policy* (London, 1976)
Gladwyn, Lord. *The Memoirs of Lord Gladwyn* (London, 1972)
Glover, M. *Invasion Scare, 1940* (London, 1990)
Gooch, G.P. *Before the War: Studies in Diplomacy*, Vol.I (London, 1936)
Graves, R. *Goodbye to All That* (London, 1963)
Grenville, J.A.S. *Europe Reshaped, 1848–1878* (Brighton, 1976)
Grey of Fallodon, Viscount. *Twenty-Five Years, 1892–1916*, Vol.I (New York, 1925)
Grigg, J. *1943. The Victory that Never Was* (London, 1980)
Guingand, Sir F. de. *Operation Victory* (London, 1947)
Haftendorn, H. *NATO and the Nuclear Revolution* (Oxford, 1996)
Hagan, K. *In Peace and War* (New York, 1978)
Hall, C. *Britain, America, and Arms Control, 1921–37* (London, 1987)
Halperin, P.G. *The Mediterranean Naval Situation, 1908–1914* (Cambridge, MA, 1971)
Hamilton, N. *Monty. Master of the Battlefield 1942–44* (London, 1983)

Hardinge of Penshurst, Lord. *Old Diplomacy* (London, 1947)
Hart, S.A. *Montgomery and Colossal Cracks: The 21st Army Group in Northwest Europe, 1944–45* (Westport, CT, 2000)
Hathaway, R.M. *Great Britain and the United States: Special Relations Since World War I* (Boston, 1990)
Head Quarters, Second British Army. *An Account of the Operations of Second British Army in Europe, 1944–45* (Germany [No city or publisher shown], 1945)
Headlam-Morley, J. *Studies in Diplomatic History* (London, 1930)
Healey, D. *The Time of My Life* (London, 1989)
Henderson, A. *Labour and the Geneva Protocol* (London, 1925)
Hennessy, P. *Cabinet* (London, 1986)
Heuser, B. *NATO, Britain, France and the FRG* (London, 1999)
Heuser, B. *Nuclear Mentalities* (London, 1998)
Heuston, R.F.V. *Lives of the Lord Chancellors* (Oxford, 1964)
Hietala, T.R. *Manifest Design: Anxious Aggrandizement in Late Jacksonian America* (Ithaca, 1985)
Hinsley, F.H. *Power and the Pursuit of Peace: Theory and Practice in the History of Relations between States* (Cambridge, 1982)
Hjelholt, H. *Treitschke und Schleswig-Holstein. Der Liberalismus und die Politik Bismarcks in der schleswig-holsteinischen Frage* (Munich, Berlin, 1929)
Holden Reid, B. *The Origins of the American Civil War* (London, 1996)
Hoppe, C. *Zwischen Teilhabe und Mitsprache: die Nuklearfrage in der Allianzpolitik Deutschlands 1959–66* (Baden-Baden, 1993)
Horn, M. *Britain, France and the Financing of the First World War* (Montreal/Kingston, 2002)
Howard, M. *The Continental Commitment: The Dilemma of British Defence Policy in the Era of Two World Wars* (Harmondsworth, 1972)
Hubbard, C.M. *The Burden of Confederate Diplomacy* (Knoxville, 1998)
Huguet, General. *Britain and the War: A French Indictment* (London, 1928)
Jacobson, J. *Locarno Diplomacy. Germany and the West 1925–1929* (Princeton, 1972)
Jones, H. *Abraham Lincoln and a New Birth of Freedom: Union and Slavery in the Diplomacy of the Civil War* (Lincoln NE, 1999)
Jungar, S. *Ryssland och den Svensk-Norsk Unionens Opplösning* (Åbo, 1969)
Kaiser, D.E. *Politics and War: European Conflict from Philip II to Hitler* (Cambridge, 1990)
Kennedy, P.M. *The Rise of the Anglo-German Antagonism, 1860–1914* (London, 1980)
Kent, B. *The Spoils of War. The Politics, Economics, and Diplomacy of Reparations, 1918–1932* (Oxford, 1989)
Kissinger, H.A. *The White House Years* (Boston, 1979)
Knott, S.F. *Secret and Sanctioned: Covert Operations and the American Presidency* (New York, 1996)
Krumeich, G. *Armaments and Politics in France on the Eve of the First World War* (Oxford, 1984)
Labour Party. *Report of the Sixty-Third Annual Conference, 12–13 December 1964* (1965)
Leffler, M.P. *The Elusive Quest. America's Pursuit of European Stability and French Security, 1919–1933* (Chapel Hill, 1979)
Lloyd, D.W. *Battlefield Tourism: Pilgrimage and the Commemoration of the Great War in Britain, Australia and Canada, 1919–1939* (Oxford, 1998)
Llewellyn Smith, Michael. *Ionian Vision: Greece in Asia Minor, 1919–1922* (London, 1973)
Lowe, C.J. and M.L. Dockrill. *The Mirage of Power*, 3 vols. (London, 1972)
Lowe, C.J. *Salisbury and the Mediterranean* (London, 1964)
Lowe, C.J. *The Reluctant Imperialists*, Vol.I: *British Foreign Policy 1878–1902* (London, 1967)
Ludwig, I. *Treitschke und Frankreich* (Munich/Berlin, 1934)

BIBLIOGRAPHY

339

Macfie, A.L. *The End of the Ottoman Empire, 1908-1923* (London, 1998)
McGhee, G.C. *At the Creation of a New Germany: From Adenauer to Brandt* (New Haven, 1989)
McKercher, B.J.C., ed. *Arms Limitation and Disarmament, 1899-1939: Restraints on War* (New York, 1992)
McKercher, B.J.C. *The Second Baldwin Government and the United States, 1924-1929: Attitudes and Diplomacy* (Cambridge, 1984)
Magnus, P. *King Edward the Seventh* (London, 1964)
Maisell, E. *The Foreign Office and Foreign Policy, 1919-1926* (Brighton, 1994)
Marder, A.J. *From Dreadnought to Scapa Flow: The Royal Navy in the Fisher Era, 1904-1919*, Vol.I (1966)
Marriott, J.A.R. *George Canning and His Times* (London, 1903)
Martin, Lieutenant-General H.G. *The History of the Fifteenth Scottish Division 1939-45* (Edinburgh, 1948)
Mathew, H.G.C. *Gladstone, 1809-98* (Oxford, 1997)
Meriggi, L. *Il conflitto lituano-polacco e la questione di vilna* (Milan, 1930)
Minault, Gail. *The Khilafat Movement: Religous Sybolism and Political Mobilization in India* (New York, 1982)
Monger, G.W. *The End of Isolation: British Foreign Policy, 1900-1907* (London, 1963)
Montgomery of Alamein, Field Marshal Viscount. *Normandy to the Baltic* (London, 1946)
Morgan, A. *Harold Wilson* (London, 1992)
Murray, D. *Kennedy, Macmillan and Nuclear Weapons* (London, 1999)
Murray, W. *The Change in the European Balance of Power, 1938-1939* (Princeton, 1984)
Neale, R.G. *British and American Imperialism, 1898-1900* (Brisbane, 1965)
Neilson, K. *Britain and the Last Tsar: British Policy and Russia, 1894-1917* (Oxford, 1995)
Neustadt, R.E. and E.R. May. *Thinking in Time: The Uses of History for Decision-Makers* (New York, 1986)
Newton, Lord. *Lord Lyons: A Record of British Diplomacy* (London, 1913)
Nicolson, Harold. *Curzon: The Last Phase, 1919-1925, A Study in Post-War Diplomacy* (London, 1937)
Nicolson, Harold. *Sir Arthur Nicolson, Bart, First Lord Carnock: A Study in the Old Diplomacy* (London, 1930)
O'Malley, O. *The Phantom Caravan* (London, 1954)
Oncken, E. *Panthersprung nach Agadir: Die deutsche Politik während der zweiten Marokkokrise 1911* (Düsseldorf, 1981)
Orde, A. *British Policy and European Reconstruction After the First World War* (London, 1990)
O'Riordan, E.Y. *Britain and the Ruhr Crisis* (Basingstoke, 2001)
Osterheld, H. *Aussenpolitik unter Bundeskanzler Ludwig Erhard* (Frankfurt, 1992)
Pantenberg, I.F. *Im Schatten des Zweibundes: Probleme österreichisch-ungarischer Bündnispolitik, 1897-1908* (Vienna, 1996)
Peden, G. *British Rearmament and the Treasury, 1932-1939* (Edinburgh, 1979)
Perkins, B. *The Great Rapprochement: England and the United States, 1895-1914* (1969)
Phillips, W.A. *George Canning* (London, 1903)
Phillips, W.A. *The Confederation of Europe* (London, 1914)
Ponting, C. *Breach of Promise* (London, 1989)
Postan, M.M. *History of the Second World War: British War Production* (London, 1952)
Raulff, H. *Zwischen Machtpolitik und Imperialismus. d. dt. Frankreich 1904-1906* (Dusseldorf, 1976)
Reynolds, D. *Britannia Overruled: British Policy and World Power in the 20th Century* (London, New York, 1991)
Rich, N. *Friedrich von Holstein: Politics and Diplomacy in the Era of Bismarck and Wilhelm II* (Cambridge, 1965)

Richardson, D. *The Evolution of British Disarmament Policy in the 1920s* (London, 1989)
Riddell, Lord. *More Pages from My Diary, 1908–1914* (London, 1934)
Ritter, G. *The Schlieffen Plan: Critique of a Myth* (London, 1958)
Robbins, K. *John Bright* (London, 1979)
Roskill, S. *Naval Policy between the Wars II: The Period of Reluctant Rearmament, 1930–1939* (London, 1976)
Rosse, Captain the Earl of, and Colonel E.R. Hill. *The Story of the Guards Armoured Division* (London, 1956)
Ruggiero, J. *Neville Chamberlain and British Rearmament: Pride, Prejudice and Politics* (Westport, CT, 1999)
Russell, Earl. *Recollections and Suggestions 1813–73* (London, 1875)
Saint-Aulaire, Comte de. *Confession d'un Vieux Diplomate* (Paris, 1953)
Satow, E.M. *An Austrian Diplomat of the 'Fifties: The Rede Lecture for 1908* (Cambridge, 1908)
Scarfe, N. *Assault Division. A History of the 3rd Division from the Invasion of Normandy to the Surrender of Germany* (London, 1947)
Scherer, P. *Lord John Russell* (London, 1999)
Schertz, S. *Die Deutschlandpolitik Kennedys und Johnsons* (Cologne, 1992)
Schmitt, B.E. *The Annexation of Bosnia, 1908–1909* (Cambridge, 1937)
Schuker, S.A. *The End of French Predominance in Europe. The Financial Crisis of 1924 and the Adoption of the Dawes Plan* (Chapel Hill, 1976)
Schwartz, D. *NATO's Nuclear Dilemmas* (Washington, 1983)
Scully, R. *The Origins of the Lloyd George Coalition* (Princeton, 1975)
Seeley, J.R. *The Growth of British Policy: An Historical Essay*, Vol.II (Cambridge, 1895)
Senn, A.E. *The Great Powers, Lithuania, and the Vilna Question, 1920–1928* (Leyden, 1966)
Shannon, Richard. *Gladstone and the Bulgarian Agitation* (Hassocks, 1975)
Shay, Jr., R.P. *British Rearmament in the Thirties: Politics and Profit* (Princeton, 1977)
Shrimsley, S. *The First Hundred Days of Harold Wilson* (London, 1965)
Silberschmidt, M. *The United States and Europe: Rivals and Partners* (London, 1972)
Smith, M. *British Air Strategy between the Wars* (Oxford, 1984)
Snyder, J. *The Ideology of the Offensive: Military Decision-Making and the Disaster of 1914* (Ithaca, 1984)
Spears, E.L. *Liaison 1914: A Narrative of the Great Retreat* (London, 1930)
Steinbruner J. *The Cybernetic Theory of Decision* (Princeton, 1974)
Steiner, Z.S. *Britain and the Origins of the First World War* (London, 1977)
Stevenson, D. *Armaments and the Coming of War: Europe, 1904–1914* (Oxford, 1996)
Stone, G. *The Oldest Ally: Britain and the Portuguese Connection, 1936–1941* (Woodbridge, 1994)
Stromseth, J. *The Origins of Flexible Response* (London, 1988)
Taylor, A.J.P. *The Struggle for Mastery in Europe, 1848–1918* (Oxford, 8th edn 1988)
Temperley, H.W.V. *Frederic the Great And Kaiser Joseph: An Episode of War and Diplomacy in the Eighteenth Century* (London, 1915)
Thorne, C. *Allies of a Kind: The United States, Britain and the War against Japan, 1941–1945* (London, 1978)
Toynbee, Arnold. *The Murderous Tyranny of the Turks* (London and New York, 1917)
Trevelyan, G.M. *Grey of Fallodon* (London, 1943)
Turner, A. *The Cost of War: British Policy on French War Debts, 1918–1932* (Brighton, 1998)
Van Deusen, G.G. *William Henry Seward* (New York, 1967)
Vansittart, R. *Lessons of My Life* (1943)
Vietsch, E. von. *Bethmann Hollweg: Staatsmann zwischen Macht und Ethos* (Boppard, 1969)

BIBLIOGRAPHY 341

Walder, D. *The Chanak Affair* (London, 1969)
Walters, F.P. *A History of the League of Nations*, Vol.I (Oxford/London/New York/Toronto, 1952)
War Office. *Training in the Army* (London, 1961)
Webster, C.K. *The Foreign Policy of Castlereagh 1815-1822: Britain and the European alliance* (London, 1925)
Wedel, O.H. *Austro-German Diplomatic Relations, 1908-1914* (Stanford, CA, 1932)
Weighly, R.F. *History of the United States Army* (London, 1968)
Williams, G. and B. Reed. *Denis Healey and the Policies of Power* (London, 1971)
Williamson, S.R. *The Politics of Grand Strategy: Britain and France Prepare for War, 1904-1914* (London, 1990)
Wills, G. *Inventing America: Jefferson's Declaration of Independence* (London, 1980)
Wilson, K.M. *Empire and Continent: Studies in British Foreign Policy* (London, 1987)
Wilson, K.M. *The Policy of the Entente: Essays on the Determinants of British Foreign Policy, 1904-1914* (Cambridge, 1985)
Wilson, H. *Labour Government, 1964-1970. A Personal Record* (London, 1971)
Winand, P. *Eisenhower, Kennedy and the United States of Europe* (New York, 1993)
Wong, J.Y. *Deadly Dreams: Opium and the Arrow War (1856-60) in China* (Cambridge, 1998)
Wood, A. *Nineteenth Century Britain 1815-1914* (London, 1960)
Ziegler, P. *Mountbatten* (London, 1985)
Ziegler, P. *Wilson: The Authorised Life* (London, 1993)
Zuckerman, S. *Monkeys, Men and Missiles* (London, 1988)

Articles and Chapters
Andrew, C.M. 'The Entente Cordiale from Its Origins to 1914', in N. Waites, ed., *Troubled Neighbours: Franco-British Relations in the Twentieth Century* (1971)
Anonymous. 'British Foreign Policy in the Last Century', *Quarterly Review*, 220/439(April 1914)
Beloff, M. 'The Special Relationship: An Anglo-American Myth', in Martin Gilbert, ed., *A Century of Conflict: Essays for A.J.P. Taylor* (1966)
Boyle, T. 'New Light on Lloyd George's Mansion House Speech', *Historical Journal*, 22(1980)
Bridge, F.R. 'Izvolsky, Aehrenthal, and the End of the Austro-Russian Entente, 1906-8', *Mitteilungen des österreichischen Staatsarchivs*, 29(1976)
Carlton, D. 'Great Britain and the Coolidge Naval Conference of 1927', *Political Science Quarterly*, 83(1968), 573-98
Cecil, R. 'The Draft Treaty of Mutual Assistance', *Journal of the Royal Insitute of International Affairs*, 4(1924), 45-82
Chamberlain, A. 'Great Britain as a European Power', *Journal of the Royal Institute of International Affairs*, 9(1930), 180-88
Coghlan, F. 'Armaments, Economic Policy and Appeasement: Background to British Foreign Policy, 1931-1937', *History*, 57(1972)
Coogan, J.W. and P.F. Coogan. 'The British Cabinet and the Anglo-French Staff Talks: Who Knew What and When did he Know it?', *Journal of British Studies*, 24(1985)
Cooper, M.B. 'British Policy in the Balkans, 1908-9', *Historical Journal*, 7(1964)
Cosgrove, R.A. 'A Note on Lloyd George's Speech at the Mansion House, 21 July 1911', *Historical Journal*, 12(1969)
Crampton, R.J. 'August Bebel and the British Foreign Office', *History*, 58(1973)
Cunliffe, M. 'New World, Old World: The Historical Antithesis', in R. Rose, ed., *Lessons from America* (1974)
d'Este, C. 'The British Army and the Challenge of War 1939-45', in D. Chandler and I.

Beckett, eds., *The Oxford Illustrated History of the British Army* (Oxford, 1994)
Dockrill, M.L. and Z.S. Steiner. 'The Foreign Office at the Paris Peace Conference in 1919', *International History Review*, 2(1980)
Dockrill, M.L. 'David Lloyd George and Foreign Policy before 1914', in A.J.P. Taylor, ed., *Lloyd George: Twelve Essays* (1971)
Dockrill, M.L. 'British Policy during the Agadir Crisis of 1911', in F.H. Hinsley, ed., *British Foreign Policy under Sir Edward Grey* (Cambridge, 1977)
Dockrill, S. 'Britain's Power and Influence: The Wilson Government's Defence Debate at Chequers in November 1964', *Diplomacy & Statecraft*, 11(2000)
Edwards, E.W. 'The Franco-German Agreement on Morocco, 1909', *English Historical Review*, 79(1963)
Fearon, P. 'Aircraft Manufacturing', in N. Buxton and D.H. Aldcroft, eds., *British Industry between the Wars: Instability and Industrial Development* (London, 1979)
Ferris, J.R. 'Between Military and Political: British Power and Diplomacy from the Chanak Crisis to the Lausanne Conference, 1922', *Proceedings of the Joint Turkish–Israeli Military History Conference* (Istanbul, 2000)
Ferris, J.R. 'Whitehall's Black Chamber: British Cryptology and the Government Code and Cypher School, 1919–1929', *Intelligence and National Security*, 2(1987)
French, D. '"Tommy is no Soldier": The Morale of the Second British Army in Normandy', *Journal of Strategic Studies*, 19(1996)
Fry, M.G. *Lloyd George and Foreign Policy: Education of a Statesman, 1890–1916* (Montreal, 1977)
Goldstein, Erik. 'Great Britain and Greater Greece', *Historical Journal*, 32/2(1989), 339–56
Gooch, G.P. 'H.W.V. Temperley, 1879–1939', *Proceedings of the British Academy*, 25(1940)
Gooch, J. 'The Weary Titan: Strategy and Policy in Great Britain, 1890–1918', in W. Murray, M. Knox, and A. Bernstein, eds., *The Making of Strategy: Rulers, States and Wars* (Cambridge, 1994)
Grayson, R.S. *Austen Chamberlain and the Commitment to Europe. British Foreign Policy 1924–29* (London, 1997)
Grayson, R.S. 'Austen Chamberlain', in T.G. Otte, ed., *The Makers of British Foreign Policy from Pitt to Thatcher* (Basingstoke, 2002)
Grenville, J.A.S. 'Diplomacy and War Plans in the United States, 1890–1917', *Transactions of the Royal Historical Society*, 5th Series, 2(1961)
Hayes, P. 'Britain, Germany and the Admiralty's Plans for Attacking German Territory, 1906–1915', in L. Freedman et al., eds., *War, State and International Politics: Essays in Honour of Sir Michael Howard* (Oxford, 1992)
Holden Reid, B. 'Civil Military Relations', in S.-M. Grant and P.J. Parish, eds., *The Legacy of the Civil War* (Baton Rouge, 2003)
Humphreys, R.A. 'Anglo-American Relations in Central America', *Transactions of the Royal Historical Society*, 5th Series, 18(1968)
Jacobson, J. 'Is There a New International History of the 1920s', *American Historical Review*, 88(1983), 617–45
Jeffery, K. and A. Sharp. 'Lord Curzon and Secret Intelligence', in C. Andrew and J. Noakes, eds., *Intelligence and International Relations, 1900–1945* (Exeter, 1987)
Johnson, D. 'Austen Chamberlain and the Locarno Agreements', *University of Birmingham Historical Journal* 8(1961), 62–81
Johnson, G. 'Lord D'Abernon, Austen Chamberlain and the Origin of the Treaty of Locarno', *Electronic Journal of International History* (www.ihrinfo.ac.uk/publications/ejihart2.html, 2000)
Joll, J. '1914: The Unspoken Assumptions', in H.W. Koch, ed., *The Origins of the First World War: Great Power Rivalry and German War Aims* (1972)

Jordan, G.H.S. 'Pensions Not Dreadnoughts: The Radicals and Naval Retrenchment', in A.J.A. Morris, ed., *Edwardian Radicalism, 1900–1914* (1974)
Lambert, A. 'The Admiralty, the *Trent* Crisis of 1861 and the Strategy of Imperial Defence', in *Les Marines Française et Britannique Face aux États-Unis: De la Guerre d'Independence a la Guerre de Secession* (Vincennes, 1999)
Langhorne, Richard. 'The Treaty of Lausanne (1923) and the Recognition of Modern Turkey: The International Context', in *Atatürk Türkiiye'sinde (1923–1983) Di° Politika Sempozyumu* (Istanbul, 1984)
Lentin, A. '"Une aberation inexplicable"? Clemenceau and the Abortive Anglo-French Guarantee Treaty of 1919', *Diplomacy and Statecraft*, 8(July 1997)
Lentin, A. 'The Treaty That Never Was: Lloyd George and the Abortive Anglo-French Alliance of 1919', in J. Loades, ed., *The Life and Times of David Lloyd George* (Bangor, 1991)
Lentin, A. 'Lloyd George, Clemenceau and the Elusive Anglo-French Guarantee Treaty: "A Disastrous Episode"?' in A. Sharp and G. Stone, eds., *Anglo-French Relations in the Twentieth Century: Rivalry and Cooperation* (2000)
Lieven, D. 'Pro-Germans and Russian Foreign Policy, 1890–1914', *International History Review*, 2(1980)
McDermott, J. 'The Revolution in British Military Thinking from the Boer War to the Moroccan Crisis', in P.M. Kennedy, ed., *The War Plans of the Great Powers, 1880–1914* (Boston, 1979)
McKale, D.M. '*Weltpolitik versus Pax Britannica*: Anglo-German Rivalry in Egypt, 1904–1914, *Canadian Journal of History*, 22(1987)
MacKenzie, S.P. 'Citizens in Arms: The Home Guard and the internal security of the United Kingdom, 1940–1941', *Intelligence & National Security*, 6(1991), 548–72
McKercher, B.J.C. 'Austen Chamberlain's Control of British Foreign Policy, 1924–1929', *International History Review*, 6(1984), 570–91
McKercher, B.J.C. 'Old Diplomacy and New: The Foreign Office in the Interwar Period', in M.L. Dockrill and B.J.C. McKercher, ed., *Diplomacy and World Power: Studies in British Foreign Policy, 1890–1951* (Cambridge, 1996), 79-114
Marchat, H. 'L'Affaire Morocaine en 1911', *Revue d'histoire diplomatique*, 77(1963)
Maslowski, P. 'To the Edge of Greatness: The United States, 1783–1865', in W. Murray, M. Knox and A. Bernstein, eds., *The Making of Strategy: Rulers, States and Wars* (Cambridge, 1994)
Mayers, S.L. 'Anglo-German Rivalry at the Algeciras Conference', in P. Gifford and W.R. Louis, eds., *Britain and Germany in Africa: Imperial Rivalry and Colonial Rule* (New Haven, 1967)
Morgan, K.O. 'Lloyd George and Germany', *Historical Journal*, 39(1996)
Murray, A.C. *Master and Brother: The Murrays of Elibank* (1945)
Neilson, K. 'Incidents and Foreign Policy: A Case Study', *Diplomacy & Statecraft*, 9(1998)
Neilson, K. '"Control the Whirlwind": Sir Edward Grey as Foreign Secretary, 1906–1916', in T.G. Otte, ed., *The Makers of Foreign Policy: From Pitt to Thatcher* (2001)
Noel-Baker, P.J. *The Geneva Protocol for the Pacific Settlement of International Disputes* (1925)
Otte, T.G. 'Eyre Crowe and British Foreign Policy: A Cognitive Map', in T.G. Otte and C.A. Pagedas, eds., *Personalities, War and Diplomacy: Essays in International History* (1997)
Otte, T.G. '"An Altogether Unfortunate Affair": Britain and the *Daily Telegraph* Affair', *Diplomacy & Statecraft*, 5(1995)
Otte, T.G. 'The Elusive Balance: British Foreign Policy and the French Entente Before the First World War', in A. Sharp and G. Stone, eds., *Anglo-French Cooperation in the Twentieth Century: Rivalry and Cooperation* (2000)
Parish, P.J. 'Gladstone and America', in P.J. Jagger, ed., *Gladstone* (1998)

Parker, R.A.C. 'Economics, Rearmament and Foreign Policy: The United Kingdom before 1939 – A Preliminary Study', *Journal of Contemporary History*, 10(1975)
Parker, R.A.C. 'British Rearmament 1936–1939: Treasury, Trade Unions and Skilled Labour', *English Historical Review*, 96(1981)
Piesche, M. Die Rolle des Reparationsagenten Parker Gilbert während der Weimarer Republik (1924-1930)', *Jahrbuch für Geschichte*, 18(1978), 135–69
Place, T.H. 'Lionel Wigram, Battle Drill, and the British Army in the Second World War', *War in History*, 7(2000)
Pogge-von Strandmann, H. 'Rathenau, die Gebrüder Mannesmann und die zweite Marokkokrise', in I. Geiss and B.J. Wendt, eds., *Deutschland in der Weltpolitik des 19. und 20. Jahrhunderts: Festschrift für Fritz Fischer* (Düsseldorf, 1973)
Ramm, A. 'Granville', in K.M. Wilson, ed., *British Foreign Secretaries and Foreign Policy: From Crimean War to First World War* (1987)
Reynolds, D. 'Churchill and the British "Decision" to Fight on in 1940', in R. Langhorne, ed., *Diplomacy and Intelligence during the Second World War* (Cambridge, 1985)
Roi, M.L. and B.J.C. McKercher. '"Ideal" and "Punch-Bag": Conflicting Views of the Balance of Power and Their Influence on Interwar British Foreign Policy', *Diplomacy & Statecraft*, 12(2001), 47–78
Rosecrance, R. and Z.S. Steiner. 'British Grand Strategy and the Origins of World War II', in R. Rosecrance and A.A. Stein, eds., *The Domestic Bases of Grand Strategy* (Ithaca/London, 1993)
Schlieffen, A. von. 'War at the Present Day', *National Review*, 52/312(1909)
Schrafstetter, S. and S. Twigge. 'Trick or Truth? The British ANF Proposal, West Germany and US Non-Proliferation Policy', *Diplomacy & Statecraft*, 11(2000)
Schwartz, T. 'Lyndon Johnson and Europe', in H.W. Brands, ed., *The Foreign Policies of Lyndon Johnson* (College Station, TX, 1999)
Senn, A.E. 'The Polish Lithuanian War Scare, 1927', *Journal of Central European Affairs*, 21(1961), 267–84
Sharp, A. 'Anglo-French Relations from Versailles to Locarno', in A. Sharp and G. Stone, eds., *Anglo-French Relations in the Twentieth Century: Rivalry and Cooperation* (2000)
Silberstein, G.E. 'Germany, France and the Casablanca Incident, 1908–9: An Investigation of a Forgotten Crisis', *Canadian Journal of History*, 11(1976)
Spring, D.W. 'Russia and the Franco-Russian Alliance, 1905–1914', *Slavonic and East European Review*, 66(1988)
Steinberg, J. 'The *Novelle* of 1908: Necessities and Choices in the Anglo-German Naval Arms Race', in *Transactions of the Royal Historical Society*, 5th Ser., 21(1971)
Steiner, Z.S. and M.L. Dockrill. 'The Foreign Office Reforms, 1919–21' *Historical Journal*, 17(1974)
Steiner, Z.S. 'Elitism and Foreign Policy: The Foreign Office before the Great War', in B.J.C. McKercher and D.J. Moss, eds., *Shadow and Substance in British Foreign Policy, 1895–1939* (Edmonton, 1984)
Stone, N. 'Moltke-Conrad: Relations between the Austro-Hungarian and German General Staffs, 1909–1914', *Historical Journal*, 9(1966)
Stone, G.A. 'Rearmament, War and the Performance of the Bristol Aeroplane Company, 1935–1945', in C.E. Harvey and J. Press, eds., *Studies in the Business History of Bristol* (Bristol, 1988)
Sweet, D.W. 'The Baltic Question in British Diplomacy before the First World War', *Historical Journal*, 13(1970)
Sweet, D.W. 'The Bosnian Crisis', in F.H. Hinsley, ed., *British Foreign Policy under Sir Edward Grey* (Cambridge, 1977)
Sweet, D.W. 'Great Britain and Germany, 1905–1911', in F.H. Hinsley, ed., *British Foreign Policy under Sir Edward Grey* (Cambridge, 1977)
Temperley, H.W.V. 'Lord Granville's Unpublished Memorandum on Foreign Policy, 1852',

Cambridge Historical Journal, 2(1928)
Tomlinson, R. 'The Disappearance of France, 1896–1940: French Politics and the Birth Rate', *Historical Journal*, 28(1985)
Turner, A. 'Anglo-French Financial Relations in the 1920s', *European History Quarterly*, 26(1996)
Weinroth, H.S. 'British Radicals and the Balance of Power, 1902–1914', *Historical Journal*, 13(1970)
Williams, B.J. 'The Revolution of 1905 and Russian Foreign Policy', in C. Abramsky (ed.), *Essays in Honour of E.H. Carr* (1974)
Williams, B.J. 'The Strategic Background to the Anglo-Russian Convention of August 1907', *Historical Journal*, 9(1966)
Williamson, S.R. 'The Origins of World War I', *Journal of Interdisciplinary History*, 18(1988)
Wilson, K.M. 'Grey', in K.M. Wilson, ed., *British Foreign Secretaries and Foreign Policy* (1987)
Wilson, K.M. 'British Power in the European Balance, 1906–1914', in D. Dilks, ed., *Retreat from Power*, vol.I (1981)
Wilson, T. 'Britain's Amoral Commitment to France in August 1914', *History*, 54 (1979)

Theses and Dissertations
Place, T.H. 'Tactical Doctrine and Training in the Infantry and Armoured Arms of the British Home Army, 1940–44' (Leeds University Ph.D., 1997)
Dockrill, M.L. 'The Formation of a Continental Foreign Policy by Great Britain, 1908–1912' (University of London Ph.D., 1969)

Index

Abyssinian crisis, 33, 256
Adair, Sir Alan, 288
Adams, Charles Francis, 57–8, 60, 61, 67, 70
Adams, Henry, 58
Adenauer, Konrad, 298
Admiralty, 33, 210, 240, 253, 263
Aegean Sea, 244
Afghanistan, 238, 243–4, 246, 248
Africa, 33
Air Ministry, 240, 253, 256, 262–3
Alabama Claims, 47, 61, 68–70
Alaska, 49
Albania, 260
Alexander, King of the Hellenes, 187
Alexander, Sir Harold, 285–6
Ali Fuad, 157, 164
Allied Demands Committee, 240, 256
Alsace-Lorraine, 29
American exceptionalism, 55, 56, 57
Amery, Lord, 133
Anderson, Sir Kenneth, 284–5
Anglo-French rivalry, 48–9, 50
Anglo-German Naval treaty (1935), 35
Anglo-Japanese alliance (1902), 3, 6, 213
Anglo-Polish staff conversations, 263–4
Anglo-Portuguese alliance, 248
Anglo-Romanian Protocol, 263
Anglo-Russian Convention (1907), 3–4
Anglo-Turkish declaration, 256
Ankara, 257
Anschluss, 254, 260
Anti-Comintern Pact (1937), 260
Appomattox, 59
Arbitration, in international relations, 70
Argyll, Duke of, 65
Arms Sales, 237–65
Army, British, 8; British Expeditionary Force (1934–38), 37, 40
Arrow War (1856–60), 67
Asquith, H.H., 186
Ashburton, Lord, 54
Athens, 259–60
Atlantic Nuclear Force, 295, 300–319
Atlantic, 244, 249
Atatürk, Kemal, 148–51, 153, 159,
163–5, 168, 171, 175–6, 178–9, 185, 188–9, 191–2, 195, 257
Austria (after 1918), 9
Austria-Hungary, 6, 7, 24, 27, 218
Austro-Prussian War, 49
Azores, 250

Balance of power, 1–3, 7, 13–14, 24–5, 31, 32–3, 34, 37–8, 41, 207–8, 213, 215, 218–20, 222–3, 226–30
Baldwin, Stanley, 208, 237
Balfour, Arthur, 121–4
Balkan entente, 248–9
Balkan States, 248
Ball, George, 296, 301, 303, 305–7, 314, 318
Baltic States, 239
Bank of England, 33
Barnes, John, 313–14
Barron, Major-General Frederick, 255
Battle bomber, 245, 259, 262, 264
Belcem, David, 271, 287
Belgium, 27, 213, 219, 230, 244, 246–7, 249–50
Belgrade, 260–62
Berlin, 243
Bermuda, 51
Bevin, Ernest, 42–3
Bimetallism, 51, 52
Birch, General Sir Noel, 251
Birkenhead, Lord, 173
Bismarck, Prince Otto von, 24, 210
Black Sea, 245
Blankenhorn, Herbert, 315, 317
Blenheim bomber, 245, 256, 258–9, 262–3
Blockade, 40; of Union, 63
Board of Trade, 239, 240, 246
Boers, 50
Bohemia, 263
Bonar Law, Andrew, 191, 201
Bosphorus, 245
Bradshaw, W.P.A., 287
Brazil, 70
Brest–Litovsk, Treaty of (1918), 27
Briand, Aristide, 31, 217–18, 223,

224–6, 229, 230
Briand Plan (1929–30), 34
Bridges, Sir Edward, 240
Bright, John, 56–7
Bristol, Mark, 187, 197
British Commonwealth, 11, 28, 42, 210, 212, 214
British Empire, 28, 29–30, 32–3, 35, 36, 41, 42, 209–10; 'British family' of nations, 60–61, 68
British guarantee to Poland (1939), 263
British Guiana, 56
British policy towards European rivals, 49, 49, 50, 54, 66, 71
British policy towards US, 35, 48–9, 50, 53, 54, 58, 61, 62, 67; criticisms of, 46, 56, 63, 64, 65; efforts to influence elections, 52; illusions of, 65; mediation considered, 58, 65, 66; pro-Confederate sympathy of, 56, 63, 64–5, 69
Brock, Sir Osmond, 143, 152, 163, 176
Brooke, Sir Alan, 275, 277, 285–6
Brooks, Preston, 69
Bruce, David, 303, 305, 309
Bruce, Sir Frederick, 67
Bruce, Stanley, 246
Bucharest, 248, 262–3
Bucknall, Gerlad, 284–5, 289
Budapest, 246
Bulgaria, 1792, 43, 245, 247–8, 250–51
Bullen-Smith, D.C., 287
Bundy, McGeorge, 301, 303, 306–8, 310–11, 314–16
Burns, Jogn, 26
Butler, Benjamin F., 67
Butler, R.A., 297

Cabinet Crisis (1862), 60
Cabinet Office, British, 309, 310, 314
Cabinet, British, 50, 304, 308, 312, 315, 317
Caccia, Harold, 309
Cadogan, Sir Alexander, 260
Cairo, 247
Cambon, Paul, 124
Campbell, Sir Ronald, 260–61
Canada, 11, American designs on, 57, 69; military reinforcement of, 61, 62, 67; Security of, 51, 52, 53–4, 60, 67, 68, 70

Cape Verde Islands, 250
Carol, King of Romania, 263
Castle, Barbara, 312
Castlereagh, Lord, 30, 218–19, 221, 222
Cecil, Robert, 216, 222, 223, 229
Chalfont, Lord, 311–12, 314, 317
Chamberlain, Austen, 5, 6, 7, 11, 12, 30, 31, 32-33, 34, 126, 134, 154, 161, 189, 207–30 passim
Chamberlain, Joseph, 71, 209–10, 211
Chamberlain, Neville, 8–9, 10, 12, 23, 36, 38–40, 210, 239, 272
Chase, Salmon P., 56, 60
Chatfield, Lord, 253–5, 257
Chicherin, G., 200
Chiefs of Staff, British, 38, 241, 244–6, 248, 259–60, 265, 299, 302
China, 7, 32–33, 211, 242, 246, 251
Churchill, Sir Winston, 12, 13, 29, 39, 41, 121, 127–30, 143, 173, 187, 189–90, 216, 273–5, 277–8, 284, 289–90
Civil War, as Anglo-American rupture, 46, 55, 58, 60, 68; levels of European interest in, 50, 55; Northern victory inevitable, 57
Clarendon, Lord, 62
Clayton–Bulwer Treaty (1850), 53, 56
Clemençeau, Georges, 28, 120, 134, 164, 210
Cobden, Richard, 48–49, 56–7
Committee of Imperial Defence, 29–30, 209, 240, 242–7
Concert of Europe, 218–19, 221, 229
Confederacy, 49, 57; belligerent rights of, 61, 63, 68; case for independence, 64, 65; failure to gain recognition, 57, 58, 60, 61, 66; self-defeating policy of, 64
Constantine, King of the Hellenes, 186–8
Constanza, 264
Cooper, Chester, 306
Corbin, Charles, 260
Craven, Sir Charles, 253–4
Crawford, Lord, 191
Crerar, Harry, 286
Crewe, Lord, 199, 201, 213, 215
Crimean War (1854–56), 49
Crocker, John, 285
Crossman, Richard, 304
Crowe, Sir Eyre, 25, 26, 191, 194–6, 201, 215

Cuba, 69
Cumming, Sir Mansfield, 147
Curzon, Lord, 5, 12, 25, 32, 120, 122, 124–5, 143–5, 152–5, 161, 163, 167–9, 174, 177, 187, 189–97, 199–204
Czech crisis (1938), 9–10', 243
Czechoslovakia, 38, 259–63

D'Abernon, Lord, 124
Daladier, Édouard, 39
Danish War (1864), 49
Danube, 245, 248
Danzig, 40
Dardanelles, 239, 250
Dawes Plan (1924), 31, 214
Declaration of Independence (1775), 55
Declaration of Neutrality (British, 1861), 63, 64
Declaration of Paris (1856), 63–4
Defence Policy Requirements Committee, 238–40
De Gaulle, Charles, 43
De Guingand, Freddie, 271, 287
Dempsey, Sir Miles, 279, 285, 288
Deputy Chiefs of Staff, 249–51, 257
Derby, Lord, 126
De Robeck, Sir John, 186
Deterrence, American reliance on, 53; British reliance on, 1861–65, 47, 62, 67
Disraeli, Benjamin, 2, 5, 71
Dix, John A., 68
Dockrill, Michael, 2, 11–15, 119
Dominions, 242, 253
Draft Treaty of Mutual Assistance (1923), 214, 228
Dunkirk, Treaty of (1947), 42

Eastern Europe, 218–19, 224–6, 228; anti-aggression front, 250, 261
Eastern Question, 1, 5–6, 50
Eden, Anthony, 241
Egypt, 6, 10–11, 140, 238, 242, 244, 246–7, 249
Eisenhower, Dwight, 278, 285
English, David, 271
English Speaking Union, 68
Entente cordiale, 3, 6, 51, 12, 213
Erhard, Ludwig, 298–9, 302, 306, 308–18

Erskine, G.W.J., 287, 289
Ethiopia, see 'Abyssinian crisis'
European Economic Community, 11, 42, 43
Export Credit Act, 246
Export Credits Guarantee Department, 241

Far East, 7, 8, 9, 32–3, 35, 249–50
Fashoda, confrontation at (1898), 50
Fathi Bey, 146, 156
Fenian Raids, 60, 69, 70
Ferid Bey, 146, 155, 165, 170, 175
Finland, 239
Fish, Hamilton, 69, 70
Fisher, Sir Warren, 245
Flandin, Étienne, 35–6
Foreign Arms Order Committee, 240, 246
Foreign Office, British, 3–4, 11, 12, 25–6, 27, 30, 31, 32–3, 34, 36, 40, 42, 215, 217, 218–19, 222–3, 297, 299–300, 304, 311–14, 316–19
Fortifications, Canadian, 50, 67
Foster, William, 312
France, 3, 7, 10, 13, 26, 27, 28–9, 30–31, 34–5, 35–6, 38, 40, 42, 119–27, 129–31, 133–5, 140, 142–3, 152, 159, 164, 179, 207, 210, 211, 212–13, 215–16, 217–18, 220, 224–6, 227–30, 247, 249–51, 259, 262–4, 272, 296, 298–9, 303, 305–6, 316–17
Franco-Austrian War (1859), 49
Franco-Prussian War (1870–71), 49–50
Franklin, Benjamin, 56
Franklin-Bouillon, Henri, 145, 189
Free trade, 58, 64, 67
Freedom of the seas, 61
French policy towards Mexico, 48; towards US, 48, 50, towards European rivals, 49, 51; US policy towards, 52

Gafencu, Grigore, 262
Gaitskell, Hugh, 297
Gandhi, Mahatma, 32
Garroni, Marchese, 171, 172, 200–201
Gazis, Colonel, 259
Geddes, Sir Eric, 129
General Staff Intelligence (GSI), 144–5, 152, 178
Geneva arbitration (1872), 70

Geneva Protocol (1924), 35, 214, 216, 228
George II, King of the Helenes, 188, 259
German Wars of Unification, 49
Germany, rivalry with GB, 3, 9–10, 50–51
Germany, West, 295–319
Germany, 3, 7, 8, 23, 24, 26–7, 28–9, 30–31, 34–5, 37–8, 40, 41, 42, 119, 123–7, 129–31,133–5, 207, 210, 212–13, 215–16, 217–18, 220, 224–26, 227–30, 238, 242–5, 247–51, 254–7, 259, 261–2, 264; rearmament (1935–39), 35, 40
Ghent, Treaty of (1814), 53
Gibraltar, 244, 250
Gladiator fighter, 245, 262
Gladstone, W.E., 2, 5–6, 11, 23, 45, 65–6, 192; as premier, 68–9, 70, 71
Godesberg meeting (1938), 38
Goldberg, Arthur, 316
Gordon Walker, Patrick, 298–311, 313, 318
Government Code and Cypher School (GC&CS), 142, 144, 146, 149, 156, 160–61, 169, 171, 179
Grant, Nellie, 71
Grant, Ulysses S., as general-in-chief, 59, 60; president, 69–70, 71
Granville, Lord, 24
Graves, Robert, 123
Great Britain, ambivalence of towards US, 45, 64; avoids war (1861–62), 48, 54, 59, 62, 66–7, 68, 69–70, 71; and balance of power, 1–3, 7, 13–14, 24–5, 31, 32–3, 34, 37–8, 41, 207–8, 213, 215, 218–20, 222–3, 226–30; conciliatoriness, 48, 49–50, 51, 52–3, 55, 71; departure from Western Hemisphere, 46–7, 51, 69, 70, 71; as a European Power, 211–13, 218–20; resolution of, 47, 62, 64; and Soviet–American relationship (post-1945), 41–2; and Anglo-American 'special relationship', 42–3
Greece, 10, 38, 42, 50, 140, 142–3, 162, 166, 170, 172, 179, 180, 237, 242–4, 246–8, 250–51, 255, 259, 261–2, 265
Grew, Joseph, 197–98, 201–2
Grey, Sir Edward, 3–4, 11, 12, 25–6, 27
Gribbon, Colonel, 151

Grigg, P.J., 278

Halifax, Lord, 38, 39, 242, 246, 248, 255, 257, 262–5
Halifax, Ont., 62
Hamid Bey, 164, 170, 179
Hamilton, Sir Ian, 192
Hampden bomber, 259
Hampton Roads Conference (1865), 57
Hankey, Sir Maurice, 126, 202
Hardinge, Charles, 12, 127
Harington, Charles, 140, 142–3, 145–6, 148, 150–55, 157–8, 163, 175–80
Harlech, Lord, 299, 303
Harrison-Place, Tim, 271
Hart, Steven, 271
Hassel, Kai-Uwe von, 300
Headlam-Morley, James, 218–19
Healey, Denis, 297–300, 304, 307, 317
Heath, Edward, 43
Henderson, Arthur, 30
Henderson, Nevile, 197
Herriot, Édouard, 216
Hetherington, Alasdair, 301, 306, 308, 310
Hindenburg, Field Marshal Paul von, 27
Historiography, 45–6, 51–2, 53, 56
Hitler, Adolph, 8, 9–10, 12, 27, 35, 36, 38, 39, 41, 230
Hoare, Sir Samuel, 239, 245–6
Holland, see 'Netherlands'
Hore Belisha, Leslie, 246, 258
Horrocks, Brian, 285–6
Humanitarian arguments to end Civil War, 65, 66
Hughes, Billy, 185, 195
Hungary, 220, 245–6, 251
Huntziger, General Charles, 257
Hurricane fighter, 256, 258, 260–64

'Indirect claims', US on GB, 69
Imbalance of power, US pursuit of, 48
India, 11, 27, 29–30, 32, 42, 242, 244
Industrial Intelligence Centre, 240, 242–3, 256, 263
Inönü, Ismet, 257
Inskip, Sir Thomas, 36–7, 239, 241–3, 245, 253, 265
Intervention, British (1861–65), 47, 48, 58, 63, 66, 57; European, 48
Iran (Persia), 238, 244, 246

INDEX

Iraq, 238, 244, 246–8
Irish Question, 57, 60, 210
Ismet Pasha, 199
Istanbul, 264
Italy, 3, 9, 33, 35–6, 140, 142–3, 152, 154, 162, 164, 216–17, 220, 238, 244–5, 248–50, 255, 259–62, 308–9, 313
Italy, reunification of (1870), 49

Japan, 7, 8, 9, 32–3, 35, 36, 220, 244, 250
Jebb, Julian, 40
Johnson–Clarendon Convention (1869), 69
Johnson, Lyndon, 134, 298, 305–9, 311–12, 315–18
Juarez, Benito, 59

Kaiser's Telegram (1896), 50–51
Kellogg–Briand Pact, 31
Kennard, Sir Howard, 263
Kennedy, John, 296
Kerr, Philip, 126
Kingston, Ontario, 62
Kirkman, S.C., 287
Kisch, Fred, 132
Kordt, Theodor, 40
Kosygin, Andrei, 311

Lago, Count, 162
Lansdowne, Lord, 3, 25–6
Laroche, Jules, 170, 174
League of Nations, 30, 35, 123, 207–8, 212, 216–18, 220–21, 222–4, 228–30, 260
League of Nations Union, 216, 222, 229
Leeper, A.W.A., 186, 192, 198–9
Leese, Oliver, 285–6
Lenin, Vladimir, 32
Limited liability, 42–3
Lincoln, Abraham, 56, 60, 64
Lindsay, Ronald, 155, 196, 224–5
Lisbon, 250, 255
Lithuania, 224–6
Lithuanian–Polish crisis (1927–28), 224–26
Litvinov, Maxim, 32
Lloyd George, David, 4–5, 12, 28–9, 120–21, 124, 126–9, 140, 143, 153, 156, 158, 161, 168, 173, 186, 189,
191, 195, 198, 208, 211
Locarno, Treaty of (1925), 30–32, 34, 36, 207–8, 216–17, 218, 220, 224–26, 227–30
London, 33, 36, 214, 257, 259, 261
Ludendorff, Field Marshal Erich, 27
Luxembourg, 28
Lynne, O., 287
Lyons, Lord, 58, 59, 61, 62, 67

MacDonald, J. Ramsay, 35, 214
Mackinder, Halford, 209–10, 220
Macmillan, Harold, 43, 296–7
Malta, 122
Manchurian crisis (1931–33), 35, 214
Manifest Destiny, 51
Mason, James M., 61
Maximilian, Emperor of Mexico, 48
McCreery, Richard, 285
McNamara, Robert, 298, 313–14
Mediterranean, 244, 247, 249–50, 258–9
Memel, 224
Mercier, Baron, 59
Metaxas, General John, 259–60
Metternich, Count, 211
Mexico, US policy towards, 48, 59; French policy towards, 48–9, 59
Middle East, 10, 28, 32, 33, 244, 247–9
Military Intelliegence Division (MID), 144
Milne, G.F., 188–9
Ministry of Defence, 297, 299, 309
Minuteman missiles, 305–6
Mohammed II, Sultan, 191
Monroe Doctrine (1823), 48, 52, 53
Montreux Straits Conference, 256
Moral superiority, question of, 46, 56, 57, 64, 65–6
Moravia, 263
Morton, Desmond, 256, 261
Montgomery, Bernard, 271, 277–9, 281, 284–9, 291
Mountbatten, Lord, 299, 306
Multilateral Force, 295–319; working group 299–300, 312
Mussolini, Benito, 200
Munich settlement (1938), 9–10, 23, 38, 40, 259
Murray, Gilbert, 222, 229
Murray, Williamson, 40
Mussolini, Benito, 217–18

Mustapha Reschid, 165, 171, 175, 177, 178

Napoleon I, 39, 49, 221
Napoleon III, 48, 49, 64
Napoleonic Wars, 23, 25, 52
Nassau agreement, 296–301, 304–5
Nasser, Abdel, 10
Naval Intelligence Division (NID), 144, 177
Nazi–Soviet Non-Aggression Pact (1939), 39, 258, 264–5
Netherlands, 239, 244, 246–7, 250
Netherlands, 38, 219, 308–9
Neustadt, Richard, 305–6
Newcastle Speech, by W.E. Gladstone, 65, 68
'New World–Old World', historical antithesis, 56
New York, 33
Nicolson, Harold, 126, 186, 198, 201
Nineteenth Century, 68
Non-Proliferation Treaty and negotiations, 295, 303–5, 310–14, 316–19
Norman, Montagu, 33
Norstad, Lauris, 296
North American Review, 68
North Atlantic Treaty Organisation, 295–319; Nuclear Planning Group, 317

O'Conor, Sir Richard, 279, 286, 288
Oregon Claims, 52
Osman Nizami Pasha, 156
Owen, Henry, 300

Paget, Sir Bernard, 275, 280, 285
Palestine, 248
Palmerston, Lord, 24, 54, 56, 58, 59, 65, 66–7
Parallel, 49th, 52, 69; 54o 40m, 52
Paris, 33, 260
Parker, R.A.C., 40
Paul, Prince Regent of Yugoslavia, 262
Permanent Court of International Justice, 223
Persian Gulf, 244
Pierre, Andrew, 304
Pilsudski, Josef, 224–25
Piracy, 63

Pitt, William (the Younger), 39
Poincaré, Raymond, 30, 148, 155, 160–62, 169, 199–200
Poland, 10, 12, 28–9, 38, 237, 242, 246–8, 250–51, 255, 261–3, 265; and Lithuanian–Polish crisis (1927–28), 224–6
Polaris missiles, 296–7, 300–302, 304–5, 315
Polish Insurrection (1863–64), 49
Portugal, 237, 242, 244, 246–8, 250, 252, 254–6, 259, 261, 265
Prague, 247, 254
Preliminary Emancipation Proclamation (1862), 66
Prince of Wales, 55
Protection, 63
Prussia, 24, 27

Quebec, 62

Raczynski, Count Edward, 264
Raglan, Lord, 123
Ramsden, W.H.C., 288
Raouf Bey, 157, 164, 165
Reading, Lord, 196
Rearmament, British (1934–39), 36–7
Red River Campaign (1864), 59
Red Sea, 244
Reform Club (London), 60
Rennie, T.G., 288
Rhineland, 28, 35–6, 215, 217
Rhineland pact, see 'Locarno, Treaty of'
Riddell, Lord, 164
Ritchie, Neil, 287
Riza Nuri, 157
Roberts, Frank, 299–300, 314–15
Roberts, G.P., 290
Robinson, Sir Arthur, 240
Romania, 10, 38, 220, 237, 242, 244, 246–8, 250–51, 255, 261–3, 265
Rome–Berlin Axis, 248
Roosevelt, Franklin, 31, 275
Rosebery, Lord, 71
Rostow, Walt, 305, 316–17
Royal Air Force, 8, 32, 40
Royal Institute of International Affairs, 212–13
Royal Navy, 2, 7, 25, 32, 52, 62, 210, 214
Ruhr Valley, 213–14, 215, 228, 230

INDEX

Rumbold, Sir Horace, 143, 152, 159, 165, 173, 177, 187–91, 195, 198, 202–3
Rusk, Dean, 301, 303, 310, 313–16
Russell, Lord John, 54, 58, 59, 62, 664, 65–6
Russia, 2, 3, 7, 10, 24, 25, 26–7, 29, 49, 66, 67, 211, 212–13, 218, 220, 224; see also Union of the Soviet Socialist Republics
Saar, 28
Sackville-West, Charles, 132
Salazar, António Oliveira, 255–6
Salisbury, 3rd Marquess of, 2–3, 5–6, 11, 24, 50, 71, 72
Salisbury, 4th Marquess of, 222
Saudi Arabia, 244, 246, 248
Schenck, Robert C., 70
Schroeder, Gerhard, 298, 310, 315–17
Scott, Kenneth, 300
Secession (1860–61), 57
Seely, John, 209
Secret Intelligence Service (SIS), 143–4, 146–9, 152, 165, 172–3, 177, 180
Self-determination, 64
Serbia, 27
Seward, William H., 47, 52, 57, 58, 59, 60–61, 62, 63, 67
Shrimsley, Anthony, 306–7
Shuckburgh, Evelyn, 299–300, 312
Siam, 239
Simon, Sir John, 257–8
Simonds, Guy, 286
Singapore, 42
Slavery, denied as Union war aim, 64
Slidell, John, 61
Smith, Sir Arthur, 288
Smuts, Jan, 126, 134
South, see also Confederacy, 57
South African War (1899–1902), 25, 50, 209
Southeast Asia, 33
Sovereignty, 47, 58, 60, 61
Spain, 244, 248, 250, 255
Spanish American War (1898), 50
Spanish Civil War, 242
Spears, Edward, 132
Spitfire fighter, 259–60, 262, 264
Stalin, Joseph, 32
Stamfordham, Lord, 199
Stanhope, Lord, 246

Stanley, Oliver, 246
Stewart, Michael, 311–17
Strauss, Franz-Josef, 317
Stresa Front (1935), 35
Stresemann, Gustav, 31, 216, 217–18, 223, 224–6, 229, 230
Suez Canal, 10, 122, 185, 244, 249
Sumner, Charles, 57, 69
Swayne, J.G., 276
Swinton, Lord, 239

Taverne, Dick, 304
Texas, 55, 56, 59
Third Reich, 261, 263
Thirteenth Amendment (1865), 57
Thorneycroft, Peter, 297, 311
Tilea, Virgil, 262–3
Tocqueveille, Alexis de, 67
Toynbee, Arnold, 192
Treasury, British, 37, 40–41, 237, 245–6, 257–8, 264–5, 302, 309
Treaties, Ashburton (1842), 54; Ghent (1814), 53; Clayton–Bulwer (1850), 53, 56; Washington (1871), 70
Treitschke, Heinrich, 210–11
Trenchard, Hugh, 130
Trend, Burke, 303
Trent Crisis (1861), 47, 61
Turkey, 1–2, 5, 6, 42, 141–203, 237, 242, 244, 246–50, 254, 256–9, 261–2, 264–5
Turkish–German alliance (1914–18), 244
Tyrrell, Sir William, 199, 227

Union of Soviet Socialist Republics, 10–11, 31–2, 38, 41–2, 140, 142–3, 149–50, 152, 154, 157, 163–4, 166, 173, 180, 244, 246, 248, 250–51, 263, 296, 303, 305, 311–14; see also Russia
Union: British supporters of, 56–7, 65; consequences of Northern victory, 46–7, 60, 67; Northern desire to restore, 57
United Nations, 42
United Nations Disarmament Conference, 313
United States Army, 53, 59, 71
United States Navy, 53, 61, 71
United States of America, 6, 10, 23–4, 27–8, 31, 33–4, 38, 40, 41–2, 121, 295–19; British policy towards, 7, 10,

24, 25, 33–4, 38, 41–3, 46–51, 67–8, 69, 71; French policy towards, 48; policy towards France, 52, 59, 62; policy towards GB, 49, 52, 60–61, 62, 663–4, 69–70, 71; power nature of, 53–4, 57–8, 62, 71–2

V-bombers, 297, 301
Vansittart, Sir Robert, 122, 252, 260
Venizelos, Eleftherios, 187, 199
Versailles, treaty of, 12, 28–9, 34, 207, 213–14, 216, 217, 218–19, 227–8, 230
Vickers (Armstrong), 237, 251–3, 265
Victoria I, 6
Vienna, Congress of (1814–15), 218–19
Vilna, 224–6
Vivian, Major, 147

'Whig' interpretation of US foreign relations, 46
War of 1812, 49, 52, 54
War of American Independence (1775–83), 54, 65
War Office, 240, 252–3, 255, 262
Warsaw, 263
Warsaw Pact, 11
Washington DC, 57, 214

Washington, George, 56
Washington, Treaty of (1871), 33, 70
Waterlow, Sir Sydney, 259
Webster, Charles, 221
Wellington bomber, 259
Western Hemisphere, struggle for, 46, 48, 51, 69, 70, 71
Whig Party (British), 56
William II, 3
Wilson, Harold, 295–319
Wilson, Sir Henry, 126, 129–33, 188
Wilson, Woodrow, 186
Wireless Observation Group (WOG), 143–6, 149–51, 156–8, 162–3, 169
World Disarmament Conference (1932–34), 35, 217; and Preparatory Commission (1926–31), 218
Wood, Sir Kingsley, 245, 247
Wright, Oliver, 299, 306

Young, Owen, 217
Young Plan (1929), 217
Youth's Companion, 68
Yugoslavia, 237, 242, 244, 246–8, 250–51, 255, 260–61, 265
Yusuf Kemal, 157

Zuckerman, Solly, 299, 30

Other Titles of Interest

Power, Conflict and Trade

Michael Gerace

Wherever international commerce flows in world politics, military power often flows with it—sometimes as a protector of commerce, sometimes as its promoter and sometimes as a tool of aggression against it. How are military power and international trade related? Do military power and commerce expand together or does military power decline as commerce (and perhaps interdependence) increases? Does this relationship vary across countries and, if so, how?

Power, Conflict and Trade is a study of the relationship between military power and international commerce among the Great Powers prior to World War I. After building an argument for a direct relationship between military power and commerce and exploring their numerous connections, the book estimates models of the relationship among the Great Powers and explores a great deal of their commercial and military data, all of which is situated in the context of their mutual rivalries. Another question investigated is whether the peacetime conflicts and rivalries of the Great Powers affected their trade relations adversely.

320 pages 2003
0 7146 5442 6 cloth

FRANK CASS PUBLISHERS
Crown House, 47 Chase Side, Southgate, London N14 5BP
Tel: +44 (0)20 8920 2100 Fax: +44 (0)20 8447 8548 E-mail: info@frankcass.com
NORTH AMERICA
920 NE 58th Avenue Suite 300, Portland, OR 97213-3786 USA
Tel: 800 944 6190 Fax: 503 280 8832 E-mail: cass@isbs.com
Website: www.frankcass.com

The Munich Crisis, 1938
Prelude to World War II

Igor Lukes and Erik Goldstein
both at Boston University (Eds)

The crises of the 1930s and especially the Munich Agreement in 1938 provoked a vast amount of writing. However, most of the classical works are almost half a century old and were written at a time when it was virtually impossible to gain access to the relevant archival collections on both sides of the Iron Curtain. Authors had to limit their scope of inquiry and had to treat as evidence politically slanted memoirs, official pronouncements, and collections of arbitrarily selected documents. This project studies the Czechoslovak–German crisis and its impact from previously neglected perspectives and celebrates the post-Cold War openness by bringing in new evidence from hitherto inaccessible archives.

416 pages 1999
0 7146 4995 3 cloth
0 7146 8056 7 paper

FRANK CASS PUBLISHERS
Crown House, 47 Chase Side, Southgate, London N14 5BP
Tel: +44 (0)20 8920 2100 Fax: +44 (0)20 8447 8548 E-mail: info@frankcass.com
NORTH AMERICA
920 NE 58th Avenue Suite 300, Portland, OR 97213-3786 USA
Tel: 800 944 6190 Fax: 503 280 8832 E-mail: cass@isbs.com
Website: www.frankcass.com